Mastering Oracle SQL

Other Oracle and SQL resources from O'Reilly

Related titles
Oracle in a Nutshell
SQL Pocket Guide
Oracle SQL*Plus: The Definitive Guide
Oracle PL/SQL Language Pocket Reference
TOAD Pocket Reference for Oracle

SQL Tuning
Oracle PL/SQL Programming
Oracle Essentials: Oracle 9i, Oracle9, and Oracle8i
Oracle SQL*Plus Pocket Reference
Learning Oracle PL/SQL

Oracle Books Resource Center
oracle.oreilly.com is a complete catalog of O'Reilly's books on Oracle and related technologies, including sample chapters and code examples.

oreillynet.com is the essential portal for developers interested in open and emerging technologies, including new platforms, programming languages, and operating systems.

Conferences
O'Reilly brings diverse innovators together to nurture the ideas that spark revolutionary industries. We specialize in documenting the latest tools and systems, translating the innovator's knowledge into useful skills for those in the trenches. Visit *conferences.oreilly.com* for our upcoming events.

Safari Bookshelf (*safari.oreilly.com*) is the premier online reference library for programmers and IT professionals. Conduct searches across more than 1,000 books. Subscribers can zero in on answers to time-critical questions in a matter of seconds. Read the books on your Bookshelf from cover to cover or simply flip to the page you need. Try it today with a free trial.

SECOND EDITION

Mastering Oracle SQL

Sanjay Mishra and Alan Beaulieu

O'REILLY®

Beijing · Cambridge · Farnham · Köln · Paris · Sebastopol · Taipei · Tokyo

Mastering Oracle SQL, Second Edition
by Sanjay Mishra and Alan Beaulieu

Copyright © 2004, 2002 O'Reilly Media, Inc. All rights reserved.
Printed in the United States of America.

Published by O'Reilly Media, Inc., 1005 Gravenstein Highway North, Sebastopol, CA 95472.

O'Reilly books may be purchased for educational, business, or sales promotional use. Online editions are also available for most titles (*safari.oreilly.com*). For more information, contact our corporate/institutional sales department: (800) 998-9938 or *corporate@oreilly.com*.

Editor:	Jonathan Gennick
Production Editor:	Matt Hutchinson
Production Services:	Octal Publishing, Inc.
Cover Designers:	Ellie Volckhausen and Emma Colby
Interior Designer:	Melanie Wang

Printing History:

April 2002:	First Edition.
July 2004:	Second Edition.

 This book uses RepKover,™ a durable and flexible lay-flat binding.

ISBN: 0-596-00632-2
[M]

Table of Contents

Preface

SQL is the language for accessing a relational database. SQL provides a set of statements for storing and retrieving data to and from a relational database. It has gained steadily in popularity ever since the first relational database was unleashed upon the world. Other languages have been put forth, but SQL is now accepted as the standard language for almost all relational database implementations, including Oracle.

SQL is different from other programming languages because it is nonprocedural. Unlike programs in other languages, where you specify the sequence of steps to be performed, a SQL program (more appropriately called a SQL statement) only expresses the desired result. The responsibility for determining how the data will be processed to generate the desired result is left to the database management system. The nonprocedural nature of SQL makes it easier to access data in application programs.

If you are using an Oracle database, SQL is the interface you use to access the data stored in your database. SQL allows you to create database structures such as tables (to store your data), views, and indexes. SQL allows you to insert data into the database, and to retrieve that stored data in a desired format (for example, you might sort it). Finally, SQL allows you to modify, delete, and otherwise manipulate your stored data. SQL is the key to everything you do with the database. It's important to know how to get the most out of that interface. Mastery over the SQL language is one of the most vital requirements of a database developer or database administrator.

Why We Wrote This Book

Our motivation for writing this book stems from our own experiences learning how to use the Oracle database and Oracle's implementation of the SQL language. Oracle's SQL documentation consists of a reference manual that doesn't go into details about the practical usefulness of the various SQL features that Oracle supports. Nor does the manual present complex, real-life examples.

When we looked for help with SQL in the computer book market, we found that there are really two types of SQL books available. Most are the reference type that describe features and syntax, but that don't tell you how to apply that knowledge to real-life problems. The other type of book, very few-in-number, discusses the application of SQL in a dry and theoretical style without using any particular vendor's implementation. Since every database vendor implements their own variation of SQL, we find books based on "standard" SQL to be of limited usefulness.

In writing this book, we decided to write a practical book focused squarely on Oracle's version of SQL. Oracle is the market-leading database, and it's also the database on which we've honed our SQL expertise. In this book, we not only cover the most important and useful of Oracle's SQL features, but we show ways to apply them to solve specific problems.

What's New in Oracle SQL?

When we wrote the first edition of this book, Oracle9*i* had just come out, and we managed to cover some of the interesting and new features in that release of the database. Now, Oracle Database 10*g* has just been released, and there are even more new features to talk about:

- A new, MODEL clause has been added to the SELECT statement, enabling you to write queries that perform spreadsheet-like calculations against multidimensional arrays created from data you select from the database.

- Oracle has added support for using regular expressions from SQL, and with a vengeance. Not only can you use regular expressions to select data, but also to manipulate data in various, useful ways. For example, you can perform regular expression search-and-replace operations. No other database vendor that we know of offers such powerful, regular expression functionality.

- XML is everywhere these days, and that hasn't gone unnoticed in the world of SQL. The ANSI/ISO folk have created the SQL/XML standard, which defines mechanisms for selecting relational data and presenting it in XML form. Oracle supports this standard, which involves several, new SQL functions. Oracle also now supports XML as a native data type.

These are just the big features, which, of course, we cover in this second edition. In addition, we cover many small updates to Oracle SQL, such as the multiset union operators that enable you to perform set operations involving nested table collections.

Finally, we've worked carefully together as a team, not only with each other, but also with our editor, to ensure that all examples in this book are drawn from a single data set. You'll be able to download that data set from this book's catalog page. You can then use it to follow along with our examples.

Objectives of This Book

The single most important objective of this book is to help you harness the power of Oracle SQL to the maximum extent possible. You will learn to:

- Understand the features and capabilities of the SQL language, as implemented by Oracle.
- Use complex SQL features, such as outer joins, correlated subqueries, hierarchical queries, grouping operations, and analytical queries.
- Use DECODE and CASE to implement conditional logic in your SQL queries.
- Write SQL statements that operate against partitions, objects, and collections, such as nested tables and variable arrays.
- Use the new SQL features introduced in Oracle Database 10*g*, such as regular expressions and interrow calculations.
- Use best-practices to write efficient, maintainable SQL queries.

One topic that is important to us and many of our readers, but which is not explicitly discussed in this book is SQL tuning. Tuning tips are sprinkled throughout the book, but we do not include a chapter on tuning for the following reasons:

- Tuning is a large topic, and reasonable coverage of SQL tuning would easily double or triple the size of this book.
- There are already many excellent Oracle-specific and general-purpose tuning books on the market, whereas there are very few books (in our opinion, exactly one) that thoroughly explore the feature set of Oracle SQL.
- In many ways, mastery of Oracle's SQL implementation is the most important tool in your tuning toolkit.

With this book under your belt, you will be less likely to write SQL statements that perform badly, and you will be able to employ multiple strategies to rework existing statements.

Audience for This Book

This book is for Oracle developers, database administrators, and anyone who needs access to data stored in an Oracle database for reporting or ad-hoc analysis. Whether you are new to the world of databases or a seasoned professional, if you use SQL to access an Oracle database, this book is for you. Whether you use simple queries to access data or embed them in PL/SQL or Java programs, SQL is the core of all data access tasks in your application. Knowing the power and flexibility of SQL will improve your productivity, allowing you to get more done in less time, and with increased certainty that the SQL statements you write are indeed correct.

Platform and Version

We used Oracle Database 10*g* in writing this book. We've covered many of Oracle Database 10*g*'s important new SQL features, including regular expressions, hierarchical query features, object and collection functionality, and interrow calculations. Most of the concepts, syntax, and examples apply to earlier releases of Oracle as well. We specifically point out the new Oracle Database 10*g* features.

Structure of This Book

This book is divided into 18 chapters and 1 appendix:

- Chapter 1, *Introduction to SQL*, introduces the SQL language and describes its brief history. This chapter is primarily for those readers who have little or no prior SQL experience. You'll find simple examples of the core SQL statements (SELECT, INSERT, UPDATE, and DELETE) and of SQL's basic features.

- Chapter 2, *The WHERE Clause*, describes ways to filter data in your SQL statements. You'll learn to restrict the results of a query to the rows you wish to see, and restrict the results of a data manipulation statement to the rows you wish to modify.

- Chapter 3, *Joins*, describes constructs used to access data from multiple, related tables. The important concepts of inner join and outer join are discussed in this chapter.

- Chapter 4, *Group Operations*, shows you how to generate summary information, such as totals and subtotals, from your data. Learn how to define groups of rows, and how to apply various aggregate functions to summarize data in those groups.

- Chapter 5, *Subqueries*, shows you how to use correlated and noncorrelated subqueries and inline views to solve complex problems that would otherwise require procedural code together with more than one query.

- Chapter 6, *Handling Temporal Data*, talks about handling date and time information in an Oracle database. Learn the tricks and traps of querying time-based data.

- Chapter 7, *Set Operations*, shows you how to use UNION, INTERSECT, and MINUS to combine results from two or more independent component queries into one.

- Chapter 8, *Hierarchical Queries*, shows you how to store and extract hierarchical information (such as in an organizational chart) from a relational table. Oracle provides many features to facilitate working with hierarchical data, including several new features introduced in Oracle Database 10*g*.

- Chapter 9, *DECODE and CASE*, talks about two very powerful yet simple features of Oracle SQL that enable you to simulate conditional logic in what is otherwise a declarative language.

- Chapter 10, *Partitioning*, discusses the issues involved with creating and accessing partitioned tables using SQL. Learn to write SQL statements that operate on specific partitions and subpartitions.

- Chapter 11, *PL/SQL*, explores the integration of SQL and PL/SQL. This chapter describes how to call PL/SQL stored procedures and functions from SQL statements, and how to write efficient SQL statements within PL/SQL programs.

- Chapter 12, *Objects and Collections*, explores the object-oriented aspects of the Oracle database server, including object types and collections.

- Chapter 13, *Advanced Group Operations*, deals with complex grouping operations used mostly in decision support systems. We show you how to use Oracle features such as ROLLUP, CUBE, and GROUPING SETS to efficiently generate various levels of summary information required by decision-support applications. We also discuss the grouping features that enable composite and concatenated groupings, including the GROUP_ID and GROUPING_ID functions.

- Chapter 14, *Advanced Analytic SQL*, deals with analytical queries and analytic functions. Learn how to use ranking, windowing, and reporting functions to generate decision-support information.

- Chapter 15, *SQL Best Practices*, talks about best practices that you should follow to write efficient and maintainable queries. Learn which SQL constructs are the most efficient for a given situation. For example, we describe when it's better to use WHERE instead of HAVING to restrict query results. We also discuss the performance implications of using bind variables vis-à-vis literal SQL.

- Chapter 16, *XML*, explores how the Oracle server can store XML documents, features used to navigate, search, and extract content from XML documents, and functions used to generate XML documents from ordinary tables.

- Chapter 17, *Regular Expressions*, shows how to write and interpret regular expressions for performing advanced text searches and substitutions.

- Chapter 18, *Model Queries*, introduces the new, MODEL clause, which lets you manipulate relational data as if it were a big, multidimensional, spreadsheet (Oracle prefers the term *model*). Model queries enable you to solve problems using a single SQL statement that previously would have required you to download data to a third-party, spreadsheet program such as Microsoft Excel.

- The Appendix, *Oracle's Old Join Syntax*, describes the SQL89 join syntax, and Oracle's proprietary, outer-join syntax. Only this syntax was available for joins until the release of Oracle9*i* Database, which introduced support for the newer, and better, SQL92 join syntax.

Conventions Used in This Book

The following typographical conventions are used in this book:

Italic

> Used for filenames, directory names, table names, field names, and URLs. It is also used for emphasis and for the first use of a technical term.

`Constant width`

> Used for examples and to show the contents of files and the output of commands. Also used for column names, XML element names, regular expressions, SQL literals mentioned in the text, and function names.

`Constant width italic`

> Used in syntax descriptions to indicate user-defined items.

`Constant width bold`

> Indicates user input in examples showing an interaction. Also indicates emphasized code elements to which you should pay particular attention.

`Constant width bold italic`

> Used in code examples to emphasize aspects of the SQL statements, or results, that are under discussion.

UPPERCASE

> In syntax descriptions, indicates keywords.

lowercase

> In syntax descriptions, indicates user-defined items, such as variables.

[ ] In syntax descriptions, square brackets enclose optional items.

{ } In syntax descriptions, curly brackets enclose a set of items from which you must choose only one.

| In syntax descriptions, a vertical bar separates the items enclosed in curly or square brackets, as in {TRUE | FALSE}.

… In syntax descriptions, ellipses indicate repeating elements.

> Indicates a tip, suggestion, or general note. For example, we use notes to point you to useful new features in Oracle Database 10g.

> Indicates a warning or caution. For example, we'll tell you if a certain SQL clause might have unintended consequences if not used carefully.

Using Code Examples

This book is here to help you get your job done. In general, you may use the code in this book in your programs and documentation. You do not need to contact us for permission unless you're reproducing a significant portion of the code. For example, writing a program that uses several chunks of code from this book does not require permission. Selling or distributing a CD-ROM of examples from O'Reilly books *does* require permission. Answering a question by citing this book and quoting example code does not require permission. Incorporating a significant amount of example code from this book into your product's documentation *does* require permission.

We appreciate, but do not require, attribution. An attribution usually includes the title, author, publisher, and ISBN. For example: "*Mastering Oracle SQL*, Second Edition, by Sanjay Mishra and Alan Beaulieu. Copyright 2004 O'Reilly Media, Inc., 0-596-00632-2."

If you feel your use of code examples falls outside fair use or the permission given above, feel free to contact us at:

permissions@oreilly.com.

Comments and Questions

We have tested and verified the information in this book to the best of our ability, but you may find that features have changed or that we have made mistakes. If so, please notify us by writing to:

O'Reilly Media, Inc.
1005 Gravenstein Highway North
Sebastopol, CA 95472
(800) 998-9938 (in the United States or Canada)
(707) 829-0515 (international or local)
(707) 829-0104 (fax)

You can also send messages electronically. To be put on the mailing list or request a catalog, send email to:

info@oreilly.com

To ask technical questions or comment on the book, send email to:

bookquestions@oreilly.com

O'Reilly has a web site for this book, where you can find examples and errata (previously reported errors and corrections are available for public view there). You can access this page at:

http://www.oreilly.com/catalog/0596006322

For more information about this book and others, see the O'Reilly web site:

http://www.oreilly.com

Acknowledgments

We are indebted to a great many people who have contributed in the development and production of this book. We owe a huge debt of gratitude to Jonathan Gennick, the editor of the book. Jonathan's vision for this book, close attention to details, and exceptional editing skills are the reasons this book is here today.

Our sincere thanks to our technical reviewers: Diana Lorentz, Jason Bucata, Trudy Pelzer, and Peter Linsley, who generously gave their valuable time to read and comment on a draft copy of this book. Their contributions have greatly improved its accuracy, readability, and value.

This book certainly would not have been possible without a lot of hard work and support from the skillful staff at O'Reilly, including Ellie Volckhausen and Emma Colby, the cover designers; David Futato, the interior designer; Julie Hawks, who converted the files; Matt Hutchinson, the production editor; Rob Romano and Jessamyn Read, the illustrators; and Sarah Sherman, Marlowe Shaeffer, and Claire Cloutier, who provided quality control.

From Sanjay

I would like to thank my coauthor Alan and my coauthor/editor Jonathan Gennick for constant cooperation and smooth execution during the first as well as the second edition of this book.

My adventure with Oracle's database started in the Tribology Workbench project at Tata Steel, Jamshedpur, India. Sincere thanks to my co-workers in the Tribology Workbench project for all the experiments and explorations we did during our learning days with Oracle. Ever since, Oracle database technology has become a way of life for me.

Special thanks the readers of the first edition whose feedback, comments, questions, and suggestions helped improve the second edition of the book. Sincere thanks to my current and previous co-workers for their support and encouragement.

Last, but not the least, I thank my wife, Sudipti, for her support, understanding, and constant encouragement.

From Alan

I would like to thank my coauthor Sanjay and my coauthor/editor Jonathan Gennick for helping to make the second edition of this book a reality. I would also like to thank the many readers of our first edition who pointed out errors, asked questions, and made suggestions; with your help, our second edition is a much better book.

Most of all, I would like to thank my wife, Nancy, for her support, patience, and encouragement, and my daughters, Michelle and Nicole, for their love and inspiration.

CHAPTER 1

Introduction to SQL

In this introductory chapter, we explore the origin and utility of the SQL language, demonstrate some of the more useful features of the language, and define a simple database design from which most examples in the book are derived.

What Is SQL?

SQL is a special-purpose language used to define, access, and manipulate data. SQL is *nonprocedural*, meaning that it describes the necessary components (i.e., tables) and desired results without dictating exactly how those results should be computed. Every SQL implementation sits atop a *database engine*, whose job it is to interpret SQL statements and determine how the various data structures in the database should be accessed to accurately and efficiently produce the desired outcome.

The SQL language includes two distinct sets of commands: *Data Definition Language* (DDL) is the subset of SQL used to define and modify various data structures, while *Data Manipulation Language* (DML) is the subset of SQL used to access and manipulate data contained within the data structures previously defined via DDL. DDL includes numerous commands for handling such tasks as creating tables, indexes, views, and constraints, while DML is comprised of just five statements:

INSERT
   Adds data to a database.

UPDATE
   Modifies data in a database.

DELETE
   Removes data from a database.

MERGE
   Adds and/or modifies data in a database. MERGE is part of the 2003 ANSI SQL standard.

SELECT
   Retrieves data from a database.

Some people feel that DDL is the sole property of database administrators, while database developers are responsible for writing DML statements, but the two are not so easily separated. It is difficult to efficiently access and manipulate data without an understanding of what data structures are available and how they are related; likewise, it is difficult to design appropriate data structures without knowledge of how the data will be accessed. That being said, this book deals almost exclusively with DML, except where DDL is presented to set the stage for one or more DML examples. The reasons for focusing on just the DML portion of SQL include:

- DDL is well represented in various books on database design and administration as well as in SQL reference guides.
- Most database performance issues are the result of inefficient DML statements.
- Even with a paltry five statements, DML is a rich enough topic to warrant not just one book, but a whole series of books.

 Anyone who writes SQL in an Oracle environment should be armed with the following three books: a reference guide to the SQL language, such as *Oracle in a Nutshell* (O'Reilly); a performance-tuning guide, such as *Optimizing Oracle Performance* (O'Reilly); and the book you are holding, which shows how to best utilize and combine the various features of Oracle's SQL implementation.

So why should you care about SQL? In this age of Internet computing and n-tier architectures, does anyone even care about data access anymore? Actually, efficient storage and retrieval of information is more important than ever:

- Many companies now offer services via the Internet. During peak hours, these services may need to handle thousands of concurrent requests, and unacceptable response times equate to lost revenue. For such systems, every SQL statement must be carefully crafted to ensure acceptable performance as data volumes increase.
- We can store a lot more data today than we could just a few years ago. A single disk array can hold tens of terabytes of data, and the ability to store hundreds of terabytes is just around the corner. Software used to load or analyze data in these environments must harness the full power of SQL to process ever-increasing data volumes within constant (or shrinking) time windows.

Hopefully, you now have an appreciation for what SQL is and why it is important. The next section will explore the origins of the SQL language and the support for the SQL standard in Oracle's products.

A Brief History of SQL

In the early 1970s, an IBM research fellow named Dr. E. F. Codd endeavored to apply the rigors of mathematics to the then-untamed world of data storage and retrieval. Codd's work led to the definition of the *relational data model* and a language called DSL/Alpha for manipulating data in a relational database. IBM liked what they saw, so they commissioned a project called System/R to build a prototype based on Codd's work. Among other things, the System/R team developed a simplified version of DSL called SQUARE, which was later renamed SEQUEL, and finally renamed SQL.

The work done on System/R eventually led to the release of various IBM products based on the relational model. Other companies, such as Oracle, rallied around the relational flag as well. By the mid 1980s, SQL had gathered sufficient momentum in the marketplace to warrant oversight by the American National Standards Institute (ANSI). ANSI released its first SQL standard in 1986, followed by updates in 1989, 1992, 1999, and 2003. There will undoubtedly be further refinements in the future.

Thirty years after the System/R team began prototyping a relational database, SQL is still going strong. While there have been numerous attempts to dethrone relational databases in the marketplace, well-designed relational databases coupled with well-written SQL statements continue to succeed in handling large, complex data sets where other methods fail.

Oracle's SQL Implementation

Given that Oracle was an early adopter of the relational model and SQL, one might think that they would have put a great deal of effort into conforming with the various ANSI standards. For many years, however, the folks at Oracle seemed content that their implementation of SQL was functionally equivalent to the ANSI standards without being overly concerned with true compliance. Beginning with the release of Oracle8*i*, however, Oracle has stepped up its efforts to conform to ANSI standards and has tackled such features as the CASE statement and the left/right/full outer join syntax.

Ironically, the business community seems to be moving in the opposite direction. A few years ago, people were much more concerned with portability and would limit their developers to ANSI-compliant SQL so that they could implement their systems on various database engines. Today, companies tend to pick a database engine to use across the enterprise and allow their developers to use the full range of available options without concern for ANSI-compliance. One reason for this change in attitude is the advent of n-tier architectures, where all database access can be contained within a single tier instead of being scattered throughout an application. Another possible reason might be the emergence of clear leaders in the DBMS market over the last decade, such that managers perceive less risk in which database engine they choose.

Theoretical Versus Practical Terminology

If you were to peruse the various writings on the relational model, you would come across terminology that you will not find used in this book (such as *relations* and *tuples*). Instead, we use practical terms such as tables and rows, and we refer to the various parts of a SQL statement by name rather than by function (i.e., "SELECT clause" instead of *projection*). With all due respect to Dr. Codd, you will never hear the word *tuple* used in a business setting, and, since this book is targeted toward people who use Oracle products to solve business problems, you won't find it here either.

A Simple Database

Because this is a practical book, it contains numerous examples. Rather than fabricating different sets of tables and columns for every chapter or section in the book, we have decided to draw from a single, simple schema for most examples. The subject area that we chose to model is a parts distributor, such as an auto-parts wholesaler or medical device distributor, in which the business fills customer orders for one or more parts that are supplied by external suppliers. Figure 1-1 shows the entity-relationship model for this business.

If you are unfamiliar with entity-relationship models, here is a brief description of how they work. Each box in the model represents an *entity*, which correlates to a database table.* The lines between the entities represent the *relationships* between tables, which correlate to foreign keys. For example, the cust_order table holds a foreign key to the employee table, which signifies the salesperson responsible for a particular order. Physically, this means that the cust_order table contains a column holding employee ID numbers, and that, for any given order, the employee ID number indicates the employee who sold that order. If you find this confusing, simply use the diagram as an illustration of the tables and columns found within our database. As you work your way through the SQL examples in this book, return occasionally to the diagram, and you should find that the relationships start making sense.

---

* Depending on the purpose of the model, entities may or may not correlate to database tables. For example, a *logical* model depicts business entities and their relationships, whereas a *physical* model illustrates tables and their primary/foreign keys. The model in Figure 1-1 is a physical model.

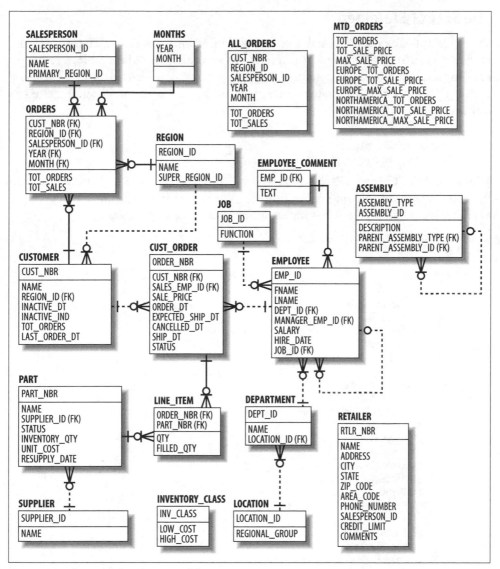

Figure 1-1. The parts distributor model

DML Statements

In this section, we will introduce the five statements that comprise the DML portion of SQL. The information presented in this section should be enough to allow you to start writing DML statements. As is discussed at the end of the section, however, DML can look deceptively simple, so keep in mind while reading the section that there are many more facets to DML than are discussed here.

The SELECT Statement

The SELECT statement is used to retrieve data from a database. The set of data retrieved via a SELECT statement is referred to as a *result set*. Like a table, a result set is comprised of rows and columns, making it possible to populate a table using the result set of a SELECT statement. The SELECT statement can be summarized as follows:

```
SELECT <one or more things>
FROM <one or more places>
WHERE <zero, one, or more conditions apply>
```

While the SELECT and FROM clauses are required, the WHERE clause is optional (although you will seldom see it omitted). We will therefore begin with a simple example that retrieves three columns from every row of the customer table:

```
SELECT cust_nbr, name, region_id
FROM customer;
```

```
CUST_NBR NAME                                REGION_ID
-------- ----------------------------------- ----------
       1 Cooper Industries                           5
       2 Emblazon Corp.                              5
       3 Ditech Corp.                                5
       4 Flowtech Inc.                               5
       5 Gentech Industries                          5
       6 Spartan Industries                          6
       7 Wallace Labs                                6
       8 Zantech Inc.                                6
       9 Cardinal Technologies                       6
      10 Flowrite Corp.                              6
      11 Glaven Technologies                         7
      12 Johnson Labs                                7
      13 Kimball Corp.                               7
      14 Madden Industries                           7
      15 Turntech Inc.                               7
      16 Paulson Labs                                8
      17 Evans Supply Corp.                          8
      18 Spalding Medical Inc.                       8
      19 Kendall-Taylor Corp.                        8
      20 Malden Labs                                 8
      21 Crimson Medical Inc.                        9
      22 Nichols Industries                          9
      23 Owens-Baxter Corp.                          9
      24 Jackson Medical Inc.                        9
      25 Worcester Technologies                      9
      26 Alpha Technologies                         10
      27 Phillips Labs                              10
      28 Jaztech Corp.                              10
      29 Madden-Taylor Inc.                         10
      30 Wallace Industries                         10
```

Since we neglected to impose any conditions via a WHERE clause, the query returns every row from the customer table. If you want to restrict the set of data returned by the query, you can include a WHERE clause with a single condition:

```
SELECT cust_nbr, name, region_id
FROM customer
WHERE region_id = 8;

  CUST_NBR NAME                             REGION_ID
---------- ------------------------------- ----------
        16 Paulson Labs                             8
        17 Evans Supply Corp.                       8
        18 Spalding Medical Inc.                    8
        19 Kendall-Taylor Corp.                     8
        20 Malden Labs                              8
```

The result set now includes only those customers residing in the region with a region_id of 8. But what if you want to specify a region by name instead of region_id? You could query the region table for a particular name and then query the customer table using the retrieved region_id. Instead of issuing two different queries, however, you can produce the same outcome using a single query by introducing a *join*, as in:

```
SELECT customer.cust_nbr, customer.name, region.name
FROM customer INNER JOIN region
  ON region.region_id = customer.region_id
WHERE region.name = 'New England';

  CUST_NBR NAME                             NAME
---------- ------------------------------- -----------
         1 Cooper Industries               New England
         2 Emblazon Corp.                  New England
         3 Ditech Corp.                    New England
         4 Flowtech Inc.                   New England
         5 Gentech Industries              New England
```

The FROM clause now contains two tables instead of one and includes a *join condition* that specifies that the customer and region tables are to be joined using the region_id column found in both tables. Joins and join conditions will be explored in detail in Chapter 3.

Since both the customer and region tables contain a column called name, you must specify which table's name column you are interested in. This is done in the previous example by using dot-notation to append the table name in front of each column name. If you would rather not type full table names, you can assign *table aliases* to each table in the FROM clause and use those aliases instead of the table names in the SELECT and WHERE clauses, as in:

```
SELECT c.cust_nbr, c.name, r.name
FROM customer c INNER JOIN region r
ON r.region_id = c.region_id
WHERE r.name = 'New England';
```

In this example, we assigned the alias c to the customer table and the alias r to the region table. Thus, we can use c. and r. instead of customer. and region. in the SELECT and WHERE clauses.

SELECT clause elements

In the examples thus far, the result sets generated by our queries have contained columns from one or more tables. While most elements in your SELECT clauses will typically be simple column references, a SELECT clause may also include:

- Literal values, such as numbers (27) or strings ('abc')
- Expressions, such as shape.diameter * 3.1415927
- Function calls, such as TO_DATE('01-JAN-2004','DD-MON-YYYY')
- Pseudocolumns, such as ROWID, ROWNUM, or LEVEL

While the first three items in this list are fairly straightforward, the last item merits further discussion. Oracle makes available several phantom columns, known as *pseudocolumns*, that do not exist in any tables. Rather, they are values visible during query execution that can be helpful in certain situations.

For example, the pseudocolumn ROWID represents the physical location of a row. This information represents the fastest possible access mechanism. It can be useful if you plan to delete or update a row retrieved via a query. However, you should never store ROWID values in the database, nor should you reference them outside of the transaction in which they are retrieved, since a row's ROWID can change in certain situations, and ROWIDs can be reused after a row has been deleted.

The next example demonstrates each of the different element types from the previous list:

```
SELECT ROWNUM,
  cust_nbr,
  1 multiplier,
  'cust # ' || cust_nbr cust_nbr_str,
  'hello' greeting,
  TO_CHAR(last_order_dt, 'DD-MON-YYYY') last_order
FROM customer;

ROWNUM CUST_NBR MULTIPLIER CUST_NBR_STR GREETING LAST_ORDER
------ -------- ---------- ------------ -------- -----------
     1        1          1 cust # 1     hello    15-JUN-2000
     2        2          1 cust # 2     hello    27-JUN-2000
     3        3          1 cust # 3     hello    07-JUL-2000
     4        4          1 cust # 4     hello    15-JUL-2000
     5        5          1 cust # 5     hello    01-JUN-2000
     6        6          1 cust # 6     hello    10-JUN-2000
     7        7          1 cust # 7     hello    17-JUN-2000
     8        8          1 cust # 8     hello    22-JUN-2000
     9        9          1 cust # 9     hello    25-JUN-2000
    10       10          1 cust # 10    hello    01-JUN-2000
```

```
11    11     1 cust # 11    hello    05-JUN-2000
12    12     1 cust # 12    hello    07-JUN-2000
13    13     1 cust # 13    hello    07-JUN-2000
14    14     1 cust # 14    hello    05-JUN-2000
15    15     1 cust # 15    hello    01-JUN-2000
16    16     1 cust # 16    hello    31-MAY-2000
17    17     1 cust # 17    hello    28-MAY-2000
18    18     1 cust # 18    hello    23-MAY-2000
19    19     1 cust # 19    hello    16-MAY-2000
20    20     1 cust # 20    hello    01-JUN-2000
21    21     1 cust # 21    hello    26-MAY-2000
22    22     1 cust # 22    hello    18-MAY-2000
23    23     1 cust # 23    hello    08-MAY-2000
24    24     1 cust # 24    hello    26-APR-2000
25    25     1 cust # 25    hello    01-JUN-2000
26    26     1 cust # 26    hello    21-MAY-2000
27    27     1 cust # 27    hello    08-MAY-2000
28    28     1 cust # 28    hello    23-APR-2000
29    29     1 cust # 29    hello    06-APR-2000
30    30     1 cust # 30    hello    01-JUN-2000
```

Note that the third through sixth columns have been given *column aliases*, which are names that you assign to a column. If you are going to refer to the columns in your query by name instead of by position, you will want to assign each column a name that makes sense to you.

Interestingly, a SELECT clause is not required to reference columns from any of the tables in the FROM clause. For example, the next query's result set is composed entirely of literals:

```
SELECT 1 num, 'abc' str
FROM customer;

       NUM STR
---------- ---
         1 abc
         1 abc
         1 abc
         1 abc
         1 abc
         1 abc
         1 abc
         1 abc
         1 abc
         1 abc
         1 abc
         1 abc
         1 abc
         1 abc
         1 abc
         1 abc
```

```
1 abc
1 abc
1 abc
1 abc
1 abc
1 abc
1 abc
1 abc
1 abc
1 abc
1 abc
1 abc
1 abc
```

Since there are 30 rows in the customer table, the query's result set includes 30 identical rows of data.

Ordering your results

In general, there is no guarantee that the result set generated by your query will be in any particular order. If you want your results to be sorted by one or more columns, you can add an ORDER BY clause after the WHERE clause. The following example sorts the results from the New England query by customer name:

```
SELECT c.cust_nbr, c.name, r.name
FROM customer c INNER JOIN region r
ON r.region_id = c.region_id
WHERE r.name = 'New England'
ORDER BY c.name;

CUST_NBR NAME                                 NAME
-------- ------------------------------- -----------
       1 Cooper Industries                    New England
       3 Ditech Corp.                         New England
       2 Emblazon Corp.                       New England
       4 Flowtech Inc.                        New England
       5 Gentech Industries                   New England
```

You may also designate the sort column(s) by their position in the SELECT clause. To sort the previous query by customer number, which is the first column in the SELECT clause, you could issue the following statement:

```
SELECT c.cust_nbr, c.name, r.name
FROM customer c INNER JOIN region r
ON r.region_id = c.region_id
WHERE r.name = 'New England'
ORDER BY 1;

  CUST_NBR NAME                                 NAME
---------- ------------------------------- -----------
         1 Cooper Industries                    New England
         2 Emblazon Corp.                       New England
         3 Ditech Corp.                         New England
```

```
4 Flowtech Inc.                        New England
5 Gentech Industries                   New England
```

Specifying sort keys by position will certainly save you some typing, but it can often lead to errors if you later change the order of the columns in your SELECT clause.

Removing duplicates

In some cases, your result set may contain duplicate data. For example, if you are compiling a list of parts that were included in last month's orders, the same part number would appear multiple times if more than one order included that part. If you want duplicates removed from your result set, you can include the DISTINCT keyword in your SELECT clause, as in:

```
SELECT DISTINCT li.part_nbr
FROM cust_order co INNER JOIN line_item li
ON co.order_nbr = li.order_nbr
WHERE co.order_dt >= TO_DATE('01-JUL-2001','DD-MON-YYYY')
  AND co.order_dt < TO_DATE('01-AUG-2001','DD-MON-YYYY');
```

This query returns the distinct set of parts ordered during July 2001. Without the DISTINCT keyword, the result set would contain one row for every line-item of every order, and the same part would appear multiple times if it was included in multiple orders. When deciding whether to include DISTINCT in your SELECT clause, keep in mind that finding and removing duplicates necessitates a sort operation, which can greatly increase the execution time of your query.

The INSERT Statement

The INSERT statement is the mechanism for loading data into your database. This section will introduce the traditional single-table INSERT statement, as well as the new multitable INSERT ALL statement introduced in Oracle 9*i*.

Single-table inserts

With the traditional INSERT statement, data can be inserted into only one table at a time, although the data being loaded into the table can be pulled from one or more additional tables. When inserting data into a table, you do not need to provide values for every column in the table; however, you need to be aware of the columns that require non-NULL* values and the ones that do not. Here's the definition of the employee table:

```
describe employee

Name                                       Null?    Type
------------------------------------------ -------- ------------
EMP_ID                                     NOT NULL NUMBER(5)
```

---

* NULL indicates the absence of a value. The use of NULL is covered in Chapter 2.

```
FNAME                           VARCHAR2(20)
LNAME                           VARCHAR2(20)
DEPT_ID               NOT NULL  NUMBER(5)
MANAGER_EMP_ID                  NUMBER(5)
SALARY                          NUMBER(5)
HIRE_DATE                       DATE
JOB_ID                          NUMBER(3)
```

The NOT NULL designation for the emp_id and dept_id columns indicates that values are required for these two columns. Therefore, you must be sure to provide values for at least these two columns in your INSERT statements, as demonstrated by the following:

```
INSERT INTO employee (emp_id, dept_id)
VALUES (101, 20);
```

Any inserts into employee may optionally include any or all of the remaining six columns, which are described as *nullable* since they may be left undefined. Thus, you could decide to add the employee's last name to the previous statement:

```
INSERT INTO employee (emp_id, lname, dept_id)
VALUES (101, 'Smith', 20);
```

The VALUES clause must contain the same number of elements as the column list, and the data types must match the column definitions. In this example, emp_id and dept_id hold numeric values while lname holds character data, so the INSERT statement will execute without error. Oracle always tries to convert data from one type to another automatically, however, so the following statement will also run without error:

```
INSERT INTO employee (emp_id, lname, dept_id)
VALUES ('101', 'Smith', '20');
```

Sometimes, the data to be inserted needs to be retrieved from one or more tables. Since the SELECT statement generates a result set consisting of rows and columns of data, you can feed the result set from a SELECT statement directly into an INSERT statement, as in:

```
INSERT INTO employee (emp_id, fname, lname, dept_id, hire_date)
SELECT 101, 'Dave', 'Smith', d.dept_id, SYSDATE
FROM department d
WHERE d.name = 'ACCOUNTING';
```

In this example, the purpose of the SELECT statement is to retrieve the department ID for the Accounting department. The other four columns in the SELECT clause are either literals (101, 'Dave', 'Smith') or function calls (SYSDATE).

Multitable inserts

While inserting data into a single table is the norm, there are situations where data from a single source must be inserted either into multiple tables or into the same table multiple times. Such tasks would normally be handled programatically using PL/SQL,

---

but Oracle9*i* introduced the concept of a multitable insert to allow complex data insertion via a single INSERT statement. For example, let's say that one of Mary Turner's customers wants to set up a recurring order on the last day of each month for the next six months. The following statement adds six rows to the cust_order table using a SELECT statement that returns exactly one row:

```
INSERT ALL
INTO cust_order (order_nbr, cust_nbr, sales_emp_id,
  order_dt, expected_ship_dt, status)
VALUES (ord_nbr, cust_nbr, emp_id,
  ord_dt, ord_dt + 7, status)
INTO cust_order (order_nbr, cust_nbr, sales_emp_id,
  order_dt, expected_ship_dt, status)
VALUES (ord_nbr + 1, cust_nbr, emp_id,
  add_months(ord_dt, 1), add_months(ord_dt, 1) + 7, status)
INTO cust_order (order_nbr, cust_nbr, sales_emp_id,
  order_dt, expected_ship_dt, status)
VALUES (ord_nbr + 2, cust_nbr, emp_id,
  add_months(ord_dt, 2), add_months(ord_dt, 2) + 7, status)
INTO cust_order (order_nbr, cust_nbr, sales_emp_id,
  order_dt, expected_ship_dt, status)
VALUES (ord_nbr + 3, cust_nbr, emp_id,
  add_months(ord_dt, 3), add_months(ord_dt, 3) + 7, status)
INTO cust_order (order_nbr, cust_nbr, sales_emp_id,
  order_dt, expected_ship_dt, status)
VALUES (ord_nbr + 4, cust_nbr, emp_id,
  add_months(ord_dt, 4), add_months(ord_dt, 4) + 7, status)
INTO cust_order (order_nbr, cust_nbr, sales_emp_id,
  order_dt, expected_ship_dt, status)
VALUES (ord_nbr + 5, cust_nbr, emp_id,
  add_months(ord_dt, 5), add_months(ord_dt, 5) + 7, status)
SELECT 99990 ord_nbr, c.cust_nbr cust_nbr, e.emp_id emp_id,
  last_day(SYSDATE) ord_dt, 'PENDING' status
FROM customer c CROSS JOIN employee e
WHERE e.fname = 'MARY' and e.lname = 'TURNER'
  and c.name = 'Gentech Industries';
```

The SELECT statement returns the data necessary for this month's order, and the INSERT statement modifies the order_nbr, order_dt, and expected_ship_dt columns for the next five months' orders. You are not obligated to insert all rows into the same table, nor must your SELECT statement return only one row, making the multitable insert statement quite flexible and powerful. The next example shows how data about a new salesperson can be entered into both the employee and salesperson tables:

```
INSERT ALL
INTO employee (emp_id, fname, lname, dept_id, hire_date)
VALUES (eid, fnm, lnm, did, TRUNC(SYSDATE))
INTO salesperson (salesperson_id, name, primary_region_id)
VALUES (eid, fnm || ' ' || lnm, rid)
SELECT 1001 eid, 'JAMES' fnm, 'GOULD' lnm,
  d.dept_id did, r.region_id rid
```

```
    FROM department d, region r
    WHERE d.name = 'SALES' and r.name = 'Southeast US';
```

So far, you have seen how multiple rows can be inserted into the same table and how the same rows can be inserted into multiple tables. The next, and final, example of multitable inserts demonstrates how a *conditional clause* can be used to direct each row of data generated by the SELECT statement into zero, one, or many tables:

```
INSERT FIRST
  WHEN order_dt < TO_DATE('2001-01-01', 'YYYY-MM-DD') THEN
    INTO cust_order_2000 (order_nbr, cust_nbr, sales_emp_id,
      sale_price, order_dt)
    VALUES (order_nbr, cust_nbr, sales_emp_id, sale_price, order_dt)
  WHEN order_dt < TO_DATE('2002-01-01', 'YYYY-MM-DD') THEN
    INTO cust_order_2001 (order_nbr, cust_nbr, sales_emp_id,
      sale_price, order_dt)
    VALUES (order_nbr, cust_nbr, sales_emp_id, sale_price, order_dt)
  WHEN order_dt < TO_DATE('2003-01-01', 'YYYY-MM-DD') THEN
    INTO cust_order_2002 (order_nbr, cust_nbr, sales_emp_id,
      sale_price, order_dt)
    VALUES (order_nbr, cust_nbr, sales_emp_id, sale_price, order_dt)
SELECT co.order_nbr, co.cust_nbr, co.sales_emp_id,
  co.sale_price, co.order_dt
FROM cust_order co
WHERE co.cancelled_dt IS NULL
  AND co.ship_dt IS NOT NULL;
```

This statement copies all customer orders prior to January 1, 2003, to one of three tables depending on the value of the order_dt column. The keyword FIRST specifies that once one of the conditions evaluates to TRUE, the statement should skip the remaining conditions and move on to the next row. If you specify ALL instead of FIRST, all conditions will be evaluated, and each row might be inserted into multiple tables if more than one condition evaluates to TRUE.

The DELETE Statement

The DELETE statement facilitates the removal of data from the database. Like the SELECT statement, the DELETE statement contains a WHERE clause that specifies the conditions used to identify rows to be deleted. If you neglect to add a WHERE clause to your DELETE statement, all rows will be deleted from the target table. The following statement will delete all employees with the last name of Hooper from the employee table:

```
DELETE FROM employee
WHERE lname = 'HOOPER';
```

In some cases, the values needed for one or more of the conditions in your WHERE clause exist in another table. For example, your company may decide to outsource its accounting functions, thereby necessitating the removal of all accounting personnel from the employee table:

```
DELETE FROM employee
WHERE dept_id =
 (SELECT dept_id
  FROM department
  WHERE name = 'ACCOUNTING');
```

The use of the SELECT statement in this example is known as a *subquery* and will be studied in detail in Chapter 5.

In certain cases, you may want to restrict the number of rows that are to be deleted from a table. For example, you may want to remove all data from a table, but you want to limit your transactions to no more than 100,000 rows. If the cust_order table contained 527,365 records, you would need to find a way to restrict your DELETE statement to 100,000 rows and then run the statement six times until all the data has been purged. The following example demonstrates how the ROWNUM pseudocolumn may be used in a DELETE statement to achieve the desired effect:

```
DELETE FROM cust_order
WHERE ROWNUM <= 100000;
COMMIT;
```

The UPDATE Statement

Modifications to existing data are handled by the UPDATE statement. Like the DELETE statement, the UPDATE statement includes a WHERE clause to specify which rows should be targeted. The following example shows how you might give a 10% raise to everyone making less than $40,000:

```
UPDATE employee
SET salary = salary * 1.1
WHERE salary < 40000;
```

If you want to modify more than one column in the table, you have two choices: provide a set of column/value pairs separated by commas, or provide a set of columns and a subquery. The following two UPDATE statements modify the inactive_dt and inactive_ind columns in the customer table for any customer who hasn't placed an order in the past year:

```
UPDATE customer
SET inactive_dt = SYSDATE, inactive_ind = 'Y'
WHERE last_order_dt < SYSDATE - 365;

UPDATE customer
SET (inactive_dt, inactive_ind) =
 (SELECT SYSDATE, 'Y' FROM dual)
WHERE last_order_dt < SYSDATE - 365;
```

The subquery in the second example is a bit forced, since it uses a query against the dual table to build a result set containing two literals, but it should give you an idea of how you would use a subquery in an UPDATE statement. In later chapters, you will see far more interesting uses for subqueries.

 dual is an Oracle-provided table containing exactly one row with one column. It comes in handy when you need to construct a query that returns exactly one row.

The MERGE Statement

There are certain situations, especially within Data Warehouse applications, where you may want to either insert a new row into a table or update an existing row depending on whether or not the data already exists in the table. For example, you may receive a nightly feed of parts data that contains both parts that are known to the system along with parts just introduced by your suppliers. If a part number exists in the part table, you will need to update the unit_cost and status columns; otherwise, you will need to insert a new row.

While you could write code that reads each record from the feed, determines whether or not the part number exists in the part table, and issues either an INSERT or UPDATE statement, you could instead issue a single MERGE statement.* Assuming that your data feed has been loaded into the part_stg staging table, your MERGE statement would look something like the following:

```
1   MERGE INTO part p_dest
2   USING part_stg p_src
3   ON (p_dest.part_nbr = p_src.part_nbr)
4   WHEN MATCHED THEN UPDATE
5     SET p_dest.unit_cost = p_src.unit_cost, p_dest.status = p_src.status
6   WHEN NOT MATCHED THEN INSERT (p_dest.part_nbr, p_dest.name,
7     p_dest.supplier_id, p_dest.status,  p_dest.inventory_qty,
8     p_dest.unit_cost, p_dest.resupply_date)
9     VALUES (p_src.part_nbr, p_src.name,
10    p_src.supplier_id, p_src.status, 0, p_src.unit_cost, null);
```

This statement looks fairly complex, so here is a description of what it is doing:

Lines 1–3

For each row in the part_stg table, see if the part_nbr column exists in the part table.

Lines 4–5

If it does, then update the matching row in the part table using data from the part_stg table.

Lines 6–10

Otherwise, insert a new row into the part table using the data from the part_stg table.

---

* MERGE was introduced in Oracle9i.

So Why Are There 17 More Chapters?

After reading this chapter, you might think that SQL looks pretty simple (at least the DML portion). At a high level, it is fairly simple, and you now know enough about the language to go write some code. However, you will learn over time that there are numerous ways to arrive at the same end point, and some are more efficient and elegant than others. The true test of SQL mastery is when you no longer have the desire to return to what you were working on the previous year, rip out all the SQL, and recode it. For one of us, it took about nine years to reach that point. Hopefully, this book will help you reach that point in far less time.

While you are reading the rest of the book, you might notice that the majority of examples use SELECT statements, with the remainder somewhat evenly distributed across INSERT, UPDATE, and DELETE statements. This disparity is not indicative of the relative importance of SELECT statements over the other three DML statements; rather, SELECT statements are favored because we can show a query's result set, which should help you to better understand the query, and because many of the points being made using SELECT statements can be applied to UPDATE and DELETE statements as well.

CHAPTER 2
The WHERE Clause

Whether you are querying, modifying, or deleting data, the WHERE clause is the mechanism for identifying what data you want to work with. This chapter explores the role of the WHERE clause in SQL statements, as well as the various options available when building a WHERE clause.

Life Without WHERE

Before delving into the WHERE clause, let's imagine life without it. Say that you are interested in doing some maintenance on the data in the part table. To inspect the data in the table, you issue the following query:

```
SELECT part_nbr, name, supplier_id, status, inventory_qty
FROM part;
```

If the part table contains 10,000 items, the result set returned by the query would consist of 10,000 rows, each with 5 columns. You would then load the 10,000 rows into memory and make your modifications.

Once you have made the required modifications to your data in memory, it is time to apply the changes to the part table. Without the ability to specify the rows to modify, you have no choice but to delete all rows in the table and re-insert all 10,000 rows:

```
DELETE FROM part;

INSERT INTO part (part_nbr, name, supplier_id, status, inventory_qty)
VALUES ('XY5-1002', 'Wonder Widget', 1, 'IN-STOCK', 1);

/* 9,999 more INSERTs on the wall, 9,999 more INSERTS... */
```

While this approach works in theory, it wreaks havoc on performance, concurrency (the ability for more than one user to modify data simultaneously), and scalability (the ability to perform predictably as load increases).

Now imagine that you want to modify data in the part table only for those parts supplied by Acme Industries. Since the supplier's name is stored in the supplier table, you must include both the part and supplier tables in the FROM clause:

```
SELECT p.part_nbr, p.name, p.supplier_id, p.status, p.inventory_qty,
    s.supplier_id, s.name
FROM part p, supplier s;
```

If 100 companies supply the 10,000 parts in the part table, this query will return 1,000,000 rows. Known as the *Cartesian product*, this number equates to every possible combination of all rows from the two tables. As you sift through the million rows, you would keep only those where the values of p.supplier_id and s.supplier_id are identical and where the s.name column matches 'Acme Industries'. If Acme Industries supplies only 50 of the 10,000 parts in your database, you will end up discarding 999,950 of the 1,000,000 rows returned by your query.

WHERE to the Rescue

Hopefully, the scenarios in the previous section give you some insight into the utility of the WHERE clause, including the ability to:

- Filter out unwanted data from a query's result set.
- Isolate one or more rows of a table for modification.
- Conditionally join two or more data sets together.

To see how these things are accomplished, let's add a WHERE clause to the previous SELECT statement, which strives to locate all parts supplied by Acme Industries. Here's the query with the new WHERE clause:

```
SELECT p.part_nbr, p.name, p.supplier_id, p.status, p.inventory_qty,
    s.supplier_id, s.name
FROM part p, supplier s
WHERE s.supplier_id = p.supplier_id
    AND s.name = 'Acme Industries';
```

The WHERE clause here is comprised of two parts, known as *conditions*, which are evaluated separately. Conditions always evaluate to either TRUE or FALSE; if there are multiple conditions in a WHERE clause, they all must evaluate to TRUE for a given row to be included in the result set. Actually, that's a bit of an oversimplification. As you will see later, using the OR and NOT operators allows the WHERE clause to evaluate to TRUE even if individual conditions evaluate to FALSE.

For this example, a row created by combining data from the part and supplier tables will only be included in the final result set if both tables share a common value for the supplier_id column, and if the value of the name column in the supplier table matches 'Acme Industries'. Any other permutation of data from the two tables would evaluate to FALSE and be discarded.

For this chapter only, we'll use the older style of join syntax in which you specify join conditions in the WHERE clause. We do this to explore the full functionality of the WHERE clause.

With the addition of the WHERE clause to the previous example, therefore, Oracle will take on the work of discarding undesired rows from the result set, and only 50 rows would be returned by the query, rather than 1,000,000. Now that you have retrieved the 50 rows of interest from the database, you can begin the process of modifying the data. Keep in mind, however, that with the WHERE clause at your disposal you will no longer need to delete and re-insert your modified data; instead, you can use the UPDATE statement to modify specific rows based on the part_nbr column, which is the unique identifier for the table:

```
UPDATE part
SET status = 'DISCONTINUED'
WHERE part_nbr = 'AI5-4557';
```

While this is certainly an improvement, you can do even better. If your intent is to modify the status for all 50 parts supplied by Acme Industries, there is no need to execute a separate query at all. Simply execute a single UPDATE statement that finds and modifies all 50 records:

```
UPDATE part
SET status = 'DISCONTINUED'
WHERE supplier_id =
  (SELECT supplier_id
   FROM supplier
   WHERE name = 'Acme Industries');
```

The WHERE clause in this statement consists of a single condition that equates the supplier_id column to the value returned by the subquery against the supplier table. Subqueries are covered extensively in Chapter 5, so don't worry if this looks a bit intimidating. The net result is that the condition will be rewritten to use the value returned by the subquery, as in:

```
UPDATE part
SET status = 'DISCONTINUED'
WHERE supplier_id = 1;
```

When executed, the condition evaluates to TRUE for exactly 50 of the 10,000 rows in the part table, and the status of those 50 rows changes to DISCONTINUED.

WHERE Clause Evaluation

Now that you have seen the WHERE clause in action, let's take a look at how it is evaluated. As previously mentioned, the WHERE clause consists of one or more conditions that evaluate independently to TRUE or FALSE. If your WHERE clause consists of multiple conditions, the conditions are separated by the logical operators

AND and OR. Depending on the outcome of the individual conditions and the placement of these logical operators, Oracle will assign a final value of TRUE or FALSE to each candidate row, thereby determining whether a row will be included in the final result set.

Here's another look at the Acme Industries query:

```
SELECT p.part_nbr, p.name, p.supplier_id, p.status, p.inventory_qty,
    s.supplier_id, s.name
FROM part p, supplier s
WHERE s.supplier_id = p.supplier_id
    AND s.name = 'Acme Industries';
```

The WHERE clause consists of two conditions separated by AND. Thus, a row will only be included if both conditions evaluate to TRUE. Table 2-1 shows the possible scenarios when conditions are replaced by their possible outcomes.

Table 2-1. Multiple-condition evaluation using AND

Intermediate result	Final result
WHERE TRUE AND TRUE	TRUE
WHERE FALSE AND FALSE	FALSE
WHERE FALSE AND TRUE	FALSE
WHERE TRUE AND FALSE	FALSE

Using basic logic rules, you can see that the only combination of outcomes that results in a final value of TRUE being assigned to a candidate row is where both conditions evaluate to TRUE. Table 2-2 demonstrates the possible outcomes if the conditions had been separated by OR rather than AND.

Table 2-2. Multiple-condition evaluation using OR

Intermediate result	Final result
WHERE TRUE OR TRUE	TRUE
WHERE FALSE OR FALSE	FALSE
WHERE FALSE OR TRUE	TRUE
WHERE TRUE OR FALSE	TRUE

Next, let's spice the query up a bit by including parts supplied by either Acme Industries or Tilton Enterprises:

```
SELECT p.part_nbr, p.name, p.supplier_id, p.status, p.inventory_qty,
    s.supplier_id, s.name
FROM part p, supplier s
WHERE s.supplier_id = p.supplier_id
    AND (s.name = 'Acme Industries'
    OR s.name = 'Tilton Enterprises');
```

There are now three separate conditions separated by AND and OR with parentheses surrounding two of the conditions. Table 2-3 illustrates the possible outcomes.

Table 2-3. Multiple-condition evaluation using AND and OR

Intermediate result	Final result
WHERE TRUE AND (TRUE OR FALSE)	TRUE
WHERE TRUE AND (FALSE OR TRUE)	TRUE
WHERE TRUE AND (FALSE OR FALSE)	FALSE
WHERE FALSE AND (TRUE OR FALSE)	FALSE
WHERE FALSE AND (FALSE OR TRUE)	FALSE
WHERE FALSE AND (FALSE OR FALSE)	FALSE

Since a particular part cannot be supplied by both Acme Industries and Tilton Enterprises, the intermediate results TRUE AND (TRUE AND TRUE) and FALSE AND (TRUE AND TRUE) were not included in Table 2-3.

To liven things up even more, here's an example using the NOT operator. The following query returns data for parts supplied by anyone other than Acme Industries or Tilton Enterprises:

```
SELECT p.part_nbr, p.name, p.supplier_id, p.status, p.inventory_qty,
  s.supplier_id, s.name
FROM part p, supplier s
WHERE s.supplier_id = p.supplier_id
  AND NOT (s.name = 'Acme Industries'
    OR s.name = 'Tilton Enterprises');
```

Table 2-4 demonstrates how the addition of the NOT operator changes the outcome.

Table 2-4. Multiple-condition evaluation using AND, OR, and NOT

Intermediate result	Final result
WHERE TRUE AND NOT (TRUE OR FALSE)	FALSE
WHERE TRUE AND NOT (FALSE OR TRUE)	FALSE
WHERE TRUE AND NOT (FALSE OR FALSE)	TRUE
WHERE FALSE AND NOT (TRUE OR FALSE)	FALSE
WHERE FALSE AND NOT (FALSE OR TRUE)	FALSE
WHERE FALSE AND NOT (FALSE OR FALSE)	FALSE

The use of the NOT operator in the previous example is a bit forced; later examples will demonstrate more natural ways of expressing the same logic.

Conditions and Expressions

Now that you understand how conditions are grouped together and evaluated, it's time to take a look at the different elements that make up a condition. A condition is comprised of one or more *expressions* along with one or more *operators*. Examples of expressions include:

- Numbers
- Columns, such as s.supplier_id
- Literals, such as 'Acme Industries'
- Functions, such as UPPER('abcd')
- Lists of simple expressions, such as (1, 2, 3)
- Subqueries

Examples of operators include:

- Arithmetic operators, such as +, -, *, and /
- Comparison operators, such as =, <, >=, !=, LIKE, and IN

The following sections explore many of the common condition types that use different combinations of the preceeding expression and operator types.

Equality/Inequality Conditions

Most of the conditions found in a WHERE clause will be equality conditions used to join data sets together or to isolate specific values. You have already encountered these types of conditions numerous times in previous examples, including:

```
s.supplier_id = p.supplier_id

s.name = 'Acme Industries'

supplier_id = (SELECT supplier_id
  FROM supplier
  WHERE name = 'Acme Industries')
```

All three conditions are comprised of a column expression followed by a comparison operator (=) followed by another expression. The conditions differ in the type of expression on the right side of the comparison operator. The first example compares one column to another, the second example compares a column to a literal, and the third example compares a column to the value returned by a subquery.

You can also build conditions that use the inequality comparison operator (!=). In a previous example, the NOT operator was used to find information about parts supplied by every supplier other than Acme Industries and Tilton Enterprises. Using the

!= operator rather than using NOT makes the query easier to understand and removes the need for the OR operator:

```
SELECT p.part_nbr, p.name, p.supplier_id, p.status, p.inventory_qty,
   s.supplier_id, s.name
FROM part p, supplier s
WHERE s.supplier_id = p.supplier_id
  AND s.name != 'Acme Industries'
  AND s.name != 'Tilton Enterprises';
```

While this is an improvement over the previous version, the next section shows an even cleaner way to represent the same logic.

Membership Conditions

Along with determining whether two expressions are identical, it is often useful to determine whether one expression can be found within a set of expressions. Using the IN operator, you can build conditions that will evaluate to TRUE if a given expression exists in a set of expressions:

```
s.name IN ('Acme Industries', 'Tilton Enterprises')
```

You may also use the NOT IN operator to determine whether an expression does not exist in a set of expressions:

```
s.name NOT IN ('Acme Industries', 'Tilton Enterprises')
```

Most people prefer to use a single condition with IN or NOT IN instead of writing multiple conditions using = or !=, so, with that in mind, here's one last stab at the Acme/Tilton query:

```
SELECT p.part_nbr, p.name, p.supplier_id, p.status, p.inventory_qty,
   s.supplier_id, s.name
FROM part p, supplier s
WHERE s.supplier_id = p.supplier_id
  AND s.name NOT IN ('Acme Industries', 'Tilton Enterprises');
```

Along with prefabricated sets of expressions, subqueries may be employed to generate sets on the fly. If a subquery returns exactly one row, you may use a comparison operator; if a subquery returns more than one row, or if you're not sure whether the subquery might return more than one row, use the IN operator. The following example updates all orders that contain parts supplied by Eastern Importers:

```
UPDATE cust_order
SET sale_price = sale_price * 1.1
WHERE cancelled_dt IS NULL
  AND ship_dt IS NULL
  AND order_nbr IN
  (SELECT li.order_nbr
   FROM line_item li, part p, supplier s
   WHERE s.name = 'Eastern Importers'
     AND s.supplier_id = p.supplier_id
     AND p.part_nbr = li.part_nbr);
```

The subquery evaluates to a (potentially empty) set of order numbers. All orders whose order number exists in that set are then modified by the UPDATE statement.

Range Conditions

If you are dealing with dates or numeric data, you may be interested in whether a value falls within a specified range rather than whether it matches a specific value or exists in a finite set. For such cases, you may use the BETWEEN operator, as in:

```
DELETE FROM cust_order
WHERE order_dt BETWEEN '01-JUL-2001' AND '31-JUL-2001';
```

To determine whether a value lies outside a specific range, you can use the NOT BETWEEN operator:

```
SELECT order_nbr, cust_nbr, sale_price
FROM cust_order
WHERE sale_price NOT BETWEEN 1000 AND 10000;
```

When using BETWEEN, make sure the first value is the lesser of the two values provided. While "BETWEEN 01-JUL-2001 AND 31-JUL-2001" and "BETWEEN 31-JUL-2001 AND 01-JUL-2001" might seem logically equivalent, specifying the higher value first guarantees that your condition will always evaluate to FALSE. Keep in mind that X BETWEEN Y AND Z is evaluated as X >= Y AND X <= Z.

Ranges may also be specified using the operators <, >, <=, and >=, although doing so requires writing two conditions rather than one. The previous query can also be expressed as:

```
SELECT order_nbr, cust_nbr, sale_price
FROM cust_order
WHERE sale_price < 1000 OR sale_price > 10000;
```

Matching Conditions

When dealing with character data, there are some situations where you are looking for an exact string match, and others where a partial match is sufficient. For the latter case, you can use the LIKE operator along with one or more pattern-matching characters, as in:

```
DELETE FROM part
WHERE part_nbr LIKE 'ABC%';
```

The pattern-matching character % matches strings of any length, so all of the following part numbers would be deleted: 'ABC', 'ABC-123', 'ABC9999999'. If you need finer control, you can use the underscore (_) pattern-matching character to match single characters, as in:

```
DELETE FROM part
WHERE part_nbr LIKE '_B_';
```

For this pattern, any part number composed of exactly three characters with a B in the middle would be deleted. Both pattern-matching characters may be utilized in numerous combinations to find the desired data. Additionally, the NOT LIKE operator may be employed to find strings that don't match a specified pattern. The following example deletes all parts whose name does not contain a Z in the third position followed later by the string "T1J":

```
DELETE FROM part
WHERE part_nbr NOT LIKE '__Z%T1J%';
```

Oracle provides a slew of built-in functions for handling character data that can be used to build matching conditions. For example, the condition part_nbr LIKE 'ABC%' could be rewritten using the SUBSTR function as SUBSTR(part_nbr, 1, 3) = 'ABC'. For definitions and examples for all of Oracle's built-in functions, see *Oracle in a Nutshell* (O'Reilly).

You may come across data that include the characters % and _ and need to include them in your patterns. For example, you might have a column called instructions in the cust_order table that may have a value such as:

Cancel order if more than 25% of parts are unavailable

If you want to find strings containing the % character, you will need to *escape* the % character within your pattern so that it isn't treated as a wildcard. To do so, you will need to use the ESCAPE clause to let Oracle know which character you have chosen as the escape character:

```
SELECT instructions
FROM cust_order
WHERE instructions LIKE '%\%%' ESCAPE '\';
```

This query would return all rows where the instructions column contains the % character anywhere in the string.

Regular Expressions

Beginning with the Oracle Database 10g release, you can use regular expressions within your conditions. Regular expressions allow for much more complex pattern matching without the need for multiple conditions. For example, if you wanted to find all customers whose name begins with W, ends in "ies" and does not include L anywhere in the string, you could use multiple conditions with the LIKE and NOT LIKE operators:

```
SELECT name
FROM customer
WHERE name LIKE 'W%ies'
  AND name NOT LIKE '%L%';

NAME
----------------------------
Worcester Technologies
Wallace Industries
```

You can achieve the same result more succinctly, in a single expression, with the new REGEXP_LIKE function:

```
SELECT name
FROM customer
WHERE REGEXP_LIKE(name, '^W([^L]*)ies$');

NAME
-----------------------------
Worcester Technologies
Wallace Industries
```

If that second argument to REGEXP_LIKE looks like gibberish, fear not: we cover regular expressions in detail in Chapter 17.

Handling NULL

The NULL expression represents the absence of a value. If, when entering an order into the database, you are uncertain when the order will be shipped, it is better to leave the ship date undefined than to fabricate a value. Until the ship date has been determined, therefore, it is best to leave the ship_dt column NULL. NULL is also useful for cases where data is not applicable. For example, a cancelled order's shipping date is no longer applicable and should be set to NULL.

When working with NULL, the concept of equality does not apply; a column may *be* NULL, but it will never *equal* NULL. Therefore, you will need to use the special operator IS NULL when looking for NULL data, as in:

```
UPDATE cust_order
SET expected_ship_dt = SYSDATE + 1
WHERE ship_dt IS NULL;
```

In this example, all orders whose shipping date hasn't been specified will have their expected shipping date set to tomorrow.

You may also use the IS NOT NULL operator to locate non-NULL data:

```
UPDATE cust_order
SET expected_ship_dt = NULL
WHERE ship_dt IS NOT NULL;
```

This example sets the expected shipping date to NULL for all orders that have already shipped. Notice that the SET clause uses the equality operator (=) with NULL, whereas the WHERE clause uses the IS NOT NULL operator. The equality operator is used to set a column to NULL, whereas the IS NOT NULL operator is used to evaluate whether a column is NULL. A great many mistakes might have been avoided had the designers of SQL chosen a special operator to be utilized when setting a column to NULL (i.e., SET expected_ship_dt TO NULL), but this is not the case. To make matters worse, Oracle doesn't complain if you mistakenly use the equality operator when evaluating for NULL. The following query will parse and execute but will never return rows:

```
SELECT order_nbr, cust_nbr, sale_price, order_dt
FROM cust_order
WHERE ship_dt = NULL;
```

Hopefully, you would quickly recognize that the previous query never returns data and replace the equality operator with IS NULL. However, there is a more subtle mistake involving NULL that is harder to spot. Say you are looking for all employees who are not managed by Marion Blake, whose employee ID is 7698. Your first instinct may be to run the following query:

```
SELECT fname, lname, manager_emp_id
FROM employee
WHERE manager_emp_id != 7698;
```

FNAME	LNAME	MANAGER_EMP_ID
JOHN	SMITH	7902
TERRY	JONES	7839
MARION	BLAKE	7839
CAROL	CLARK	7839
DONALD	SCOTT	7566
DIANE	ADAMS	7788
JENNIFER	FORD	7566
BARBARA	MILLER	7782

While this query returns rows, it leaves out those employees who are top-level managers and, thus, are not managed by anyone. Since NULL is neither equal nor not equal to 7698, this set of employees is absent from the result set. To ensure that all employees are considered, you will need to explicitly handle NULL, as in:

```
SELECT fname, lname, manager_emp_id
FROM employee
WHERE manager_emp_id IS NULL OR manager_emp_id != 7698;
```

FNAME	LNAME	MANAGER_EMP_ID
JOHN	SMITH	7902
TERRY	JONES	7839
MARION	BLAKE	7839
CAROL	CLARK	7839
DONALD	SCOTT	7566
FRANCIS	KING	
DIANE	ADAMS	7788
JENNIFER	FORD	7566
BARBARA	MILLER	7782

Including two conditions for every nullable column in your WHERE clause can get a bit tiresome. Instead, you can use Oracle's built-in function NVL, which substitutes a specified value for columns that are NULL, as in:

```
SELECT fname, lname, manager_emp_id
FROM employee
WHERE NVL(manager_emp_id, -999) != 7698;
```

FNAME	LNAME	MANAGER_EMP_ID
JOHN	SMITH	7902
TERRY	JONES	7839
MARION	BLAKE	7839
CAROL	CLARK	7839
DONALD	SCOTT	7566
FRANCIS	KING	
DIANE	ADAMS	7788
JENNIFER	FORD	7566
BARBARA	MILLER	7782

In this example, the value -999 is substituted for all NULL values, which, since -999 is never equal to 7698, guarantees that all rows whose manager_emp_id column is NULL will be included in the result set. Thus, all employees whose manager_emp_id column is NULL or is *not* NULL and has a value other than 7698 will be retrieved by the query.

Placement of Join Conditions

Throughout this chapter, all examples that join multiple tables have had their join conditions included in the WHERE clause along with various filter conditions. Beginning with the Oracle9*i* release, you have the option of using the ANSI join syntax, which specifies that all join conditions be included in the FROM clause, as illustrated by the following:

```
SELECT p.part_nbr, p.name, p.supplier_id, p.status, p.inventory_qty,
  s.supplier_id, s.name
FROM part p INNER JOIN supplier s
ON s.supplier_id = p.supplier_id
WHERE s.name NOT IN ('Acme Industries', 'Tilton Enterprises');
```

As you can see, the join condition s.supplier_id = p.supplier_id has been moved to the ON subclause, and the FROM clause specifies that the part and supplier tables be joined via an inner join. This syntax may look a bit strange at first, but it greatly improves the readability and maintainability of your queries. Therefore, for the remainder of this book, all examples will employ the ANSI join syntax.

WHERE to Go from Here

This chapter has introduced the role of the WHERE clause in different types of SQL statements as well as the various components used to build a WHERE clause. Because the WHERE clause plays such an important role in many SQL statements, however, the topic is far from exhausted. Additional coverage of WHERE clause topics may be found in:

- Chapter 3, in which various flavors of join conditions are studied in detail
- Chapter 5, which probes the different types of subqueries along with the appropriate operators for evaluating their results
- Chapter 6, in which various methods of handling date/time data are explored
- Chapter 15, which explores certain aspects of the WHERE clause from the standpoint of performance and efficiency

Additionally, here are a few tips to help you make the most of your WHERE clauses:

Check your join conditions carefully. Make sure that each data set in the FROM clause is properly joined. Keep in mind that some joins require multiple conditions. See Chapter 3 for more information.

Avoid unnecessary joins. Just because two data sets in your FROM clause contain the same column does not necessitate a join condition be added to your FROM/WHERE clause. In some designs, redundant data has been propagated to multiple tables through a process called *denormalization*. Take the time to understand the database design, and ask your DBA or database designer for a current data model.

Use parentheses. Oracle maintains both operator precedence and condition precedence, meaning there are clearly defined rules for the order in which things will be evaluated, but the safest route for you and for those who will later maintain your code is to dictate evaluation order using parentheses. For operators, specifying (5 * p.inventory_qty) + 2 rather than 5 * p.inventory_qty + 2 makes the order in which the operations should be performed clear. For conditions, use parentheses any time the OR operator is employed.

Use consistent indentation. For example, if the previous line contains a left parenthesis without a matching right parenthesis, indent the current line to show that it is a continuation of the previous line.

Handle NULLs properly. After writing your WHERE clause, inspect each condition with respect to its ability to properly handle NULL values. Take the time to understand the table definitions in your database so that you know which columns allow NULLs.

Pick up introductory books on logic and set theory at your local library. While understanding these two topics won't necessarily get you invited to more cocktail parties, it will certainly make you a better SQL programmer.

CHAPTER 3

Joins

Most things in life are not self-contained. There is not one shop where you will find all your requirements. This is valid for database tables as well. Quite often, you need information from more than one table. The SQL construct that combines data from two or more tables is called a *join*. This chapter takes you into the details of joins, their types, and their usage.

What Is a Join Query?

A *join query* extracts information from two or more tables or views. A join query differs from a regular query in at least the following two ways:

- The FROM clause of a join query refers to two or more tables or views.
- A condition is specified in the join query (known as join condition) that relates the rows of one table to the rows of another table.

The following example illustrates a simple join query:

```
SELECT department.location_id, department.name, location.regional_group
FROM department JOIN location
ON department.location_id = location.location_id;

LOCATION_ID NAME                 REGIONAL_GROUP
----------- -------------------- ---------------
        122 ACCOUNTING           NEW YORK
        124 RESEARCH             DALLAS
        167 OPERATIONS           BOSTON
```

This example queries two tables. The department name is stored in the department table, whereas each department's region is stored in the location table. Notice the JOIN keyword between the two tables names in the FROM clause. The SELECT list may include columns from any of the tables specified in the FROM clause. The clause starting with the keyword ON specifies the join condition.

 The syntax shown in the preceding example is the standard SQL join syntax supported from Oracle9*i* onwards. The Appendix describes an older syntax that you should avoid using, but will often encounter in older code.

Join Conditions

Usually, when you write a join query, you specify a condition that conveys a relationship between the tables specified in the FROM clause. This condition is referred to as the join condition. The join condition specifies how the rows from one table will be combined with the rows of another table. This join condition is usually applied to the foreign key columns of one table and the primary or unique key columns of another table. In the previous example, the ON clause specifies the join condition by which the `location_id` column of the `department` table is equated with the `location_id` column of the `location` table:

```
ON department.location_id = location.location_id;
```

To perform the join, Oracle picks up one combination of rows from the two tables, and checks to see whether the join condition is true. If the join condition is true, Oracle includes this combination of rows in the result set. This process is repeated for all combinations of rows from the two tables. Some of the things that you should know about join conditions are discussed in the following list:

- The columns specified in a join condition need not be specified in the SELECT list. In the following example, the join condition involves the `location_id` column from the `department` and `location` tables; however, the `location_id` column is not selected:

  ```
  SELECT d.dept_id, d.name, l.regional_group
  FROM department d JOIN location l
  ON d.location_id = l.location_id;
  ```

- Usually a join condition is specified on the foreign key columns of one table and the primary key or unique key columns of another table. However, you can join on other columns as well. A join condition involves columns that relate two tables in some logical way.

- A join condition may involve more than one column. This is usually the case when a foreign key constraint consists of multiple columns.

- The total number of join conditions in a query is always equal to the total number of tables less one.

Table Aliases

It is a common practice to use table aliases when selecting data from multiple tables. Whenever there is an ambiguity in the column names, you must use a table alias (or the table name) to qualify any ambiguous column name. For example:

```
SELECT d.dept_id, d.name, l.regional_group
FROM department d JOIN location l
ON d.location_id = l.location_id;
```

In this example, the column name location_id appears in both the tables. Therefore, the table aliases d and l are used in the ON clause to ask Oracle to equate the location_id column from the department table with the location_id column from the location table. The table aliases have been used with the columns in the SELECT clause as well, even though those column names are unambiguous. It is a good practice to use table aliases everywhere in a query if you are using them at all.

- The data types of the columns involved in a join condition need to be *compatible*, but not necessarily *the same*. Oracle performs implicit data type conversion between the join columns, if required.

- It is not necessary that a join condition involve the equal-to (=) operator. A join condition may contain other operators as well. Joins involving other operators are discussed later in this chapter in the section "Equi-Joins Versus Non-Equi-Joins."

The USING Clause

In this chapter's first example, the join condition was specified in the ON clause, which contained an expression defining the relationship between the two tables. Specifying the join condition can be simplified if the following conditions hold true:

- The join depends on an equality condition between two columns, or between sets of two columns, to relate the rows from the two tables.

- The names of the join columns are identical in both the tables.

If these two conditions are satisfied, you can apply the USING clause to specify the join condition. Earlier, you saw the following example of a join query:

```
SELECT department.location_id, department.name, location.regional_group
FROM department JOIN location
ON department.location_id = location.location_id;
```

The column involved in the join condition (location_id) is named identically in both the tables, and its value must be the same in both tables. Therefore, this join query can be rewritten as:

```
SELECT location_id, department.name, location.regional_group
FROM department JOIN location
USING (location_id);
```

The USING clause affects the semantics of the SELECT clause. The USING clause tells Oracle that the tables in the join have identical names for the column in the USING clause. Oracle then merges those two columns, and recognizes only one such column with the given name. If you include a join column in the SELECT list, Oracle doesn't allow you to qualify that column with a table name (or table alias). If you attempt to qualify a join column name in the SELECT list using either an alias or a table name, you will get an error:

```
SELECT department.location_id, department.name, location.regional_group
FROM department JOIN location
USING (location_id);
SELECT department.location_id, department.name, location.regional_group
       *
ERROR at line 1:
ORA-25154: column part of USING clause cannot have qualifier
```

This is why our USING query did not alias the location_id column in the SELECT list.

Conditions Involving Multiple Columns

Quite often you will encounter a join condition that involves multiple columns from each table. If a join condition consists of multiple columns, you need to specify all the predicates in the ON clause. For example, if tables A and B are joined based on columns c1 and c2, the join condition would be:

```
SELECT ...
FROM A JOIN B
ON A.c1 = B.c1 AND A.c2 = B.c2;
```

If the column names are identical in the two tables, you can use the USING clause and specify all the columns in one USING clause, separated by commas. The previous join condition can be rewritten as:

```
SELECT ...
FROM A JOIN B
USING (c1, c2);
```

The Natural Join Clause

A *natural join* between two tables relates the rows from the two tables based on all pairs of columns, one column from each table, with matching names. You don't specify a join condition. The following example illustrates a natural join:

```
SELECT department.name, location.regional_group
FROM department NATURAL JOIN location;

NAME                 REGIONAL_GROUP
-------------------- ---------------
ACCOUNTING           NEW YORK
RESEARCH             DALLAS
OPERATIONS           BOSTON
```

In this example, the two tables—department and location—have the same name for the column location_id. Therefore, the join takes place by equating the location_id from the department table to the location_id from the location table. The preceding query is equivalent to the following queries:

```
SELECT department.name, location.regional_group
FROM department JOIN location
ON department.location_id = location.location_id;

SELECT department.name, location.regional_group
FROM department JOIN location
USING (location_id);
```

While using a natural join, you are not allowed to qualify the common columns with table names or aliases (similar to the effect of the USING clause). For example, if you want to include the location_id column in the SELECT list, and you specify department.location_id, you will get an error:

```
SELECT department.location_id, department.name, location.regional_group
FROM department NATURAL JOIN location;
SELECT department.location_id, department.name, location.regional_group
       *
ERROR at line 1:
ORA-25155: column used in NATURAL join cannot have qualifier
```

You need to remove the department qualifier so the location_id column can include it in the SELECT list:

```
SELECT location_id, department.name, location.regional_group
FROM department NATURAL JOIN location;

LOCATION_ID NAME                 REGIONAL_GROUP
----------- -------------------- ---------------
        122 ACCOUNTING           NEW YORK
        124 RESEARCH             DALLAS
        167 OPERATIONS           BOSTON
```

Implicit specification of join conditions can have some unwanted side affects. Let's take the example of join between the supplier and part tables to illustrate this:

```
DESC supplier
Name                                               Null?     Type
-------------------------------------------------- --------- --------------
SUPPLIER_ID                                        NOT NULL  NUMBER(5)
NAME                                               NOT NULL  VARCHAR2(30)

DESC part
Name                                               Null?     Type
-------------------------------------------------- --------- --------------
PART_NBR                                           NOT NULL  VARCHAR2(20)
NAME                                               NOT NULL  VARCHAR2(30)
SUPPLIER_ID                                        NOT NULL  NUMBER(5)
STATUS                                             NOT NULL  VARCHAR2(20)
INVENTORY_QTY                                                NUMBER(6)
UNIT_COST                                                    NUMBER(8,2)
RESUPPLY_DATE                                                DATE
```

An inner join between these two tables, generates the following result:

```
SELECT supplier.supplier_id, part.part_nbr
FROM supplier JOIN part
ON supplier.supplier_id = part.supplier_id;

SUPPLIER_ID PART_NBR
----------- -----------
          1 AI5-4557
          2 TZ50828
          3 EI-T5-001
```

The following example illustrates a natural join between these two tables:

```
SELECT supplier_id, part.part_nbr
FROM supplier NATURAL JOIN part;

no rows selected
```

No output. What happened? The reason lies in the fact that, aside from supplier_id, these two tables have another pair of columns with a common name. That column is name. So, when you ask for a natural join between the supplier and the part tables, the join takes place not only by equating the supplier_id column of the two tables, but the name column from the two tables is equated as well. Since, no supplier name is the same as a part name from that same supplier, no rows are returned by the query. The equivalent inner join of the preceding natural join is:

```
SELECT supplier.supplier_id, part.part_nbr
FROM supplier JOIN part
ON supplier.supplier_id = part.supplier_id
AND supplier.name = part.name;
```

or, expressed via the USING clause:

```
SELECT supplier_id, part.part_nbr
FROM supplier JOIN part
USING (supplier_id, name);
```

By looking at the inner join queries we've just presented, you can very well understand why the natural join between the supplier and part tables didn't return any rows. You must be aware of this potential for error when using natural joins. To avoid such problems, we recommend explicitly specifying join conditions, using either the ON or the USING clauses.

Types of Joins

There are several types of joins to be aware of:

Cross joins

Cross joins are joins without a join condition. Each row of one table is combined with each row of another table. The result is referred to as a Cartesian product.

Inner joins

Inner joins are the regular joins. An inner join returns the rows that satisfy the join condition. Each row returned by an inner join contains data from all the tables involved in the join.

Outer joins

Outer joins are an extension to inner joins. An outer join returns the rows that satisfy the join condition and also the rows from one table for which no corresponding rows (i.e., that satisfy the join condition) exist in the other table.

Equi- and non-equi-joins

An *equi-join* is a join where the join condition uses the equal to (=) operator to relate the rows of two tables. When a join condition uses any other operator to relate the rows of two tables, the join is called a *non-equi-join*.

Self joins

A self join is a join of a table to itself.

Partition outer joins

A new type of join introduced in Oracle Database 10g that is slated to be part of the next ANSI/ISO SQL standard after SQL:2003. A partition outer join divides your result set into groups, or partitions, and repeats the same outer join for each of these groups. Such joins are extremely handy for generating missing rows.

The following sections discuss each of these joins in detail, and with examples.

Cross Joins/Cartesian Products

If you don't specify a join condition when joining two tables, Oracle combines each row from the first table with each row from the second table. This type of result set is called a cross join or a Cartesian product; either term is acceptable. The number of rows in a cross join is the product of the number of rows in each table. Here's an example of a cross join:

```
SELECT e.lname, d.name
FROM employee e CROSS JOIN department d;

LNAME       NAME
----------  --------------
SMITH       ACCOUNTING
ALLEN       ACCOUNTING
WARD        ACCOUNTING
JONES       ACCOUNTING
MARTIN      ACCOUNTING
BLAKE       ACCOUNTING
...
...
...
SCOTT       OPERATIONS
KING        OPERATIONS
TURNER      OPERATIONS
ADAMS       OPERATIONS
JAMES       OPERATIONS
FORD        OPERATIONS
MILLER      OPERATIONS

56 rows selected.
```

Since the query didn't specify a join condition, each row from the employee table is combined with each row from the department table. Needless to say, this result set is of little use. More often than not, a cross join produces a result set containing misleading rows. Therefore, unless you are sure that you want a Cartesian product, don't use a cross join.

Notice the use of the keyword CROSS before the JOIN keyword in the previous example. If you omit the CROSS keyword, and don't specify a join condition, Oracle will throw an error, because it thinks that you are attempting a regular join and have inadvertently omitted the join condition. For example:

```
SELECT e.lname, d.name
FROM employee e JOIN department d;
FROM employee e JOIN department d
                                *
ERROR at line 2:
ORA-00905: missing keyword
```

What happens when you specify the CROSS keyword as well as a join condition through an ON or USING clause? Oracle rejects your query with an error, and rightly so, because cross joins are joins without join conditions. For example:

```
SELECT e.lname, d.name
FROM employee e CROSS JOIN department d
ON e.dept_id = d.dept_id;
ON e.dept_id = d.dept_id
*
ERROR at line 3:
ORA-00933: SQL command not properly ended
```

Be aware that it's easily possible to inadvertently specify a cross join when using the old join syntax described in the Appendix. Using that syntax, a cross join occurs when you list two tables in the FROM clause separated by commas, and you forget to write a join condition into the query's WHERE clause.

Inner Joins

Inner joins are the most commonly used joins. When people refer simply to a "join," they most likely mean an "inner join." An inner join relates the rows from the source tables based on the join condition, and returns the rows that satisfy it. For example, to list the name and department for each employee, you would use the following SQL statement:

```
SELECT e.lname, d.name
FROM employee e JOIN department d
ON e.dept_id = d.dept_id;
```

```
LNAME                 NAME
-------------------   -------------------
CLARK                 ACCOUNTING
KING                  ACCOUNTING
MILLER                ACCOUNTING
SMITH                 RESEARCH
ADAMS                 RESEARCH
FORD                  RESEARCH
SCOTT                 RESEARCH
JONES                 RESEARCH
ALLEN                 SALES
BLAKE                 SALES
MARTIN                SALES
JAMES                 SALES
TURNER                SALES
WARD                  SALES

14 rows selected.
```

In this example, each row of the employee table is combined with each row of the department table, and if the combination satisfies the join condition (dept_id in the employee table matches the dept_id in the department table), then it is included in the result set.

The JOIN keyword, unless prefixed with another keyword, means an inner join. Optionally, you can use the INNER keyword before the JOIN keyword to explicitly indicate an inner join, as in the following example:

```
SELECT e.lname, d.name
FROM employee e INNER JOIN department d
ON e.dept_id = d.dept_id;
```

Let's look at another example to go a bit deeper in the concept behind an inner join:

```
SELECT * FROM department;
```

```
    DEPT_ID NAME                   LOCATION_ID
 ---------- --------------------   -----------
         10 ACCOUNTING                     122
         20 RESEARCH                       124
         30 SALES
         40 OPERATIONS                     167
```

```
SELECT * FROM  location;
```

```
LOCATION_ID REGIONAL_GROUP
----------- --------------------
        122 NEW YORK
        124 DALLAS
        123 CHICAGO
        167 BOSTON
        144 SAN FRANCISCO
```

```
SELECT d.name, l.regional_group
FROM department d JOIN location l
ON d.location_id = l.location_id;
```

```
NAME                 REGIONAL_GROUP
-------------------- --------------------
ACCOUNTING           NEW YORK
RESEARCH             DALLAS
OPERATIONS           BOSTON
```

Our department table has four rows, and our location table has five rows. However, the inner join returns only three rows. The inner join returns only those rows from the two tables that satisfy the join condition. What this means, with respect to this example, is that only those departments that have a corresponding location, and only those locations that have a corresponding department, are returned by the inner join query. The "SALES" department doesn't have a location_id, and therefore has no corresponding entry in the location table, so it is not included in the result set of the inner join. Similarly, the locations "CHICAGO" and "SAN FRANCISCO" don't have corresponding entries in the department table, and are not included in the result set of the inner join.

> The concept of an inner join is easier to understand in terms of the Cartesian product (or cross join). While performing a join of the department and location tables, a Cartesian product is first formed (conceptually, Oracle doesn't physically materialize this Cartesian product), and then the join conditions in the ON (or USING) clause restrict the results to only those rows for which the location_id values match.

The most important concept to understand about joins, and especially about inner joins, is that a join is all about matching rows from one table with corresponding rows in another table.

Outer Joins

Sometimes, while performing a join between two tables, you need to return all the rows from one table even when there are no corresponding rows in the other table. For example, you may want to see all the departments even if they are not related to any particular location. Oracle provides a special type of join to include rows from one table that don't have matching rows from the other table. This type of join is known as an *outer join*.

The syntax of an outer join is:

```
FROM table1 { LEFT | RIGHT | FULL } [OUTER] JOIN table2
```

The syntax elements are:

table1, table2
    Specifies the tables between which you are performing the outer join.

LEFT
    Specifies that the results be generated using all rows from *table1*. For those rows in *table1* that don't have corresponding rows in *table2*, NULLs are returned in the result set for the *table2* columns.

RIGHT
    Specifies that the results be generated using all rows from *table2*. For those rows in *table2* that don't have corresponding rows in *table1*, NULLs are returned in the result set for the *table1* columns.

FULL
    Specifies that the results be generated using all rows from *table1* and *table2*. For those rows in *table1* that don't have corresponding rows in *table2*, NULLs are returned in the result set for the *table2* columns. Additionally, for those rows in

table2 that don't have corresponding rows in *table1*, NULLs are returned in the result set for the *table1* columns.

OUTER

Specifies that you are performing an OUTER join. This keyword is optional. If you use LEFT, RIGHT, or FULL, Oracle automatically assumes an outer join. The OUTER keyword is for completeness' sake, and complements the INNER keyword.

Left outer joins

To list all departments even if they are not related to any particular location, you can perform a LEFT OUTER JOIN between the `department` and the `location` tables. For example:

```
SELECT d.dept_id, d.name, l.regional_group
FROM department d LEFT OUTER JOIN location l
ON d.location_id = l.location_id;
```

```
   DEPT_ID NAME                 REGIONAL_GROUP
---------- -------------------- --------------
        10 ACCOUNTING           NEW YORK
        20 RESEARCH             DALLAS
        30 SALES
        40 OPERATIONS           BOSTON
```

This query lists all the rows from the `department` table together with their corresponding locations from the `location` table. For the rows from `department` with no corresponding rows in `location`, NULLs are returned for the `l.regional_group` column in the result set.

Right outer joins

Likewise, to list all the locations even if they are not related to any particular department, you can perform a RIGHT OUTER JOIN between the `location` and the `department` tables. For example:

```
SELECT d.dept_id, d.name, l.regional_group
FROM department d RIGHT OUTER JOIN location l
ON d.location_id = l.location_id;
```

```
   DEPT_ID NAME                 REGIONAL_GROUP
---------- -------------------- --------------
        10 ACCOUNTING           NEW YORK
                                CHICAGO
        20 RESEARCH             DALLAS
                                SAN FRANCISCO
        40 OPERATIONS           BOSTON
```

This query lists all the rows from the `location` table, and their corresponding departments from the `department` table. For the rows from `location` that don't have corresponding rows in department, NULLs are returned for the d.dept_id and d.name columns in the result set.

The LEFT and RIGHT keywords in an outer join query are relative to the position of the tables in the FROM clause. The same result can be achieved using either a LEFT OUTER JOIN or a RIGHT OUTER JOIN, by switching the position of the tables. For example, the following two queries are equivalent:

```
SELECT d.dept_id, d.name, l.regional_group
FROM department d LEFT OUTER JOIN location l
ON d.location_id = l.location_id;

SELECT d.dept_id, d.name, l.regional_group
FROM location l RIGHT OUTER JOIN department d
ON d.location_id = l.location_id;
```

In each case, the directional word, either LEFT or RIGHT, points toward the anchor table, the table that is required. The other table is then the optional table in the join.

Full outer joins

Ocassionally, you may need the effect of an outer join in both directions, which you can think of as a combination of LEFT and RIGHT outer joins. For example, you may need to list all the departments (with or without a location), as well as all the locations (with or without a department). Use a FULL OUTER JOIN to generate such a result set:

```
SELECT d.dept_id, d.name, l.regional_group
FROM department d FULL OUTER JOIN location l
ON d.location_id = l.location_id;

   DEPT_ID NAME                 REGIONAL_GROUP
---------- -------------------- ----------------
        10 ACCOUNTING           NEW YORK
        20 RESEARCH             DALLAS
        30 SALES
        40 OPERATIONS           BOSTON
                                CHICAGO
                                SAN FRANCISCO

6 rows selected.
```

This query performs a FULL OUTER JOIN between the two tables, and lists:

- All the rows that satisfy the join condition
- The rows in the department table that don't have a corresponding location
- The rows in the location table that don't have a corresponding department

A full outer join is bidirectional in the sense that the result is the same irrespective of the position of the tables in the FROM clause. In mathematical terms, you would consider the FULL OUTER JOIN operator to be "commutative."

Equi-Joins Versus Non-Equi-Joins

The join condition determines whether a join is an equi-join or a non-equi-join. When a join condition relates two tables by equating the columns from the tables, it is an equi-join. When a join condition relates two tables by an operator other than equality, it is a non-equi-join. A query may contain equi-joins as well as non-equi-joins.

Equi-joins are the most common join type. For example, if you want to list all the parts supplied by all the suppliers, you can join the supplier table with the part table by equating the supplier_id from one table to that of the other:

```
SELECT s.name supplier_name, p.name part_name
FROM supplier s JOIN part p
ON s.supplier_id = p.supplier_id;

SUPPLIER_NAME                       PART_NAME
----------------------------------  -----------------------
Acme Industries                     Acme Part AI5-4557
Tilton Enterprises                  Tilton Part TZ50828
Eastern Importers                   Eastern Part EI-T5-001
```

However, there are situations in which you need non-equi-joins to get the required information. For example, if you want to list the inventory_class of each part, and the inventory_class is based on a range of unit costs, you need to execute the following query:

```
SELECT p.name part_name, c.inv_class inv_class
FROM part p JOIN inventory_class c
ON p.unit_cost BETWEEN c.low_cost AND c.high_cost;

PART_NAME                       INV
------------------------------  ---
Acme Part AI5-4557              A
Tilton Part TZ50828             B
Eastern Part EI-T5-001          B
```

The use of the BETWEEN operator to relate the unit_cost column from the part table to the low_cost and high_cost columns of the inventory_class table makes this query a non-equi-join. (You can achieve the same result by using the combination of >= and <= operators instead of BETWEEN. Try this as an exercise.)

Self Joins

There are situations in which one row of a table is related to another row of the same table. The employee table is a good example. The manager of one employee is also an employee. The rows for both are in the same employee table. This relationship is indicated in the manager_emp_id column:

```
CREATE TABLE employee (
emp_id          NUMBER (5) NOT NULL PRIMARY KEY,
```

```
fname              VARCHAR2 (20),
lname              VARCHAR2 (20),
dept_id            NUMBER (5),
manager_emp_id     NUMBER (5) REFERENCES employee(emp_id),
salary             NUMBER (5),
hire_date          DATE,
job_id             NUMBER (3));
```

To get information about an employee and his manager, you have to join the employee table with itself. You can do that by specifying the employee table twice in the FROM clause and using two different table aliases, thereby treating employee as if it were two separate tables. The following example lists the name of each employee and his manager:

```
SELECT e.lname employee, m.lname manager
FROM employee e JOIN employee m
ON e.manager_emp_id = m.emp_id;
```

```
EMPLOYEE             MANAGER
-------------------- --------------------
SCOTT                JONES
FORD                 JONES
ALLEN                BLAKE
WARD                 BLAKE
JAMES                BLAKE
TURNER               BLAKE
MARTIN               BLAKE
MILLER               CLARK
ADAMS                SCOTT
JONES                KING
CLARK                KING
BLAKE                KING
SMITH                FORD
```

```
13 rows selected.
```

Note that the employee table is used twice in the FROM clause with two different aliases. Also note the join condition that reads as: "Where the employee's manager_emp_id is the same as his manager's emp_id."

Self outer joins

Even though the employee table has 14 rows, the previous query returned only 13 rows. This is because there is an employee without a manager_emp_id. Oracle excludes that employee's row from the result set while performing the self inner join. To include employees without manager_emp_id values, in other words, without managers, you need an outer join:

```
SELECT e.lname employee, m.lname manager
FROM employee e LEFT OUTER JOIN employee m
ON e.manager_emp_id = m.emp_id;
```

```
EMPLOYEE              MANAGER
--------------------  --------------------
FORD                  JONES
SCOTT                 JONES
JAMES                 BLAKE
TURNER                BLAKE
MARTIN                BLAKE
WARD                  BLAKE
ALLEN                 BLAKE
MILLER                CLARK
ADAMS                 SCOTT
CLARK                 KING
BLAKE                 KING
JONES                 KING
SMITH                 FORD
KING

14 rows selected.
```

Be careful when using a LEFT or RIGHT outer join to join a table to itself. If you choose the wrong direction, you may get an absurd result set that makes no sense. In this case, we want to list all the employees irrespective of whether they have a manager or not. Therefore, the employee table we need to make optional is the one from which we are drawing manager names.

Self non-equi-joins

The previous example showed self equi-joins. However, there are situations when you need to perform self non-equi-joins. We will illustrate this by an example. Let's assume that you are in charge of organizing interdepartmental basketball competition within your organization. It is your responsibility to draw the teams and schedule the competition. You query the department table and get the following result:

```
SELECT name FROM department;

NAME
--------------
ACCOUNTING
RESEARCH
SALES
OPERATIONS
```

You find that there are four departments, and to make a fair competition, you decide that each department plays against the other three departments once, and at the end, the department with the maximum wins is declared the winner. You have been to an Oracle SQL training class recently, and decide to apply the concept of self join you learned there. You execute the following query:

```
SELECT d1.name team1, d2.name team2
FROM department d1 CROSS JOIN department d2;
```

```
TEAM1                TEAM2
-------------------- --------------------
ACCOUNTING           ACCOUNTING
ACCOUNTING           RESEARCH
ACCOUNTING           SALES
ACCOUNTING           OPERATIONS
RESEARCH             ACCOUNTING
RESEARCH             RESEARCH
RESEARCH             SALES
RESEARCH             OPERATIONS
SALES                ACCOUNTING
SALES                RESEARCH
SALES                SALES
SALES                OPERATIONS
OPERATIONS           ACCOUNTING
OPERATIONS           RESEARCH
OPERATIONS           SALES
OPERATIONS           OPERATIONS

16 rows selected.
```

Disappointing results. From your knowledge of high school mathematics, you know that four teams each playing once with the other three makes six combinations. However, your SQL query returned 16 rows. Now you realize that since you used a cross join (or didn't specify any join condition), you got a Cartesian product from your query. You put in a join condition, and your query and results now look as follows:

```
SELECT d1.name team1, d2.name team2
FROM department d1 JOIN department d2
ON d1.dept_id = d2.dept_id;

TEAM1          TEAM2
-------------- --------------
ACCOUNTING     ACCOUNTING
RESEARCH       RESEARCH
SALES          SALES
OPERATIONS     OPERATIONS
```

Oops! The equi-join returned a very unwanted result. A team can't play against itself. You realize your mistake, and this sparks the idea that you can use non-equi-joins in this situation. You rewrite the query as a non-equi-join. You don't want a team to play against itself, and therefore replace the = operator in the join condition with !=. Let's look at the results:

```
SELECT d1.name team1, d2.name team2
FROM department d1 JOIN department d2
ON d1.dept_id != d2.dept_id;

TEAM1          TEAM2
-------------- --------------
RESEARCH       ACCOUNTING
SALES          ACCOUNTING
```

```
OPERATIONS      ACCOUNTING
ACCOUNTING      RESEARCH
SALES           RESEARCH
OPERATIONS      RESEARCH
ACCOUNTING      SALES
RESEARCH        SALES
OPERATIONS      SALES
ACCOUNTING      OPERATIONS
RESEARCH        OPERATIONS
SALES           OPERATIONS
```

```
12 rows selected.
```

Still not done. In this result set, you have permutations such as (RESEARCH, ACCOUNTING) and (ACCOUNTING, RESEARCH), and so on. Therefore, each team plays against the others twice. You need to remove these permutations, which you rightly consider to be duplicates. You think about using DISTINCT. DISTINCT will not help here, because the row (RESEARCH, ACCOUNTING) is different from the row (ACCOUNTING, RESEARCH) from the viewpoint of DISTINCT; but not from the viewpoint of your requirement. After some thought, you want to try out an inequality operator other than !=. You decide to go with the less-than (<) operator. Here are the results you get:

```
SELECT d1.name team1, d2.name team2
FROM department d1 JOIN department d2
ON D1.DEPT_ID < D2.DEPT_ID;
```

```
TEAM1                 TEAM2
-------------------- -----------
ACCOUNTING            RESEARCH
ACCOUNTING            SALES
ACCOUNTING            OPERATIONS
RESEARCH              SALES
RESEARCH              OPERATIONS
SALES                 OPERATIONS
```

```
6 rows selected.
```

That's it! Now you have six combinations: each team plays against the other three just once. Let's examine why this version of the query works. Conceptually, when Oracle executes this query, a Cartesian product is first formed with 16 rows. Then the less-than (<) operator in the join condition restricts the result set to those rows in which the dept_id of Team 1 is less than the dept_id of Team 2. The less-than (<) operator eliminates the duplicates, because for any given permutation of two departments this condition is satisfied for only one. Using greater-than (>) instead of less-than (<) will also give you the required result, but the team1 and team2 values will be reversed:

```
SELECT d1.name team1, d2.name team2
FROM department d1 JOIN department d2
ON d1.dept_id > d2.dept_id;
```

```
TEAM1                TEAM2
-------------------- -----------
OPERATIONS           SALES
OPERATIONS           RESEARCH
OPERATIONS           ACCOUNTING
SALES                RESEARCH
SALES                ACCOUNTING
RESEARCH             ACCOUNTING

6 rows selected.
```

Don't be disheartened by the painful process you had to go through to get this result. Sometimes you have to go through an agonizing experience to get simple results such as these. That's life. Now that you have the team combinations right, go a bit further and assign a date for each match. Use "tomorrow" as the starting date:

```
SELECT d1.name team1, d2.name team2, SYSDATE + ROWNUM match_date
FROM department d1 JOIN department d2
ON d1.dept_id < d2.dept_id;

TEAM1                TEAM2                MATCH_DAT
-------------------- -------------------- ---------
ACCOUNTING           RESEARCH             10-NOV-03
ACCOUNTING           SALES                11-NOV-03
ACCOUNTING           OPERATIONS           12-NOV-03
RESEARCH             SALES                13-NOV-03
RESEARCH             OPERATIONS           14-NOV-03
SALES                OPERATIONS           15-NOV-03

6 rows selected.
```

Now publish these results on the corporate intranet along with the rules and regulations for the competition, and you are done.

Partition Outer Joins

Partition outer joins are an interesting new feature in Oracle Database 10g. They're useful for *data densification*, which is a fancy way of saying that they are useful for filling in rows that do not exist. This is a common requirement for data warehousing queries.

Part of our example database is an employee_expense table with summary information from employee expense reports. The data in that table looks as follows:

```
SELECT * FROM employee_expense;

    EMP_ID       YEAR      MONTH EXPENSE_CLAIM APPROVED_AMT PAID_DATE
---------- ---------- ---------- ------------- ------------ ---------
      7369       2002          2       3072.43      3072.43 03-MAR-02
      7369       2002          4            30           30 01-JUN-02
      7369       2002          5        235.03        35.03 01-JUN-02
      7369       2002          9       5095.98      5095.08 31-OCT-02
      7369       2002         12       1001.01      1001.01 01-FEB-03
```

```
7782      2002       1      111.09      111.09 01-FEB-02
7782      2002       3        9.85        9.85 01-APR-02
7782      2002       7     3987.32     3987.32 01-AUG-02
7782      2002       9        1200        1200 01-OCT-02
```

Management wants to review expenses, and you've been asked to generate a data extract of employee expense claims for the year 2002. Furthermore, to facilitate some analysis that management wishes to do using Excel, you've been asked to ensure that your extract contains one row per month per employee, but only for those employees who actively submit expense reports. Most do not.

You think about these requirements for a while, and realize that you have a months table containing one row for each month in 2002:

```
SELECT *
FROM months
WHERE year = 2002;

    YEAR      MONTH
---------- ----------
    2002        1
    2002        2
    2002        3
    2002        4
    2002        5
    2002        6
    2002        7
    2002        8
    2002        9
    2002       10
    2002       11
    2002       12
```

You can use this months table in an outer join to generate 12 rows for each employee. For example, to generate one row per month for employee 7782, you can write the following query:

```
SELECT NVL(ee.emp_id, 7782), m.year, m.month, NVL(ee.expense_claim,0)
FROM (SELECT * FROM months WHERE year = 2002) m
     LEFT OUTER JOIN (SELECT *
                      FROM employee_expense
                      WHERE emp_id = 7782) ee
     ON m.year = ee.year AND m.month = ee.month
ORDER BY m.month;

NVL(EE.EMP_ID,7782)      YEAR      MONTH NVL(EE.EXPENSE_CLAIM,0)
-------------------- ---------- ---------- -----------------------
               7782      2002        1                  111.09
               7782      2002        2                       0
               7782      2002        3                    9.85
               7782      2002        4                       0
               7782      2002        5                       0
               7782      2002        6                       0
               7782      2002        7                 3987.32
```

7782	2002	8	0
7782	2002	9	1200
7782	2002	10	0
7782	2002	11	0

NVL(EE.EMP_ID,7782)	YEAR	MONTH	NVL(EE.EXPENSE_CLAIM,0)
7782	2002	12	0

The query in this example is a bit intense. It performs a join of two nested SELECT statements, called *subqueries*. The first subquery returns the 12 rows from months for the year 2002. Those 12 rows are the mandatory rows in the outer join. The second subquery returns the actual expense rows for employee #7782. The outer join ensures that 12 rows are returned, and the two NVL functions ensure that each of those 12 rows has a value for the potentially NULL employee_expense fields. Expense claims for months in which no report was filed are simply set to zero.

 Subqueries are discussed in detail in Chapter 5. We hated to have to bring them up now, but we felt the preceding example was necessary to help you understand what a partition outer join is all about.

The previous query is all well and good, but to generate your report you'd need to execute the preceding query many times, once for each employee who has submitted at least one expense report in the year 2002. This is where partition outer joins come into play. They make it trivial to do the *equivalent* of executing the preceding query once per employee. Here's how:

```
SELECT ee.emp_id, m.year, m.month, NVL(ee.expense_claim,0)
FROM (SELECT * FROM months WHERE year = 2002) m
     LEFT OUTER JOIN employee_expense ee
        PARTITION BY (ee.emp_id)
        ON m.year = ee.year AND m.month = ee.month
ORDER BY ee.emp_id, m.month;
```

EMP_ID	YEAR	MONTH	NVL(EE.EXPENSE_CLAIM,0)
7369	2002	1	0
7369	2002	2	3072.43
7369	2002	3	0
7369	2002	4	30
7369	2002	5	235.03
7369	2002	6	0
7369	2002	7	0
7369	2002	8	0
7369	2002	9	5095.98
7369	2002	10	0
7369	2002	11	0
7369	2002	12	1001.01
7782	2002	1	111.09
7782	2002	2	0

7782	2002	3	9.85
7782	2002	4	0
7782	2002	5	0
7782	2002	6	0
7782	2002	7	3987.32
7782	2002	8	0
7782	2002	9	1200
7782	2002	10	0
7782	2002	11	0
7782	2002	12	0

Notice the PARTITION BY clause in this query. That clause is new in Oracle Database 10g, and in this example it causes the database engine to conceptually perform the following steps:

1. Divide the rows from employee_expense into groups based on their emp_id values, one group per value.

2. Outer join each group to the months table as a separate operation.

The key here is that rather than one outer join, you are getting the equivalent of many outer joins, but with a much simpler syntax, and from one query. The preceding query is logically equivalent to the following UNION ALL query:

```
SELECT NVL(ee.emp_id, 7369), m.year, m.month, NVL(ee.expense_claim,0)
FROM (SELECT * FROM months WHERE year = 2002) m
    LEFT OUTER JOIN (SELECT *
                      FROM employee_expense
                      WHERE emp_id = 7369) ee
    ON m.year = ee.year AND m.month = ee.month
ORDER BY m.month
UNION ALL
SELECT NVL(ee.emp_id, 7782), m.year, m.month, NVL(ee.expense_claim,0)
FROM (SELECT * FROM months WHERE year = 2002) m
    LEFT OUTER JOIN (SELECT *
                      FROM employee_expense
                      WHERE emp_id = 7782) ee
    ON m.year = ee.year AND m.month = ee.month
ORDER BY m.month;
```

You'll learn more about UNION queries in Chapter 7, so don't worry if you don't fully understand this example now. Our point here is to illustrate that, given the two employees represented in our example employee_expense table, our partition outer join query performs the equivalent of two outer joins, one for each employee.

 Unlike the case with our UNION ALL code, you do not need to apply NVL to the partition columns when doing a partition outer join. The correct emp_id values were filled in automatically, for all new rows generated in each partition.

Because they make it easy to fill in gaps in your data, partition outer joins are particularly helpful when writing lag and lead queries, which are a type of query particularly sensitive to gaps in data. You'll learn more about lag and lead queries in Chapter 14.

Joins and Subqueries

Joins can sometimes be used to good advantage in reformulating SELECT statements that would otherwise contain subqueries. Consider the problem of obtaining a list of suppliers of parts for which your inventory has dropped below 10 units. You might begin by writing a query such as the following:

```
SELECT supplier_id, name
FROM supplier s
WHERE EXISTS (SELECT *
             FROM part p
             WHERE p.inventory_qty < 10
               AND p.supplier_id = s.supplier_id);
```

The subquery in this SELECT statement is a correlated subquery, which means that it will be executed once for each row in the supplier table. Assuming that you have no indexes on the inventory_qty and supplier_id columns of the part table, this query could result in multiple, full-table scans of the part table. It's possible to restate the query using a join. For example:

```
SELECT s.supplier_id, s.name
FROM supplier s JOIN part p
ON p.supplier_id = s.supplier_id
WHERE p.inventory_qty < 10;
```

Whether the join version or the subquery version of a query is more efficient depends on the specific situation. It may be worth your while to test both approaches to see which query runs faster.

DML Statements on a Join View

A join view is a view based on a join. Special considerations apply when you issue a DML (INSERT, UPDATE, or DELETE) statement against a join view. Ever thought about what happens when you insert a row into a join view—which table does the row go into? And what happens when you delete a row from a join view—from which table is it deleted? This section deals with these questions.

To be modifiable (also referred to as updatable), a join view must not contain any of the following:

* Hierarchical query clauses, such as START WITH or CONNECT BY
* GROUP BY or ORDER BY clauses
* MODEL query

- Set operations, such as UNION, UNION ALL, INTERSECT, MINUS
- Aggregate functions, such as AVG, COUNT, MAX, MIN, SUM, and so on
- Analytical functions, such as CUME_DIST, and so on
- A subquery or a collection expression in the SELECT list
- The DISTINCT operator
- WITH READ ONLY option
- The ROWNUM pseudocolumn

A DML statement on a join view can modify only one base table of the view. Thus, to be modifiable, a join view must also preserve a key from at least one of its tables.

Key-Preserved Tables

A *key-preserved table* is the most important requirement for a join view to be modifiable. In a join, a table is called a key-preserved table if its keys are preserved through the join—every key of the table can also be a key of the resultant join result set. Every primary key or unique key value in the base table must also be unique in the result set of the join. Here's an example that better demonstrates the concept of key preserved tables:

```
DESC employee
Name                                     Null?     Type
---------------------------------------- --------- -------------
EMP_ID                                   NOT NULL  NUMBER(5)
FNAME                                              VARCHAR2(20)
LNAME                                              VARCHAR2(20)
DEPT_ID                                  NOT NULL  NUMBER(5)
MANAGER_EMP_ID                                     NUMBER(5)
SALARY                                             NUMBER(5)
HIRE_DATE                                          DATE
JOB_ID                                             NUMBER(3)


DESC retailer
Name                                     Null?     Type
---------------------------------------- --------- -------------
RTLR_NBR                                 NOT NULL  NUMBER(6)
NAME                                               VARCHAR2(45)
ADDRESS                                            VARCHAR2(40)
CITY                                               VARCHAR2(30)
STATE                                              VARCHAR2(2)
ZIP_CODE                                           VARCHAR2(9)
AREA_CODE                                          NUMBER(3)
PHONE_NUMBER                                       NUMBER(7)
SALESPERSON_ID                                     NUMBER(4)
CREDIT_LIMIT                                       NUMBER(9,2)
COMMENTS                                           LONG

CREATE OR REPLACE VIEW v_rtlr_emp AS
SELECT c.rtlr_nbr, c.name, c.city, e.emp_id,
       c.salesperson_id, e.lname sales_rep
```

```
FROM retailer c JOIN employee e
ON c.salesperson_id = e.emp_id;
```

View created.

```
SELECT * FROM v_rtlr_emp;
```

RTLR_NBR	NAME	CITY	EMP_ID	SALES_REP
104	EVERY MOUNTAIN	CUPERTINO	7499	ALLEN
107	WOMENS SPORTS	SUNNYVALE	7499	ALLEN
201	STADIUM SPORTS	NEW YORK	7499	ALLEN
203	REBOUND SPORTS	NEW YORK	7499	ALLEN
207	FAST BREAK	CONCORD	7499	ALLEN
216	THE ALL AMERICAN	CHELSEA	7499	ALLEN
223	VELO SPORTS	MALDEN	7499	ALLEN
227	THE TOUR	SOMERVILLE	7499	ALLEN
218	THE OUTFIELD	FLUSHING	7499	ALLEN
211	AT BAT	BROOKLINE	7499	ALLEN
206	THE COLISEUM	SCARSDALE	7499	ALLEN
205	POINT GUARD	YONKERS	7499	ALLEN
202	HOOPS	LEICESTER	7499	ALLEN
101	TKB SPORT SHOP	REDWOOD CITY	7521	WARD
228	FITNESS FIRST	JACKSON HEIGHTS	7521	WARD
226	CENTURY SHOP	HUNTINGTON	7521	WARD
106	SHAPE UP	PALO ALTO	7521	WARD
103	JUST TENNIS	BURLINGAME	7521	WARD
102	VOLLYRITE	BURLINGAME	7654	MARTIN
208	AL AND BOB'S SPORTS	AUSTIN	7654	MARTIN
204	THE POWER FORWARD	DALLAS	7654	MARTIN
215	BOB'S FAMILY SPORTS	HOUSTON	7654	MARTIN
217	HIT name, THROW addr, AND RUN	GRAPEVINE	7654	MARTIN
214	AL'S PRO SHOP	SPRING	7654	MARTIN
100	JOCKSPORTS	BELMONT	7844	TURNER
212	ALL SPORT	BROOKLYN	7844	TURNER
221	WHEELS AND DEALS	HOUSTON	7844	TURNER
224	JOE'S BIKE SHOP	GRAND PRAIRIE	7844	TURNER
225	BOB'S SWIM, CYCLE AND RUN	IRVING	7844	TURNER
222	JUST BIKES	DALLAS	7844	TURNER
213	GOOD SPORT	SUNNYSIDE	7844	TURNER
105	K + T SPORTS	SANTA CLARA	7844	TURNER

32 rows selected.

The view v_rtlr_emp is a join of retailer and employee tables on the retailer. salesperson_id and employee.emp_id columns. Is there a key-preserved table in this join view? Which one—or is it both? If you observe the relationship between the two tables and the join query, you will notice that rtlr_nbr is the key of the retailer table, as well as the key of the result of the join. This is because there is only one row in the retailer table for every row in the join view v_rtlr_emp, and every row in the view has a unique rtlr_nbr. Therefore, the table retailer is a key-preserved table in this join view. How about the employee table? The key of the employee table is not preserved through the join because emp_id is not unique in the view, consequently emp_id can't be a key for the result of the join. Therefore, the table employee is not a key-preserved table in this view.

You must remember the following important points regarding key-preserved tables:

- Key-preservation is a property of the table inside the join view, not the table itself independently. A table may be key-preserved in one join view, and may not be key-preserved in another join view. For example, if we create a join view by joining the employee table with the department table on the dept_id column, then in the resulting view the employee table will be key-preserved, but the department table will not be a key-preserved table.
- It is not necessary for the key column(s) of a table to be SELECTed in the join view for the table to be key-preserved. For example, in the v_rtlr_emp view discussed previously, the retailer table would have been the key-preserved table even if we had not included the rtlr_nbr column in the SELECT list.
- On the other hand, if you select the key column(s) of a table in the view definition, your doing so doesn't make that table key-preserved. In the v_rtlr_emp view, even though we have included emp_id in the SELECT list, the employee table is not key-preserved.
- The key-preserved property of a table in a join view doesn't depend on the data inside the table. It depends on the schema design and the relationship between the tables.

A join view may SELECT data from many tables. However, any DML operation can modify the data from only one underlying table. The following sections discuss how you can use INSERT, UPDATE, and DELETE statements on a join view.

INSERT Statements on a Join View

Let's issue an INSERT statement against the join view v_rtlr_emp, that attempts to insert a record into the retailer table:

```
INSERT INTO v_rtlr_emp (rtlr_nbr, name, salesperson_id)
VALUES (345, 'X-MART STORES', 7820);

1 row created.
```

That worked. Now let's try the following INSERT statement, which also supplies a value for a column from the employee table:

```
INSERT INTO v_rtlr_emp (rtlr_nbr, name, salesperson_id, sales_rep)
VALUES (456, 'LEE PARK RECREATION CENTER', 7599, 'JAMES');
INSERT INTO v_rtlr_emp (rtlr_nbr, name, salesperson_id, sales_rep)
                                                        *
ERROR at line 1:
ORA-01776: cannot modify more than one base table through a join view
```

This INSERT statement attempts to insert values into two tables (retailer and employee), which is not allowed. You can't refer to the columns of a non-key-preserved table in an INSERT statement.

DELETE Statements on a Join View

DELETE operations can be performed on a join view if the join view has one and only one key-preserved table. The view v_rtlr_emp discussed previously has only one key-preserved table, retailer; therefore, you can delete from this join view as in the following example:

```
DELETE FROM v_rtlr_emp
WHERE rtlr_nbr = 214;
```

```
1 row deleted.
```

But wait! The view joined two tables? What row then, did we just delete? The answer is that we deleted a row from the key-preserved table, in this case from the retailer table.

Let's take another example where there is more than one key-preserved table. We will create a join view that involves two key-preserved tables, and then attempt to delete from that view.

```
CREATE VIEW v_cust_disputed_ord AS
SELECT d.order_nbr, d.cust_nbr, c.cancelled_dt
FROM disputed_orders d JOIN cust_order c
ON d.order_nbr = c.order_nbr;
```

```
View created.
```

In the view v_cust_disputed_ord both the tables are key-preserved, because the key of each of the tables is also a key of the result set of the join. Now try deleting a row from this view:

```
DELETE FROM v_cust_disputed_ord
WHERE order_nbr = 1003;
```

```
1 row deleted.
```

Since there are two key-preserved tables, which table did the row get deleted from? After querying the individual tables, you will find that a row has been deleted from the disputed_orders table. Why? This is a bit tricky. The rule is that if you attempt to delete a row from a join view having more than one key-preserved table, the row will be deleted from the first table in the join. If you reverse the order of the tables in the join, and then issue a delete, you will find that the row will be deleted from the cust_order table. This is strange, but it's the rule. Keep this unexpected behavior in mind when you write applications that need to delete from a join view with multiple key-preserved tables.

UPDATE Statements on a Join View

An UPDATE operation can be performed on a join view if it attempts to update a column in the key-preserved table. For example:

```
UPDATE v_rtlr_emp
SET name = 'PRO SPORTS'
WHERE rtlr_nbr = 215;

1 row updated.
```

This UPDATE is successful since it updated the name column of the retailer table, which is key-preserved. However, the following UPDATE statement will fail because it attempts to modify the sales_rep column that maps to the employee table, which is non-key-preserved:

```
UPDATE v_rtlr_emp
SET sales_rep = 'ANDREW'
WHERE rtlr_nbr = 214;
SET sales_rep = 'ANDREW'
    *
ERROR at line 2:
ORA-01779: cannot modify a column which maps to a non-key-preserved table
```

Data Dictionary Views to Find Updatable Columns

Oracle provides the data dictionary view USER_UPDATABLE_COLUMNS that shows all modifiable columns in all tables and views in a user's schema. This can be helpful if you have a view that you wish to update, but aren't sure whether it's updatable. USER_UPDATABLE_COLUMNS has the following definition:

```
DESC USER_UPDATABLE_COLUMNS

Name              Null?      Type
---------------   --------   -------------
OWNER             NOT NULL   VARCHAR2(30)
TABLE_NAME        NOT NULL   VARCHAR2(30)
COLUMN_NAME       NOT NULL   VARCHAR2(30)
UPDATABLE                    VARCHAR2(3)
INSERTABLE                   VARCHAR2(3)
DELETABLE                    VARCHAR2(3)
```

 ALL_UPDATABLE_COLUMNS shows modifiable columns from all the views you can access (as opposed to just those you own), and DBA_UPDATABLE_COLUMNS (for DBAs only) shows such columns for all the views in the database.

The following example shows USER_UPDATABLE_COLUMNS being queried for a list of updatable columns in the v_rtlr_emp view:

```
SELECT * FROM USER_UPDATABLE_COLUMNS
WHERE TABLE_NAME = 'V_RTLR_EMP';
```

```
OWNER    TABLE_NAME     COLUMN_NAME        UPD INS DEL
-------  -------------  ----------------   --- ---
DEMO     V_RTLR_EMP     RTLR_NBR           YES YES YES
DEMO     V_RTLR_EMP     NAME               YES YES YES
DEMO     V_RTLR_EMP     CITY               YES YES YES
DEMO     V_RTLR_EMP     EMP_ID             NO  NO  NO
DEMO     V_RTLR_EMP     SALESPERSON_ID     YES YES YES
DEMO     V_RTLR_EMP     SALES_REP          NO  NO  NO
```

Impact of WITH CHECK OPTION

WITH CHECK OPTION is an optional clause in the CREATE VIEW statement that prevents any changes to the data in the view that could cause rows to be not included in the view. For example, you have a view with the following definition:

```
CREATE VIEW emp_20 AS
SELECT * FROM employee
WHERE dept_id = 20
WITH CHECK OPTION;
```

Using this view you can't insert a row that has dept_id = 30, or update the existing rows to have dept_id = 30, as shown in the following example:

```
INSERT INTO emp_20 VALUES
(8765, 'SANJAY','MISHRA', 30, 7656, 4000, '01-JAN-88', 765);
INSERT INTO emp_20 VALUES
               *
ERROR at line 1:
ORA-01402: view WITH CHECK OPTION where-clause violation

UPDATE emp_20 SET dept_id = 30;
UPDATE emp_20 SET dept_id = 30
          *
ERROR at line 1:
ORA-01402: view WITH CHECK OPTION where-clause violation
```

Since the WHERE clause of the view definition restricts the data in the view to dept_id = 20, and the view is defined with the clause WITH CHECK OPTION, you are not allowed to insert or update rows that could cause the rows not to be included in this view.

The purpose of WITH CHECK OPTION is to prevent DML operations as shown in the preceding example. However, this clause has some side effects on the updatability of join views in general.

If a join view is created using the WITH CHECK OPTION clause, INSERT statements are not allowed on the view at all, even if you are attempting to insert into the key-preserved table only. For example:

```
CREATE VIEW v_rtlr_emp_wco AS
SELECT c.rtlr_nbr, c.name, c.city, c.salesperson_id, e.lname sales_rep
FROM retailer c JOIN employee e
ON c.salesperson_id = e.emp_id
WITH CHECK OPTION;
```

```
View created.

INSERT INTO v_rtlr_emp_wco (rtlr_nbr, name, salesperson_id)
VALUES (345, 'X-MART STORES', 7820);
INSERT INTO v_rtlr_emp_wco (rtlr_nbr, name, salesperson_id)
                          *
ERROR at line 1:
ORA-01733: virtual column not allowed here
```

The error message "ORA-01733: virtual column not allowed here" may not be very comprehensible, but it indicates that you are not allowed to insert into this join view.

WITH CHECK OPTION as such doesn't prevent you from deleting rows from a join view, as shown in the following example:

```
DELETE FROM v_rtlr_emp_wco
WHERE rtlr_nbr = 215;

1 row deleted.
```

However, WITH CHECK OPTION prevents deletion if the join view involves a self join of the key-preserved table. For example, the view emp_mgr_wco involves a self join of the table employee (which is the key-preserved table in this view definition).

```
CREATE VIEW emp_mgr_wco AS
SELECT e.lname employee, e.salary salary, m.lname manager
FROM employee e, employee m
WHERE e.manager_emp_id = m.emp_id
WITH CHECK OPTION;

View created.

DELETE FROM emp_mgr_wco WHERE employee = 'JONES';
DELETE FROM emp_mgr_wco WHERE employee = 'JONES'
                              *
ERROR at line 1:
ORA-01752: cannot delete from view without exactly one key-preserved table
```

You get an error while trying to delete a row from the view emp_mgr_wco, as it involves a self join of the key-preserved table.

Furthermore, the WITH CHECK OPTION restricts your ability to modify a join view. If a join view is created using the WITH CHECK OPTION clause, you can't modify any of the join columns, nor any of the columns from the tables involved in a self join. The following example illustrates the error you get when trying to update the join column of such a view.

```
UPDATE v_rtlr_emp_wco
SET salesperson_id = 7784
WHERE rtlr_nbr = 215;
SET salesperson_id = 7784
    *
ERROR at line 2:
ORA-01733: virtual column not allowed here
```

The error message "ORA-01733: virtual column not allowed here" indicates that you are not allowed to update the indicated column. Since the view is created with the WITH CHECK OPTION clause, and the column salesperson_id is a join column, you are not allowed to update it. You will get a similar error if you try to update a column of a table involved in a self join, as illustrated in the following example:

```
UPDATE emp_mgr_wco
SET salary = 4800
WHERE employee = 'JONES';
SET salary = 4800
    *
ERROR at line 2:
ORA-01733: virtual column not allowed here
```

In this example, since the view definition involves a self join of the employee table, and the view is created with the WITH CHECK OPTION clause, you are not allowed to update any columns of the employee table.

CHAPTER 4
Group Operations

Group operations are quite common in the day-to-day life of a SQL programmer. When you use SQL to access a database, it is quite common to expect questions such as:

- What is the maximum salary in this department?
- How many managers are there in each department?
- What is the number of customers for each product?
- Can you print the monthly aggregate sales for each region?

You need *group operations* to answer these questions. Oracle provides a rich set of features to handle group operations. These features include aggregate functions, the GROUP BY clause, the HAVING clause, and the extensions to the GROUP BY clause—ROLLUP, CUBE, and GROUPING SETS.

This chapter deals with simple group operations involving the aggregate functions, the GROUP BY and HAVING clauses. Advanced group operations such as ROLLUP, CUBE, and GROUPING SETS are discussed in Chapter 13.

Aggregate Functions

An *aggregate function* summarizes the results of an expression over a number of rows, returning a single value. The general syntax for most of the aggregate functions is as follows:

```
aggregate_function([DISTINCT | ALL] expression)
```

The syntax elements are:

aggregate_function
    Gives the name of the function—e.g., SUM, COUNT, AVG, MAX, MIN

DISTINCT
    Specifies that the aggregate function should consider only distinct values of the argument expression.

ALL

Specifies that the aggregate function should consider all values, including all duplicate values, of the argument expression. The default is ALL.

expression

Specifies a column, or any other expression, on which you want to perform the aggregation.

Let's look at a simple example. The following SQL uses the MAX function to find the maximum salary of all employees:

```
SELECT MAX(salary) FROM employee;

MAX(SALARY)
-----------
       5000
```

In subsequent sections, we use a series of slightly more involved examples that illustrate various aspects of aggregate function behavior. For those examples, we use the following cust_order table:

```
DESC cust_order
```

Name	Null?	Type
ORDER_NBR	NOT NULL	NUMBER(7)
CUST_NBR	NOT NULL	NUMBER(5)
SALES_EMP_ID	NOT NULL	NUMBER(5)
SALE_PRICE		NUMBER(9,2)
ORDER_DT	NOT NULL	DATE
EXPECTED_SHIP_DT	NOT NULL	DATE
CANCELLED_DT		DATE
SHIP_DT		DATE
STATUS		VARCHAR2(20)

```
SELECT order_nbr, cust_nbr, sales_emp_id, sale_price,
order_dt, expected_ship_dt
FROM cust_order;
```

ORDER_NBR	CUST_NBR	SALES_EMP_ID	SALE_PRICE	ORDER_DT	EXPECTED_
1001	1	7354	99	22-JUL-01	23-JUL-01
1000	1	7354		19-JUL-01	24-JUL-01
1002	5	7368		12-JUL-01	25-JUL-01
1003	4	7654	56	16-JUL-01	26-JUL-01
1004	4	7654	34	18-JUL-01	27-JUL-01
1005	8	7654	99	22-JUL-01	24-JUL-01
1006	1	7354		22-JUL-01	28-JUL-01
1007	5	7368	25	20-JUL-01	22-JUL-01
1008	5	7368	25	21-JUL-01	23-JUL-01
1009	1	7354	56	18-JUL-01	22-JUL-01
1012	1	7354	99	22-JUL-01	23-JUL-01
1011	1	7354		19-JUL-01	24-JUL-01
1015	5	7368		12-JUL-01	25-JUL-01

1017	4	7654	56 16-JUL-01 26-JUL-01
1019	4	7654	34 18-JUL-01 27-JUL-01
1021	8	7654	99 22-JUL-01 24-JUL-01
1023	1	7354	22-JUL-01 28-JUL-01
1025	5	7368	25 20-JUL-01 22-JUL-01
1027	5	7368	25 21-JUL-01 23-JUL-01
1029	1	7354	56 18-JUL-01 22-JUL-01

20 rows selected.

NULLs and Aggregate Functions

Notice that the column sale_price in the cust_order table is nullable, and that it contains NULL values for some rows. To examine the effect of NULLs in an aggregate function, execute the following SQL:

```
SELECT COUNT(*), COUNT(sale_price) FROM cust_order;

COUNT(*) COUNT(SALE_PRICE)
-------- -----------------
      20                14
```

Notice the difference in the output of COUNT(*) and COUNT(sale_price). This is because COUNT(sale_price) ignores NULLs, whereas COUNT(*) doesn't. The reason COUNT(*) doesn't ignore NULLs is because it counts rows, not column values. The concept of NULL doesn't apply to a row as a whole. Other than COUNT(*), there is only one other aggregate function that doesn't ignore NULLs, and that is GROUP-ING. All other aggregate functions ignore NULLs. We will discuss GROUPING in Chapter 13. For now, let's examine the effect of NULLs when they are ignored.

SUM, MAX, MIN, AVG, etc., all ignore NULLs. Therefore, if you are trying to find a value such as the average sale price in the cust_order table, the average will be of the 14 rows that have a value for that column. The following example shows the count of all rows, the total of all sale prices, and the average of all sale prices:

```
SELECT COUNT(*), SUM(sale_price), AVG(sale_price)
FROM cust_order;

COUNT(*) SUM(SALE_PRICE) AVG(SALE_PRICE)
--------------- --------------- ---------------
             20             788       56.2857143
```

Note that AVG(sale_price) is not equal to SUM(sale_price) / COUNT(*). If it were, the result of AVG(sale_price) would have been 788 / 20 = 39.4. But, since the AVG function ignores NULLS, it divides the total sale price by 14, and not by 20. AVG(sale_price) is equal to SUM(sale_price) / COUNT(sale_price) (788 / 14 = 56.2857143).

There may be situations where you want an average to be taken over all the rows in a table, not just the rows with non-NULL values for the column in question. In those situations you have to use the NVL function within the AVG function call to assign 0 (or some other useful value) to the column in place of any NULL values. (DECODE,

CASE, or the COALESCE function can be used in place of NVL. See Chapter 9 for details.) Here's an example:

```
SELECT AVG(NVL(sale_price,0)) FROM cust_order;

AVG(NVL(SALE_PRICE,0))
----------------------
                  39.4
```

Notice that the use of NVL causes all 20 rows to be considered for average computation, and the rows with NULL values for sale_price are assumed to have a 0 value for that column.

Use of DISTINCT and ALL

Most aggregate functions allow the use of DISTINCT or ALL along with the expression argument. DISTINCT allows you to disregard duplicate expression values, while ALL causes duplicate expression values to be included in the result. Notice that the column cust_nbr has duplicate values. Observe the result of the following SQL:

```
SELECT COUNT(cust_nbr), COUNT(DISTINCT cust_nbr), COUNT(ALL cust_nbr)
FROM cust_order;

COUNT(CUST_NBR) COUNT(DISTINCTCUST_NBR) COUNT(ALLCUST_NBR)
--------------- ----------------------- ------------------
             20                       4                 20
```

There are four distinct values in the cust_nbr column. Therefore, COUNT(DISTINCT cust_nbr) returns 4, whereas COUNT(cust_nbr) and COUNT(ALL cust_nbr) both return 20. ALL is the default, which means that if you don't specify either DISTINCT or ALL before the expression argument in an aggregate function, the function will consider all the rows that have a non-NULL value for the expression.

An important thing to note here is that ALL doesn't cause an aggregate function to consider NULL values. For example, COUNT(ALL SALE_PRICE) in the following example still returns 14, and not 20:

```
SELECT COUNT(ALL sale_price) FROM cust_order;

COUNT(ALLSALE_PRICE)
--------------------
                  14
```

Since ALL is the default, you can explicitly use ALL with every aggregate function. However, the aggregate functions that take more than one argument as input don't allow the use of DISTINCT. These include CORR, COVAR_POP, COVAR_SAMP, and all the linear regression functions.

In addition, some functions that take only one argument as input don't allow the use of DISTINCT. This category includes STTDEV_POP, STDDEV_SAMP, VAR_POP, VAR_SAMP, and GROUPING.

If you try to use DISTINCT with an aggregate function that doesn't allow it, you will get an error. For example:

```
SELECT STDDEV_POP(DISTINCT sale_price)
FROM cust_order;

SELECT STDDEV_POP(DISTINCT sale_price)
           *
ERROR at line 1:
ORA-30482: DISTINCT option not allowed for this function
```

However, using ALL with such a function doesn't cause any error. For example:

```
SELECT STDDEV_POP(ALL sale_price)
FROM cust_order;

STDDEV_POP(ALLSALE_PRICE)
-------------------------
                29.5282639
```

The GROUP BY Clause

The GROUP BY clause, along with the aggregate functions, groups a result set into multiple groups, and then produces a single row of summary information for each group. For example, if you want to find the total number of orders for each customer, execute the following query:

```
SELECT cust_nbr, COUNT(order_nbr)
FROM cust_order
GROUP BY cust_nbr;

  CUST_NBR COUNT(ORDER_NBR)
---------- ----------------
         1                8
         4                4
         5                6
         8                2
```

This query produces one summary line of output for each customer. This is the essence of a GROUP BY query. You asked Oracle to GROUP the results BY cust_nbr; therefore, it produced one output row for each distinct value of cust_nbr. Each data value for a given customer represents a summary based on all rows for that customer.

Correspondence Between SELECT and GROUP BY

When you write a query with a GROUP BY clause, there are a number of rules you need to be aware of that govern the correspondence between the columns in the

SELECT and GROUP BY clauses. Generally speaking, any nonaggregate expression in your SELECT clause must also be reflected in your GROUP BY clause.

Aggregate expressions generally require a GROUP BY clause

The nonaggregate expression cust_nbr in the SELECT list of the query in our most recent example also appears in the GROUP BY clause. If you have a mix of aggregate and nonaggregate expressions in the SELECT list, SQL expects that you are trying to perform a GROUP BY operation, and you must also include a GROUP BY clause in your query. Oracle returns an error if you fail to do so. For example, if you omit the GROUP BY clause, the following error is returned:

```
SELECT cust_nbr, sales_emp_id, COUNT(order_nbr)
FROM cust_order;

SELECT cust_nbr, sales_emp_id, COUNT(order_nbr)
       *
ERROR at line 1:
ORA-00937: not a single-group group function
```

There is one case in which you can write aggregate expressions in a SELECT list without also writing a GROUP BY clause and that is when you wish those aggregate expressions to apply to the entire result set. In such a case, your SELECT list must consist *only* of aggregate expressions. The queries earlier in this chapter, introducing the aggregate functions, are good examples of this case.

GROUP BY clause must include all nonaggregate expressions

If you forget to include *all* nonaggregate expressions from the SELECT list in the GROUP BY clause, SQL returns the following error:

```
SELECT cust_nbr, sales_emp_id, COUNT(order_nbr)
FROM cust_order
GROUP BY cust_nbr;

SELECT cust_nbr, sales_emp_id, COUNT(order_nbr)
                     *
ERROR at line 1:
ORA-00979: not a GROUP BY expression
```

Aggregate functions not allowed in GROUP BY clause

You can't use a group function (aggregate function) in the GROUP BY clause. You will get an error if you attempt to do so, as in the following example:

```
SELECT cust_nbr, COUNT(order_nbr)
FROM cust_order
GROUP BY cust_nbr, COUNT(order_nbr);

GROUP BY cust_nbr, COUNT(order_nbr)
                      *
```

```
ERROR at line 3:
ORA-00934: group function is not allowed here
```

Constants can be omitted from the GROUP BY clause

If you have a constant in your SELECT list, you don't need to include it in the
GROUP BY clause. However, including the constant in the GROUP BY clause
doesn't alter the result. Therefore, both the following statements will produce the
same output:

```
SELECT 'CUSTOMER', cust_nbr, COUNT(order_nbr)
FROM cust_order
GROUP BY cust_nbr;

SELECT 'CUSTOMER', cust_nbr, COUNT(order_nbr)
FROM cust_order
GROUP BY 'CUSTOMER', cust_nbr;
```

```
'CUSTOMER'   CUST_NBR COUNT(ORDER_NBR)
---------- ---------- ----------------
CUSTOMER            1                8
CUSTOMER            4                4
CUSTOMER            5                6
CUSTOMER            8                2
```

Scalar functions may be grouped by their underlying column

If a scalar function has been applied to a column in the SELECT list, the syntax
doesn't force you to include the scalar function in the GROUP BY clause. For example:

```
SELECT SUBSTR(lname,1,1), COUNT(*)
FROM employee
GROUP BY lname;
```

```
S   COUNT(*)
- ----------
A          1
A          1
B          1
C          1
F          1
J          1
J          1
K          1
M          1
M          1
S          1
S          1
T          1
W          1
```

```
14 rows selected.
```

In this example, the SELECT list has SUBSTR(lname,1,1); however, the GROUP BY clause contains just lname, without the SUBSTR function on it. Though this query is syntactically correct, if you look at the result set, you will notice that there are multiple rows with the same value for SUBSTR(lname,1,1). This means that the GROUP BY operation takes place for the entire lname, but only the substring is displayed. If you really want the result set to be grouped by the substring expression, you should include that expression in the GROUP BY clause, as shown in the following example:

```
SELECT SUBSTR(lname,1,1), COUNT(*)
FROM employee
GROUP BY SUBSTR(lname,1,1);

S   COUNT(*)
-   ----------
A          2
B          1
C          1
F          1
J          2
K          1
M          2
S          2
T          1
W          1

10 rows selected.
```

Notice the difference. This time, there is only one row in the result set for each value returned by SUBSTR(lname,1,1). The rows have been grouped on the exact same expression as is displayed.

Concatenated columns may be grouped in either of two ways

If an expression in a SELECT list concatenates two columns, you can specify the GROUP BY clause in one of the following two ways—both giving the same result:

```
SELECT manager_emp_id || job_id, COUNT(*)
FROM employee
GROUP BY manager_emp_id || job_id;

SELECT manager_emp_id || job_id, COUNT(*)
FROM employee
GROUP BY manager_emp_id, job_id;

MANAGER_EMP_ID||JOB_ID       COUNT(*)
-------------------------   ----------
672                                 1
7566669                             2
7698                                1
7698667                             1
7698670                             3
7782667                             1
```

```
7788                           1
7839671                        3
7902667                        1
```

You can sometimes exclude a nonaggregate expression from the GROUP BY clause

There are certain situations in which you want an expression in the SELECT list, but don't want to group by the same. For example, you might want to display a line number along with summary information for each customer. Attempt to do so using the following query, and you will get an error:

```
SELECT ROWNUM, cust_nbr, COUNT(order_nbr)
FROM cust_order
GROUP BY cust_nbr;

SELECT ROWNUM, cust_nbr, COUNT(order_nbr)
       *
ERROR at line 1:
ORA-00979: not a GROUP BY expression
```

If you include ROWNUM in the GROUP BY clause, you'll get the following, unexpected result:

```
SELECT ROWNUM, cust_nbr, COUNT(order_nbr)
FROM cust_order
GROUP BY ROWNUM, cust_nbr;
```

ROWNUM	CUST_NBR	COUNT(ORDER_NBR)
1	1	1
2	1	1
3	5	1
4	4	1
5	4	1
6	8	1
7	1	1
8	5	1
9	5	1
10	1	1
11	1	1
12	1	1
13	5	1
14	4	1
15	4	1
16	8	1
17	1	1
18	5	1
19	5	1
20	1	1

```
20 rows selected.
```

You certainly didn't want this result, did you? You wanted to receive one summary row for each customer, and then to display ROWNUM for those lines. But when you include ROWNUM in the GROUP BY clause, it produces one summary row for each row selected from the table cust_order. To get the expected result, you should use the following SQL:

```
SELECT ROWNUM, v.*
FROM (SELECT cust_nbr, COUNT(order_nbr)
      FROM cust_order GROUP BY cust_nbr) v;
```

```
  ROWNUM    CUST_NBR COUNT(ORDER_NBR)
---------- ---------- ----------------
        1          1                8
        2          4                4
        3          5                6
        4          8                2
```

The construct in the FROM clause is called an *inline view*. Read more about inline views in Chapter 5.

You are not required to show your GROUP BY columns

Syntactically, it is not mandatory to include all the expressions of the GROUP BY clause in the SELECT list. However, those expressions not in the SELECT list will not be represented in the output; therefore, the output may not make much sense. For example:

```
SELECT COUNT(order_nbr)
FROM cust_order
GROUP BY cust_nbr;
```

```
COUNT(ORDER_NBR)
----------------
               8
               4
               6
               2
```

This query produces a count of orders for each customer (by grouping based on cust_nbr), but without the cust_nbr in the output you can't associate the counts with the customers. Extending the previous example, you can see that without a consistent SELECT list and GROUP BY clause, the output may be a bit confusing. The following example produces output that at first glance seems useful:

```
SELECT cust_nbr, COUNT(order_nbr)
FROM cust_order
GROUP BY cust_nbr, order_dt;
```

```
  CUST_NBR COUNT(ORDER_NBR)
---------- ----------------
        1                2
        1                2
        1                4
        4                2
        4                2
```

```
        5              2
        5              2
        5              2
        8              2
```

9 rows selected.

From the output, it appears that you are trying to obtain a count of orders for each customer. However, there are multiple rows in the output for some cust_nbr values. The fact that you have included order_dt in the GROUP BY clause, and therefore generated a summary result for each combination of cust_nbr and order_dt, is missing from the output. You can't make sense of the output unless the output and the SQL statement are looked at together. You can't expect all readers of SQL output to understand SQL syntax, can you? Therefore, we always recommend maintaining consistency between the nonaggregate expressions in the SELECT list and the expressions in the GROUP BY clause. A more meaningful version of the previous SQL statement would be as follows:

```
SELECT cust_nbr, order_dt, COUNT(order_nbr)
FROM cust_order
GROUP BY cust_nbr, order_dt;

CUST_NBR ORDER_DT  COUNT(ORDER_NBR)
-------- --------- ----------------
       1 18-JUL-01                2
       1 19-JUL-01                2
       1 22-JUL-01                4
       4 16-JUL-01                2
       4 18-JUL-01                2
       5 12-JUL-01                2
       5 20-JUL-01                2
       5 21-JUL-01                2
       8 22-JUL-01                2
```

9 rows selected.

This output is consistent with the GROUP BY clause in the query. Readers of the report are more likely to make the correct assumption about what this output represents.

GROUP BY Clause and NULL Values

When you GROUP BY a column that contains NULL values for some rows, all the rows with NULL values are placed into a single group and presented as one summary row in the output. For example:

```
SELECT sale_price, COUNT(order_nbr)
FROM cust_order
GROUP BY sale_price;
```

```
SALE_PRICE COUNT(ORDER_NBR)
---------- ----------------
        25                4
        34                2
        56                4
        99                4
                          6
```

Notice that the last row in the output consists of a NULL value for the column sale_price. If you want the row containing the NULL value to be the first row in the output, you can perform an ORDER BY on sale_price in descending order:

```
SELECT sale_price, COUNT(order_nbr)
FROM cust_order
GROUP BY sale_price
ORDER BY sale_price DESC;

SALE_PRICE COUNT(ORDER_NBR)
---------- ----------------
                          6
        99                4
        56                4
        34                2
        25                4
```

Whether you are using a GROUP BY or not, the ORDER BY clause can have an optional NULLS FIRST or NULLS LAST option to put the NULLs either at the beginning or at the end of the result set, respectively. For example, to sort NULLs first:

```
SELECT sale_price, COUNT(order_nbr)
FROM cust_order
GROUP BY sale_price
ORDER BY sale_price NULLS FIRST;

SALE_PRICE COUNT(ORDER_NBR)
---------- ----------------
                          6
        25                4
        34                2
        56                4
        99                4
```

Or, to sort NULLs last:

```
SELECT sale_price, COUNT(order_nbr)
FROM cust_order
GROUP BY sale_price
ORDER BY sale_price NULLS LAST;

SALE_PRICE COUNT(ORDER_NBR)
---------- ----------------
        25                4
        34                2
```

```
               56              4
               99              4
                               6
```

GROUP BY Clause with WHERE Clause

While producing summary results using the GROUP BY clause, you can filter records from the table based on a WHERE clause, as in the following example, which produces a count of orders in which the sale price exceeds $25 for each customer:

```
SELECT cust_nbr, COUNT(order_nbr)
FROM cust_order
WHERE sale_price > 25
GROUP BY cust_nbr;

  CUST_NBR COUNT(ORDER_NBR)
---------- ----------------
         1                4
         4                4
         8                2
```

While executing a SQL statement with a WHERE clause and a GROUP BY clause, Oracle first applies the WHERE clause and filters out the rows that don't satisfy the WHERE condition. The rows that satisfy the WHERE clause are then grouped using the GROUP BY clause.

SQL syntax requires that the WHERE clause must come before the GROUP BY clause. Otherwise, the following error is returned:

```
SELECT cust_nbr, COUNT(order_nbr)
FROM cust_order
GROUP BY cust_nbr
WHERE sale_price > 25;

WHERE sale_price > 25
*
ERROR at line 4:
ORA-00933: SQL command not properly ended
```

The HAVING Clause

The HAVING clause is closely associated with the GROUP BY clause. The HAVING clause is used to put a filter on the groups created by the GROUP BY clause. If a query has a HAVING clause along with a GROUP BY clause, the result set will include only the groups that satisfy the condition specified in the HAVING clause. Let's look at some examples that illustrate this. The following query returns the number of orders per customer:

```
SELECT cust_nbr, COUNT(order_nbr)
FROM cust_order
GROUP BY cust_nbr
HAVING cust_nbr < 6;
```

```
CUST_NBR  COUNT(ORDER_NBR)
--------- ----------------
        1                8
        4                4
        5                6
```

Notice that the output only includes customers with numbers below 6. That's because the HAVING clause specified cust_nbr < 6 as a condition. Orders for all customers were counted, but only those groups that matched the specified HAVING condition were returned as the result.

The previous example is a poor use of the HAVING clause, because that clause references only unsummarized data. It's more efficient to use WHERE cust_nbr < 6 instead of HAVING cust_nbr < 6, because the WHERE clause eliminates rows prior to summarization, whereas HAVING eliminates groups post-summarization. A better version of the previous query would be:

```
SELECT cust_nbr, COUNT(order_nbr)
FROM cust_order
WHERE cust_nbr < 6
GROUP BY cust_nbr;
```

The next example shows a more appropriate use of the HAVING clause:

```
SELECT cust_nbr, COUNT(order_nbr)
FROM cust_order
GROUP BY cust_nbr
HAVING COUNT(order_nbr) > 2;
```

```
CUST_NBR  COUNT(ORDER_NBR)
--------- ----------------
        1                8
        4                4
        5                6
```

See the use of the aggregate function COUNT in the HAVING clause? This is an appropriate use for HAVING, because the results of the aggregate function cannot be determined until after the grouping takes place.

The syntax for the HAVING clause is similar to that of the WHERE clause. However, there is one restriction on the conditions you can write in the HAVING clause. A HAVING condition can refer only to an expression in the SELECT list, or to an expression involving an aggregate function. If you specify an expression in the HAVING clause that isn't in the SELECT list, or that isn't an aggregate expression, you will get an error. For example:

```
SELECT cust_nbr, COUNT(order_nbr)
FROM cust_order
GROUP BY cust_nbr
HAVING order_dt < SYSDATE;
```

```
HAVING order_dt < SYSDATE
       *
```

```
ERROR at line 4:
ORA-00979: not a GROUP BY expression
```

However, you can use an aggregate expression in the HAVING clause, even if it doesn't appear in the SELECT list, as illustrated in the following example:

```
SELECT cust_nbr
FROM cust_order
GROUP BY cust_nbr
HAVING COUNT(order_nbr) < 5;


  CUST_NBR
----------
         4
         8
```

In the preceding example, the HAVING clause refers to COUNT(order_nbr), which is not in the SELECT list. You are not required to show in your result set all the columns or expressions that determine which rows end up in that result set.

The order of the GROUP BY clause and the HAVING clause in a SELECT statement is not important. You can specify the GROUP BY clause before the HAVING clause, or vice versa. Therefore, the following two queries are the same and produce the same result:

```
SELECT cust_nbr, COUNT(order_nbr)
FROM cust_order
GROUP BY cust_nbr
HAVING COUNT(order_nbr) > 2;

SELECT cust_nbr, COUNT(order_nbr)
FROM cust_order
HAVING COUNT(order_nbr) > 2
GROUP BY cust_nbr;


  CUST_NBR COUNT(ORDER_NBR)
---------- ----------------
         1                8
         4                4
         5                6
```

Even though Oracle doesn't care whether the HAVING clause comes before the GROUP BY clause or after, the HAVING clause is applied to the groups created by the GROUP BY clause, so it is a good programming practice to always put the HAVING clause after the GROUP BY clause. Another reason for placing HAVING after GROUP BY is that SQL Standard requires that particular order. Thus, putting HAVING after GROUP BY makes your code more portable.

You can use a WHERE clause and a HAVING clause together in a query. When you do, it is important to understand the impact of the two clauses. The WHERE clause is executed first, and the rows that don't satisfy the WHERE condition are not passed to the GROUP BY clause. The GROUP BY clause summarizes the filtered data into groups, and then the HAVING clause is applied to the groups to eliminate the groups that don't satisfy the HAVING condition. The following example illustrates this:

```
SELECT cust_nbr, COUNT(order_nbr)
FROM cust_order
WHERE sale_price > 25
GROUP BY cust_nbr
HAVING COUNT(order_nbr) > 1;

 CUST_NBR COUNT(ORDER_NBR)
---------- ----------------
        1                4
        4                4
        8                2
```

In this example, the WHERE clause first eliminates all the orders that don't satisfy the condition sale_price > 25. The rest of the rows are grouped on cust_nbr. The HAVING clause eliminates the customers that don't have more than one order.

Nested Group Operations

The examples discussed in this chapter so far all involved one group operation on a column of a table. SQL also allows you to nest group functions, which means that one group function can enclose an expression that is itself a group operation on another expression or column. Let's consider the following example:

> An economic slowdown has resulted in budget constraints for many employers, especially in the IT industry. Budget constraints have forced companies to take a second look at the money spent on employee compensation. Some companies have had to downsize their workforce, others have had to cut down employee bonuses, while still others have cut the employee base salaries. Your company is no exception, and is also under financial pressure. Your CEO must take a serious look at the compensation structure of the employees at various levels in various departments in the company.

> Your CEO calls on you to query the Human Resources database and help him collect data. By this time, you've already heard the rumors of upcoming "reductions in force" (RIFs) and compensation cuts. This is your golden opportunity to impress your CEO with your skills, to make sure you are not affected by the RIFs. Mess up now, and you can be pretty sure that you have to start looking for another job in this increasingly competitive job market.

Here's your CEO's first question: What is the maximum amount of money spent by any department on employee salaries?

To answer this question, you know that you need to compute the sum of the salaries of all the employees in each department, and then find the maximum of those individual sums. Now that you know about the GROUP BY clause, finding the sum of salaries for all the employees in each department is easy:

```
SELECT dept_id, SUM(salary)
FROM employee
GROUP BY dept_id;
```

```
DEPT_ID SUM(SALARY)
---------- -----------
        10        8750
        20        9900
        30        9400
```

However, your task is half done. You next need to find the maximum of the SUM(salary) values returned by this query. One way to do that is to use the preceding query as an inline view. (Inline views are discussed in detail in Chapter 5.) The following SELECT takes the results from the earlier query, which is now a nested query, and applies the MAX function to retrieve the highest SUM(salary) value:

```
SELECT MAX(sal) FROM
(SELECT dept_id, SUM(salary) sal
FROM employee
GROUP BY dept_id);
```

```
  MAX(SAL)
----------
      9900
```

However, you don't even need to write a subquery. Another, simpler way of writing the query you need is:

```
SELECT MAX(SUM(salary))
FROM employee
GROUP BY dept_id;
```

```
MAX(SUM(SALARY))
----------------
            9900
```

The MAX(SUM(salary)) in this query is a nested group operation. When the query executes, the rows are aggregated by department. The innermost group function, in this case the SUM function, is used to generate one salary value per department. This is no different than in previous examples, but this time you have a MAX function seemingly left over. That MAX function is applied to the entire collection of SUM(salary) values produced by the initial aggregation. The result is a single value, the maximum amount of money that any one department spends on employee salaries, which is just what your CEO wanted.

 It never makes sense to use more than one level of nested group function. MAX(SUM(salary)) returns a single value. One group function enclosing another will always return a single value. No further aggregation is possible.

Knowing only the maximum of the total salaries paid by a department isn't going to help much. So, your CEO's next question is to ask about the minimum and average amounts of money spent by any department on employee salaries. That should be an easy one to answer now. Just apply the same pattern as used in the previous query:

```
SELECT MIN(SUM(salary)), AVG(SUM(salary))
FROM employee
GROUP BY dept_id;

MIN(SUM(SALARY)) AVG(SUM(SALARY))
---------------- ----------------
            8750             9350
```

Observing that the maximum (9900) is not too large compared to the minimum (8750) and the average (9350), your CEO realizes that all the departments spend pretty much uniformly on employee salaries. He next asks: What is the maximum, minimum, and average number of employees in any department? Use the following query to answer that question:

```
SELECT MAX(COUNT(*)), MIN(COUNT(*)), AVG(COUNT(*))
FROM employee
GROUP BY dept_id;

MAX(COUNT(*)) MIN(COUNT(*)) AVG(COUNT(*))
------------- ------------- -------------
            6             3    4.66666667
```

The information that some departments have double the number of employees than some others may give your CEO some ideas about how he wants to reorganize the company and reduce cost. Hopefully, you have impressed your CEO with your SQL skills to the point that you are sleeping better at nights now, secure that you, at least, will still be employed in the morning.

CHAPTER 5
Subqueries

Some endeavors require a certain level of preparation before the main activity can commence. Cooking, for example, often involves pre-mixing sets of ingredients before they are combined. Similarly, certain types of SQL statements benefit from the creation of intermediate result sets to aid in statement execution. The structure responsible for generating intermediate result sets is the subquery. This chapter will define and illustrate the use of subqueries in SQL statements.

What Is a Subquery?

As we mentioned in Chapter 1, a subquery is a SELECT statement that is nested within another SQL statement. For the purpose of this discussion, we will call the SQL statement that contains a subquery the *containing statement*. Subqueries are executed prior to execution of their containing SQL statement (see "Correlated Subqueries" later in this chapter for the exception to this rule), and the result set generated by a subquery is discarded after its containing SQL statement has finished execution. Thus, a subquery can be thought of as a temporary table with statement scope.

Syntactically, subqueries are enclosed within parentheses. For example, the following SELECT statement contains a simple subquery in its WHERE clause:

```
SELECT * FROM customer
WHERE cust_nbr = (SELECT 123 FROM dual);
```

The subquery in this statement is absurdly simple, and completely unnecessary, but it does serve to illustrate a point. When this statement is executed, the subquery is evaluated first. The result of that subquery then becomes a value in the WHERE clause expression:

```
SELECT * FROM customer
WHERE cust_nbr = 123;
```

With the subquery out of the way, the containing query can now be evaluated. In this case, it would bring back information about customer number 123.

Subqueries are most often found in the WHERE clause of a SELECT, UPDATE, or DELETE statement, as well as in the SET clause of an UPDATE statement. A subquery may either be *correlated* with its containing SQL statement, meaning that it references one or more columns from the containing statement, or it might reference nothing outside itself, in which case it is called a *noncorrelated* subquery. A less commonly used but powerful variety of subquery, called the *inline view*, occurs in the FROM clause of a SELECT statement. Inline views are always noncorrelated; they are evaluated first and behave like unindexed tables cached in memory for the remainder of the query.

Noncorrelated Subqueries

Noncorrelated subqueries allow each row from the containing SQL statement to be compared to a set of values. You can divide noncorrelated subqueries into the following three categories, depending on the number of rows and columns returned in their result set:

- Single-row, single-column subqueries
- Multiple-row, single-column subqueries
- Multiple-column subqueries

Depending on the category, different sets of operators may be employed by the containing SQL statement to interact with the subquery.

Single-Row, Single-Column Subqueries

A subquery that returns a single row with a single column is treated like a scalar by the containing statement; not surprisingly, these types of subqueries are known as *scalar subqueries*. Such a subquery may appear on either side of a condition, and the usual comparison operators (=, <, >, !=, <=, >=) are employed. The following query illustrates the utility of single-row, single-column subqueries by finding all employees earning an above-average salary. The subquery returns the average salary, and the containing query then returns all employees who earn more than that amount:

```
SELECT lname
FROM employee
WHERE salary > (SELECT AVG(salary)
                FROM employee);


LNAME
--------------------
BLAKE
```

```
CLARK
SCOTT
KING
FORD
```

As this query demonstrates, it can be perfectly reasonable for a subquery to reference the same tables as the containing query. In fact, subqueries are frequently used to isolate a subset of records within a table. For example, many applications include maintenance routines that clean up operational data, such as exception or load logs. Every week, a script might delete all but the latest day's activity. For example:

```
DELETE FROM load_log
WHERE load_dt < (SELECT MAX(TRUNC(load_dt))
                 FROM load_log);
```

Noncorrelated subqueries are also commonly found outside the WHERE clause, as illustrated by the following query, which identifies the salesperson responsible for the most orders:

```
SELECT sales_emp_id, COUNT(*)
FROM cust_order
GROUP BY sales_emp_id
HAVING COUNT(*) = (SELECT MAX(COUNT(*))
                   FROM cust_order
                   GROUP BY sales_emp_id);

SALES_EMP_ID   COUNT(*)
------------  ----------
        7354          8
```

This subquery calculates the number of orders attributable to each salesperson, and then applies the MAX function to return only the highest number of orders. The containing query performs the same aggregation as the subquery and then keeps only those salespeople whose total sales count matches the maximum value returned by the subquery. Interestingly, the containing query can return more than one row if multiple salespeople tie for the maximum sales count, while the subquery is guaranteed to return a single row and column. If it seems wasteful that the subquery and containing query both perform the same aggregation, it is; see Chapter 14 for more efficient ways to handle these types of queries.

So far, you have seen scalar subqueries in the WHERE and HAVING clauses of SELECT statements, along with the WHERE clause of a DELETE statement. Before delving deeper into the different types of subqueries, let's explore where else subqueries can and can't be utilized in SQL statements:

- The FROM clause may contain any type of noncorrelated subquery.
- The SELECT and ORDER BY clauses may contain scalar subqueries.
- The GROUP BY clause may not contain subqueries.
- The START WITH and CONNECT BY clauses, used for querying hierarchical data, may contain subqueries and will be examined in detail in Chapter 8.

- The WITH clause contains a named noncorrelated subquery that can be referenced multiple times within the containing query but executes only once (see the examples later in this chapter).
- The USING clause of a MERGE statement may contain noncorrelated subqueries.
- The SET clause of UPDATE statements may contain scalar or single-row, multiple-column subqueries.
- INSERT statements may contain scalar subqueries in the VALUES clause.

Multiple-Row, Single-Column Subqueries

Now that you know how to use single-row, single-column subqueries, let's explore how to use subqueries that return multiple rows. When a subquery returns more than one row, it is not possible to use only comparison operators, since a single value cannot be directly compared to a set of values. However, a single value *can* be compared to each value in a set. To accomplish this, the special keywords ANY and ALL are used with comparison operators to determine if a value is equal to (or less than, greater than, etc.) *any* member of the set or *all* members of the set. Consider the following query:

```
SELECT fname, lname
FROM employee
WHERE dept_id = 30 AND salary >= ALL
  (SELECT salary
   FROM employee
   WHERE dept_id = 30);
```

```
FNAME                LNAME
-------------------- --------------------
MARION               BLAKE
```

The subquery returns the set of salaries for department 30, and the containing query checks each employee in the department to see if her salary is greater or equal to every salary returned by the subquery. Thus, this query retrieves the name of the highest paid person in department 30. While every employee has a salary >= *any* of the salaries in the department, only the highest paid employee has a salary >= *all* of the salaries in the department. If multiple employees tie for the highest salary in the department, multiple names will be returned.

Another way to phrase the previous query is to find the employee whose salary is not less than any other salary in her department. You can do this using the ANY operator:

```
SELECT fname, lname
FROM employee
WHERE dept_id = 30 AND NOT salary < ANY
  (SELECT salary
   FROM employee
   WHERE dept_id = 30);
```

There are almost always multiple ways to phrase the same query. One of the challenges of writing SQL is striking the right balance between efficiency and readability. In this case, we might prefer using AND salary >= ALL over AND NOT salary < ANY because the first variation is easier to understand; however, the latter form might prove more efficient, since each evaluation of the subquery results requires from 1 to N comparisons when using ANY versus exactly N comparisons when using ALL.

> If there are 100 people in the department, each of the 100 salaries needs to be compared to the entire set of 100. When using ANY, the comparison can be suspended as soon as a larger salary is identified in the set, whereas using ALL requires 100 comparisons to ensure that there are no smaller salaries in the set.

The next query uses the ANY operator to find all employees who have been with the company longer than any top-level manager:

```
SELECT fname, lname
FROM employee
WHERE manager_emp_id IS NOT NULL
  AND hire_date < ANY
 (SELECT hire_date
  FROM employee
  WHERE manager_emp_id IS NULL);
```

FNAME	LNAME
JOHN	SMITH
KEVIN	ALLEN
CYNTHIA	WARD
TERRY	JONES
KENNETH	MARTIN
MARION	BLAKE
CAROL	CLARK
MARY	TURNER

The subquery returns the set of hire dates for all top-level managers, and the containing query returns the names of non-top-level managers whose hire date is previous to any returned by the subquery.

For the previous three queries, failure to include either the ANY or ALL operators may result in the following error:

```
ORA-01427: single-row subquery returns more than one row
```

The wording of this error message is a bit confusing. After all, how can a single-row subquery return multiple rows? What the error message is trying to convey is that a multiple-row subquery has been identified where only a single-row subquery is allowed. If you are not absolutely certain that your subquery will return exactly one row, you must include ANY or ALL to ensure your code doesn't fail in the future.

Along with ANY and ALL, you may also use the IN operator for working with multi-row subqueries. Using IN with a subquery is functionally equivalent to using = ANY, and returns TRUE if a match is found in the set returned by the subquery. The following query uses IN to postpone shipment of all orders containing parts that are not currently in stock:

```
UPDATE cust_order
SET expected_ship_dt = TRUNC(SYSDATE) + 1
WHERE ship_dt IS NULL
  AND order_nbr IN
  (SELECT l.order_nbr
   FROM line_item l INNER JOIN part p
   ON l.part_nbr = p.part_nbr
   WHERE p.inventory_qty = 0);
```

The subquery returns the set of orders requesting out-of-stock parts, and the containing UPDATE statement modifies the expected ship date of all orders in the set. We think you will agree that IN is more intuitive than = ANY, which is why IN is almost always used in such situations. Similarly, you can use NOT IN instead of using != ALL as demonstrated by the next query, which deletes all customers who haven't placed an order in the past five years:

```
DELETE FROM customer
WHERE cust_nbr NOT IN
  (SELECT cust_nbr
   FROM cust_order
   WHERE order_dt >= TRUNC(SYSDATE) - (365 * 5));
```

The subquery returns the set of customers that *have* placed an order in the past five years, and the containing DELETE statement removes all customers that are not in the set returned by the subquery.

Finding members of one set that do *not* exist in another set is referred to as an *anti-join*. As the name implies, an anti-join is the opposite of a join; rows from table A are returned if the specified data is *not* found in table B. The Oracle optimizer can employ multiple strategies for formulating execution plans for such queries, including a *merge anti-join* or a *hash anti-join*.

 Since this is not explicitly a tuning book (in our opinion, mastering the SQL implementation is the best tuning tool available), we will refrain from delving into the inner workings of the Oracle optimizer and how the optimizer can be influenced via hints. For more information, see *Oracle SQL Tuning Pocket Reference* (O'Reilly).

Multiple-Column Subqueries

While all of the previous examples compare a single column from the containing SQL statement to the result set returned by the subquery, it is also possible to issue a subquery against multiple columns. Consider the following UPDATE statement, which rolls up data from an operational table into an aggregate table:

```
UPDATE monthly_orders SET
  tot_orders = (SELECT COUNT(*)
    FROM cust_order
    WHERE order_dt >= TO_DATE('01-JUL-2001','DD-MON-YYYY')
      AND order_dt < TO_DATE('01-AUG-2001','DD-MON-YYYY')
      AND cancelled_dt IS NULL),
  max_order_amt = (SELECT MAX(sale_price)
    FROM cust_order
    WHERE order_dt >= TO_DATE('01-JUL-2001','DD-MON-YYYY')
      AND order_dt < TO_DATE('01-AUG-2001','DD-MON-YYYY')
      AND cancelled_dt IS NULL),
  min_order_amt = (SELECT MIN(sale_price)
    FROM cust_order
    WHERE order_dt >= TO_DATE('01-JUL-2001','DD-MON-YYYY')
      AND order_dt < TO_DATE('01-AUG-2001','DD-MON-YYYY')
      AND cancelled_dt IS NULL),
  tot_amt = (SELECT SUM(sale_price)
    FROM cust_order
    WHERE order_dt >= TO_DATE('01-JUL-2001','DD-MON-YYYY')
      AND order_dt < TO_DATE('01-AUG-2001','DD-MON-YYYY')
      AND cancelled_dt IS NULL)
WHERE month = 7 and year = 2001;
```

The UPDATE statement modifies four columns in the monthly_orders table, and values for each of the four columns are calculated by aggregating data in the cust_order table. Looking closely, you can see that the WHERE clauses for all four subqueries are identical; only the aggregation function differs in the four queries. The next query demonstrates how all four columns can be populated with a single trip through the cust_order table by using a single subquery that returns four columns:

```
UPDATE monthly_orders
SET (tot_orders, max_order_amt, min_order_amt, tot_amt) =
  (SELECT COUNT(*), MAX(sale_price), MIN(sale_price), SUM(sale_price)
   FROM cust_order
   WHERE order_dt >= TO_DATE('01-JUL-2001','DD-MON-YYYY')
     AND order_dt < TO_DATE('01-AUG-2001','DD-MON-YYYY')
     AND cancelled_dt IS NULL)
WHERE month = 7 and year = 2001;
```

This second statement achieves the same result more efficiently than the first by performing four aggregations during one trip through the cust_order table, rather than one aggregation during each of four separate trips.

Whereas the previous example demonstrates the use of a multiple-column subquery in the SET clause of an UPDATE statement, such subqueries may also be utilized in the WHERE clause of a SELECT, UPDATE, or DELETE statement. The next statement deletes all items from open orders that include discontinued parts:

```
DELETE FROM line_item
WHERE (order_nbr, part_nbr) IN
```

```
(SELECT c.order_nbr, p.part_nbr
 FROM cust_order c INNER JOIN line_item li
 ON c.order_nbr = li.order_nbr
 INNER JOIN part p
 ON li.part_nbr = p.part_nbr
 WHERE c.ship_dt IS NULL AND c.cancelled_dt IS NULL
   AND p.status = 'DISCONTINUED');
```

Note the use of the IN operator in the WHERE clause. Two columns are listed together in parentheses prior to the IN keyword. Values in these two columns are compared to the set of two values returned by each row of the subquery. If a match is found, the row is removed from the line_item table.

The WITH Clause

You may find yourself in a situation where you need to reference the same noncorrelated subquery multiple times in the same query. For example, let's say you want to show all employees making more than the average salary, and you want to show how much above the average each employee makes. You can formulate this using the same subquery in both the FROM and WHERE clauses:

```
SELECT e.emp_id, e.lname, e.fname,
  ROUND(e.salary - (SELECT AVG(salary) FROM employee)) above_avg
FROM employee e
WHERE e.salary > (SELECT AVG(salary) FROM employee);
```

EMP_ID	LNAME	FNAME	ABOVE_AVG
7698	BLAKE	MARION	846
7782	CLARK	CAROL	446
7788	SCOTT	DONALD	996
7839	KING	FRANCIS	2996
7902	FORD	JENNIFER	996

To eliminate the inefficiency of executing the same subquery multiple times, Oracle introduced the WITH clause in the Oracle9*i* release. Using the WITH clause, you can place the subquery that calculates the average salary at the top of the query and reference it throughout the query:

```
WITH avg_sal AS (SELECT AVG(salary) val FROM employee)
SELECT e.emp_id, e.lname, e.fname,
  (SELECT ROUND(e.salary - val) FROM avg_sal) above_avg
FROM employee e
WHERE e.salary > (SELECT val FROM avg_sal);
```

EMP_ID	LNAME	FNAME	ABOVE_AVG
7698	BLAKE	MARION	846
7782	CLARK	CAROL	446
7788	SCOTT	DONALD	996
7839	KING	FRANCIS	2996
7902	FORD	JENNIFER	996

The WITH clause creates a temporary data set called, in this case, avg_sal, which, in this case, consists of a single row of data having a single column, val. This data set is generated once and can be referenced throughout the containing query. To access the data in avg_sal, you query it as if it were a table. In this regard, it acts like a temporary table with statement scope. As you will see shortly, the WITH clause acts in many ways like another type of subquery called the inline view.

Correlated Subqueries

A subquery that references one or more columns from its containing SQL statement is called a *correlated subquery*. Unlike noncorrelated subqueries, which are executed exactly once prior to execution of the containing statement, a correlated subquery is executed once for each candidate row in the intermediate result set of the containing query. For example, consider the following query, which locates all parts supplied by Acme Industries that have been purchased 10 or more times since July 2001:

```
SELECT p.part_nbr, p.name
FROM supplier s INNER JOIN part p
ON s.supplier_id = p.supplier_id
WHERE s.name = 'Acme Industries'
  AND 10 <=
    (SELECT COUNT(*)
     FROM cust_order co INNER JOIN line_item li
     ON li.order_nbr = co.order_nbr
     WHERE li.part_nbr = p.part_nbr
       AND co.order_dt >= TO_DATE('01-JUL-2001','DD-MON-YYYY'));
```

The reference to p.part_nbr is what makes the subquery correlated; values for p.part_nbr must be supplied by the containing query before the subquery can execute. If there are 10,000 parts in the part table, but only 100 are supplied by Acme Industries, the subquery will be executed once for each of the 100 rows in the intermediate result set created by joining the part and supplier tables.

 It is possible to ask for the subquery to be evaluated earlier in the execution plan using the PUSH_SUBQ hint; once again, we suggest you pick up a good book on Oracle tuning if you are interested in learning more about how Oracle actually executes subqueries.

Correlated subqueries are often used to test whether relationships exist without regard to cardinality. We might, for example, want to find all parts that have shipped at least once since January 2002. The EXISTS operator is used for these types of queries, as illustrated by the following query:

```
SELECT p.part_nbr, p.name, p.unit_cost
FROM part p
WHERE EXISTS
 (SELECT 1
  FROM line_item li INNER JOIN cust_order co
```

```
   ON li.order_nbr = co.order_nbr
 WHERE li.part_nbr = p.part_nbr
   AND co.ship_dt >= TO_DATE('01-JAN-2002','DD-MON-YYYY'));
```

As long as the subquery returns one or more rows, the EXISTS condition is satisfied without regard for how many rows were actually returned by the subquery. Since the EXISTS operator returns TRUE or FALSE depending on the number of rows returned by the subquery, the actual columns returned by the subquery are irrelevant. The SELECT clause requires at least one column, however, so it is common practice to use either the literal "1" or the wildcard "*".

Conversely, you can test whether a relationship does not exist:

```
UPDATE customer c
SET c.inactive_ind = 'Y', c.inactive_dt = TRUNC(SYSDATE)
WHERE c.inactive_dt IS NULL
  AND NOT EXISTS (SELECT 1 FROM cust_order co
    WHERE co.cust_nbr = c.cust_nbr
      AND co.order_dt > TRUNC(SYSDATE) - 365);
```

This statement makes all customer records inactive for those customers who haven't placed an order in the past year. Such queries are commonly found in maintenance routines. For example, foreign key constraints might prevent child records from referring to a nonexistent parent, but it is possible to have parent records without children. If business rules prohibit this situation, you might run a utility each week that removes these records, as in:

```
DELETE FROM cust_order co
WHERE co.order_dt > TRUNC(SYSDATE) - 7
  AND co.cancelled_dt IS NULL
  AND NOT EXISTS
    (SELECT 1 FROM line_item li
    WHERE li.order_nbr = co.order_nbr);
```

A query that includes a correlated subquery using the EXISTS operator is referred to as a *semi-join*. A semi-join includes rows in table A for which corresponding data is found *one or more* times in table B. Thus, the size of the final result set is unaffected by the number of matches found in table B. Similar to the anti-join discussed earlier, the Oracle optimizer can employ multiple strategies for formulating execution plans for such queries, including a *merge semi-join* or a *hash semi-join*.

Although they are very often used together, the use of correlated subqueries does not require the EXISTS operator. If your database design includes denormalized columns, for example, you might run nightly routines to recalculate the denormalized data, as in:

```
UPDATE customer c
SET (c.tot_orders, c.last_order_dt) =
 (SELECT COUNT(*), MAX(co.order_dt)
  FROM cust_order co
  WHERE co.cust_nbr = c.cust_nbr
    AND co.cancelled_dt IS NULL);
```

Because a SET clause assigns values to columns in the table, the only operator allowed is =. The subquery returns exactly one row (thanks to the aggregation functions), so the results may be safely assigned to the target columns. Rather than recalculating the entire sum each day, a more efficient method might be to update only those customers who placed orders today:

```
UPDATE customer c SET (c.tot_orders, c.last_order_dt) =
 (SELECT c.tot_orders + COUNT(*), MAX(co.order_dt)
  FROM cust_order co
  WHERE co.cust_nbr = c.cust_nbr
    AND co.cancelled_dt IS NULL
    AND co.order_dt >= TRUNC(SYSDATE))
WHERE c.cust_nbr IN
 (SELECT co.cust_nbr
  FROM cust_order co
  WHERE co.order_dt >= TRUNC(SYSDATE)
    AND co.cancelled_dt IS NULL);
```

As the previous statement shows, data from the containing query can be used for other purposes in the correlated subquery than just join conditions in the WHERE clause. In this example, the SELECT clause of the correlated subquery adds today's sales totals to the previous value of tot_orders in the customer table to arrive at the new value.

Along with the WHERE clause of SELECT, UPDATE, and DELETE statements, and the SET clause of UPDATE statements, another potent use of correlated subqueries is in the SELECT clause, as illustrated by the following:

```
SELECT d.dept_id, d.name,
 (SELECT COUNT(*) FROM employee e
  WHERE e.dept_id = d.dept_id) empl_cnt
FROM department d;
```

```
   DEPT_ID NAME                  EMPL_CNT
---------- -------------------- ----------
        10 ACCOUNTING                   3
        20 RESEARCH                     5
        30 SALES                        6
        40 OPERATIONS                   0
```

The empl_cnt column returned from this query is derived from a correlated subquery that returns the number of employees assigned to each department. Note that the OPERATIONS department has no assigned employees, so the subquery returns 0.

To appreciate the value of subqueries in the SELECT clause, let's compare the previous query to a more traditional method using GROUP BY:

```
SELECT d.dept_id, d.name, COUNT(e.emp_id) empl_cnt
FROM department d LEFT OUTER JOIN employee e
  ON d.dept_id = e.dept_id
GROUP BY d.dept_id, d.name;
```

```
DEPT_ID NAME                   EMPL_CNT
---------- -------------------- ----------
      10 ACCOUNTING                   3
      20 RESEARCH                     5
      30 SALES                        6
      40 OPERATIONS                   0
```

To include every department in the result set, and not just those with assigned employees, you must perform an outer join from department to employee. The results are sorted by department ID and name, and the number of employees are counted within each department. In our opinion, the previous query employing the scalar correlated subquery is easier to understand. It does not need an outer join (or any join at all), and does not necessitate a sort operation, making it an attractive alternative to the GROUP BY version.

Inline Views

Most texts covering SQL define the FROM clause of a SELECT statement as containing a list of tables and/or views. Please abandon this definition and replace it with the following:

> The FROM clause contains a list of data sets.

In this light, it is easy to see how the FROM clause can contain tables (permanent data sets), views (virtual data sets), and SELECT statements (temporary data sets). SELECT statements, or inline views as mentioned earlier, are one of the most powerful, yet underutilized features of Oracle SQL.

 In our opinion, the name "inline view" is confusing and tends to intimidate people. Since it is a subquery that executes prior to the containing query, a more palatable name might have been "pre-query."

Here's a simple example of an inline view:

```
SELECT d.dept_id, d.name, emp_cnt.tot
FROM department d INNER JOIN
  (SELECT dept_id, COUNT(*) tot
   FROM employee
   GROUP BY dept_id) emp_cnt
  ON d.dept_id = emp_cnt.dept_id;
```

```
DEPT_ID NAME                        TOT
---------- -------------------- ----------
      10 ACCOUNTING                   3
      20 RESEARCH                     5
      30 SALES                        6
```

In this example, the FROM clause references the department table and an inline view called emp_cnt, which calculates the number of employees in each department. The two sets are joined using `dept_id` and the ID, name, and employee count are returned for each department. While this example is fairly simple, inline views allow you to do things in a single query that might otherwise require multiple select statements or a procedural language to accomplish.

Inline View Basics

Because the result set from an inline view is referenced by other elements of the containing query, you must give your inline view a name and provide aliases for all ambiguous columns. In the previous example, the inline view was given the name "emp_cnt", and the alias "tot" was assigned to the `COUNT(*)` column. Similar to other types of subqueries, inline views may join multiple tables, call built-in and user-defined functions, specify optimizer hints, and include GROUP BY, HAVING, and CONNECT BY clauses. Unlike other types of subqueries, an inline view may also contain an ORDER BY clause, which opens several interesting possibilities (see "Subquery Case Study: The Top N Performers" later in the chapter for an example using ORDER BY in a subquery).

Inline views are particularly useful when you need to combine data at different levels of aggregation. In the previous example, we needed to retrieve all rows from the `department` table and include aggregated data from the `employee` table, so we chose to do the aggregation within an inline view and join the results to the `department` table. Anyone involved in report generation or data warehouse extraction, transformation, and load (ETL) applications has doubtless encountered situations where data from various levels of aggregation needs to be combined; with inline views, you should be able to produce the desired results in a single SQL statement rather than having to break the logic into multiple pieces or write code in a procedural language.

When considering using an inline view, ask yourself the following questions:

- What value does the inline view add to the readability and, more importantly, the performance of the containing query?
- How large will the result set generated by the inline view be?
- How often, if ever, will I have need of this particular data set?

Generally, using an inline view should enhance the readability and performance of the query, and it should generate a manageable data set that is of no value to other statements or sessions; otherwise, you may want to consider building a permanent or temporary table so that you can share the data between sessions and build additional indexes as needed.

Query Execution

Inline views are always executed prior to the containing query and, thus, may not reference columns from other tables or inline views from the same query. After execution, the containing query interacts with an inline view as if it were an unindexed, in-memory table. If inline views are nested, the innermost inline view is executed first, followed by the next-innermost inline view, and so on. Consider the following query:

```
SELECT d.dept_id dept_id, d.name dept_name,
  dept_orders.tot_orders tot_orders
FROM department d INNER JOIN
  (SELECT e.dept_id dept_id, SUM(emp_orders.tot_orders) tot_orders
   FROM employee e INNER JOIN
    (SELECT sales_emp_id, COUNT(*) tot_orders
     FROM cust_order
     WHERE order_dt >= TO_DATE('01-JAN-2001','DD-MON-YYYY')
       AND cancelled_dt IS NULL
     GROUP BY sales_emp_id
    ) emp_orders
   ON e.emp_id = emp_orders.sales_emp_id
   GROUP BY e.dept_id
  ) dept_orders
ON d.dept_id = dept_orders.dept_id;

DEPT_ID DEPT_NAME             TOT_ORDERS
---------- -------------------- ----------
       30 SALES                          6
```

If you're new to inline views, this query might be intimidating. Start with the innermost query, understand the result set generated by that query, and move outward to the next level. Since inline views must be noncorrelated, you can run each inline view's SELECT statement individually and look at the results. (From the standpoint of the inline view, this would constitute an "out-of-query experience.") For the previous query, executing the emp_orders inline view generates the following result set:

```
SELECT sales_emp_id, COUNT(*) tot_orders
FROM cust_order
WHERE order_dt >= TO_DATE('01-JAN-2001','DD-MON-YYYY')
  AND cancelled_dt IS NULL
GROUP BY sales_emp_id;

SALES_EMP_ID TOT_ORDERS
------------ ----------
        7354          4
        7368          4
        7654          6
```

The emp_orders set contains all salespeople who booked orders since 2001, along with the total number of orders booked. The next level up is the dept_orders inline view, which joins the emp_orders data set to the employee table and aggregates the number of orders up to the department level. The resulting data set looks as follows:

```
SELECT e.dept_id dept_id, SUM(emp_orders.tot_orders) tot_orders
FROM employee e INNER JOIN
  (SELECT sales_emp_id, COUNT(*) tot_orders
   FROM cust_order
```

```
  WHERE order_dt >= TO_DATE('01-JAN-2001','DD-MON-YYYY')
    AND cancelled_dt IS NULL
  GROUP BY sales_emp_id
 ) emp_orders
ON e.emp_id = emp_orders.sales_emp_id
GROUP BY e.dept_id;

  DEPT_ID TOT_ORDERS
---------- ----------
      30          6
```

Finally, the dept_orders set is joined to the department table, and the final result set is:

```
  DEPT_ID DEPT_NAME            TOT_ORDERS
---------- -------------------- ----------
      30 SALES                         6
```

After query execution completes, the emp_orders and dept_orders result sets are discarded.

Data Set Fabrication

Along with querying existing tables, inline views may be used to fabricate special-purpose data sets that don't exist in the database. For example, you might want to aggregate orders over the past year by small, medium, and large orders, but the concept of order sizes may not have been defined in your database. You could build a table with three records to define the different sizes and their boundaries, but you only need this information for a single query, and you don't want to clutter the database with dozens of small, special-purpose tables. One solution is to use the UNION set operator to combine individual sets of data into a single set. (Set operators will be covered in detail in Chapter 7.) For example:

```
SELECT 'SMALL' name, 0 lower_bound, 29 upper_bound from dual
UNION ALL
SELECT 'MEDIUM' name, 30 lower_bound, 79 upper_bound from dual
UNION ALL
SELECT 'LARGE' name, 80 lower_bound, 9999999 upper_bound from dual;

NAME   LOWER_BOUND UPPER_BOUND
------ ----------- -----------
SMALL            0          29
MEDIUM          30          79
LARGE           80     9999999
```

You can then wrap this query in an inline view and use it to do your aggregations:

```
SELECT sizes.name order_size, SUM(co.sale_price) tot_dollars
FROM cust_order co INNER JOIN
  (SELECT 'SMALL' name, 0 lower_bound, 29 upper_bound from dual
   UNION ALL
   SELECT 'MEDIUM' name, 30 lower_bound, 79 upper_bound from dual
   UNION ALL
   SELECT 'LARGE' name, 80 lower_bound, 9999999 upper_bound from dual
  ) sizes
```

```
   ON co.sale_price BETWEEN sizes.lower_bound AND sizes.upper_bound
WHERE co.cancelled_dt IS NULL
   AND co.order_dt >= TO_DATE('01-JAN-2001','DD-MON-YYYY')
   AND co.order_dt < TO_DATE('01-JAN-2002','DD-MON-YYYY')
GROUP BY sizes.name
ORDER BY sizes.name DESC;

ORDER_ TOT_DOLLARS
------ -----------
SMALL          100
MEDIUM         292
LARGE          396
```

One word of caution: when constructing a set of ranges, make sure there are no gaps through which data may slip. For example, an order totaling $29.50 would not appear in either the small or medium categories, since $29.50 is neither between $0 and $29 nor between $30 and $79. One solution is to overlap the region boundaries so that there is no gap through which data can slip. Note that you can no longer use BETWEEN with this approach:

```
SELECT sizes.name order_size, SUM(co.sale_price) tot_dollars
FROM cust_order co INNER JOIN
(SELECT 'SMALL' name, 0 lower_bound, 30 upper_bound from dual
   UNION ALL
   SELECT 'MEDIUM' name, 30 lower_bound, 80 upper_bound from dual
   UNION ALL
   SELECT 'LARGE' name, 80 lower_bound, 9999999 upper_bound from dual
  ) sizes
ON co.sale_price >= sizes.lower_bound
     AND co.sale_price < sizes.upper_bound
WHERE co.cancelled_dt IS NULL
   AND co.order_dt >= TO_DATE('01-JAN-2001', 'DD-MON-YYYY')
   AND co.order_dt < TO_DATE('01-JAN-2002', 'DD-MON-YYYY')
GROUP BY sizes.name
ORDER BY sizes.name DESC;

ORDER_ TOT_DOLLARS
------ -----------
SMALL          100
MEDIUM         292
LARGE          396
```

Now that you have neither an overlap nor a gap between the buckets, you can be sure that no data will be left out of the aggregations.

Fabricated data sets can also be useful for determining what data is *not* stored in a database. For example, your manager might ask for a report listing the aggregate sales for each day of the year 2001, including days with no sales. Although the cust_order table contains records for every day that had orders, there is no table in the database containing a record for every day of the year. To provide your manager with an answer, you will need to fabricate a driving table containing a record for every day in 2001, and then outer join it to the set of aggregated sales for the same period.

Since a year contains either 365 or 366 days, we will build the set {0, 1, 2, ..., 399}, add each member of the set to the start date of 01-JAN-2001, and let Oracle throw away the rows that don't belong in 2001. To build the set {0, 1, 2, ..., 399}, we will create the sets {0, 1, 2, ..., 10}, {0, 10, 20, 30, ..., 90}, and {0, 100, 200, 300} and add members of the three sets across the Cartesian product:

```
SELECT ones.x + tens.x + hundreds.x tot
FROM
 (SELECT 0 x FROM dual UNION ALL
  SELECT 1 x FROM dual UNION ALL
  SELECT 2 x FROM dual UNION ALL
  SELECT 3 x FROM dual UNION ALL
  SELECT 4 x FROM dual UNION ALL
  SELECT 5 x FROM dual UNION ALL
  SELECT 6 x FROM dual UNION ALL
  SELECT 7 x FROM dual UNION ALL
  SELECT 8 x FROM dual UNION ALL
  SELECT 9 x FROM dual) ones
CROSS JOIN
 (SELECT 0 x FROM dual UNION ALL
  SELECT 10 x FROM dual UNION ALL
  SELECT 20 x FROM dual UNION ALL
  SELECT 30 x FROM dual UNION ALL
  SELECT 40 x FROM dual UNION ALL
  SELECT 50 x FROM dual UNION ALL
  SELECT 60 x FROM dual UNION ALL
  SELECT 70 x FROM dual UNION ALL
  SELECT 80 x FROM dual UNION ALL
  SELECT 90 x FROM dual) tens
CROSS JOIN
 (SELECT 0 x FROM dual UNION ALL
  SELECT 100 x FROM dual UNION ALL
  SELECT 200 x FROM dual UNION ALL
  SELECT 300 x FROM dual) hundreds;

       TOT
----------
         0
         1
         2
         3
         4
         5
         6
         7
         8
         9
        10
...
```

```
390
391
392
393
394
395
396
397
398
399
```

Since this query has no join conditions, every combination of the rows in the ones, tens, and hundreds sets will be generated, and the sum of the three numbers in each row will produce the set {0, 1, 2, ..., 399}. The next query generates the set of days in 2001 by adding each number in the set to the base date and then discarding days that fall in 2002:

```sql
SELECT days.dt
FROM
  (SELECT TO_DATE('01-JAN-2001', 'DD-MON-YYYY') +
    ones.x + tens.x + hundreds.x dt
  FROM
    (SELECT 0 x FROM dual UNION ALL
     SELECT 1 x FROM dual UNION ALL
     SELECT 2 x FROM dual UNION ALL
     SELECT 3 x FROM dual UNION ALL
     SELECT 4 x FROM dual UNION ALL
     SELECT 5 x FROM dual UNION ALL
     SELECT 6 x FROM dual UNION ALL
     SELECT 7 x FROM dual UNION ALL
     SELECT 8 x FROM dual UNION ALL
     SELECT 9 x FROM dual) ones
  CROSS JOIN
    (SELECT 0 x FROM dual UNION ALL
     SELECT 10 x FROM dual UNION ALL
     SELECT 20 x FROM dual UNION ALL
     SELECT 30 x FROM dual UNION ALL
     SELECT 40 x FROM dual UNION ALL
     SELECT 50 x FROM dual UNION ALL
     SELECT 60 x FROM dual UNION ALL
     SELECT 70 x FROM dual UNION ALL
     SELECT 80 x FROM dual UNION ALL
     SELECT 90 x FROM dual) tens
  CROSS JOIN
    (SELECT 0 x FROM dual UNION ALL
     SELECT 100 x FROM dual UNION ALL
     SELECT 200 x FROM dual UNION ALL
     SELECT 300 x FROM dual) hundreds) days
WHERE days.dt < TO_DATE('01-JAN-2002', 'DD-MON-YYYY');

DT
---------
01-JAN-01
02-JAN-01
```

```
03-JAN-01
04-JAN-01
05-JAN-01
06-JAN-01
07-JAN-01
08-JAN-01
09-JAN-01
10-JAN-01
...
20-DEC-01
21-DEC-01
22-DEC-01
23-DEC-01
24-DEC-01
25-DEC-01
26-DEC-01
27-DEC-01
28-DEC-01
29-DEC-01
30-DEC-01
31-DEC-01
```

Since 2001 is not a leap year, the result set will contain 365 rows, one for each day of 2001. This query can then be wrapped in another inline view and used as the driving table for generating the report. Whether you would actually want to use such a strategy in your code is up to you; the main purpose of this example is to help get the creative juices flowing.

Overcoming SQL Restrictions

The use of certain features of Oracle SQL can impose restrictions on our SQL statements. When these features are isolated from the rest of the query inside an inline view, however, these restrictions can be sidestepped. This section explores how inline views can overcome limitations with hierarchical and aggregation queries.

Hierarchical queries

Hierarchical queries allow recursive relationships to be traversed. As an example of a recursive relationship, consider a table called region that holds data about sales territories. Regions are arranged in a hierarchy, and each record in the region table references the region in which it is contained, as illustrated by the following data:

```
SELECT * FROM region;

REGION_ID NAME                 SUPER_REGION_ID
--------- -------------------- ---------------
        1 North America
        2 Canada                             1
        3 United States                      1
        4 Mexico                             1
        5 New England                        3
```

```
 6 Mid-Atlantic                3
 7 Southeast US                3
 8 Southwest US                3
 9 Northwest US                3
10 Central US                  3
11 Europe
12 France                     11
13 Germany                    11
14 Spain                      11
```

Each record in the customer table references the smallest of its applicable regions. Given a particular region, it is possible to construct a query that traverses up or down the hierarchy by utilizing the START WITH and CONNECT BY clauses:

```
SELECT region_id, name, super_region_id
  FROM region
  START WITH name = 'North America'
  CONNECT BY PRIOR region_id = super_region_id;

REGION_ID NAME                  SUPER_REGION_ID
---------- --------------------- ---------------
         1 North America
         2 Canada                             1
         3 United States                      1
         5 New England                        3
         6 Mid-Atlantic                       3
         7 Southeast US                       3
         8 Southwest US                       3
         9 Northwest US                       3
        10 Central US                         3
         4 Mexico                             1
```

The query just shown traverses the region hierarchy starting with the North America region and working down the tree. Looking carefully at the results, you can see that the Canada, United States, and Mexico regions all point to the North America region via the super_region_id field. The remainder of the rows all point to the United States region. Thus, we have identified a three-level hierarchy with one node at the top, three nodes in the second level, and six nodes in the third level underneath the United States node. For a detailed look at hierarchical queries, see Chapter 8.

Imagine that you have been asked to generate a report showing total sales in 2001 for each subregion of North America. However, hierarchical queries have the restriction that the table being traversed cannot be joined to other tables within the same query, so it might seem impossible to generate the report from a single query. Using an inline view, however, you can isolate the hierarchical query on the region table from the customer and cust_order tables, as in:

```
SELECT na_regions.name region_name,
  SUM(co.sale_price) total_sales
FROM cust_order co INNER JOIN customer c
  ON co.cust_nbr = c.cust_nbr
INNER JOIN
```

```
(SELECT region_id, name
 FROM region
 START WITH name = 'North America'
 CONNECT BY PRIOR region_id = super_region_id) na_regions
 ON c.region_id = na_regions.region_id
WHERE co.cancelled_dt IS NULL
  AND co.order_dt >= TO_DATE('01-JAN-2001','DD-MON-YYYY')
  AND co.order_dt < TO_DATE('01-JAN-2002','DD-MON-YYYY')
GROUP BY na_regions.name;

REGION_NAME          TOTAL_SALES
-------------------- -----------
Mid-Atlantic                 198
New England                  590
```

Even though the na_regions set includes the North America and United States regions, customer records always point to the smallest applicable region, which is why these particular regions do not show up in the final result set.

By placing the hierarchical query within an inline view, you are able to temporarily flatten the region hierarchy to suit the purposes of the query, which allows you to bypass the restriction on hierarchical queries without resorting to splitting the logic into multiple pieces. The next section will demonstrate a similar strategy for working with aggregate queries.

Aggregate queries

Queries that perform aggregations have the following restriction: all nonaggregate columns in the SELECT clause must be included in the GROUP BY clause. Consider the following query, which aggregates sales data by customer and salesperson, and then adds supporting data from the customer, region, employee, and department tables:

```
SELECT c.name customer, r.name region,
  e.fname || ' ' || e.lname salesperson, d.name department,
  SUM(co.sale_price) total_sales
FROM cust_order co INNER JOIN customer c
  ON co.cust_nbr = c.cust_nbr
  INNER JOIN region r
  ON c.region_id = r.region_id
  INNER JOIN employee e
  ON co.sales_emp_id = e.emp_id
  INNER JOIN department d
  ON e.dept_id = d.dept_id
WHERE co.cancelled_dt IS NULL
  AND co.order_dt >= TO_DATE('01-JAN-2001','DD-MON-YYYY')
GROUP BY c.name, r.name, e.fname || ' ' || e.lname, d.name;

CUSTOMER         REGION        SALESPERSON     DEPARTMENT   TOTAL_SALES
---------------- ------------- --------------- ------------ -----------
Zantech Inc.     Mid-Atlantic  KENNETH MARTIN  SALES                198
Flowtech Inc.    New England   KENNETH MARTIN  SALES                180
```

Since every nonaggregate in the SELECT clause must be included in the GROUP BY clause, you are forced to sort on five columns, since a sort is needed to generate the groupings. Because every customer is in one and only one region and every employee is in one and only one department, you really only need to sort on the customer and employee columns to produce the desired results. So the Oracle engine is wasting its time sorting on the region and department names.

However, by isolating the aggregation from the supporting tables, you can create a more efficient and more understandable query:

```
SELECT c.name customer, r.name region,
  e.fname || ' ' || e.lname salesperson, d.name department,
  cust_emp_orders.total total_sales
FROM
 (SELECT cust_nbr, sales_emp_id, SUM(sale_price) total
  FROM cust_order
  WHERE cancelled_dt IS NULL
    AND order_dt >= TO_DATE('01-JAN-2001','DD-MON-YYYY')
  GROUP BY cust_nbr, sales_emp_id) cust_emp_orders
  INNER JOIN customer c
  ON cust_emp_orders.cust_nbr = c.cust_nbr
  INNER JOIN region r
  ON c.region_id = r.region_id
  INNER JOIN employee e
  ON cust_emp_orders.sales_emp_id = e.emp_id
  INNER JOIN department d
  ON e.dept_id = d.dept_id;
```

CUSTOMER	REGION	SALESPERSON	DEPARTMENT	TOTAL_SALES
Flowtech Inc.	New England	KENNETH MARTIN	SALES	180
Zantech Inc.	Mid-Atlantic	KENNETH MARTIN	SALES	198

Since the cust_order table includes the customer number and salesperson ID, you can perform the aggregation against these two columns without the need to include the other four tables. Not only are you sorting on fewer columns, you are sorting on numeric fields (customer number and employee ID) rather than potentially lengthy strings (customer name, region name, employee name, and department name). The containing query uses the cust_nbr and sales_emp_id columns from the inline view to join to the customer and employee tables, which in turn are used to join to the region and department tables.

By performing the aggregation within an inline view, you have sidestepped the restriction that all nonaggregates be included in the GROUP BY clause. You have also shortened execution time by eliminating unnecessary sorts and minimized the number of joins to the customer, region, employee, and department tables. Depending on the amount of data in the tables, these improvements could yield significant performance gains.

Inline Views in DML Statements

Now that you are comfortable with inline views, it's time to add another wrinkle: inline views may also be used in INSERT, UPDATE, and DELETE statements. In most cases, using an inline view in a DML statement improves readability but otherwise adds little value to statement execution. To illustrate, we'll begin with a fairly simple UPDATE statement and then show the equivalent statement using an inline view:

```
UPDATE cust_order co
SET co.expected_ship_dt = co.expected_ship_dt + 7
WHERE co.cancelled_dt IS NULL AND co.ship_dt IS NULL
  AND EXISTS (SELECT 1
    FROM line_item li INNER JOIN part p
    ON li.part_nbr = p.part_nbr
    WHERE li.order_nbr = co.order_nbr
    AND p.inventory_qty = 0);
```

This statement uses an EXISTS condition to locate orders that include out-of-stock parts. The next version uses an inline view called suspended_orders to identify the same set of orders:

```
UPDATE (SELECT co.expected_ship_dt exp_ship_dt
  FROM cust_order co
  WHERE co.cancelled_dt IS NULL AND co.ship_dt IS NULL
    AND EXISTS (SELECT 1
      FROM line_item li INNER JOIN part p
      ON li.part_nbr = p.part_nbr
      WHERE li.order_nbr = co.order_nbr
        AND p.inventory_qty = 0)) suspended_orders
SET suspended_orders.exp_ship_dt = suspended_orders.exp_ship_dt + 7;
```

In the first statement, the WHERE clause of the UPDATE statement determines the set of rows to be updated, whereas in the second statement, the result set returned by the SELECT statement determines the target rows. Otherwise, the two statements are identical. For the inline view to add extra value to the statement, it must be able to do something that the simple update statement cannot do: join multiple tables. The following version attempts to do just that by replacing the subquery with a three-table join:

```
UPDATE (SELECT co.expected_ship_dt exp_ship_dt
  FROM cust_order co INNER JOIN line_item li
    ON co.order_nbr = li.order_nbr
    INNER JOIN part p
    ON li.part_nbr = p.part_nbr
  WHERE co.cancelled_dt IS NULL AND co.ship_dt IS NULL
    AND p.inventory_qty = 0) suspended_orders
SET suspended_orders.exp_ship_dt = suspended_orders.exp_ship_dt + 7;
```

However, statement execution results in the following error:

```
ORA-01779: cannot modify a column which maps to a non key-preserved table
```

As is often the case in life, we can't get something for nothing. To take advantage of the ability to join multiple tables within a DML statement, we must abide by the following rules:

- Only one of the joined tables in an inline view may be modified by the containing DML statement.
- To be modifiable, the target table's key must be preserved in the result set of the inline view.

Although the previous UPDATE statement attempts to modify only one table (cust_order), that table's key (order_nbr) is not preserved in the result set, since an order has multiple line items. In other words, rows in the result set generated by the three-table join cannot be uniquely identified using just the order_nbr field, so it is not possible to update the cust_order table via this particular three-table join. However, it is possible to update or delete from the line_item table using the same join, since the key of the line_item table matches the key of the result set returned from the inline view (order_nbr and part_nbr). The next statement deletes rows from the line_item table using an inline view nearly identical to the one that failed for the previous UPDATE attempt:

```
DELETE FROM (SELECT li.order_nbr order_nbr, li.part_nbr part_nbr
  FROM cust_order co INNER JOIN line_item li
    ON co.order_nbr = li.order_nbr
    INNER JOIN part p
    ON li.part_nbr = p.part_nbr
  WHERE co.cancelled_dt IS NULL AND co.ship_dt IS NULL
    AND p.inventory_qty = 0) suspended_orders;
```

The column(s) referenced in the SELECT clause of the inline view are actually irrelevant. Since the line_item table is the only key-preserved table of the three tables listed in the FROM clause, this is the table on which the DELETE statement operates. Although utilizing an inline view in a DELETE statement can be more efficient, it's somewhat disturbing that it is not immediately obvious which table is the focus of the DELETE statement. A reasonable convention when writing such statements would be to always select the key columns from the target table.

Restricting Access Using WITH CHECK OPTION

Another way in which inline views can add value to DML statements is by restricting both the rows and columns that may be modified. For example, most companies only allow members of Human Resources to see or modify salary information. By restricting the columns visible to a DML statement, we can effectively hide the salary column:

```
UPDATE (SELECT emp_id, fname, lname, dept_id, manager_emp_id
  FROM employee) emp
SET emp.manager_emp_id = 11
WHERE emp.dept_id = 4;
```

Although this statement executes cleanly, attempting to add the salary column to the SET clause would yield the following error:

```
UPDATE (SELECT emp_id, fname, lname, dept_id, manager_emp_id
  FROM employee) emp
SET emp.manager_emp_id = 11, emp.salary = 1000000000
WHERE emp.dept_id = 4;

ORA-00904: "EMP"."SALARY": invalid identifier
```

Of course, the person writing the UPDATE statement has full access to the table; the intent here is to protect against unauthorized modifications by the users. This might prove useful in an n-tier environment, where the interface layer interacts with a business-logic layer.

Although this mechanism is useful for restricting access to particular columns, it does not limit access to particular rows in the target table. To restrict the rows that may be modified using a DML statement, you can add a WHERE clause to the inline view and specify WITH CHECK OPTION. For example, you may want to restrict the users from modifying data for any employee in the Accounting department:

```
UPDATE (SELECT emp_id, fname, lname, dept_id, manager_emp_id
  FROM employee
  WHERE dept_id !=
   (SELECT dept_id FROM department WHERE name = 'ACCOUNTING')
  WITH CHECK OPTION) emp
SET emp.manager_emp_id = 7698
WHERE emp.dept_id = 30;
```

The addition of WITH CHECK OPTION to the inline view protects against any data modifications that would not be visible via the inline view. For example, attempting to modify an employee's department assignment from Sales to Accounting would generate an error, since the data would no longer be visible via the inline view:

```
UPDATE (SELECT emp_id, fname, lname, dept_id, manager_emp_id
  FROM employee
  WHERE dept_id !=
   (SELECT dept_id FROM department WHERE name = 'ACCOUNTING')
  WITH CHECK OPTION) emp
SET dept_id = (SELECT dept_id FROM department WHERE name = 'ACCOUNTING')
WHERE emp_id = 7900;

ORA-01402: view WITH CHECK OPTION where-clause violation
```

Global Inline Views

Earlier in the chapter, you saw how the WITH clause can be used to allow the same subquery to be referenced multiple times within the same query. Another way to utilize the WITH clause is as an inline view with global scope. To illustrate, we will rework one of the previous inline view examples to show how the subquery can be moved from the FROM clause to the WITH clause. Here's the original example, which comes from the section "Hierarchical queries":

```
SELECT na_regions.name region_name,
  SUM(co.sale_price) total_sales
FROM cust_order co INNER JOIN customer c
ON co.cust_nbr = c.cust_nbr
INNER JOIN
  (SELECT region_id, name
   FROM region
   START WITH name = 'North America'
   CONNECT BY PRIOR region_id = super_region_id) na_regions
ON c.region_id = na_regions.region_id
WHERE co.cancelled_dt IS NULL
  AND co.order_dt >= TO_DATE('01-JAN-2001','DD-MON-YYYY')
  AND co.order_dt < TO_DATE('01-JAN-2002','DD-MON-YYYY')
GROUP BY na_regions.name;
```

```
REGION_NAME          TOTAL_SALES
-------------------- -----------
Mid-Atlantic                 198
New England                  590
```

Here's the same query with the na_regions subquery moved to the WITH clause:

```
WITH na_regions AS (SELECT region_id, name
   FROM region
   START WITH name = 'North America'
   CONNECT BY PRIOR region_id = super_region_id)
SELECT na_regions.name region_name,
  SUM(co.sale_price) total_sales
FROM cust_order co INNER JOIN customer c
ON co.cust_nbr = c.cust_nbr
INNER JOIN na_regions
ON c.region_id = na_regions.region_id
WHERE co.cancelled_dt IS NULL
  AND co.order_dt >= TO_DATE('01-JAN-2001','DD-MON-YYYY')
  AND co.order_dt < TO_DATE('01-JAN-2002','DD-MON-YYYY')
GROUP BY na_regions.name;
```

```
REGION_NAME          TOTAL_SALES
-------------------- -----------
Mid-Atlantic                 198
New England                  590
```

Note that the FROM clause must include the inline view alias for you to reference the inline view's columns in the SELECT, WHERE, GROUP BY, or ORDER BY clauses.

To show how the na_regions subquery has global scope, the join between the na_regions inline view and the customer table has been moved to another inline view (called cust) in the FROM clause:

```
WITH na_regions AS (SELECT region_id, name
   FROM region
```

```
  START WITH name = 'North America'
  CONNECT BY PRIOR region_id = super_region_id)
SELECT cust.region_name region_name,
  SUM(co.sale_price) total_sales
FROM cust_order co INNER JOIN
  (SELECT c.cust_nbr cust_nbr, na_regions.name region_name
   FROM customer c INNER JOIN na_regions
   ON c.region_id = na_regions.region_id) cust
ON co.cust_nbr = cust.cust_nbr
WHERE co.cancelled_dt IS NULL
  AND co.order_dt >= TO_DATE('01-JAN-2001','DD-MON-YYYY')
  AND co.order_dt < TO_DATE('01-JAN-2002','DD-MON-YYYY')
GROUP BY cust.region_name;

REGION_NAME            TOTAL_SALES
-------------------- -----------
Mid-Atlantic                 198
New England                  590
```

Earlier in this section, we stated that inline views "are always executed prior to the containing query and, thus, may not reference columns from other tables or inline views from the same query." Using the WITH clause, however, you are able to break this rule, since the na_regions inline view is visible everywhere within the query. This makes the na_regions inline view act more like a temporary table than a true inline view.

Subquery Case Study: The Top N Performers

Certain queries that are easily described in English have traditionally been difficult to formulate in SQL. One common example is the "Find the top five salespeople" query. The complexity stems from the fact that data from a table must first be aggregated, and then the aggregated values must be sorted and compared to one another to identify the top or bottom performers. In this section, you will see how subqueries may be used to answer such questions. At the end of the section, we introduce ranking functions, a feature of Oracle SQL that was specifically designed for these types of queries.

A Look at the Data

Consider the problem of finding the top five salespeople. Let's assume that we are basing our evaluation on the amount of revenue each salesperson brought in during the previous year. The first task, then, would be to sum the dollar amount of all orders booked by each salesperson during the year in question. To do so, we will dip into our data warehouse, in which orders have been aggregated by salesperson, year, month, customer, and region. The following query generates total sales per salesperson for the year 2001:

```
SELECT s.name employee, SUM(o.tot_sales) total_sales
FROM orders o INNER JOIN salesperson s
```

```
ON o.salesperson_id = s.salesperson_id
WHERE o.year = 2001
GROUP BY s.name
ORDER BY 2 DESC;

EMPLOYEE                      TOTAL_SALES
----------------------------- -----------
Jeff Blake                        1927580
Sam Houseman                      1814327
Mark Russell                      1784596
John Boorman                      1768813
Carl Isaacs                       1761814
Tim McGowan                       1761814
Chris Anderson                    1757883
Bill Evans                        1737093
Jim Fletcher                      1735575
Mary Dunn                         1723305
Dave Jacobs                       1710831
Chuck Thomas                      1695124
Greg Powers                       1688252
Don Walters                       1672522
Alex Fox                          1645204
Barbara King                      1625456
Lynn Nichols                      1542152
Karen Young                       1516776
Bob Grossman                      1501039
Eric Iverson                      1468316
Tom Freeman                       1461898
Andy Levitz                       1458053
Laura Peters                      1443837
Susan Jones                       1392648
```

It appears that Isaacs and McGowan have tied for fifth place, which, as you will see, adds an interesting wrinkle to the problem.

Your Assignment

It seems that the boss was so tickled with this year's sales that she has asked you, the IT manager, to see that each of the top five salespeople receive a bonus equal to 1% of their yearly sales. No problem, you say. You quickly throw together the following report using your favorite feature, the inline view, and send it off to the boss:

```
SELECT s.name employee, top5_emp_orders.tot_sales total_sales,
  ROUND(top5_emp_orders.tot_sales * 0.01) bonus
FROM
 (SELECT all_emp_orders.salesperson_id emp_id,
    all_emp_orders.tot_sales tot_sales
  FROM
   (SELECT salesperson_id, SUM(tot_sales) tot_sales
    FROM orders
    WHERE year = 2001
    GROUP BY salesperson_id
    ORDER BY 2 DESC
```

```
  ) all_emp_orders
 WHERE ROWNUM <= 5
) top5_emp_orders INNER JOIN salesperson s
ON top5_emp_orders.emp_id = s.salesperson_id
ORDER BY 2 DESC;
```

```
EMPLOYEE                          TOTAL_SALES     BONUS
------------------------------ ----------- ----------
Jeff Blake                         1927580      19276
Sam Houseman                       1814327      18143
Mark Russell                       1784596      17846
John Boorman                       1768813      17688
Tim McGowan                        1761814      17618
```

The howl emitted by Isaacs can be heard for five square blocks. The boss, looking a bit harried, asks you to take another stab at it. Upon reviewing your query, the problem becomes immediately evident; the inline view aggregates the sales data and sorts the results, and the containing query grabs the first five sorted rows and discards the rest. Although it could easily have been McGowan, since there is no second sort column, Isaacs was arbitrarily omitted from the result set.

Second Attempt

You console yourself with the fact that you gave the boss exactly what she asked for: the top five salespeople. However, you realize that part of your job as IT manager is to give people what they need, not necessarily what they ask for, so you rephrase the boss's request as follows: give a bonus to all salespeople whose total sales ranked in the top five last year. This will require two steps: find the fifth highest sales total last year, and then find all salespeople whose total sales meet or exceed that figure. You write a new query as follows:

```
SELECT s.name employee, top5_emp_orders.tot_sales total_sales,
  ROUND(top5_emp_orders.tot_sales * 0.01) bonus
FROM salesperson s INNER JOIN
 (SELECT salesperson_id, SUM(tot_sales) tot_sales
  FROM orders
  WHERE year = 2001
  GROUP BY salesperson_id
  HAVING SUM(tot_sales) IN
    (SELECT all_emp_orders.tot_sales
     FROM
      (SELECT SUM(tot_sales) tot_sales
       FROM orders
       WHERE year = 2001
       GROUP BY salesperson_id
       ORDER BY 1 DESC
      ) all_emp_orders
    WHERE ROWNUM <= 5)
 ) top5_emp_orders
ON top5_emp_orders.salesperson_id = s.salesperson_id
ORDER BY 2 DESC;
```

EMPLOYEE	TOTAL_SALES	BONUS
Jeff Blake	1927580	19276
Sam Houseman	1814327	18143
Mark Russell	1784596	17846
John Boorman	1768813	17688
Tim McGowan	1761814	17618
Carl Isaacs	1761814	17618

Thus, there are actually six top five salespeople. The main difference between your first attempt and the second is the addition of the HAVING clause in the inline view. The subquery in the HAVING clause returns the five highest sales totals, and the inline view then returns all salespeople (potentially more than five) whose total sales exist in the set returned by the subquery.

Although you are confident in your latest results, there are several aspects of the query that bother you:

- The aggregation of sales data is performed twice.
- The query will never contend for Most Elegant Query of the Year.
- You could've sworn you read about some sort of feature just for handling these types of queries…

In fact, there is a feature, an analytic SQL feature, for performing ranking queries that became available with Oracle8*i*. That feature is the RANK function.

Final Answer

The RANK function is specifically designed to help you write queries to answer questions like the one posed in this case study. Part of a set of analytic functions (all of which will be explored in Chapter 14), the RANK function may be used to assign a ranking to each element of a set. The RANK function understands that there may be ties in the set of values being ranked and leaves gaps in the ranking to compensate. The following query illustrates how rankings would be assigned to the entire set of salespeople; notice how the RANK function leaves a gap between the fifth and seventh rankings to compensate for the fact that two rows share the fifth spot in the ranking:

```
SELECT salesperson_id, SUM(tot_sales) tot_sales,
  RANK( ) OVER (ORDER BY SUM(tot_sales) DESC) sales_rank
FROM orders
WHERE year = 2001
GROUP BY salesperson_id;
```

SALESPERSON_ID	TOT_SALES	SALES_RANK
1	1927580	1
14	1814327	2
24	1784596	3
8	1768813	4

15	1761814	5
16	1761814	5
20	1757883	7
11	1737093	8
9	1735575	9
10	1723305	10
17	1710831	11
4	1695124	12
5	1688252	13
12	1672522	14
19	1645204	15
18	1625456	16
21	1542152	17
13	1516776	18
3	1501039	19
22	1468316	20
2	1461898	21
7	1458053	22
23	1443837	23
6	1392648	24

Leaving gaps in the rankings whenever ties are encountered is critical for properly handling these types of queries. (If you do not wish to have gaps in the ranking, you can use the DENSE_RANK function intead.) Table 5-1 shows the number of rows that would be returned for this data set for various top-N queries.

Table 5-1. Rows returned for N = {1,2,3,...,9}

Top-N salespeople	Rows returned
1	1
2	2
3	3
4	4
5	6
6	6
7	7
8	8
9	9

As you can see, the result sets would be identical for both the "top five" and "top six" versions of this query for this particular data set.

By wrapping the previous RANK query in an inline view, you can retrieve the salespeople with a ranking of five or less and join the results to the salesperson table to generate the final result set:

```
SELECT s.name employee, top5_emp_orders.tot_sales total_sales,
  ROUND(top5_emp_orders.tot_sales * 0.01) bonus
FROM
```

```
(SELECT all_emp_orders.salesperson_id emp_id,
   all_emp_orders.tot_sales tot_sales
 FROM
  (SELECT salesperson_id, SUM(tot_sales) tot_sales,
     RANK( ) OVER (ORDER BY SUM(tot_sales) DESC) sales_rank
   FROM orders
   WHERE year = 2001
   GROUP BY salesperson_id
   ) all_emp_orders
  WHERE all_emp_orders.sales_rank <= 5
 ) top5_emp_orders INNER JOIN salesperson s
ON top5_emp_orders.emp_id = s.salesperson_id
ORDER BY 2 DESC;

EMPLOYEE                           TOTAL_SALES   BONUS
------------------------------     -----------   ----------
Jeff Blake                            1927580      19276
Sam Houseman                          1814327      18143
Mark Russell                          1784596      17846
John Boorman                          1768813      17688
Tim McGowan                           1761814      17618
Carl Isaacs                           1761814      17618
```

If this query looks familiar, that's because it's almost identical to the first attempt, except that the RANK function is used instead of the pseudocolumn ROWNUM to determine where to draw the line between the top five salespeople and the rest of the pack.

Now that you are happy with your query and confident in your results, you show your findings to your boss. "Nice work," she says. "Why don't you give yourself a bonus as well? In fact, you can have Isaacs's bonus, since he quit this morning." Salespeople can be so touchy.

CHAPTER 6

Handling Temporal Data

As the old saying goes, "Time and tide wait for no man." As database developers, we may not deal with tide-related information every day, but we deal with time-related information almost every single day. The hire date of an employee, your pay day, the rent or mortgage payment date, the time duration required for a financial investment to mature, and the start date and time of your new car insurance are all examples of temporal data that we deal with every single day.

The need for effective management of temporal information became critical at the turn of the century, when most of us had to devise ways to handle the two-digit year correctly as it increased from 99 to 00, and then to 01. In this age of global e-business, the concepts of time are even more involved than ever before, because business is carried out around the clock across time zone boundaries.

A database needs to effectively and efficiently handle the storage, retrieval, and manipulation of the following types of temporal data:

- Dates
- Times
- Date and time intervals
- Time zones

Oracle's support for temporal data is mature and efficient. Oracle8*i* supports convenient manipulation of date and time data. Oracle9*i* enhanced this support by introducing a new set of features including support for fractional seconds, date and time intervals, and time zones.

Time Zones

In the global economy, business is carried out across geographical boundaries and time zones. It is common for a customer in Los Angeles to order an item through a supplier's web site, and the supplier's database could be located in New York. A manufacturer in China could update the status of an order of one of its U.S. customers. Conducting business across the globe is a requirement in today's global economy, and the evolution of the Internet and related technologies have made it simple. Databases can't be far behind, can they?

Oracle facilitates global business through its support for time zones. With Oracle 9*i* Database and higher, a database and a session can be associated with time zones. Having database and session time zones enables users in geographically distant regions to exchange temporal data with the database without having to bother about the time differences between the location of their clients and the location of the database server.

 The list of valid time zone region names is provided in the data dictionary view V$TIMEZONE_NAMES.

Database Time Zone

The time zone of a database is usually set at the time of creation of the database. Alternatively, a database administrator can change the time zone using the ALTER DATABASE command, after a database is created. Both CREATE DATABASE and ALTER DATABASE commands take an optional SET TIME_ZONE clause:

```
SET TIME_ZONE = '+ | - HH:MI' | 'time_zone_region'
```

You can specify a time zone in one of two ways:

• By specifying a displacement from Coordinated Universal Time (UTC) in hours and minutes. For example, United States Eastern Standard Time is UTC –05:00.

• By specifying a time zone name or time zone abbreviation (columns TZNAME and TZABBREV in V$TIMEZONE_NAMES, respectively). Every time zone is given a name and abbreviation. For example, "U.S./Eastern" is the time zone name, and EST is the time zone abbreviation for Eastern Standard Time. You can use either the time zone name or the abbreviation to set the time zone of a database.

The following examples use the SET TIME_ZONE clause to set the time zone of a database:

```
CREATE DATABASE ... SET TIME_ZONE = '-05:00';

ALTER DATABASE ... SET TIME_ZONE = 'EST';
```

Both of these examples set the time zone to Eastern Standard Time. The first example uses a displacement (–05:00) from UTC. The second example uses the time zone abbreviation (EST). EST is 5 hours behind UTC, and is therefore equivalent to "–5:00".

If you do not explicitly set the database time zone, Oracle defaults to the operating system time zone. If the operating system time zone is not a valid Oracle time zone, UTC is used as the default time zone.

Session Time Zone

Each session can have a time zone as well. You can set the time zone of a session by using the ALTER SESSION SET TIME_ZONE statement. The syntax for the SET TIME_ZONE clause in the ALTER SESSION statement is the same as that in the CREATE DATABASE and ALTER DATABASE statements.

The following example shows two ways to set the time zone of a session to Pacific Standard Time:

```
ALTER SESSION SET TIME_ZONE = '-08:00';

ALTER SESSION SET TIME_ZONE = 'PST';
```

To set the session time zone to the local operating system time zone (e.g., the time zone of a PC initiating a remote user session), you can use the LOCAL keyword in the SET TIME_ZONE clause, as in the following example:

```
ALTER SESSION SET TIME_ZONE = LOCAL;
```

To set the session time zone to the database time zone, use the DBTIMEZONE keyword in the SET TIME_ZONE clause, as in the following example:

```
ALTER SESSION SET TIME_ZONE = DBTIMEZONE;
```

 If you do not explicitly set the session time zone, Oracle defaults to the local operating system time zone. If the local operating system time zone is not a valid Oracle time zone, UTC is used as the default session time zone.

Temporal Data Types in Oracle

Oracle provides the following categories of data types to represent temporal data inside an Oracle database:

- The DATE data type
- The TIMESTAMP data types:
  — TIMESTAMP
  — TIMESTAMP WITH TIME ZONE
  — TIMESTAMP WITH LOCAL TIME ZONE
- The INTERVAL data types:
  — INTERVAL YEAR TO MONTH
  — INTERVAL DAY TO SECOND

Up to release Oracle8i, Oracle had only one temporal data type: DATE, which held date as well as time information. Oracle9i introduced several new data types—three TIMESTAMP data types to hold time data with fractional seconds, and two INTERVAL data types to hold time intervals. The following sections discuss all these data types in detail.

The DATE Data Type

Oracle's DATE data type holds date as well as time information. Regardless of the date format you use for display purposes, Oracle stores dates internally in one standard format. Internal to the database, a date is a fixed-length, 7-byte field. The seven bytes represent the following pieces of information:

- The Century
- The Year
- The Month
- The Day
- The Hour
- The Minute
- The Second

Even though the data type is called a DATE, it also stores the time. You choose the components to display (the date, the time, the date and the time, etc.) when you retrieve a DATE value from the database. Or, if you are putting a DATE value into a program (e.g., a Java program) you might choose to extract the components of interest after transferring the entire date/time value to that program.

The TIMESTAMP Data Types

To provide support for fractional seconds along with date and time data, and also to provide support for time zones, Oracle9i introduced the following temporal data types:

- TIMESTAMP
- TIMESTAMP WITH TIME ZONE
- TIMESTAMP WITH LOCAL TIME ZONE

TIMESTAMP

The TIMESTAMP data type extends the DATE type to support more precise time values. A TIMESTAMP includes all the components of the DATE data type (century, year, month, day, hour, minute, second) plus fractional seconds. A TIMESTAMP data type is specified as:

```
TIMESTAMP [ (precision for fractional seconds) ]
```

The *precision for fractional seconds* is optional and is specified in parentheses. You can specify integer values between 0 and 9 for fractional precision. A precision of 9 means that you can have 9 digits to the right of the decimal—i.e., up to nanoseconds precision. If you don't specify the precision, it defaults to 6 (microseconds precision)—i.e., TIMESTAMP is the same as TIMESTAMP(6).

The following example creates a table with a column of type TIMESTAMP:

```
CREATE TABLE transaction (
transaction_id NUMBER(10),
transaction_timestamp TIMESTAMP,
status VARCHAR2(12));

Table created.

DESC transaction
```

Name	Null?	Type
TRANSACTION_ID		NUMBER(10)
TRANSACTION_TIMESTAMP		TIMESTAMP(6)
STATUS		VARCHAR2(12)

Since we don't specify a precision in this example for the column transaction_ timestamp, Oracle uses the default precision for the TIMESTAMP data type, and it appears as TIMESTAMP(6) when we describe the table.

TIMESTAMP WITH TIME ZONE

The TIMESTAMP WITH TIME ZONE data type further extends the TIMESTAMP type to include a time zone displacement. A TIMESTAMP WITH TIME ZONE data type is specified as:

```
TIMESTAMP [ (precision for fractional seconds) ] WITH TIME ZONE
```

The *precision for fractional seconds* is the same as that for the TIMESTAMP data type. The time zone displacement is the time difference in hours and minutes between the local time and UTC. You supply such displacements when you store values in the column, and the database retains the displacements so that those values can later be translated into any target time zone desired by your system's users.

The following example creates a table with a column of type TIMESTAMP WITH TIME ZONE:

```
CREATE TABLE transaction_time_zone (
transaction_id NUMBER(10),
transaction_timestamp TIMESTAMP(3) WITH TIME ZONE,
status VARCHAR2(12));

Table created.

DESC transaction_time_zone
```

```
Name                          Null?    Type
----------------------------- -------- -----------------------
TRANSACTION_ID                         NUMBER(10)
TRANSACTION_TIMESTAMP                  TIMESTAMP(3) WITH TIME ZONE
STATUS                                 VARCHAR2(12)
```

TIMESTAMP WITH LOCAL TIME ZONE

The TIMESTAMP WITH LOCAL TIME ZONE data type is a variant of the TIME-STAMP WITH TIME ZONE data type. A TIMESTAMP WITH LOCAL TIME ZONE data type is specified as:

```
TIMESTAMP [ (precision for fractional seconds) ] WITH LOCAL TIME ZONE
```

The *precision for fractional seconds* is the same as that in the TIMESTAMP data type. TIMESTAMP WITH LOCAL TIME ZONE differs from TIMESTAMP WITH TIME ZONE in the following ways:

- The time zone displacement is not stored as part of the column data.
- The data stored in the database is normalized to the time zone of the database. To normalize an input value to the database time zone, the input time is converted to a time in the database time zone. The original time zone is not preserved.
- When the data is retrieved, Oracle returns the data in the time zone of the user session.

The following example creates a table with a column of type TIMESTAMP WITH LOCAL TIME ZONE:

```
CREATE TABLE transaction_local_time_zone (
transaction_id NUMBER(10),
transaction_timestamp TIMESTAMP(3) WITH LOCAL TIME ZONE,
status VARCHAR2(12));

Table created.

DESC transaction_local_time_zone
```

```
Name                          Null?    Type
----------------------------- -------- -----------------------
TRANSACTION_ID                         NUMBER(10)
TRANSACTION_TIMESTAMP                  TIMESTAMP(3) WITH LOCAL TIME ZONE
STATUS                                 VARCHAR2(12)
```

The INTERVAL Data Types

Date and time interval data are an integral part of our day-to-day life. Common examples of interval data are the age of a person, the maturity period of a bond or certificate of deposit, and the warranty period of your car. Prior to Oracle9*i* Database, we all used the NUMBER data type to represent such data, and the logic needed to deal with interval data had to be coded at the application level. Oracle9*i* Database introduced two new data types to handle interval data:

- INTERVAL YEAR TO MONTH
- INTERVAL DAY TO SECOND

The following sections discuss the use of these data types.

INTERVAL YEAR TO MONTH

The INTERVAL YEAR TO MONTH type stores a period of time expressed as a number of years and months. An INTERVAL YEAR TO MONTH data type is specified as:

```
INTERVAL YEAR [ (precision for year) ] TO MONTH
```

The *precision for year* specifies the number of digits in the year field. The precision can range from 0 to 9, and the default value is 2. The default precision of two allows for a maximum interval of 99 years, 11 months.

The following example creates a table with a column of type INTERVAL YEAR TO MONTH:

```
CREATE TABLE event_history (
event_id NUMBER(10),
event_duration INTERVAL YEAR TO MONTH);

Table created.

DESC event_history

Name                           Null?    Type
------------------------------ -------- ------------------------
EVENT_ID                                NUMBER(10)
EVENT_DURATION                          INTERVAL YEAR(2) TO MONTH
```

The next example uses the NUMTOYMINTERVAL (NUMBER-TO-YEAR-MONTH INTERVAL) function to insert data into a database column of type INTERVAL YEAR TO MONTH. This function converts a NUMBER value into a value of type INTERVAL YEAR TO MONTH, using the units specified by the second argument:

```
INSERT INTO event_history VALUES (5001, NUMTOYMINTERVAL(2,'YEAR'));

1 row created.

INSERT INTO event_history VALUES (5002, NUMTOYMINTERVAL(2.5,'MONTH'));

1 row created.

SELECT * FROM event_history;
```

```
EVENT_ID EVENT_DURATION
---------- ------------------
      5001 +02-00
      5002 +00-02
```

The second argument to the NUMTOYMINTERVAL function specifies the unit of the first argument. Therefore, in the first example, the number 2 is treated as 2 years, and in the second example, the number 2.5 is treated as 2 months. Any fractional part of a month is ignored. An INTERVAL YEAR TO MONTH value is only in terms of years and months, not fractional months.

INTERVAL DAY TO SECOND

The INTERVAL DAY TO SECOND type stores a period of time expressed as a number of days, hours, minutes, seconds, and fractions of a second. An INTERVAL DAY TO SECOND data type is specified as:

```
INTERVAL DAY [(precision for day)]
TO SECOND [(precision for fractional seconds)]
```

The *precision for day* specifies the number of digits in the day field. This precision can range from 0 to 9, and the default value is 2. The *precision for fractional seconds* is the number of digits in the fractional part of a second. It can range from 0 to 9, and the default value is 6.

The following example creates a table with an INTERVAL DAY TO SECOND column:

```
CREATE TABLE batch_job_history (
job_id NUMBER(6),
job_duration INTERVAL DAY(3) TO SECOND(6));

Table created.

DESC batch_job_history
```

```
Name                    Null?    Type
----------------------- -------- ----------------------------
JOB_ID                           NUMBER(6)
JOB_DURATION                     INTERVAL DAY(3) TO SECOND(6)
```

Here's how to insert data into a table with an INTERVAL DAY TO SECOND column:

```
INSERT INTO batch_job_history VALUES
(6001, NUMTODSINTERVAL(5369.2589,'SECOND'));

1 row created.

SELECT * FROM batch_job_history;

    JOB_ID JOB_DURATION
---------- ----------------------------------------
      6001 +00 01:29:29.258900
```

For the INSERT in this example we used the function NUMTODSINTERVAL (NUMBER-TO-DAY-SECOND-INTERVAL). This function converts a NUMBER value into a value of type INTERVAL DAY TO SECOND, using the units specified in the second argument. It's analogous to NUMTOYMINTERVAL discussed in the previous section.

Literals of Temporal Types

Using literals of character and number types is pretty simple, because they don't involve any special formatting. However, when using literals of temporal type, you need to pay special attention to the formats in which they are specified. The following sections describe date, timestamp, and interval literals.

DATE Literals

DATE literals are specified in the format specified by SQL Standard, and take the following form:

```
DATE 'YYYY-MM-DD'
```

Unlike Oracle's DATE data type, a DATE literal doesn't specify any time information. You also can't specify a format. If you want to specify a date literal, you must always use the *YYYY-MM-DD* date format. The following example illustrates the use of a DATE literal in a SQL statement:

```
INSERT INTO employee
(emp_id, fname, lname, dept_id, manager_emp_id, salary, hire_date)
VALUES
(2304, 'John', 'Smith', 20, 1258, 20000, DATE '1999-10-22');

1 row created.

SELECT * FROM employee;

 EMP_ID FNAME    LNAME     DEPT_ID MANAGER_EMP_ID   SALARY HIRE_DATE
------- -------- ------- ---------- -------------- ---------- ---------
   2304 John     Smith           20           1258      20000 22-OCT-99
```

In this example, the date literal DATE '1999-10-22' is interpreted as 22-OCT-99.

TIMESTAMP Literals

A TIMESTAMP literal takes the following format:

```
TIMESTAMP 'YYYY-MM-DD HH:MI:SS.xxxxxxxxx'
```

A TIMESTAMP literal can have up to nine digits of fractional seconds. The fractional part is optional, but the date and time elements are mandatory and must be

ISO Standard for Date and Time Notation

The International Standard ISO 8601 specifies date and time notation. The date is specified by four-digit year, two-digit month, and two-digit day of the month:

YYYY-MM-DD

The time of the day is specified by two-digit hour, two-digit minute, and two-digit second:

hh:mi:ss

For detailed information on ISO Standard 8601, refer to the following documents on the Internet:

* *http://www.iso.ch/iso/en/prods-services/popstds/datesandtime.html*
* *http://www.cl.cam.ac.uk/~mgk25/iso-time.html*
* *http://www.saqqara.demon.co.uk/datefmt.htm*
* *http://www.mcs.vuw.ac.nz/technical/software/SGML/doc/iso8601/ISO8601.html*

provided in the given format. Here's an example in which data is inserted into a table with a TIMESTAMP column:

```
INSERT INTO transaction
VALUES (1001, TIMESTAMP '1998-12-31 08:23:46.368', 'OPEN');

1 row created.

SELECT * FROM transaction;

TRANSACTION_ID TRANSACTION_TIMESTAMP            STATUS
-------------- -------------------------------- ---------
          1001 31-DEC-98 08.23.46.368000 AM     OPEN
```

A TIMESTAMP literal with a time zone displacement can be used to represent a literal of type TIMESTAMP WITH TIME ZONE. It takes the following form:

```
TIMESTAMP 'YYYY-MM-DD HH:MI:SS.xxxxxxxxx {+|-} HH:MI'
```

Here is an example that shows how to insert data into a table with a TIMESTAMP WITH TIME ZONE column:

```
INSERT INTO transaction_time_zone
VALUES (1002, TIMESTAMP '1998-12-31 08:23:46.368 -10:30', 'NEW');

1 row created.

SELECT * FROM transaction_time_zone;

TRANSACTION_ID TRANSACTION_TIMESTAMP            STATUS
-------------- -------------------------------- -------
          1002 31-DEC-98 08.23.46.368 AM -10:30 NEW
```

Even though the data type is called TIMESTAMP WITH TIME ZONE, the literal still uses just the TIMESTAMP keyword. However, the literal also specifies a date/time displacement for time zone using the {+|-} *HH:MI* notation.

If you are specifying a time zone displacement in a TIMESTAMP literal, you must specify the sign of the displacement (i.e., + or −). The range of the hour in a time zone displacement is −12 to +13, and the range of a minute is 0 to 59. A displacement outside these ranges will generate an error.

> The valid range of time zone displacement in Oracle differs from that specified by the SQL Standard. The SQL Standard requires the valid range to be from −12:59 to +13:00. However, Oracle enforces the range on the hour (−12 to +13) and minute (0 to 59) components separately. Therefore, the valid range of time zone displacement in Oracle is from −12:00 to +13:59.

When you don't specify a time zone displacement, the displacement is not assumed to be zero; instead, the timestamp is assumed to be in your session time zone, and the value of the displacement defaults to the displacement of that time zone. For example, the TIMESTAMP literal in the following INSERT specifies no time zone displacement, yet the SELECT statement proves that a time zone is, in fact, assumed:

```
INSERT INTO transaction_time_zone
VALUES (1003, TIMESTAMP '1999-12-31 08:23:46.368', 'NEW');

1 row created.

SELECT * FROM transaction_time_zone;

TRANSACTION_ID TRANSACTION_TIMESTAMP                      STATUS
-------------- ------------------------------------------ -------
          1003 31-DEC-99 08.23.46.368 AM -05:00           NEW
```

There is no literal specifically for the TIMESTAMP WITH LOCAL TIME ZONE data type. To insert data into a column of this type, you use a TIMESTAMP literal with a time zone displacement. For example:

```
INSERT INTO transaction_local_time_zone
VALUES (2001, TIMESTAMP '1998-12-31 10:00:00 -3:00', 'NEW');

1 row created.

SELECT * FROM transaction_local_time_zone;

TRANSACTION_ID TRANSACTION_TIMESTAMP     STATUS
-------------- ------------------------- -------
          2001 31-DEC-98 08.00.00 AM     NEW
```

In a case like this, the time zone displacement is not stored in the database. The data is stored in the database in normalized form with respect to the database time zone.

By "normalized form" we mean the input time is converted into a time in the database time zone before being stored in the database. The database time zone in this example is –5:00. Therefore, –3:00 is 2 hours ahead of the database time zone, and 10:00:00 – 3:00 is the same as 08:00:00 – 5:00. Since the time is normalized with respect to the database time zone, the displacement doesn't need to be stored in the database.

 When TIMESTAMP WITH LOCAL TIME ZONE data is normalized to the database time zone, the time zone of the original data is not preserved.

INTERVAL Literals

Just as Oracle supports DATE and TIMESTAMP literals, it supports INTERVAL literals, too. There are two interval data types, and two types of corresponding interval literals: YEAR TO MONTH and DAY TO SECOND.

YEAR TO MONTH interval literals

A YEAR TO MONTH interval literal represents a time period in terms of years and months. A YEAR TO MONTH interval literal takes one of the following two forms:

```
INTERVAL 'y [-m]' YEAR[(precision)] [TO MONTH]
INTERVAL 'm' MONTH[(precision)]
```

The syntax elements are:

y   An integer value specifying the years.

m   An integer value specifying the months. You must include the TO MONTH keywords if you specify a month value.

precision
    Specifies the number of digits to allow for the year or month. The default is 2. The valid range is from 0 to 9.

The default precision for the year value is 2. If the literal represents a time period greater than 99 years, then you must specify a high-enough precision to accommodate the number of years in question. The integer value for the month, as well as the MONTH keyword, are optional. If you specify a month value, it must be between 0 and 11. You do need to use the MONTH keyword when you specify a month value.

The following example inserts a YEAR TO MONTH interval literal into an INTERVAL YEAR TO MONTH column:

```
INSERT INTO event_history
VALUES (6001, INTERVAL '5-2' YEAR TO MONTH);

1 row created.

SELECT * FROM event_history;
```

```
EVENT_ID EVENT_DURATION
---------- ---------------------------------------
      6001 +05-02
```

The following example uses a YEAR TO MONTH interval literal to specify a time period of exactly four years. No value for months is included:

```
SELECT INTERVAL '4' YEAR FROM DUAL;

INTERVAL'4'YEAR
---------------------------------------------
+04-00
```

A YEAR TO MONTH interval literal can also be used to represent months only:

```
SELECT INTERVAL '3' MONTH FROM DUAL;

INTERVAL'3'MONTH
---------------------------------------------
+00-03

SELECT INTERVAL '30' MONTH FROM DUAL;

INTERVAL'30'MONTH
---------------------------------------------
+02-06
```

Notice that when you use a YEAR TO MONTH interval literal to represent only months, you can actually specify a month value larger than 11. In such a situation, Oracle normalizes the value into an appropriate number of years and months. This is the only situation in which the number of months can be greater than 11.

DAY TO SECOND interval literals

A DAY TO SECOND interval literal represents a time period in terms of days, hours, minutes, seconds, and fractions of seconds. DAY TO SECOND interval literals take on the following form:

```
INTERVAL 'd [h[:m[:s]]]' unit1[(precision1)] TO unit2[(frac_precision)]
```

The syntax elements are:

d   An integer value specifying the days.

h   An integer value specifying the hours.

m   An integer value specifying the minutes.

s   A number value specifying the seconds and fractional seconds.

unit1, unit2
    Can be DAY, HOUR, MINUTE, or SECOND. The leading unit (*unit1*) must always be greater than the trailing unit (*unit2*). For example, INTERVAL HOUR TO MINUTE is valid, but INTERVAL HOUR TO DAY is not valid.

precision1
> The number of digits to allow for the leading unit. The default is 2. The valid range is from 0 to 9.

frac_precision
> The number of digits to allow for fractional seconds. The default is 6. The valid range is from 0 to 9.

By default, two digits are allowed for the number of days. If a literal represents a time period of greater than 99 days, then you must specify a precision high enough to accommodate the number of digits that you need. There's no need to specify the precision for the hour and minute values. The value for hours can be between 0 and 23, and the value for the minutes can be between 0 and 59. While specifying fractional seconds, you can specify a precision for the fractional seconds as well. The precision for the fractional seconds can be between 0 and 9 (default 6), and the seconds value can be between 0 and 59.999999999.

The following example inserts a DAY TO SECOND interval literal into a column of data type INTERVAL DAY TO SECOND. The time period being represented is 0 days, 3 hours, 16 minutes, 23.45 seconds.

```
INSERT INTO batch_job_history
VALUES (2001, INTERVAL '0 3:16:23.45' DAY TO SECOND);

1 row created.

SELECT * FROM batch_job_history;

    JOB_ID JOB_DURATION
---------- -------------------------------------------------
      2001 +00 03:16:23.450000
```

The previous example uses all elements of the DAY TO SECOND interval literal. However, you can use fewer elements if that's all you need. The following example shows several valid permutations:

```
SELECT INTERVAL '400' DAY(3) FROM DUAL;

INTERVAL'400'DAY(3)
-----------------------------------------------------------------
+400 00:00:00

SELECT INTERVAL '11:23' HOUR TO MINUTE FROM DUAL;

INTERVAL'11:23'HOURTOMINUTE
-----------------------------------------------------------------
+00 11:23:00

SELECT INTERVAL '11:23' MINUTE TO SECOND FROM DUAL;
```

```
INTERVAL'11:23'MINUTETOSECOND
----------------------------------------------------------------
+00 00:11:23.000000

SELECT INTERVAL '20' MINUTE FROM DUAL;

INTERVAL'20'MINUTE
----------------------------------------------------------------
+00 00:20:00
```

The only requirement is that you must use a range of contiguous elements. You cannot, for example, specify an interval in terms of only hours and seconds, because you can't omit the intervening minutes value. An interval of 4 hours, 36 seconds would need to be expressed as 4 hours, 0 minutes, 36 seconds.

Getting Temporal Data In and Out of a Database

In the real world, temporal data are not always represented using Oracle's DATE, TIMESTAMP, and INTERVAL data types. At various times, you'll need to convert temporal values to other data types, especially to character types, and vice versa. This is particularly true when you interface an Oracle database with an external system, for example when you are accepting date input from an external system in which dates are represented as strings of characters (or even as numbers), or when you are sending output from an Oracle database to another application that doesn't understand Oracle's native temporal data types. You also need to convert DATE and TIMESTAMP values to text when you display them on a screen or generate a printed report.

Oracle provides some extremely useful functions to enable such conversions:

- TO_DATE
- TO_TIMESTAMP
- TO_TIMESTAMP_TZ
- TO_YMINTERVAL
- TO_DSINTERVAL
- NUMTOYMINTERVAL
- NUMTODSINTERVAL
- TO_CHAR

The purpose of each of these functions is more or less self-explanatory. The following sections discuss each of these functions in detail.

TO_DATE, TO_TIMESTAMP, and TO_TIMESTAMP_TZ

TO_DATE, TO_TIMESTAMP, and TO_TIMESTAMP_TZ are built-in SQL functions that convert, respectively, a character string into a DATE, a TIMESTAMP, and a TIMESTAMP WITH TIME ZONE. Input to these functions can be string literals, PL/SQL variables, and database columns of the CHAR and VARCHAR2 data types.

These three conversion functions are similar in operation. The difference is only in the data type of the return value. You call them as follows:

```
TO_DATE(string [,format])
TO_TIMESTAMP (string [,format])
TO_TIMESTAMP_TZ (string [,format])
```

The syntax elements are:

string

> Specifies a string literal, a PL/SQL variable, or a database column containing character data (or even numeric data) convertible to a date or timestamp.

format

> Specifies the format of the input string. The format must be a valid combination of format codes shown in Table 6-1, which you'll find later in the section on "Date and Time Formats."

Through the *format* argument, Oracle provides a great deal of flexibility when it comes to converting between date and time values and text. Oracle provides far more flexibility, at least in our experience, than do competing platforms, such as DB2 and SQL Server.

Specifying a format is optional. When you don't specify a format, the input string is assumed to be in a default format as specified by the NLS_DATE_FORMAT, NLS_TIMESTAMP_FORMAT, or NLS_TIMESTAMP_TZ parameter settings.

> You can view your current NLS parameter settings by querying the view named NLS_SESSION_PARAMETERS.

Using the default formats

Every Oracle session has a set of default formats to use in converting date and timestamp values to and from their textual representations. You can query the NLS_SESSION_PARAMETERS view as follows to see the default formats currently in effect:

```
SELECT parameter, value
FROM nls_session_parameters
WHERE parameter LIKE '%FORMAT';
```

```
PARAMETER                    VALUE
---------------------------- ------------------------------
NLS_DATE_FORMAT              DD-MON-RR
NLS_TIME_FORMAT              HH.MI.SSXFF AM
NLS_TIMESTAMP_FORMAT         DD-MON-RR HH.MI.SSXFF AM
NLS_TIME_TZ_FORMAT           HH.MI.SSXFF AM TZR
NLS_TIMESTAMP_TZ_FORMAT      DD-MON-RR HH.MI.SSXFF AM TZR
```

Session-specific formats derive from settings for language and territory. If you connect without specifying a language and territory, your session will inherit the default conversion formats established for the database. You can query NLS_DATABASE_PARAMETERS for those.

When you invoke one of the TO_ conversion functions, say TO_DATE, without explicitly specifying a format, Oracle expects your input string to be in the default format for the target data type. The following INSERT statement converts a string in the default date format into a DATE, which is then inserted into the employee table:

```
INSERT INTO employee
(emp_id, fname, lname, dept_id, manager_emp_id, salary, hire_date)
VALUES
(2304, 'John', 'Smith', 20, 1258, 20000, TO_DATE('22-OCT-99'));

1 row created.

SELECT * FROM employee;

 EMP_ID FNAME    LNAME   DEPT_ID MANAGER_EMP_ID   SALARY HIRE_DATE
------- -------- ------- ---------- -------------- ---------- ---------
   2304 John     Smith        20           1258    20000 22-OCT-99
```

The hire_date column, into which our date was inserted, is of type DATE. Because the input character string of '22-OCT-99' matched Oracle's default date format, the string could be converted without reference to a format string. In fact, since the supplied string is in the default date format, you don't even need the TO_DATE function. Oracle automatically performs an implicit type conversion, as in this example:

```
INSERT INTO employee
(emp_id, fname, lname, dept_id, manager_emp_id, salary, hire_date)
VALUES
(2304, 'John', 'Smith', 20, 1258, 20000, '22-OCT-99');

1 row created.
```

Even though Oracle provides means for implicit data type conversions, we recommend always using explicit conversions, because implicit conversions are not obvious and may lead to confusion. They may also suddenly fail should a DBA change the database's default date format.

Specifying a format

If you wish to specify a format to use in converting from text to one of the temporal data types, there are at least two approaches you can take:

- Specify the format at the session level, in which case it applies to all implicit conversions, and to all TO_DATE, TO_TIMESTAMP, or TO_TIMESTAMP_TZ conversions for which you do not explicitly specify some other format.
- Specify the format as a parameter in a TO_X function call.

The following example changes the default date format for the session, and then uses TO_DATE to convert a number to date:

```
ALTER SESSION SET NLS_DATE_FORMAT = 'MMDDYY';

Session altered.

INSERT INTO employee
(emp_id, fname, lname, dept_id, manager_emp_id, salary, hire_date)
VALUES
(2304, 'John', 'Smith', 20, 1258, 20000, TO_DATE(102299));

1 row created.
```

Since the default date format has been changed prior to the conversion, the conversion function TO_DATE doesn't need the date format as an input parameter.

 Although it is possible to pass a number such as 102299 to the TO_DATE function, relying on Oracle's implicit conversion to change the number to a string, and then into a date, it's probably best to pass a string as input to the TO_DATE function.

If you do not wish to change your session's default date format, you must specify the date format as the second input parameter to whichever of the three functions you are using. For example, the following SELECT specifies a format as the second input parameter to the TO_TIMESTAMP_TZ function:

```
SELECT
    TO_TIMESTAMP_TZ('12/10/01 08:15:00.50 EST','MM/DD/YY HH:MI:SSXFF TZR')
FROM DUAL;

TO_TIMESTAMP_TZ('12/10/0108:15:00.50EST','MM/DD/YYHH:MI:SSXFFTZR')
-------------------------------------------------------------------------
10-DEC-01 08.15.00.500000000 AM EST
```

Let's look at one more example to see how a database character column can be converted to a TIMESTAMP. Let's assume that the report_id column in the report table actually stores the date on which the report was generated, and that the date is in the format "MMDDYYYY." Now, you can use TO_TIMESTAMP on that column to convert that date into a TIMESTAMP, which is then displayed using the default timestamp format:

```
SELECT sent_to, report_id,
       TO_TIMESTAMP(report_id,'MMDDYYYY') date_generated
FROM report;

SENT_TO               REPORT_I DATE_GENERATED
--------------------- -------- --------------------------------
Manager               01011999 01-JAN-99 12.00.00.000000000 AM
Director              01121999 12-JAN-99 12.00.00.000000000 AM
Vice President        01231999 23-JAN-99 12.00.00.000000000 AM
```

In this example, the TO_TIMESTAMP function converts the MMDDYYYY data in the column to a TIMESTAMP. That TIMESTAMP value is then implicitly converted into a character string for display purposes, using the default timestamp format.

 Later, in the section on the TO_CHAR function, you'll learn how you can use formats to exercise great control over the textual representation of date and timestamp values.

Converting to TIMESTAMP WITH LOCAL TIME ZONE

Interestingly, Oracle provides no function specifically to convert a text value into the TIMESTAMP WITH LOCAL TIME ZONE data type. To convert a value to TIMESTAMP WITH LOCAL TIME ZONE, you must use the CAST function, as in the following example:

```
SELECT CAST('10-DEC-01' AS TIMESTAMP WITH LOCAL TIME ZONE) FROM DUAL;

CAST('10-DEC-01'ASTIMESTAMPWITHLOCALTIMEZONE)
-----------------------------------------------------------------------------
10-DEC-01 12.00.00 AM
```

In this example, the input string is in the default date format. Therefore, no date format is required for conversion. Indeed, CAST does not support date formats.

What then do you do if you wish to convert to TIMESTAMP WITH LOCAL TIME ZONE and you also need to specify a format? One solution here is to use a conversion function along with a format to convert the string into a value TIMESTAMP WITH TIME ZONE, which you can then cast to a TIMESTAMP WITH LOCAL TIME ZONE:

```
SELECT CAST(TO_TIMESTAMP_TZ('12/10/01','MM/DD/YY')
            AS TIMESTAMP WITH LOCAL TIME ZONE)
FROM DUAL;

CAST(TO_TIMESTAMP_TZ('12/10/01','MM/DD/YY')ASTIMESTAMPWITHLOCALTIMEZONE)
-----------------------------------------------------------------------------
10-DEC-01 12.00.00 AM
```

The CAST function used in these examples is not a SQL function in the truest sense. CAST is actually a SQL expression like DECODE and CASE. The CAST expression converts a value in one data type to a value in another data type. You can generally CAST between any two, compatible data types.

TO_YMINTERVAL and TO_DSINTERVAL

The TO_YMINTERVAL and TO_DSINTERVAL functions are similar in purpose to the TO_DATE family of functions, and serve to convert character strings to the INTERVAL YEAR TO MONTH and INTERVAL DAY TO SECOND data types. You can pass literals, PL/SQL variables, and database columns of CHAR or VARCHAR2 data type to these functions, which you invoke as follows:

```
TO_YMINTERVAL (string)
TO_DSINTERVAL (string)
```

In these invocations, *string* must contain character data convertible to an INTERVAL YEAR TO MONTH or INTERVAL DAY TO SECOND value, and in one of the following formats:

TO_YMINTERVAL
> The input string must be in *Y-M* format—i.e., the year and month values must be separated by a dash (-). All components (year, month, and -) must be present in the string.

TO_DSINTERVAL
> The input string must be in *D HH:MI:SS* format. The day value of the interval is separated by a space from the time value, which is expressed in hours, minutes, and seconds, and is delimited by ":". All components must be present in the string for it to be converted to an INTERVAL DAY TO SECOND value.

The following two INSERT statements demonstrate the use of these functions:

```
INSERT INTO event_history VALUES (5001, TO_YMINTERVAL('02-04'));

INSERT INTO batch_job_history VALUES (6001, TO_DSINTERVAL('0 2:30:43'));
```

In this example, the string '02-04' represents an interval of 2 years and 4 months, while the string '0 2:30:43' represents an interval of 0 days, 2 hours, 30 minutes, and 43 seconds.

NUMTOYMINTERVAL and NUMTODSINTERVAL

The NUMTOYMINTERVAL (NUMBER-TO-YEAR-MONTH-INTERVAL) and NUMTODSINTERVAL (NUMBER-TO-DAY-SECOND-INTERVAL) functions convert numeric values into INTERVAL YEAR TO MONTH and INTERVAL DAY TO SECOND values, respectively. You invoke these functions as follows:

```
NUMTOYMINTERVAL (n, unit)
NUMTODSINTERVAL (n, unit)
```

The syntax elements are:

n Specifies a numeric value, or a value that is convertible to a numeric type.

unit
   Specifies the unit of time that *n* represents. When converting to an INTERVAL YEAR TO MONTH, *unit* may be either `'YEAR'` or `'MONTH'`. When converting to an INTERVAL DAY TO SECOND, *unit* may be any of `'DAY'`, `'HOUR'`, `'MINUTE'`, or `'SECOND'`. Case does not matter. Upper, lower, or mixed-case are all the same.

The following example demonstrates the use of these two functions. The first INSERT specifies an interval of two years, while the second specifies an interval of 5369.2589 seconds:

```
INSERT INTO event_history VALUES
    (5001, NUMTOYMINTERVAL(2,'YEAR'));

INSERT INTO batch_job_history VALUES
    (6001, NUMTODSINTERVAL(5369.2589,'SECOND'));
```

Unlike the case with TO_YMINTERVAL and TO_DSINTERVAL, you cannot pass mixed units to these NUMTOXXINTERVAL functions. However, you can build up values from mixed units as follows:

```
INSERT INTO event_history VALUES
    (7001, NUMTOYMINTERVAL(2,'YEAR') + NUMTOYMINTERVAL (4, 'MONTH'));
```

This INSERT creates a two-year and four-month interval by adding a two-year interval to a four-month interval.

 Remember, that there is a "break" in the interval model between days and months. You cannot add an INTERVAL DAY TO SECOND value to an INTERVAL YEAR TO MONTH value.

TO_CHAR

The TO_CHAR function is the opposite of the TO_DATE and TO_TIMESTAMP functions, and converts a DATE, TIMESTAMP, TIMESTAMP WITH TIME ZONE, or TIMESTAMP WITH LOCAL TIME ZONE value into a string of characters. Call TO_CHAR as follows:

```
TO_CHAR(temporal_data [,format])
```

The syntax elements are:

temporal_data
> Specifies a literal, PL/SQL variable, or a database column of type DATE, TIMESTAMP, TIMESTAMP WITH TIME ZONE, or TIMESTAMP WITH LOCAL TIME ZONE.

format
> Specifies the format of the output string. The format must be a valid combination of date or timestamp format elements as described later in the section "Date and Time Formats."

The format is optional. When the format is not specified, the format of the output depends upon the type of the input data:

DATE
> The output string takes the format specified by the parameter NLS_DATE_FORMAT.

TIMESTAMP
> The output string takes the format specified by the parameter NLS_TIMESTAMP_FORMAT.

TIMESTAMP WITH TIME ZONE
> The output string takes the format specified by the parameter NLS_TIMESTAMP_TZ_FORMAT.

TIMESTAMP WITH LOCAL TIME ZONE
> The output string takes the format specified by the parameter NLS_TIMESTAMP_FORMAT.

The database parameters NLS_DATE_FORMAT, NLS_TIMESTAMP_FORMAT, and NLS_TIMESTAMP_TZ_FORMAT are discussed in the section "Database Parameters."

The following example uses TO_CHAR to convert an input date into a string using the default date format:

```
SELECT fname, TO_CHAR(hire_date) FROM employee;

FNAME                TO_CHAR(H
-------------------- ---------
John                 22-OCT-99
```

The following example uses TO_CHAR to convert a timestamp into a string, and explicitly specifies a timestamp format:

```
SELECT TO_CHAR(SYSTIMESTAMP, 'MM/DD/YYYY HH24:MI:SS.FF') FROM DUAL;

TO_CHAR(SYSTIMESTAMP,'MM/DD/Y
-----------------------------
12/12/2003 10:18:36.070000
```

The format element `FF` in the preceding example represents fractional seconds. Timestamp-specific formats are discussed in the section "Date and Time Formats."

There are situations when you may need to combine TO_CHAR with TO_DATE. For example, if you want to know on what day of the week January 1, 2000, fell, you can use the following query:

```
SELECT TO_CHAR(TO_DATE('01-JAN-2000','DD-MON-YYYY'),'Day') FROM DUAL;

TO_CHAR(T
---------
Saturday
```

In this example, the input string `'01-JAN-2000'` is first converted into a date and then the TO_CHAR function is used to convert this date into a string representing the day of the week.

Printing Numeric Amounts in Words

By using the date formats and the functions innovatively, you can generate very interesting and useful outputs. For example, say that you are writing a check-printing application, and you need to print each check amount in words. You can do that using an expression such as in the following SELECT statement:

```
SELECT TO_CHAR(TO_DATE(TRUNC(3456.34),'J'),'Jsp') || ' Dollars and ' ||
TO_CHAR(TO_DATE(ROUND(MOD(3456.34,1)*100),'J'),'Jsp') || ' Cents'
"Check Amount"
FROM DUAL;

Check Amount
-----------------------------------------------------------------
Three Thousand Four Hundred Fifty-Six Dollars and Thirty-Four Cents
```

This example splits the input number into two components – the first consisting of the whole number and the second consisting of the fractional number. The whole number component is converted to words using the `Jsp` format. The fractional component is multiplied by 100 and rounded to extract the two digit cents, and then the same technique is applied to convert that number to words.

Date and Time Formats

You can display dates and times in a number of ways. Every country, every industry has its own standard for representing temporal data. Oracle provides you with date and time format codes so that you can interpret and display dates and timestamps in a wide variety of formats.

A simple example of displaying a date is:

```
SELECT SYSDATE FROM DUAL;

SYSDATE
---------
03-OCT-01
```

By default, the date is displayed using the DD-MON-RR format. This format uses two digits for the date (zero padded on the left), three characters for the month (the first three characters of the English, or your local language, name of the month in uppercase), and two digits for the year of the century (zero padded on the left). The default date format for the database is controlled by the NLS_DATE_FORMAT initialization parameter. You can use ALTER SYSTEM or ALTER SESSION commands to change the default date format for the instance or the session, respectively. You can also use the TO_CHAR function to specify a format on a per-call basis:

```
SELECT TO_CHAR(SYSDATE,'MM/DD/YYYY') FROM DUAL;

TO_CHAR(SY
----------
10/03/2001
```

This example converts the current date into the format *MM/DD/YYYY* using the TO_CHAR function. The second argument is a format string specifying how we want the date to be presented. Table 6-1 describes the various date format elements at your disposal. Most of the examples in Table 6-1 are based on 03-OCT-2001 03:34:48 P.M. Those that involve B.C. dates use the year 2105 B.C. Those that specifically demonstrate A.M. times are based on 03-OCT-2001 11:00:00 AM.

Table 6-1. Oracle date, timestamp, and time zone format elements

Component	Options	Description	Format	Output
Punctuation	-/,;:.*	Simply reproduced in the output	DD-MON-YY	03-OCT-01
	Space	Simply reproduced in the output	DD MM YYYY	03 10 2001
	"Text"	Simply reproduced in the output	DD "of" Month	03 of October
Day	DD	Day of the month	MM/DD/YY	10/03/01
	DDD	Day of the year; starts with 1st January as 1	DDD/YY	276/01
	D	Day of the week; starts with Sunday as 1	D MM/YY	4 10/01
	DAY	Name of the day, in uppercase	DAY MM/YY	WEDNESDAY 10/01
	Day	Name of the day, in mixed case	Day MM/YY	Wednesday 10/01
	DY	Abbreviated name of the day, in uppercase	DY MM/YY	WED 10/01
	Dy	Abbreviated name of the day, in mixed case	Dy MM/YY	Wed 10/01

Component	Options	Description	Format	Output
Month	MM	Two-digit month	MM/DD/YY	10/03/01
	MONTH	Name of the month, in uppercase	MONTH YY	OCTOBER 0
	Month	Name of the month, in mixed case	Month YY	October 0
	MON	Abbreviated name of the month, in uppercase	MON YY	OCT 0
	Mon	Name of the month, in mixed case	Mon YY	Oct 01
	RM	Roman-numeral month	DD-RM-YY	03-X-01
Year	Y	Last one digit of year	MM Y	10 1
	YY	Last two digits of year	MM YY	10 01
	YYY	Last three digits of year	MM YYY	10 001
	YYYY	Four digits of year	MM YYYY	10 2001
	Y,YYY	Year with comma	MM Y,YYY	10 2,001
	YEAR	Year spelled out, in uppercase	MM YEAR	10 TWO THOUSAND ONE
	Year	Year spelled out, in mixed case	MM Year	10 Two Thousand One
	SYYYY	Four digits of year with "−" sign for BC	SYYYY	−2105
	RR	Round year depending on the current year	DD-MON-RR	03-OCT-01
	RRRR	Round year depending on the current year	DD-MON-RRRR	03-OCT-2001
	I	Last one digit of the ISO Standard year	MM I	10 1
	IY	Last two digits of the ISO Standard year	MM IY	10 01
	IYY	Last three digits of the ISO Standard year	MM IYY	10 001
	IYYY	Four digits of the ISO Standard year	MM IYYY	10 2001
Century	CC	Century	CC	21
	SCC	Century with "−" sign for BC	SCC	−22
Wtdeek	W	Week of the month	W	1
	WW	Week of the year	WW	40
	IW	Week of the year in ISO standard	IW	40
Quarter	Q	Quarter of the year	Q	4
Hour	HH	Hour of the day 1–12	HH	03
	HH12	Hour of the day 1–12	HH12	03
	HH24	Hour of the day 0–23	HH24	15
Minute	MI	Minute of hour 0–59	MI	34

Component	Options	Description	Format	Output
Second	SS	Second of minute 0–59	SS	48
	SSSSS	Seconds past midnight	SSSSS	42098
AM/PM	AM	Meridian indicator	HH:MI AM	11:00 AM
	A.M.	Meridian indicator with dots	HH:MI A.M.	11:00 A.M.
	PM	Meridian indicator	HH:MI PM	03:34 PM
	P.M.	Meridian indicator with dots	HH:MI P.M.	03:34 P.M.
AD/BC	AD	AD indicator	YY AD	01 AD
	A.D.	AD indicator with dots	YY A.D.	01 A.D.
	BC	BC indicator	YY BC	05 BC
	B.C.	BC indicator with dots	YY B.C.	05 B.C.
Julian day	J	Number of days since January 1, 4712 BC	J	2452186
Suffix	TH or th	Ordinal number	DDTH or DDth	03RD
	SP or sp	Spelled number	MMSP or MMsp	TEN
	SPTH	Spelled ordinal number	DDSPTH	THIRD
	THSP	Spelled ordinal number	DD THSP	THIRD
Fractional seconds	FF	Always use FF, with two Fs.	HH:MI:SS.FF or HH:MI:SSXFF	11:47:26.336000
Time zone	TZH	Time zone hour	HH:MI:SS.FF TZH	08:23:46.368 –10
	TZ	Time zone minute	HH:MI:SS.FF TZH:TZM	08:23:46.368 –10:30

AD/BC Indicators

Oracle provides two formats, AD and BC (two more with dots—A.D., B.C.), to characterize a year with respect to the year 0. However, they both serve the same purpose, and you can use either of them with equivalent results. If you have used the format BC in a query, and the date you are applying this format to comes out to be an AD year, Oracle is intelligent enough to print AD instead of BC, and vice versa. For example:

```
SELECT TO_CHAR(SYSDATE, 'YYYY AD'),
       TO_CHAR(SYSDATE, 'YYYY BC') FROM DUAL;

TO_CHAR( TO_CHAR(
-------- --------
 2001 AD  2001 AD

SELECT TO_CHAR(ADD_MONTHS(SYSDATE,-50000), 'YYYY AD'),
       TO_CHAR(ADD_MONTHS(SYSDATE,-50000), 'YYYY BC') FROM DUAL;
```

```
TO_CHAR( TO_CHAR(
-------- --------
  2165 BC  2165 BC
```

In the first example, even though we supplied the BC format with the SYSDATE, it printed 2001 AD in the output, and in the second example, even though we supplied AD with a date 50,000 months earlier (in the BC), it printed BC in the output. The function ADD_MONTHS is discussed later in the chapter.

AM/PM Indicators

The AM/PM indicators (as well as A.M. and P.M.) behave exactly the same as the AD/BC indicators. If you have used the AM format in a query, and the time you are applying this format to comes out to be a PM time, Oracle is intelligent enough to print PM instead of AM, and vice versa. For example:

```
SELECT TO_CHAR(SYSDATE, 'HH:MI:SS AM'),
       TO_CHAR(SYSDATE, 'HH:MI:SS PM'),
       TO_CHAR(SYSDATE - 8/24, 'HH:MI:SS AM'),
       TO_CHAR(SYSDATE - 8/24, 'HH:MI:SS PM')
FROM DUAL;

TO_CHAR(SYS TO_CHAR(SYS TO_CHAR(SYS TO_CHAR(SYS
----------- ----------- ----------- -----------
06:58:07 PM 06:58:07 PM 10:58:07 AM 10:58:07 AM
```

Case-Sensitivity of Formats

Some date formats are case-sensitive while others aren't. The formats that represent numbers are not case-sensitive. For example:

```
SELECT TO_CHAR(SYSDATE, 'HH:MI') UPPER,
TO_CHAR(SYSDATE, 'hh:mi') LOWER,
TO_CHAR(SYSDATE, 'Hh:mI') MIXED
FROM DUAL;

UPPER LOWER MIXED
----- ----- -----
03:17 03:17 03:17
```

You can see that the format *HH:MI* is case-insensitive—no matter which case you use for the format, the output is the same. The same applies to all other format elements that represent numbers, for example, DD, MM, YY, etc.

The Year 0

At our graduation party in 1990, all of our classmates agreed to meet after 10 years on January 1, 2000. Some even suggested that since it would be the start of the new Millennium, it would be a great idea to have a millennium get-together.

Ten years passed by. Some of us, who had kept in touch after graduation, remembered our millennium plan and decided to have a get-together on January 1, 2000. The party was well organized, and everyone was having a great time, untill someone came up with the thought that our party wasn't actually a millennium party. It was one year earlier than the actual start of the millennium. There was no year "0," and therefore, the year 2000 was the last year of the then current millennium. The new millennium actually began a year later January 1, 2001. Debate over this issue continued till the wee hours in the morning, and four years later we still debate it.

When the millennium began is an interesting topic for discussion, and the basis for that discussion lies in the convention we use in numbering our years. The common convention is the BC/AD convention, in which the sequence of years is ..., 2 BC, 1 BC, 1 AD, 2 AD, ... In this convention, there is no year 0—1 AD comes right after 1 BC. However, the convention used by astronomers includes a year 0. And, instead of representing BC and AD, astronomers prefer using the "-" and "+" notation. In the astronomical convention, the sequence of years is ..., −1, 0, +1, +2, ...

Oracle uses the BC/AD convention, and doesn't allow the year 0, as shown in the following example:

```
SELECT TO_DATE('0000-12-10','YYYY-MM-DD') FROM DUAL;
SELECT TO_DATE('0000-12-10','YYYY-MM-DD') FROM DUAL
                *
ERROR at line 1:
ORA-01841: (full) year must be between -4713 and +9999, and not be 0
```

Since there is no year 0 in the Oracle calendar, the year after 1 BC must be the year 1 AD. Therefore, the difference between the date "January 1, 0001 AD" and the date "December 31, 0001 BC" should be 1 day. However, the following example is in complete contrast to this:

```
SELECT TO_DATE('0001-01-01 AD','YYYY-MM-DD AD')
     - TO_DATE('0001-12-31 BC', 'YYYY-MM-DD BC')
FROM DUAL;

TO_DATE('0001-01-01AD','YYYY-
-----------------------------
                          367
```

Where does 367 come from? You were expecting 1, right? 367 is the result of 366 (the number of days in the year 0, being a leap year) plus 1. The existence of year 0 indicates that Oracle's date arithmetic uses the astronomical convention. This contradiction is known as Oracle's year-zero bug.

—continued—

Refer to an enlightening article by Peter Gulutzan and Trudy Pelzer at *http://www.orafaq.net/papers/dates_o.doc* for details on this and other interesting facts involving Oracle's calendar.

Date formats that represent textual date components are case-sensitive. For example, the format DAY is different from day. The following rules apply for determining the case of the output when a textual date format is used:

- If the first character of the format is lowercase, then the output will be lowercase, regardless of the case of the other characters in the format:

```
SELECT TO_CHAR(SYSDATE, 'month'),
       TO_CHAR(SYSDATE, 'mONTH'),
       TO_CHAR(SYSDATE, 'moNTh')
FROM DUAL;

TO_CHAR(S TO_CHAR(S TO_CHAR(S
--------- --------- ---------
october   october   october
```

- If the first character of the format element is uppercase and the second character is also uppercase, then the output will be uppercase, regardless of the case of the other characters in the format:

```
SELECT TO_CHAR(SYSDATE, 'MOnth'),
       TO_CHAR(SYSDATE, 'MONTH')
FROM DUAL;

TO_CHAR(S TO_CHAR(S
--------- ---------
OCTOBER   OCTOBER
```

- If the first character of the format element is uppercase and the second character is lowercase, then the output will have an uppercase first character and all other characters lowercase, regardless of the case of the other characters in the format:

```
SELECT TO_CHAR(SYSDATE, 'MoNTH'), TO_CHAR(SYSDATE, 'Month')
FROM DUAL;

TO_CHAR(S TO_CHAR(S
--------- ---------
October   October
```

These rules apply to all text elements, such as those used to represent month names, day names, and so forth.

Two-Digit Years

Even though Oracle stores the century of the year internally, it allows you to use two-digit years. Therefore, it is important to know how the century is handled when

MINUTES: MI or MM

Many SQL beginners assume that since HH represents hours and SS represents seconds, MM would represent minutes, and try to write the following SQL queries to print the current time:

```
SELECT TO_CHAR(SYSDATE, 'HH:MM:SS') FROM DUAL;

TO_CHAR(
--------
02:10:32
```

However, this is wrong. MM represents months and not minutes. The format for minutes is MI. Therefore, remember to use MI instead of MM when attempting to get the minutes part of the date. The correct query is:

```
SELECT TO_CHAR(SYSDATE, 'HH:MI:SS') FROM DUAL;

TO_CHAR(
--------
02:57:21
```

It becomes extremely difficult to debug an application if the MM format is embedded in the code instead of MI.

you use a two-digit year. Oracle provides two two-digit year formats that you can use: YY and RR.

With the YY year format, the century is assumed to be the current century:

```
ALTER SESSION SET NLS_DATE_FORMAT = 'DD-MON-YY';

Session altered.

SELECT SYSDATE, TO_CHAR(SYSDATE,'DD-MON-YYYY') FROM DUAL;

SYSDATE    TO_CHAR(SYS
---------  -----------
06-OCT-01 06-OCT-2001

SELECT TO_CHAR(TO_DATE('10-DEC-99'),'DD-MON-YYYY'),
       TO_CHAR(TO_DATE('10-DEC-01'),'DD-MON-YYYY') FROM DUAL;

TO_CHAR(TO_ TO_CHAR(TO_
----------- -----------
10-DEC-2099 10-DEC-2001
```

Since the current date was 06-OCT-2001 when these examples were executed, the first two digits of the years (the century component) in this example are assumed to be 20.

With the RR year format, the first two digits of the specified year are determined based upon the last two digits of the current year and the last two digits of year specified. The following rules apply:

- If the specified year is less than 50, and the last two digits of the current year are less than 50, then the first two digits of the return date are the same as the first two digits of the current date.

- If the specified year is less than 50, and the last two digits of the current year are greater than or equal to 50, then first two digits of the return date are one greater than the first two digits of the current date.

- If the specified year is greater than or equal to 50, and the last two digits of the current year are less than 50, then first two digits of the return date are one less than the first two digits of the current date.

- If the specified year is greater than or equal to 50, and the last two digits of the current year are greater than or equal to 50, then the first two digits of the return date are the same as the first two digits of the current date.

The following example demonstrates these rules:

```
ALTER SESSION SET NLS_DATE_FORMAT = 'DD-MON-RR';

Session altered.

SELECT SYSDATE, TO_CHAR(SYSDATE,'DD-MON-YYYY') FROM DUAL;

SYSDATE    TO_CHAR(SYS
---------- -----------
06-OCT-01 06-OCT-2001

SELECT TO_CHAR(TO_DATE('10-DEC-99'),'DD-MON-YYYY'),
       TO_CHAR(TO_DATE('10-DEC-01'),'DD-MON-YYYY') FROM DUAL;

TO_CHAR(TO_ TO_CHAR(TO_
----------- -----------
10-DEC-1999 10-DEC-2001
```

The ALTER SESSION command sets the default date format to DD-MON-RR. The next SELECT uses SYSDATE to show the current date at the time the example was executed. The final SELECT demonstrates the use of the RR date format (both TO_DATE calls rely on the default format set earlier). Note that the DD-MON-RR date format treats 10-DEC-99 as 10-DEC-1999, whereas it treats 10-DEC-01 as 10-DEC-2001. Compare this output to the rules we just listed.

The year format RRRR (four Rs) allows you to enter either a two-digit year or a four-digit year. If you enter a four-digit year, Oracle behaves as if the year format was YYYY. If you enter a two-digit year, Oracle behaves as if the year format is RR. The RRRR format is rarely used. Most SQL programmers prefer to use either YYYY, or to explicitly specify RR.

ISO Standard Issues

The ISO 8601 standard determines the start date of the first week of the year based upon whether most of the days in the week belong to the new year or to the previous year. If January 1 is a Monday, Tuesday, Wednesday, or a Thursday, then January 1 belongs to the first week of the new ISO year. The first day of the ISO year is either January 1 (if it is a Monday) or the previous Monday (which actually goes back to the last calendar year). For example, if January 1 is a Tuesday, then the first day of the ISO year is Monday, December 31, of the prior calendar year.

If January 1 is a Friday, Saturday, or a Sunday, then January 1 belongs to the last week of the previous ISO year. The first day of the first week of the new ISO year is then considered to be the Monday following January 1. For example, if January 1 falls on a Saturday, then the first day of the ISO year is considered to be Monday, January 3.

If you need to work with ISO dates, Oracle provides date formats that treat ISO years differently from calendar years. These ISO formats are:

IW
> Represents the week of the year in ISO standard.

I, IY, IYY, and IYYY
> Represents the ISO year.

The following sections describe ISO weeks and years with examples.

ISO standard weeks

In the ISO standard, weeks of the year are counted differently than regular calendar weeks. In a regular calendar, the first week of the year starts on January 1. 01-JAN is the first date of the first week. However, in the ISO standard, a week always starts on a Monday and ends on a Sunday. Therefore, the first date of the first week is considered to be the date of the nearest Monday. This date could be a couple of days later than 01-JAN, or it could be a couple of days earlier (in the previous year).

The format WW returns the week of the year in terms of the regular calendar, and the format IW returns the week of the year in terms of the ISO standard. Since 01-JAN-2001 was a Monday, it was considered the start date of the first week in terms of the regular calendar as well as in terms of the ISO standard. Therefore, if you compute the week number of any date in the year 2001, the results will be the same whether you use the regular calendar or the ISO calendar. For example:

```
SELECT TO_CHAR(TO_DATE('10-DEC-01'),'WW'),
       TO_CHAR(TO_DATE('10-DEC-01'),'IW')
FROM DUAL;

TO TO
-- --
50 50
```

However, the year 1999 didn't start on a Monday. Therefore, for some dates, the week number in the ISO standard could be different from that of the regular calendar. For example:

```
SELECT TO_CHAR(TO_DATE('10-DEC-99'),'WW'),
       TO_CHAR(TO_DATE('10-DEC-99'),'IW')
FROM DUAL;

TO TO
-- --
50 49
```

The ISO Standard can cause a year to have 53 weeks. Here's an example:

```
SELECT TO_CHAR(TO_DATE('01-JAN-99'),'IW'),
       TO_CHAR(TO_DATE('01-JAN- 99'),'Day')
FROM DUAL;

TO TO_CHAR(T
-- ---------
53 Friday
```

Note that the ISO standard treats January 1, 1999 to be in the 53rd week of 1998, because it falls on a Friday. The first week of 1999 starts on the subsequent Monday, which is January 4, as per the ISO standard.

ISO standard year

The year formats I, IY, IYY, and IYYY represent the ISO year. IYYY represents the four-digit ISO year, IYY represents the last three digits of the ISO year, IY represents the last two digits of the ISO year, and I represents the last digit of the ISO year. Remember that the start date of an ISO year is not necessarily January 1. The following example returns the ISO and calendar years for January 1, 1999:

```
SELECT TO_CHAR(TO_DATE('01-JAN-99'),'IYYY'),
       TO_CHAR(TO_DATE('01-JAN-99'),'YYYY') FROM DUAL;

TO_C TO_C
---- ----
1998 1999
```

Notice that even though the calendar year is 1999, the ISO year is considered to be 1998. That's because 01-Jan-1999 fell on a Friday—late in the week, which causes the week to be considered part of the previous ISO year. The following example demonstrates the opposite situation:

```
SELECT TO_CHAR(TO_DATE('31-DEC-90'),'IYYY'),
       TO_CHAR(TO_DATE('31-DEC-90'),'YYYY') FROM DUAL;

TO_C TO_C
---- ----
1991 1990
```

This time, the calendar year is 1990, but the date 31-Dec-1990 is considered to be in ISO year 1991. This is because 01-Jan-1991 fell on a Tuesday, early enough in the week for the entire week to be considered part of the next ISO year.

Database Parameters

The default formats to use when converting temporal data to character form are determined by database parameters. The key parameters are:

NLS_DATE_FORMAT
Specifies the default format used by TO_DATE and TO_CHAR functions when converting character data into data of type DATE or vice versa.

NLS_TIMESTAMP_FORMAT
Specifies the default format used by TO_TIMESTAMP and TO_CHAR functions when converting character data into data of type TIMESTAMP and TIMESTAMP WITH LOCAL TIME ZONE or vice versa.

NLS_TIMESTAMP_TZ_FORMAT
Specifies the default format used by TO_TIMESTAMP_TZ and TO_CHAR when converting character data into data of type TIMESTAMP WITH TIME ZONE or vice versa.

If any of these parameters are not set explicitly, its default value is derived from the setting for the NLS_TERRITORY parameter. The NLS_TERRITORY parameter specifies the territory, such as "AMERICA" or "CZECH REPUBLIC." For more details on the NLS parameters, refer to Oracle's *Globalization Support Guide*.

You or your DBA can specify values for these default date format parameters in one of the following three ways:

- By specifying a value in the instance's initialization parameter file. For example:

    ```
    NLS_DATE_FORMAT = 'YYYY-MM-DD'
    ```

    A format string specified using this approach becomes the instance-wide default.

- By issuing an ALTER SESSION command to change the default for your current session:

    ```
    ALTER SESSION SET NLS_TIMESTAMP_FORMAT = 'YYYY-MM-DD HH24:MI:SS.FF';
    ```

- By setting an environment variable on your client, to change the default value for all sessions initiated from your client:

    ```
    setenv NLS_DATE_FORMAT 'YYYY-MM-DD'
    ```

The NLS_LANG environment variable must be set for any other NLS_ environment variable setting to take effect. Unless NLS_LANG is set, all settings for other NLS_ environment variables are ignored.

The session-level setting overrides the environment variable setting, and the environment variable setting overrides the initialization parameter setting.

Manipulating Temporal Data

Date arithmetic is an important aspect of our day-to-day life. We find the age of a person by subtracting his date of birth from today's date. We compute the date a warranty expires by adding the warranty period to the purchase date. Drivers' license expirations, bank interest calculation, and a host of other things all depend on date arithmetic. It is extremely important for any database to support such common date arithmetic operations.

Using the Built-in Temporal Functions

Oracle provides a number of helpful functions, some of which you've seen used earlier in this chapter, that you can use to manipulate temporal values:

ADD_MONTHS(*date_value, months*)
> Adds months to a date. Add negative values to subtract months. If the initial date represents the last day of a month, the result is forced to the final day of the result month. The upcoming section on "Addition" discusses this function in detail.

CURRENT_DATE
> Returns the current date in the session time zone, as a DATE value.

CURRENT_TIMESTAMP
> Returns the current date and time in the session time zone, as a TIMESTAMP WITH TIME ZONE value.

DBTIMEZONE
> Returns the database time zone.

EXTRACT(*element* FROM *temporal_value*)
> Returns the specified element from a date, timestamp, or interval. Valid elements, which are SQL keywords and not string values, are: YEAR, MONTH, DAY, HOUR, MINUTE, SECOND, TIMEZONE_HOUR, TIMEZONE_MINUTE, TIMEZONE_REGION, and TIMEZONE_ABBR. The temporal value may be any of Oracle's date, timestamp, or interval types.

FROM_TZ(*timestamp, time_zone*)
> Converts a TIMESTAMP into a TIMESTAMP WITH TIME ZONE, essentially merging the two values you provide into one. The *time_zone* argument must be a string in the form [+|-]*hh:mi*.

LAST_DAY(*date_value*)
> Computes the last day of the month in which the given DATE value falls.

LOCALTIMESTAMP

Returns the current date and time in the session timezone, as a TIMESTAMP value.

MONTHS_BETWEEN(*later_date, earlier_date*)

Determines the number of months between two dates. The calculation is performed as: *later_date* − *earlier_date*. If *later_date* is actually earlier, than you'll get a negative result. See the section "Subtraction" for a detailed look at this function.

NEW_TIME(*date, source_time_zone, target_time_zone*)

Translates the time component of *date* from the *source_time_zone* to the *target_time_zone*. The time zone arguments must be strings containing time zone abbreviations such as PST, EST, CST. The list of time zones supported for use with NEW_TIME is shorter, and distinct from, the list of time zones supported for the timestamp types.

NEXT_DAY(*date, weekday*)

Returns the date of the next specified weekday following the given *date*. The *weekday* argument must be a valid weekday name or abbreviation in the current language—e.g., "Monday," "Tuesday," "Wed," "Thu."

ROUND(*temporal_value, format_element*)

Rounds a date or timestamp value to the specified element. See the section "Rounding and Truncating Dates."

SESSIONTIMEZONE

Returns the session timezone.

SYSDATE

Returns the current date and time for the operating system on which the database resides.

SYSTIMESTAMP

Returns the current date and timestamp time for the operating system on which the database resides as a TIMESTAMP WITH TIME ZONE value.

SYS_EXTRACT_UTC (*timestamp_with timezone_value*)

Returns the UTC data and time value with respect to the input TIMESTAMP WITH TIME ZONE value.

TRUNC(*temporal_value, format_element*)

Truncates a date/time value to a specific element. See the section "Rounding and Truncating Dates."

TZ_OFFSET([*tz_name*|*tz_offset*])

Returns the time zone offset with respect to UTC. Input may be a time zone name from V$TIMEZONE_NAMES or a time zone offset in the form [+|-]*hh*:*mi*.

SYSDATE is one of the most commonly used functions, and returns the current date and time as a DATE value:

```
ALTER SESSION SET NLS_DATE_FORMAT = 'DD-MON-RR HH:MI:SS';

Session altered.

SELECT SYSDATE FROM  DUAL;

SYSDATE
------------------
11-NOV-01 01:00:10
```

The following is an example of a function that takes arguments. The FROM_TZ function is used to add time zone information to the timestamp returned by a call to SYSTIMESTAMP. You can see that LOCALTIMESTAMP by itself returns no time zone information. FROM_TZ combines the TIMESTAMP with the time zone we specified, and returns a TIMESTAMP WITH TIME ZONE:

```
SELECT LOCALTIMESTAMP FROM dual;

LOCALTIMESTAMP
---------------------------------------------------------
18-DEC-03 03.31.24.974000 PM

SELECT FROM_TZ(LOCALTIMESTAMP,'-5:00') FROM dual;

FROM_TZ(LOCALTIMESTAMP,'-5:00')
---------------------------------------------------------
18-DEC-03 03.31.25.024000 PM -05:00
```

The EXTRACT function is unusual in that its first argument is actually a SQL keyword, and the delimiter between arguments is also a keyword:

```
SELECT EXTRACT(YEAR FROM SYSDATE) FROM dual;

EXTRACT(YEARFROMSYSDATE)
------------------------
                    2003
```

A more useful and interesting example of EXTRACT is shown at the end of the section "Subtraction."

Many of Oracle's temporal functions take only DATE values as inputs. This harks back to the day when DATE was the only temporal type. You have to be careful about this, because Oracle will implicitly convert timestamp types to DATEs, leading you to inadvertently write erroneous code. For example:

```
SELECT ADD_MONTHS(SYSTIMESTAMP,1) FROM dual;

ADD_MONTH
---------
18-JAN-04
```

The problem here isn't terribly obvious, but what's happened is that SYSTIMESTAMP has returned a TIMESTAMP WITH TIME ZONE value, which has been implicitly cast to a DATE, and thus both fractional seconds and the time zone have been lost. The results are the same as if you'd executed:

```
SELECT ADD_MONTHS(CAST(SYSTIMESTAMP AS DATE),1) FROM dual;
```

Be careful about passing TIMESTAMP values to functions that expect DATEs. If your code depends on fractional seconds or time zone information, you'll lose that information, and your code won't work as you expect.

 We rather wish Oracle had overloaded all the existing DATE functions, such as ADD_MONTHS, to also accept the various TIMESTAMP data types.

Addition

Adding two datetime values doesn't make sense. However, you can add days, months, years, hours, minutes, and seconds to a datetime to generate a future date and time. How you go about adding time intervals to datetime values depends on whether you are working with a DATE or one of the TIMESTAMP values.

Adding numbers to a DATE

The + operator allows you to add numbers to a DATE. The unit of a number added to a DATE is assumed to be days. Therefore, to find tomorrow's date, you can add 1 to SYSDATE:

```
SELECT SYSDATE, SYSDATE+1 FROM DUAL;

SYSDATE    SYSDATE+1
---------  ---------
05-OCT-01 06-OCT-01
```

Any time you add a number to a DATE, Oracle assumes that the number represents a number of days. Therefore, if you want to add multiples of a day (week, month, year, etc.) to a DATE, you first need to multiply by a conversion factor. For example, to add one week to today's date, you add 7 (7 days in a week times 1 day) to SYSDATE:

```
SELECT SYSDATE+7 FROM DUAL;

SYSDATE+7
---------
12-OCT-01
```

Similarly, if you want to add fractions of a day (hour, minute, second) to a DATE, you first need to convert such fractions into a fractional number of days. Do this by dividing by a conversion factor. For example, to add 20 minutes to the current date and time, you need to add (20 minutes/1,440 minutes in a day) to SYSDATE:

```
SELECT TO_CHAR(SYSDATE,'DD-MON-YY HH:MI:SS'),
TO_CHAR(SYSDATE+(20/1440),'DD-MON-YY HH:MI:SS')
FROM DUAL;

TO_CHAR(SYSDATE,'D TO_CHAR(SYSDATE+(2
------------------ ------------------
05-OCT-01 01:22:03 05-OCT-01 01:42:03
```

 Oracle allows you to use the + operator to add a number (number of days) to a TIMESTAMP value. However, when you do that, the TIMESTAMP value will be implicitly converted to a DATE value, with consequent loss of information.

Adding months to a DATE

Adding months to a DATE is not as easy as adding weeks, because all months don't have the same number of days—some have 30, some 31, some 28, and at times even 29. To add one month to a DATE, you need to know how many days that calendar month will have. Therefore, adding months to a DATE by converting those months to a number of days involves lots of homework, which is error-prone. Fortunately, Oracle does all the homework for us, and provides a built-in SQL function to add months to DATE values. This function is called ADD_MONTHS, and you call it as follows:

```
SELECT fname, hire_date, ADD_MONTHS(hire_date, 6) review_date
FROM employee;

FNAME                HIRE_DATE REVIEW_DA
-------------------- --------- ---------
John                 22-OCT-99 22-APR-00
```

This example shows the computation of an employee's biannual review date by using ADD_MONTHS to add six months to the employee's hire_date. The input DATE and the result DATE both fall on the 22nd of the month. This would not have happened if we had added 180 days to the input DATE. ADD_MONTHS is "smart" in one other way, too. The following example adds 6 months to 31 December 1999:

```
SELECT ADD_MONTHS('31-DEC-99',6) FROM DUAL;

ADD_MONTH
---------
30-JUN-00
```

The ADD_MONTHS function is intelligent enough to know that adding 6 months to 31 December should result in the last day of June. And since the last day of June is the 30th (not 31st), it returns 30 June, 2000.

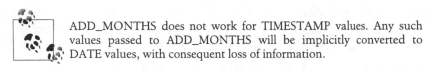 ADD_MONTHS does not work for TIMESTAMP values. Any such values passed to ADD_MONTHS will be implicitly converted to DATE values, with consequent loss of information.

Adding true INTERVAL values rather than numbers

You can use the + operator to add INTERVALs to DATE or TIMESTAMP values. For example, assume the flight time between New York and Los Angeles is 6 hours and 27 minutes. To find the arrival time of the flight, leaving New York now (3:39 PM in the example), at Los Angeles, you add the flight time to the current time:

```
select sysdate, sysdate + INTERVAL '0 6:27:00' DAY TO SECOND
from dual;

SYSDATE             SYSDATE+INTERVAL'06
------------------- -------------------
12/29/2003 15:39:00 12/29/2003 22:06:00
```

The preceding example adds an interval literal INTERVAL '0 6:27:00' DAY TO SECOND (6 hours and 27 minutes) to the DATE value returned by SYSDATE. The result of the addition is a DATE value and is in the New York (EST) time zone. However, since the destination is Los Angeles, you would like the output to be in the local time zone of the destination (PST). To achieve this, you can use the NEW_TIME function, as shown in the following example:

```
select sysdate,
       new_time(sysdate + INTERVAL '0 6:27:00' DAY TO SECOND, 'EST','PST')
from dual;

SYSDATE             NEW_TIME(SYSDATE+IN
------------------- -------------------
12/29/2003 15:39:00 12/29/2003 19:06:00
```

Therefore, a flight with flight time of 6 hours and 27 minutes that leaves New York at 3:39 PM will reach Los Angeles at 7:06 PM local time.

Similarly to adding intervals to DATE values, you can add intervals to TIMESTAMP values. For example:

```
SELECT LOCALTIMESTAMP, LOCALTIMESTAMP + INTERVAL '0 3:16:23' DAY TO SECOND
FROM DUAL;

LOCALTIMESTAMP
----------------------------------------------
LOCALTIMESTAMP+INTERVAL'03:16:23'DAYTOSECOND
----------------------------------------------
28-MAR-04 04.30.19.208000 PM
28-MAR-04 07.46.42.208000000 PM
```

If you need to add some number of days to a TIMESTAMP value, you shouldn't just directly add the number to the TIMESTAMP. In doing so, the TIMESTAMP will be implicitly converted to a DATE, which results in the loss of information. Specifically, you'll lose your fractional seconds. Rather, you should convert the number to an interval, and then add the interval to the TIMESTAMP. The result will be a TIMESTAMP value, and no information will be lost. For example:

```
SELECT LOCALTIMESTAMP + INTERVAL '1 0:00:00' DAY TO SECOND
FROM DUAL;

LOCALTIMESTAMP+INTERVAL'10:00:00'DAYTOSECOND
--------------------------------------------
29-MAR-04 04.36.46.211000000 PM
```

As an alternative to using an INTERVAL literal as in the preceding example, you can use the NUMTODSINTERVAL function to convert a number to an interval, as shown in the following example:

```
SELECT LOCALTIMESTAMP + NUMTODSINTERVAL(1,'DAY')
FROM DUAL;

LOCALTIMESTAMP+NUMTODSINTERVAL(1,'DAY')
-----------------------------------------
29-MAR-04 04.37.16.077000000 PM
```

Subtraction

Even though no other arithmetic operation (addition, multiplication, division) between two DATEs makes any sense, subtracting one DATE from another DATE is a very common and useful operation. The - operator allows you to subtract a DATE from a DATE, or a number from a DATE, a TIMESTAMP from a TIMESTAMP, an interval from a DATE and an interval from a TIMESTAMP.

Subtracting one DATE from another

Subtracting one DATE from another DATE returns the number of days between those two DATEs. The following example displays the lead time of a set of orders by subtracting the date on which the order was placed (order_dt) from the expected ship date (expected_ship_dt):

```
SELECT order_nbr, expected_ship_dt - order_dt lead_time
FROM cust_order;

ORDER_NBR  LEAD_TIME
---------- ----------
      1001          1
      1000          5
      1002         13
      1003         10
      1004          9
      1005          2
      1006          6
      1007          2
      1008          2
```

1009	4
1012	1
1011	5
1015	13
1017	10
1019	9
1021	2
1023	6
1025	2
1027	2
1029	4

Subtracting one TIMESTAMP from another

Subtracting one TIMESTAMP from another TIMESTAMP returns an interval of type INTERVAL DAY TO SECOND. For example:

```
SELECT LOCALTIMESTAMP - transaction_timestamp FROM transaction;

SYSTIMESTAMP-TRANSACTION_TIMESTAMP
-----------------------------------
+000000453 07:04:39.086000
```

Subtracting a number from a DATE

Along with subtracting one DATE from another, you can also subtract a number from a DATE. Subtracting a number from a DATE returns a DATE that number of days in the past. For example, subtracting 1 from SYSDATE gives yesterday, and subtracting 7 from SYSDATE yields the same day last week:

```
SELECT SYSDATE, SYSDATE - 1, SYSDATE - 7 FROM DUAL;

SYSDATE    SYSDATE-1 SYSDATE-7
--------- --------- ---------
05-OCT-01 04-OCT-01 28-SEP-01
```

Oracle lets you use the - operator to subtract a number (of days) from a TIMESTAMP value. However, when you do that, the TIMESTAMP value will be implicitly converted to a DATE value, with consequent loss of information.

Subtracting months from a DATE

Unlike ADD_MONTHS, Oracle doesn't provide a SUBTRACT_MONTHS function. To subtract months from a DATE, use the ADD_MONTHS function, and pass a negative number as the second parameter:

```
SELECT SYSDATE, ADD_MONTHS(SYSDATE, -6) FROM DUAL;

SYSDATE    ADD_MONTH
--------- ---------
05-OCT-01 05-APR-01
```

Number of months between two DATEs

Earlier in this section you saw that subtracting a DATE from another DATE returns the number of days between the two dates. There are times when you may want to know the number of months between two DATEs. Consider that subtracting an employee's `hire_date` from SYSDATE yields the number of days of experience the employee has with her employer:

```
SELECT SYSDATE-hire_date FROM employee;

SYSDATE-HIRE_DATE
-----------------
         714.0786
```

It's better, in most cases, to find the number of months of experience rather than the number of days. You know that dividing the number of days between two DATEs by 30 won't accurately calculate the number of months between those two DATEs. Therefore, Oracle provides the built-in SQL function MONTHS_BETWEEN for finding the number of months between two DATEs. MONTHS_BETWEEN is called as follows:

```
SELECT MONTHS_BETWEEN(SYSDATE,hire_date),
       MONTHS_BETWEEN(hire_date, SYSDATE)
FROM employee;

MONTHS_BETWEEN(SYSDATE,HIRE_DATE) MONTHS_BETWEEN(HIRE_DATE,SYSDATE)
--------------------------------- ---------------------------------
                        267.83499                        -267.83499
```

MONTHS_BETWEEN subtracts the second DATE from the first. So, if the second DATE comes later than the first, then MONTHS_BETWEEN will return a negative value. You can see that behavior in this example. Both calls use the same two DATEs, but in different orders, and the difference in results is that one result is negative while the other is positive.

There is no YEARS_BETWEEN function. To find the number of years between two DATEs, you can either subtract the two DATEs to find the number of days and then divide by 365, or use MONTHS_BETWEEN to find the number of months and then divide by 12. All years don't have the same number of days—some have 365 days and others have 366 days. Therefore, it is not accurate to divide the number of days by 365 to get the number of years. On the other hand, all years have 12 months, whether a leap year or not. Therefore, the most accurate way to calculate the number of years between two DATEs is to use the MONTHS_BETWEEN function to find the number of months and then divide by 12 to get the number of years.

Time interval between two DATEs

As you saw in the preceding examples, subtracting one DATE from another returns the number of days. However, at times, if the difference is a fractional day, you would like to find the number of hours, minutes, and seconds between two points in time. In

---

the next example, a pizza delivery center keeps track of the order_receive_time and the delivery_time of the orders it receives:

```
CREATE TABLE pizza_delivery (
order_id             NUMBER(10),
order_receive_time   DATE,
delivery_time        DATE);

Table created.

INSERT INTO pizza_delivery VALUES
(1, TO_DATE('12/20/03 08:47:53','MM/DD/YY HH:MI:SS'),
TO_DATE ('12/20/03 10:30:34','MM/DD/YY HH:MI:SS'));

1 row created.

COMMIT;

Commit complete.
```

The manager of the pizza delivery center wants to know the time difference between the order_receive_time and the delivery_time. You can use the date subtraction operation as in the following query:

```
SELECT delivery_time - order_receive_time FROM pizza_delivery;

DELIVERY_TIME-ORDER_RECEIVE_TIME
--------------------------------
                       .07130787
```

The fractional days returned by the preceding query doesn't make much sense. The manager wants to know the time difference in hours, minutes, and seconds. One way to find this would be to convert the number returned by the date subtraction into an interval using the NUMTODSINTERVAL function, and then extract the hour, minute, and second components of this interval using the EXTRACT function:

```
SELECT EXTRACT(HOUR FROM
               NUMTODSINTERVAL(delivery_time - order_receive_time, 'DAY'))
       ||':'||
       EXTRACT(MINUTE FROM
               NUMTODSINTERVAL(delivery_time - order_receive_time, 'DAY'))
       ||':'||
       EXTRACT(SECOND FROM
               NUMTODSINTERVAL(delivery_time - order_receive_time, 'DAY'))
       "Lead Time"
FROM pizza_delivery;

Lead Time
--------------------------------------------------------------------------
1:42:41
```

This example uses three expressions to extract hour, minute, and second, respectively, and then concatenates those values using the : delimiter to return the result in the HH:MI:SS format, which is much easier to comprehend compared to a fractional day.

Subtracting an INTERVAL from a DATE or TIMESTAMP

You can use the - operator to subtract an INTERVAL from a DATE or TIMESTAMP value. For example, if you need to reach your office at 8:00 AM, and it takes 30 minutes to reach from your home to office, you can use the following example to back calculate the start time:

```
SELECT TO_DATE('12/29/2003 08:00:00') - INTERVAL '0 0:30:00' DAY TO SECOND
FROM DUAL;

TO_DATE('12/29/2003
-------------------
12/29/2003 07:30:00
```

The preceding example subtracts an interval literal (INTERVAL '0 0:30:00' DAY TO SECOND) from a DATE value, and returns a DATE value. Similarly, you can subtract an interval from a TIMESTAMP value, using the "-" operator, as shown in the following example:

```
SELECT LOCALTIMESTAMP - INTERVAL '0 0:30:00' DAY TO SECOND
FROM DUAL;

LOCALTIMESTAMP-INTERVAL'00:30:00'DAYTOSECOND
--------------------------------------------
28-MAR-04 03.42.59.819000000 PM
```

The preceding example subtracts an interval literal (INTERVAL '0 0:30:00' DAY TO SECOND) from a TIMESTAMP value, and returns a TIMESTAMP value.

If you need to subtract some number of days from a TIMESTAMP value, you shouldn't just directly subtract the number from the TIMESTAMP. In doing so, the TIMESTAMP will be implicitly converted to a DATE and result in loss of information. Rather, you should convert the number to an interval, and then subtract the interval from the TIMESTAMP. This way, the result will be a TIMESTAMP value, and no information will be lost, as illustrated in the following example:

```
SELECT LOCALTIMESTAMP - INTERVAL '1 0:00:00' DAY TO SECOND
FROM DUAL;

LOCALTIMESTAMP-INTERVAL'10:00:00'DAYTOSECOND
--------------------------------------------
27-MAR-04 04.23.09.248000000 PM
```

As an alternative to the preceding example, you can use the NUMTODSINTERVAL function to convert a number to an interval, as shown in the following example:

```
SELECT LOCALTIMESTAMP - NUMTODSINTERVAL(1,'DAY')
FROM DUAL;
```

```
LOCALTIMESTAMP-NUMTODSINTERVAL(1,'DAY')
----------------------------------------
27-MAR-04 04.27.41.052000000 PM
```

Determining the First Day of the Month

Oracle provides a built-in function to get the last day of a month. The function returns the last day of the month containing the input date. For example, to find the last date of the current month, you can use the following SQL statement:

```
SELECT LAST_DAY(SYSDATE) "Next Payment Date" FROM DUAL;

Next Paym
---------
31-OCT-01
```

Sometimes it's useful to be able to determine the first day of a given month; it would be nice if Oracle would provide a FIRST_DAY function. One approach to getting the first day of the month for a given date is to use the TRUNC function:

```
TRUNC(SYSDATE,'MM')
```

A side-effect of this approach is that any time-of-day component of the input value is eliminated; the result will always have a time of midnight at the beginning of the day. Such a truncation of time may be good, especially if you are doing a range comparison. For example, to find all employees hired in the current month, without applying any sort of function to the hire_date column:

```
SELECT * FROM employee
WHERE hire_date >= TRUNC(SYSDATE,'MM')
  AND hire_date < TRUNC(LAST_DAY(SYSDATE)+1);
```

This SELECT statement works because TRUNC(SYSDATE,'MM') sets the time-of-day to the very beginning of the first day of the month. The second TRUNC expression resolves to the very beginning of the first day of the following month, which is why less-than rather than less-than-or-equal-to is used when comparing hire_date to that value.

In many cases, TRUNC(*date*,'MM') will work just fine for getting to the first day of a month. However, if you need to determine the first day of the month in which a given DATE value falls while also preserving the time-of-day, you can use the following expression:

```
ADD_MONTHS((LAST_DAY(SYSDATE)+1), -1)
```

This expression finds the last day of the month represented by date. It then adds 1 to get to the first day of the subsequent month, and finally uses ADD_MONTHS with an argument of –1 to go back to the beginning of the month in which you started. The result is the first day of the month in which the given date falls. Other approaches to this problem are possible; this is just one that works well for us. This approach has the advantage of preserving the time component of the date in question.

Rounding and Truncating Dates

Rounding and truncating dates is similar in concept to the rounding and truncating of numbers, but more involved because an Oracle DATE contains date as well as time information. Use the ROUND function to round a date/time value to a specific element; use the TRUNC function to truncate a date/time value to a specific element.

 Take care when using ROUND and TRUNC on TIMESTAMP values. Such values are implicitly converted to type DATE before being passed to ROUND or TRUNC, and you'll lose any information, such as time zone and fractional seconds, that a DATE value cannot hold.

The return value from ROUND or TRUNC depends upon the specified format, which is an optional parameter. If you don't specify a format in the call to ROUND, the function returns a date by rounding the input to the nearest day. If you don't specify a format in the call to TRUNC, that function returns the input date by setting the time component to the beginning of the day.

When using ROUND and TRUNC to round to the nearest day, or to truncate a date, the functions set the time fields of the return value to the beginning of the returned day—i.e., 12:00:00 AM (00:00:00 in HH24 format). For example:

```
SELECT TO_CHAR(SYSDATE, 'DD-MON-YY HH:MI:SS AM'),
       TO_CHAR(ROUND(SYSDATE), 'DD-MON-YY HH:MI:SS AM'),
       TO_CHAR(TRUNC(SYSDATE), 'DD-MON-YY HH:MI:SS AM')
FROM DUAL;

TO_CHAR(SYSDATE,'DD-M TO_CHAR(ROUND(SYSDATE TO_CHAR(TRUNC(SYSDATE
-------------------- -------------------- --------------------
06-OCT-01 07:35:48 AM 06-OCT-01 12:00:00 AM 06-OCT-01 12:00:00 AM
```

Notice that since the input time (SYSDATE) is before 12 noon, the output of ROUND and TRUNC are the same. However, if the input time were after 12 noon, the output of ROUND and TRUNC would be different, as in the following example:

```
SELECT TO_CHAR(SYSDATE, 'DD-MON-YY HH:MI:SS AM'),
       TO_CHAR(ROUND(SYSDATE), 'DD-MON-YY HH:MI:SS AM'),
       TO_CHAR(TRUNC(SYSDATE), 'DD-MON-YY HH:MI:SS AM')
FROM DUAL;

TO_CHAR(SYSDATE,'DD-M TO_CHAR(ROUND(SYSDATE TO_CHAR(TRUNC(SYSDATE
-------------------- -------------------- --------------------
06-OCT-01 05:35:48 PM 07-OCT-01 12:00:00 AM 06-OCT-01 12:00:00 AM
```

Since the input time is past 12 noon, ROUND returns the beginning of the next day. However, TRUNC still returns the beginning of the input date. This is similar to the rounding and truncating of numbers.

When you specify a format as an input to the ROUND and TRUNC functions, things become a bit more involved, but the concepts of rounding and truncating still remain the same. The difference is that the rounding and truncating are now based on the format you specify. For example, if you specify the format as YYYY, the input date will be truncated or rounded based on the year, which means that if the input date is before the middle of the year (July 1), both ROUND and TRUNC will return the first day of the year. If the input date is after July 1, ROUND will return the first day of the next year, whereas TRUNC will return the first day of the input year. For example:

```
SELECT TO_CHAR(SYSDATE-180, 'DD-MON-YYYY HH24:MI:SS'),
       TO_CHAR(ROUND(SYSDATE-180,'YYYY'),'DD-MON-YYYY HH24:MI:SS'),
       TO_CHAR(TRUNC(SYSDATE-180,'YYYY'),'DD-MON-YYYY HH24:MI:SS')
FROM DUAL;

TO_CHAR(SYSDATE-180, TO_CHAR(ROUND(SYSDAT TO_CHAR(TRUNC(SYSDAT
-------------------- -------------------- --------------------
09-APR-2001 20:58:33 01-JAN-2001 00:00:00 01-JAN-2001 00:00:00

SELECT TO_CHAR(SYSDATE, 'DD-MON-YYYY HH24:MI:SS'),
       TO_CHAR(ROUND(SYSDATE,'YYYY'),'DD-MON-YYYY HH24:MI:SS'),
       TO_CHAR(TRUNC(SYSDATE,'YYYY'),'DD-MON-YYYY HH24:MI:SS')
FROM DUAL;

TO_CHAR(SYSDATE,'DD- TO_CHAR(ROUND(SYSDAT TO_CHAR(TRUNC(SYSDAT
-------------------- -------------------- --------------------
06-OCT-2001 20:58:49 01-JAN-2002 00:00:00 01-JAN-2001 00:00:00
```

Similarly, you can round or truncate a date to a specific month, quarter, week, century, hour, minute, and so forth by using the appropriate format. Table 6-2 lists the formats (and their meanings) that can be used with the ROUND and TRUNC functions.

Table 6-2. Date formats for use with ROUND and TRUNC

Rounding unit	Format	Remarks
Century	CC SCC	TRUNC returns the first date of the century.
		ROUND returns the first date of the century if the input date is before the middle of the century (01-JAN-xx51); otherwise, ROUND returns the first date of the next century.
Year	SYYYY YYYY YEAR SYEAR YYY YY Y	TRUNC returns the first date of the year.
		ROUND returns the first date of the year if the input date is before the middle of the year (01-JUL); otherwise, ROUND returns the first date of the next year.
ISO	IYYY IYY IY I	TRUNC returns the first date of the ISO year.
		ROUND returns the first date of the ISO year if the input date is before the middle of the ISO year; otherwise, ROUND returns the first date of the next ISO year.

Table 6-2. Date formats for use with ROUND and TRUNC (continued)

Rounding unit	Format	Remarks
Quarter	Q	TRUNC returns the first date of the quarter.
		ROUND returns the first date of the quarter if the input date is before the middle of the quarter (the 16th day of the second month of the quarter); otherwise, ROUND returns the first date of the next quarter.
Month	MONTH MON MM RM	TRUNC returns the first date of the month.
		ROUND returns the first date of the month if the input date is before the middle of the month (the 16th day of the month); otherwise, ROUND returns the first date of the next month.
Week	WW	TRUNC returns the first date of the week.
		ROUND returns the first date of the week if the input date is on or before the middle of the week (based on the first day of the year); otherwise, the first date of the next week.
ISO Week	IW	TRUNC returns the first date of the ISO week.
		ROUND returns the first date of the week if the input date is before the middle of the week (based on the first day of the ISO year); otherwise, ROUND returns the first date of the next week.
Week	W	TRUNC returns the first date of the week.
		ROUND returns the first date of the week if the input date is before the middle of the week (based on the first day of the month); otherwise, ROUND returns the first date of the next week.
Day	DDD DD J	TRUNC returns the beginning of the day.
		ROUND returns the beginning of the day if the input time is before the middle of the day (12:00 noon); otherwise, ROUND returns the beginning of the next day.
Day of the week	DAY DY D	TRUNC returns the first date of the week.
		ROUND returns the first date of the week if the input date is before the middle of the week (based on the first day of the month); otherwise, ROUND returns the first date of the next week.
Hour	HH HH12 HH24	TRUNC returns the beginning of the hour.
		ROUND returns the beginning of the hour if the input time is before the middle of the hour (00:30); otherwise, ROUND returns the beginning of the next hour.
Minute	MI	TRUNC returns the beginning of the minute.
		ROUND returns the beginning of the minute if the input time is before the middle of the minute (00:00:30); otherwise, ROUND returns the beginning of the next minute.

SELECTing Data Based on Date Ranges

There are times when you need to SELECT data from a table based on a given date range. Let's say you have been asked to print all disputed orders placed on a given date, say 22-JUL-01. Most likely, your immediate response would be a query such as the following:

```
SELECT * FROM disputed_orders
WHERE order_dt = '22-JUL-01';

no rows selected
```

There's no output. Surprised? Although you know there are orders on 22-JUL-01, this query didn't return any rows. The reason is that order_dt is a DATE column, and contains time as well as date information. On the other hand, the date literal '22-JUL-01' doesn't contain any time information. When you don't specify the time portion in a date literal, the time portion is assumed to be beginning of the day—i.e., 12:00:00 A.M. (or 00:00:00 in 24 hour format). In the disputed_orders table, the time components in the order_dt column are other than 12:00:00 A.M. In this case, the correct query to print orders placed on 22-JUL-01 is:

```
SELECT order_nbr, cust_nbr, order_dt, expected_ship_dt
FROM disputed_orders
WHERE order_dt BETWEEN
            TO_DATE('22-JUL-01 00:00:00','DD-MON-YY HH24:MI:SS') AND
            TO_DATE('22-JUL-01 23:59:59','DD-MON-YY HH24:MI:SS');
```

```
ORDER_NBR   CUST_NBR ORDER_DT   EXPECTED_
---------   -------- ---------  ---------
     1001          1 22-JUL-01  23-JUL-01
     1005          8 22-JUL-01  24-JUL-01
     1006          1 22-JUL-01  28-JUL-01
     1012          1 22-JUL-01  23-JUL-01
     1021          8 22-JUL-01  24-JUL-01
     1023          1 22-JUL-01  28-JUL-01
```

The query treats the one day as a range: 22-JUL-01 00:00:00 through 22-JUL-01 23:59:59. Thus, the query returns any order placed at any time during 22-JUL-01.

Another way to solve this problem of needing to ignore the time components in a DATE column is to truncate the date, and then compare the truncated result with the input literal:

```
SELECT order_nbr, cust_nbr, order_dt, expected_ship_dt
FROM disputed_orders
WHERE TRUNC(order_dt) = '22-JUL-01';
```

```
ORDER_NBR   CUST_NBR ORDER_DT   EXPECTED_
---------   -------- ---------  ---------
     1001          1 22-JUL-01  23-JUL-01
     1005          8 22-JUL-01  24-JUL-01
     1006          1 22-JUL-01  28-JUL-01
     1012          1 22-JUL-01  23-JUL-01
     1021          8 22-JUL-01  24-JUL-01
     1023          1 22-JUL-01  28-JUL-01
```

The TRUNC function sets the time portion to the beginning of the day. Therefore, the equality comparison with the date literal '22-JUL-01' returns the expected output. The same result can be achieved by converting order_dt to a character string in a format matching that of the input data:

```
SELECT * FROM disputed_orders
WHERE TO_CHAR(order_dt,'DD-MON-YY') = '22-JUL-01';
```

The downside to the approach of using the TRUNC and TO_CHAR functions is that the resulting query cannot make use of any index that happens to be on the order_dt column. This can have significant performance implications. On the other hand, the date range solution, while more complex to code, does not preclude the use of any index on the column in question.

 Oracle8*i* and higher support the use of function-based indexes, which, if created correctly, allow for the use of indexes even when functions are applied to columns in query predicates.

You can use the same techniques shown in this section to SELECT data based on any given date range, even if that range spans more than just one day.

Creating a Date Pivot Table

For certain types of queries, it's helpful to have a table with one row for each date over a period of time. For example, you might wish to have one row for each date in the current year. You can use the TRUNC function in conjunction with some PL/SQL code to create such a table:

```
CREATE TABLE dates_of_year (one_day DATE);

Table created.

DECLARE
  i NUMBER;
  start_day DATE := TRUNC(SYSDATE,'YY');
BEGIN
  FOR i IN 0 .. (TRUNC(ADD_MONTHS(SYSDATE,12),'YY') - 1) - (TRUNC(SYSDATE,'YY'))
  LOOP
    INSERT INTO dates_of_year VALUES (start_day+i);
  END LOOP;
END;
/

PL/SQL procedure successfully completed.

SELECT COUNT(*) FROM dates_of_year;

  COUNT(*)
----------
       365
```

The dates_of_year table is now populated with the 365 days of the year 2001. You can now use this table to generate various useful lists of dates.

Let's say there are two paydays where you work—the 15th of each month and the last day of each month. Use the following query against the dates_of_year table to generate a list of all paydays in the year 2001:

```
SELECT one_day payday FROM dates_of_year
WHERE TO_CHAR(one_day,'DD') = '15'
OR one_day = LAST_DAY(one_day);

PAYDAY
---------
15-JAN-01
31-JAN-01
15-FEB-01
28-FEB-01
15-MAR-01
31-MAR-01
15-APR-01
30-APR-01
15-MAY-01
31-MAY-01
15-JUN-01
30-JUN-01
15-JUL-01
31-JUL-01
15-AUG-01
31-AUG-01
15-SEP-01
30-SEP-01
15-OCT-01
31-OCT-01
15-NOV-01
30-NOV-01
15-DEC-01
31-DEC-01

24 rows selected.
```

Quite often you are told by a government organization that the processing of a document will take "x" number of days. When someone says something like that, they usually mean "x" number of working days. Therefore, to calculate the expected completion date, you need to count "x" days from the current date, skipping Saturdays and Sundays. Obviously, you can't use simple date arithmetic, because simple date subtraction doesn't exclude weekend days. What you can do is use the dates_of_year table. For example:

```
SELECT COUNT(*) FROM dates_of_year
WHERE RTRIM(TO_CHAR(one_day,'DAY')) NOT IN ('SATURDAY', 'SUNDAY')
AND one_day BETWEEN '&d1' AND '&d2';

Enter value for d1: 18-FEB-01
Enter value for d2: 15-MAR-01
old   3: AND one_day BETWEEN '&d1' AND '&d2'
new   3: AND one_day BETWEEN '18-FEB-01' AND '15-MAR-01'
```

```
   COUNT(*)
----------
        19
```

This query counts the number of days between the two dates you enter, excluding Saturdays and the Sundays. The TO_CHAR function with the 'DAY' format converts each candidate date (from the dates_of_year table) to a day of the week, and the NOT IN operator excludes the days that are Saturdays and Sundays. Notice the use of the RTRIM function with TO_CHAR. We used RTRIM because TO_CHAR produces the DAY as a nine-character string, blank padded to the right. RTRIM eliminates those extra spaces.

There could be holidays between two dates, and the queries shown in this section don't deal with that possibility. To take holidays into account, you need another table (perhaps named holidays) that lists all the holidays in the year. You can then modify the previous query to exclude days listed in the holidays table. Try this as an exercise.

Summarizing by a Date/Time Element

Let's say you want to print a quarterly summary of all your orders. You want to print the total number of orders and total sale price for each quarter. The order table is as follows:

```
SELECT * FROM cust_order;

ORDER CUST  SALES  PRICE ORDER_DT  EXPECTED_ CANCELLED SHIP STATUS
----- ----  ------ ----- --------- --------- --------- ---- -----------
 1001    1  7354      99 22-JUL-01 23-JUL-01                 DELIVERED
 1000    1  7354         19-JUL-01 24-JUL-01 21-JUL-01       CANCELLED
 1002    5  7368         12-JUL-01 25-JUL-01 14-JUL-01       CANCELLED
 1003    4  7654      56 16-JUL-01 26-JUL-01                 DELIVERED
 1004    4  7654      34 18-JUL-01 27-JUL-01                 PENDING
 1005    8  7654      99 22-JUL-01 24-JUL-01                 DELIVERED
 1006    1  7354         22-JUL-01 28-JUL-01 24-JUL-01       CANCELLED
 1007    5  7368      25 20-JUL-01 22-JUL-01                 PENDING
 1008    5  7368      25 21-JUL-01 23-JUL-01                 PENDING
 1009    1  7354      56 18-JUL-01 22-JUL-01                 DELIVERED
 1012    1  7354      99 22-JUL-01 23-JUL-01                 DELIVERED
 1011    1  7354         19-JUL-01 24-JUL-01 21-JUL-01       CANCELLED
 1015    5  7368         12-JUL-01 25-JUL-01 14-JUL-01       CANCELLED
 1017    4  7654      56 16-JUL-01 26-JUL-01                 DELIVERED
 1019    4  7654      34 18-JUL-01 27-JUL-01                 PENDING
 1021    8  7654      99 22-JUL-01 24-JUL-01                 DELIVERED
 1023    1  7354         22-JUL-01 28-JUL-01 24-JUL-01       CANCELLED
 1025    5  7368      25 20-JUL-01 22-JUL-01                 PENDING
 1027    5  7368      25 21-JUL-01 23-JUL-01                 PENDING
 1029    1  7354      56 18-JUL-01 22-JUL-01                 DELIVERED

20 rows selected.
```

There is no quarter column in the cust_order table. You have to manipulate the order_dt column to generate the quarter. The following SQL statement does this using the TO_CHAR function along with a date format. In addition to being used in the SELECT list, notice that TO_CHAR is used in the GROUP BY clause to group the results by quarter:

```
SELECT 'Q'||TO_CHAR(order_dt, 'Q') quarter, COUNT(*),
       SUM(NVL(sale_price,0))
FROM cust_order
GROUP BY 'Q'||TO_CHAR(order_dt, 'Q');

QU   COUNT(*) SUM(NVL(SALE_PRICE,0))
--   -------- ----------------------
Q3        20                    788
```

Using this same technique, you can summarize data by week, month, year, hour, minute, or any other date/time unit that you choose.

CHAPTER 7
Set Operations

There are situations when we need to combine the results from two or more SELECT statements. SQL enables us to handle these requirements by using set operations. The result of each SELECT statement can be treated as a set, and SQL set operations can be applied on those sets to arrive at a final result. Oracle SQL supports the following four set operations:

- UNION ALL
- UNION
- MINUS
- INTERSECT

SQL statements containing these set operators are referred to as *compound queries*, and each SELECT statement in a compound query is referred to as a *component query*. Two SELECTs can be combined into a compound query by a set operation only if they satisfy the following two conditions:

- The result sets of both the queries must have the same number of columns.
- The data type of each column in the second result set must match the data type of its corresponding column in the first result set.

These conditions are also referred to as *union compatibility* conditions. The term union compatibility is used even though these conditions apply to other set operations as well. Set operations are often called *vertical joins*, because the result combines data from two or more SELECTS based on columns instead of rows. The generic syntax of a query involving a set operation is:

```
component_query
{UNION | UNION ALL | MINUS | INTERSECT}
component_query
```

The keywords UNION, UNION ALL, MINUS, and INTERSECT are set operators. You can have more than two component queries in a composite query; you will always use one less set operator than the number of component queries.

There is an exception to the second union compatibility condition. Two data types do not need to be the same if they are in the same *data type group*. By data type group, we mean the general categories such as numbers, strings, and datetimes. For example, it is ok to have a column in the first component query of data type CHAR, that corresponds to a VARCHAR2 column in the second component query (or vice versa). Oracle performs implicit type conversion in such a case.

However, Oracle will not perform implicit type conversion if corresponding columns in the component queries belong to different data type groups. For example, if a column in the first component query is of data type DATE, and the corresponding column in the second component query is of data type CHAR, Oracle will not perform implicit conversion, and you will get an error as a result of violation of data type compatibility. This is illustrated in the following example:

```
SELECT TO_DATE('12-OCT-03') FROM DUAL
UNION
SELECT '13-OCT-03' FROM DUAL;

SELECT TO_DATE('12-OCT-03') FROM DUAL
                   *
ERROR at line 1:
ORA-01790: expression must have same datatype as corresponding expression
```

The following sections discuss syntax, examples, rules, and restrictions for the four set operations.

Set Operators

The following list briefly describes the four set operations supported by Oracle SQL:

UNION ALL
:   Combines the results of two SELECT statements into one result set.

UNION
:   Combines the results of two SELECT statements into one result set, and then eliminates any duplicate rows from that result set.

MINUS
:   Takes the result set of one SELECT statement, and removes those rows that are also returned by a second SELECT statement. Duplicate rows are eliminated.

INTERSECT
:   Returns only those rows that are returned by each of two SELECT statements. Duplicate rows are eliminated.

Before moving on to the details on these set operators, let's look at the following two queries, which we'll use as component queries in our subsequent examples. The first query retrieves all the customers in region 5:

```
SELECT cust_nbr, name
FROM customer
WHERE region_id = 5;
```

```
   CUST_NBR NAME
---------- -----------------------------
         1 Cooper Industries
         2 Emblazon Corp.
         3 Ditech Corp.
         4 Flowtech Inc.
         5 Gentech Industries
```

The second query retrieves all the customers with the sales representative 'MARTIN':

```
SELECT c.cust_nbr, c.name
FROM customer c
WHERE c.cust_nbr IN (SELECT o.cust_nbr
                     FROM cust_order o, employee e
                     WHERE o.sales_emp_id = e.emp_id
                     AND e.lname = 'MARTIN');
```

```
   CUST_NBR NAME
---------- -----------------------------
         4 Flowtech Inc.
         8 Zantech Inc.
```

If you look at the results returned by these two queries, you will notice that there is one common row (for Flowtech Inc.). The following sections discuss the effects of the various set operations between these two result sets.

UNION ALL

The UNION ALL operator merges the result sets of two component queries. This operation returns rows retrieved by either of the component queries, without eliminating duplicates. The following example illustrates the UNION ALL operation:

```
SELECT cust_nbr, name
FROM customer
WHERE region_id = 5
UNION ALL
SELECT c.cust_nbr, c.name
FROM customer c
WHERE c.cust_nbr IN (SELECT o.cust_nbr
                     FROM cust_order o, employee e
                     WHERE o.sales_emp_id = e.emp_id
                     AND e.lname = 'MARTIN');
```

```
CUST_NBR NAME
---------- ------------------------------
        1 Cooper Industries
        2 Emblazon Corp.
        3 Ditech Corp.
        4 Flowtech Inc.
        5 Gentech Industries
        4 Flowtech Inc.
        8 Zantech Inc.

7 rows selected.
```

As you can see from the result set, there is one customer, which is retrieved by both the SELECTs, and therefore appears twice in the result set. The UNION ALL operator simply merges the output of its component queries, without caring about any duplicates in the final result set.

UNION

The UNION operator returns all distinct rows retrieved by two component queries. The UNION operation eliminates duplicates while merging rows retrieved by either of the component queries. The following example illustrates the UNION operation:

```
SELECT cust_nbr, name
FROM customer
WHERE region_id = 5
UNION
SELECT c.cust_nbr, c.name
FROM customer c
WHERE c.cust_nbr IN (SELECT o.cust_nbr
                     FROM cust_order o, employee e
                     WHERE o.sales_emp_id = e.emp_id
                     AND e.lname = 'MARTIN');

CUST_NBR NAME
---------- ------------------------------
        1 Cooper Industries
        2 Emblazon Corp.
        3 Ditech Corp.
        4 Flowtech Inc.
        5 Gentech Industries
        8 Zantech Inc.

6 rows selected.
```

This query is a modification of the query from the preceding section; the keywords UNION ALL have been replaced with UNION. Now, the result set contains only distinct rows (no duplicates). To eliminate duplicate rows, a UNION operation needs to do some extra tasks as compared to the UNION ALL operation. These extra tasks include sorting and filtering the result set. If you observe carefully, you will notice that the result set of the UNION ALL operation is not sorted, whereas the result set of the UNION operation is sorted. (The result set of a UNION is sorted on the combination of all the columns in the SELECT list. In the preceeding example, the UNION result set will be sorted on the combination cust_nbr and name.) These extra tasks introduce a performance overhead to the UNION operation. A query involving UNION will take more time than the same query with UNION ALL, even if there are no duplicates to remove.

Unless you have a valid need to retrieve only distinct rows, use UNION ALL instead of UNION for better performance.

INTERSECT

INTERSECT returns only the rows retrieved by *both* component queries. Compare this with UNION, which returns the rows retrieved by *any* of the component queries. If UNION acts like "OR," INTERSECT acts like "AND." For example:

```
SELECT cust_nbr, name
FROM customer
WHERE region_id = 5
INTERSECT
SELECT c.cust_nbr, c.name
FROM customer c
WHERE c.cust_nbr IN (SELECT o.cust_nbr
                     FROM cust_order o, employee e
                     WHERE o.sales_emp_id = e.emp_id
                     AND e.lname = 'MARTIN');


  CUST_NBR NAME
---------- -----------------------------
         4 Flowtech Inc.
```

As you saw earlier, "Flowtech Inc." was the only customer retrieved by both SELECT statements. Therefore, the INTERSECT operator returns just that one row.

MINUS

MINUS returns all rows from the first SELECT that are not also returned by the second SELECT.

Oracle's use of MINUS does not follow the ANSI/ISO SQL standard. The corresponding ANSI/ISO SQL keyword is EXCEPT.

The following example illustrates how MINUS works:

```
SELECT cust_nbr, name
FROM customer
WHERE region_id = 5
```

```
MINUS
SELECT c.cust_nbr, c.name
FROM customer c
WHERE c.cust_nbr IN (SELECT o.cust_nbr
                     FROM cust_order o, employee e
                     WHERE o.sales_emp_id = e.emp_id
                     AND e.lname = 'MARTIN');

  CUST_NBR NAME
---------- ------------------------------
         1 Cooper Industries
         2 Emblazon Corp.
         3 Ditech Corp.
         5 Gentech Industries
```

You might wonder why you don't see "Zantech Inc." in the output. An important thing to note here is that the execution order of component queries in a set operation is from top to bottom. The results of UNION, UNION ALL, and INTERSECT will not change if you alter the ordering of component queries. However, the result of MINUS will be different if you alter the order of the component queries. If you rewrite the previous query by switching the positions of the two SELECTs, you get a completely different result:

```
SELECT c.cust_nbr, c.name
FROM customer c
WHERE c.cust_nbr IN (SELECT o.cust_nbr
                     FROM cust_order o, employee e
                     WHERE o.sales_emp_id = e.emp_id
                     AND e.lname = 'MARTIN')
MINUS
SELECT cust_nbr, name
FROM customer
WHERE region_id = 5;

  CUST_NBR NAME
---------- ------------------------------
         8 Zantech Inc.
```

In the second MINUS example, the first component query adds "Flowtech Inc." and "Zantech Inc." to the result set while the second component query removes "Flowtech Inc.", leaving "Zantech Inc." as the sole remaining row.

> In a MINUS operation, rows may be returned by the second SELECT that are not also returned by the first. These rows are not included in the output.

Precedence of Set Operators

If more than two component queries are combined using set operators, then Oracle evaluates the set operators from left to right. In the following example, the UNION is evaluated before the INTERSECT:

```
SELECT cust_nbr, name
FROM customer
WHERE region_id = 5
UNION
SELECT c.cust_nbr, c.name
FROM customer c
WHERE c.cust_nbr IN (SELECT o.cust_nbr
                     FROM cust_order o, employee e
                     WHERE o.sales_emp_id = e.emp_id
                     AND e.lname = 'MARTIN')
INTERSECT
SELECT cust_nbr, name
FROM customer
WHERE region_id = 6;

CUST_NBR NAME
-------- ------------------------------
       8 Zantech Inc.
```

To influence a particular order of evaluation of the set operators, you can use parentheses. Looking at the preceding example, if you want the INTERSECT to be evaluated before the UNION, you should introduce parentheses into the query such that the component queries involving the INTERSECT are enclosed in parentheses, as shown in the following example:

```
SELECT cust_nbr, name
FROM customer
WHERE region_id = 5
UNION
(
SELECT c.cust_nbr, c.name
FROM customer c
WHERE c.cust_nbr IN (SELECT o.cust_nbr
                     FROM cust_order o, employee e
                     WHERE o.sales_emp_id = e.emp_id
                     AND e.lname = 'MARTIN')
INTERSECT
SELECT cust_nbr, name
FROM customer
WHERE region_id = 6
);

CUST_NBR NAME
-------- ------------------------------
       1 Cooper Industries
       2 Emblazon Corp.
       3 Ditech Corp.
```

```
4 Flowtech Inc.
5 Gentech Industries
8 Zantech Inc.
```

The operation within the parentheses is evaluated first. The result is then combined with the component queries outside the parentheses.

The ANSI/ISO SQL standard gives higher precedence to the INTERSECT operator. However, Oracle, at least through Oracle Database 10g, doesn't implement that higher precedence. All set operations currently have equal precedence.

In the future, Oracle may change the precedence of INTERSECT to comply with the standard. To prepare for that possibility, we recommend using parentheses to control the order of evaluation of set operators whenever you use INTERSECT in a query with any other set operator.

Comparing Two Tables

Developers, and even DBAs, occasionally need to compare the contents of two tables to determine whether the tables contain the same data. The need to do this is especially common in test environments, as developers may want to compare a set of data generated by a program under test with a set of "known good" data. Comparison of tables is also useful for automated testing purposes, when you have to compare actual results with a given set of expected results. SQL's set operations provide an interesting solution to this problem of comparing two tables.

The following query uses both MINUS and UNION ALL to compare two tables for equality. The query depends on each table having either a primary key or at least one unique index.

```
(SELECT * FROM customer_known_good
MINUS
SELECT * FROM customer_test)
UNION ALL
(SELECT * FROM customer_test
MINUS
SELECT * FROM customer_known_good);
```

You can look at this query as the union of two compound queries. The parentheses ensure that both MINUS operations take place first before the UNION ALL operation is performed. The result of the first MINUS query will be those rows in customer_known_good that are not also in customer_test. The result of the second MINUS query will be those rows in customer_test that are not also in customer_known_good. The UNION ALL operator simply combines these two result sets for convenience. If no rows are returned by this query, then we know that both tables have identical rows. Any rows returned by this query represent differences between the customer_test and customer_known_good tables.

If the possibility exists for one or both tables to contain duplicate rows, you must use a more general form of this query to test the two tables for equality. This more general form uses row counts to detect duplicates:

```
(SELECT c1.*,COUNT(*)
 FROM customer_known_good
 GROUP BY c1.cust_nbr, c1.name...
MINUS
 SELECT c2.*, COUNT(*)
 FROM customer_test c2
 GROUP BY c2.cust_nbr, c2.name...)
UNION ALL
(SELECT c3.*,COUNT(*)
 FROM customer_test c3
 GROUP BY c3.cust_nbr, c3.name...
MINUS
 SELECT c4.*, COUNT(*)
 FROM customer_known_good c4
 GROUP BY c4.cust_nbr, c4.name...)
```

This query is getting complex! The GROUP BY clause (see Chapter 4) for each SELECT must list *all* columns for the table being selected. Any duplicate rows will be grouped together, and the count will reflect the number of duplicates. If the number of duplicates is the same in both tables, the MINUS operations will cancel those rows out. If any rows are different, or if any occurrence counts are different, the resulting rows will be reported by the query.

Let's look at an example to illustrate how this query works. We'll start with the following tables and data:

DESC customer_known_good

```
Name                          Null?     Type
--------------------------- -------- ----------------
CUST_NBR                    NOT NULL NUMBER(5)
NAME                        NOT NULL VARCHAR2(30)
```

SELECT * FROM customer_known_good;

```
  CUST_NBR NAME
----------- ------------------------------
         1 Sony
         1 Sony
         2 Samsung
         3 Panasonic
         3 Panasonic
         3 Panasonic

6 rows selected.
```

DESC customer_test

```
Name                            Null?     Type
------------------------------- --------  ----------------
CUST_NBR                        NOT NULL  NUMBER(5)
NAME                            NOT NULL  VARCHAR2(30)
```

SELECT * FROM customer_test;

```
CUST_NBR NAME
----------- ------------------------------
          1 Sony
          1 Sony
          2 Samsung
          2 Samsung
          3 Panasonic
```

As you can see the customer_known_good and customer_test tables have the same structure, but different data. Also notice that none of these tables has a primary or unique key; there are duplicate records in both. The following SQL will compare these two tables effectively:

```
(SELECT c1.*, COUNT(*)
FROM customer_known_good c1
GROUP BY c1.cust_nbr, c1.name
MINUS
SELECT c2.*, COUNT(*)
FROM customer_test c2
GROUP BY c2.cust_nbr, c2.name)
UNION ALL
(SELECT c3.*, COUNT(*)
FROM customer_test c3
GROUP BY c3.cust_nbr, c3.name
MINUS
SELECT c4.*, COUNT(*)
FROM customer_known_good c4
GROUP BY c4.cust_nbr, c4.name);
```

```
CUST_NBR NAME                             COUNT(*)
----------- ------------------------------ ----------
          2 Samsung                               1
          3 Panasonic                             3
          2 Samsung                               2
          3 Panasonic                             1
```

These results indicate that one table (customer_known_good) has one record for "Samsung," whereas the second table (customer_test) has two records for the same customer. Also, one table (customer_known_good) has three records for "Panasonic," whereas the second table (customer_test) has one record for the same customer. Both the tables have the same number of rows (two) for "Sony," and therefore "Sony" doesn't appear in the output.

Duplicate rows are not possible in tables that have a primary key or at least one unique index. Use the short form of the table comparison query for such tables.

Using NULLs in Compound Queries

We discussed union compatibility conditions at the beginning of this chapter. The union compatibility issue gets interesting when NULLs are involved. As you know, NULL doesn't have a data type, and NULL can be used in place of a value of any data type. If you purposely select NULL as a column value in a component query, Oracle no longer has two data types to compare to see whether the two component queries are compatible. This is particularly an issue with older Oracle releases. Oracle9*i* Database, and also later releases of Oracle, are "smart enough" to know which flavor of NULL to use in a compound query. The following examples, generated from an Oracle9*i* database, demonstrate this:

```
SELECT 1 num, 'DEFINITE' string FROM DUAL
UNION
SELECT NULL num, 'UNKNOWN' string FROM DUAL;

       NUM STRING
---------- --------
         1 DEFINITE
           UNKNOWN

SELECT 1 num, SYSDATE dates FROM DUAL
UNION
SELECT 2 num, NULL dates FROM DUAL;

       NUM DATES
---------- ---------
         1 06-JAN-02
         2
```

If you are using Oracle8*i* or prior, these queries may cause errors. The examples in the rest of this section are executed against an Oracle8*i* database.

When your set operation includes a character column that corresponds to a NULL literal, you won't have any problems from the use of NULL. All releases of Oracle handle this case. For example, from an Oracle8*i* installation:

```
SELECT 1 num, 'DEFINITE' string FROM DUAL
UNION
SELECT 2 num, NULL string FROM DUAL;

       NUM STRING
---------- --------
         1 DEFINITE
         2
```

Notice that Oracle8*i* considers the character string `'DEFINITE'` from the first component query to be compatible with the NULL value supplied for the corresponding column in the second component query.

However, if a NUMBER or a DATE column of a component query is set to NULL, you must explicitly tell Oracle what "flavor" of NULL to use. Otherwise, you'll encounter errors. For example:

```
SELECT 1 num, 'DEFINITE' string FROM DUAL
UNION
SELECT NULL num, 'UNKNOWN' string FROM DUAL;
SELECT 1 num, 'DEFINITE' string FROM DUAL
       *
ERROR at line 1:
ORA-01790: expression must have same datatype as corresponding expression
```

Note that the use of NULL in the second component query causes a data type mismatch between the first column of the first component query, and the first column of the second component query. Using NULL for a DATE column causes the same problem, as in the following example:

```
SELECT 1 num, SYSDATE dates FROM DUAL
UNION
SELECT 2 num, NULL dates FROM DUAL;
SELECT 1 num, SYSDATE dates FROM DUAL
              *
ERROR at line 1:
ORA-01790: expression must have same datatype as corresponding expression
```

In these cases, you need to cast the NULL to a suitable data type to fix the problem, as in the following examples:

```
SELECT 1 num, 'DEFINITE' string FROM DUAL
UNION
SELECT TO_NUMBER(NULL) NUM, 'UNKNOWN' string FROM DUAL;

       NUM STRING
---------- --------
         1 DEFINITE
           UNKNOWN

SELECT 1 num, SYSDATE dates FROM DUAL
UNION
SELECT 2 num, TO_DATE(NULL) dates FROM DUAL;

       NUM DATES
---------- ---------
         1 06-JAN-02
         2
```

Remember, you'll only encounter these problems of union compatibility when using literal NULL values in Oracle8*i* and earlier releases. The problems go away beginning with the Oracle9*i* Database release.

Rules and Restrictions on Set Operations

Other than the union compatibility conditions discussed at the beginning of the chapter, there are some other rules and restrictions that apply to the set operations. These rules and restrictions are described in this section.

Column names for the result set are derived from the first SELECT:

```
SELECT cust_nbr "Customer ID", name "Customer Name"
FROM customer
WHERE region_id = 5
UNION
SELECT c.cust_nbr "ID", c.name "Name"
FROM customer c
WHERE c.cust_nbr IN (SELECT o.cust_nbr
                     FROM cust_order o, employee e
                     WHERE o.sales_emp_id = e.emp_id
                     AND e.lname = 'MARTIN');

Customer ID Customer Name
----------- ---------------------
          1 Cooper Industries
          2 Emblazon Corp.
          3 Ditech Corp.
          4 Flowtech Inc.
          5 Gentech Industries
          8 Zantech Inc.

6 rows selected.
```

Although both SELECTs use column aliases, the result set takes the column names from the first SELECT. The same thing happens when you create a view based on a set operation. The column names in the view are taken from the first SELECT:

```
CREATE VIEW v_test_cust AS
SELECT cust_nbr "Customer_ID", name "Customer_Name"
FROM customer
WHERE region_id = 5
UNION
SELECT c.cust_nbr "ID", c.name "Name"
FROM customer c
WHERE c.cust_nbr IN (SELECT o.cust_nbr
                     FROM cust_order o, employee e
                     WHERE o.sales_emp_id = e.emp_id
                     AND e.lname = 'MARTIN');

View created.

DESC v_test_cust

Name                             Null?    Type
-------------------------------- -------- ----
Customer_ID                               NUMBER
Customer_Name                             VARCHAR2(45)
```

If you want to use ORDER BY in a query involving set operations, you must place the ORDER BY at the end of the entire statement. The ORDER BY clause can appear only once at the end of the compound query. The component queries can't have individual ORDER BY clauses. For example:

```
SELECT cust_nbr, name
FROM customer
WHERE region_id = 5
UNION
SELECT emp_id, lname
FROM employee
WHERE lname = 'MARTIN'
ORDER BY cust_nbr;

 CUST_NBR NAME
---------- ---------------------
        1 Cooper Industries
        2 Emblazon Corp.
        3 Ditech Corp.
        4 Flowtech Inc.
        5 Gentech Industries
     7654 MARTIN

6 rows selected.
```

Note that the column name used in the ORDER BY clause of this query is taken from the first SELECT. You couldn't order these results by emp_id. If you attempt to ORDER BY emp_id, you will get an error, as in the following example:

```
SELECT cust_nbr, name
FROM customer
WHERE region_id = 5
UNION
SELECT emp_id, lname
FROM employee
WHERE lname = 'MARTIN'
ORDER BY emp_id;
ORDER BY EMP_ID
         *
ERROR at line 8:
ORA-00904: invalid column name
```

The ORDER BY clause doesn't recognize the column names of the second SELECT. To avoid confusion over column names, it is a common practice to ORDER BY column positions:

```
SELECT cust_nbr, name
FROM customer
WHERE region_id = 5
UNION
SELECT emp_id, lname
FROM employee
WHERE lname = 'MARTIN'
ORDER BY 1;
```

```
   CUST_NBR NAME
---------- --------------------
         1 Cooper Industries
         2 Emblazon Corp.
         3 Ditech Corp.
         4 Flowtech Inc.
         5 Gentech Industries
      7654 MARTIN

6 rows selected.
```

For better readability and maintainability of your queries, we recommend that you explicitly use identical column aliases in all the component queries, and then use these column aliases in the ORDER BY clause.

 Unlike ORDER BY, you can use GROUP BY and HAVING clauses in component queries.

The following list summarizes some simple rules, restrictions, and notes that don't require examples:

- Set operations are not permitted on columns of type BLOB, CLOB, BFILE, and VARRAY, nor are set operations permitted on nested table columns.

- Since UNION, INTERSECT, and MINUS operators involve sort operations, they are not allowed on LONG columns. However, UNION ALL is allowed on LONG columns.

- Set operations are not allowed on SELECT statements containing TABLE collection expressions.

- SELECT statements involved in set operations can't use the FOR UPDATE clause.

- The number and size of columns in the SELECT list of component queries are limited by the block size of the database. The total bytes of the columns SELECTed can't exceed one database block.

CHAPTER 8

Hierarchical Queries

A relational database is based upon sets, with each table representing a set. However, there are some types of information that are not directly amenable to the set data structure. Think, for example, of an organization chart, a bill of material in a manufacturing and assembly plant, or a family tree. These types of information are hierarchical in nature, and most conveniently represented in a tree structure. In this chapter we discuss how to represent such hierarchical information in a relational table. We also discuss in detail various SQL constructs that you can use to extract hierarchical information from a relational table.

Representing Hierarchical Information

Let's look at an example to understand how we can represent hierarchical information in a relational database. As a basis for the example, we'll use an organization chart showing how one employee reports to another within a large organization, as shown in Figure 8-1.

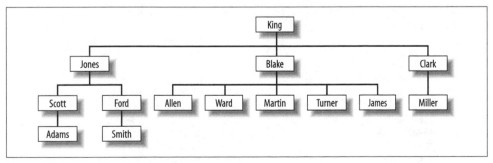

Figure 8-1. An organization chart

Figure 8-1 represents a hierarchy of employees. The information regarding an employee, his manager, and the reporting relationship need to be represented in one table, employee, as shown in the Entity Relationship Diagram in Figure 8-2.

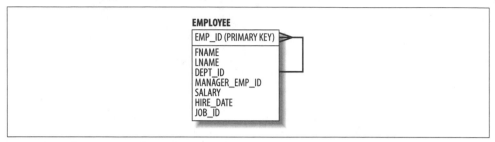

Figure 8-2. The reporting relationship

In Figure 8-2, the employee table refers to itself. The column manager_emp_id refers to the emp_id column of the same table. To represent hierarchical data, you need to make use of a relationship such as when one column of a table references another column of the same table. When such a relationship is implemented using a data-base constraint, it is known as *self-referential integrity constraint*. The corresponding CREATE TABLE statement will look as follows:

```
CREATE TABLE employee (
emp_id          NUMBER (4) CONSTRAINT emp_pk PRIMARY KEY,
fname           VARCHAR2 (15) NOT NULL,
lname           VARCHAR2 (15) NOT NULL,
dept_id         NUMBER (2) NOT NULL,
manager_emp_id  NUMBER (4) CONSTRAINT emp_fk REFERENCES employee(emp_id),
salary          NUMBER (7,2) NOT NULL,
hire_date       DATE NOT NULL,
job_id          NUMBER (3));
```

As a basis for the examples in this chapter, we'll use the following sample data:

```
SELECT emp_id, lname, dept_id, manager_emp_id, salary, hire_date
FROM employee;
```

EMP_ID	LNAME	DEPT_ID	MANAGER_EMP_ID	SALARY	HIRE_DATE
7369	SMITH	20	7902	800	17-DEC-80
7499	ALLEN	30	7698	1600	20-FEB-81
7521	WARD	30	7698	1250	22-FEB-81
7566	JONES	20	7839	2000	02-APR-81
7654	MARTIN	30	7698	1250	28-SEP-81
7698	BLAKE	30	7839	2850	01-MAY-80
7782	CLARK	10	7839	2450	09-JUN-81
7788	SCOTT	20	7566	3000	19-APR-87
7839	KING	10		5000	17-NOV-81
7844	TURNER	30	7698	1500	08-SEP-81

7876 ADAMS	20	7788	1100 23-MAY-87
7900 JAMES	30	7698	950 03-DEC-81
7902 FORD	20	7566	3000 03-DEC-81
7934 MILLER	10	7782	1300 23-JAN-82

The employee table has two important aspects:

- The column manager_emp_id
- The emp_fk constraint

The column manager_emp_id stores the emp_id of the employee's manager. For example, the manager_emp_id for Smith is 7902, which means that Ford is Smith's manager. The employee King doesn't have a manager_emp_id, which indicates that King is the uppermost employee. To be able to represent the uppermost employee, the manager_emp_id column must be nullable.

There is a foreign key constraint on the manager_emp_id column. This enforces the rule that any value put in the manager_emp_id column must be the emp_id of a valid employee. Such a constraint is not mandatory when representing hierarchical information. However, it is a good practice to define database constraints to enforce such business rules.

Before moving on to the following sections on manipulating hierarchies, we will introduce some hierarchy terminology. The following list defines terms that we'll use often when working with hierarchical data:

Node
    A row in a table that represents a specific entry in a hierarchical tree structure. For example, in Figure 8-1 each employee is considered to be a node.

Parent
    A node that is one level up in a tree. In Figure 8-1, King is the parent of Blake, and Blake is the parent of Martin. The term *parent node* is sometimes used in place of just *parent*.

Child
    A node that is one level down in a tree. In Figure 8-1, Blake is a child of King. Blake, in turn, has five children: Allen, Ward, Martin, Turner, and James. The term *child node* is sometimes used in place of just *child*.

Root
    The uppermost node in a hierarchical structure. The definition of a root is that it has no parent. In Figure 8-1, King is the root. You can have only one root in any given tree, but it's worth noting that you can have multiple trees in a hierarchical table. If our employee table stored information on employees from multiple companies, we would have one root per company. The term *root node* is sometimes used in place of *root*.

Leaf

A node with no children, and sometimes called a *leaf node*. Leaf nodes are the antitheses of root nodes, and represent the lowest levels of a tree structure. The leaf nodes in Figure 8-1 are Adams, Smith, Allen, Ward, Martin, Turner, James, and Miller. Leaf nodes do not all need to be at the same level, but they do need to be without children.

Level

A layer of nodes. In Figure 8-1, King constitutes one level. Jones, Blake, and Clark constitute the next level down, and so forth.

Simple Hierarchy Operations

The processes for extracting some types of information from a table storing hierarchical data are relatively simple, and can be performed using the techniques that we have discussed so far in this book. Extracting more complex information requires using some new SQL constructs, which we'll discuss in the section "Oracle SQL Extensions." In this section, we'll discuss the hierarchy operations that can be performed using what you've learned so far.

Finding Root Nodes

Finding the root nodes of a hierarchy tree is easy; look for the nodes with no parents. You may have more than one hierarchy in a table, and consequently more than one root node. In the employee table we discussed earlier, the value for manager_emp_id is NULL for the uppermost employee, and only for the uppermost employee. The following query searches for cases where manager_emp_id is NULL, thereby returning the root node:

```
SELECT emp_id, lname, dept_id, manager_emp_id, salary, hire_date
FROM employee
WHERE manager_emp_id IS NULL;
```

EMP_ID	LNAME	DEPT_ID	MANAGER_EMP_ID	SALARY	HIRE_DATE
7839	KING	10		5000	17-NOV-81

Because the manager_emp_id column defines the hierarchy, it's important that it always contain correct data. While populating data in this table, we must make sure to specify a manager_emp_id for every row other than the row for the uppermost employee. The uppermost employee doesn't report to anyone (doesn't have a manager), and hence manager_emp_id is not applicable for him. If we leave out manager_emp_id values for employees that do have managers, those employees will erroneously show up as root nodes.

Finding a Node's Immediate Parent

You may wish to link nodes to their immediate parents. For example, you might want to print a report showing each employee's manager. The name of each employee's manager can be derived by joining the employee table to itself. This type of join is a self join (discussed in Chapter 3). The following query returns the desired result:

```
SELECT e.lname "Employee", m.lname "Manager"
FROM employee e, employee m
WHERE e.manager_emp_id = m.emp_id;
```

```
Employee    Manager
----------  ----------
SMITH       FORD
ALLEN       BLAKE
WARD        BLAKE
JONES       KING
MARTIN      BLAKE
BLAKE       KING
CLARK       KING
SCOTT       JONES
TURNER      BLAKE
ADAMS       SCOTT
JAMES       BLAKE
FORD        JONES
MILLER      CLARK

13 rows selected.
```

Note this query results in only 13 rows, although the employee table has 14 rows:

```
SELECT COUNT(*) FROM employee;

  COUNT(*)
----------
        14
```

The reason that only 13 rows are returned from the self join is simple. Our query lists employees and their managers. But since the uppermost employee KING doesn't have any manager, that row is not produced in the output. If you want all the employees to be produced in the result, you need an outer join, as in the following example:

```
SELECT e.lname "Employee", m.lname "Manager"
FROM employee e LEFT OUTER JOIN employee m
ON e.manager_emp_id = m.emp_id ;
```

```
Employee              Manager
--------------------  --------------------
SMITH                 FORD
ALLEN                 BLAKE
WARD                  BLAKE
```

```
JONES           KING
MARTIN          BLAKE
BLAKE           KING
CLARK           KING
SCOTT           JONES
KING
TURNER          BLAKE
ADAMS           SCOTT
JAMES           BLAKE
FORD            JONES
MILLER          CLARK
```

14 rows selected.

Outer joins were discussed in detail in Chapter 3.

Finding Leaf Nodes

The opposite problem from finding root nodes, which have no parents, is to find leaf nodes, which have no children. Employees who do not manage anyone are the leaf nodes in the hierarchy tree shown in Figure 8-1. At first glance, the following query seems like it should list all employees from the employee table who are not managers of any other employee:

```
SELECT * FROM employee
WHERE emp_id NOT IN (SELECT manager_emp_id FROM employee);
```

However, when you execute this statement, you will see "No rows selected." Why? It is because the manager_emp_id column contains a NULL value in one row (for the uppermost employee), and NULLs can't be compared to any data value. Therefore, to get the employees who don't manage anyone, you need to rewrite the query as follows:

```
SELECT emp_id, lname, dept_id, manager_emp_id, salary, hire_date
FROM employee e
WHERE emp_id NOT IN
(SELECT manager_emp_id FROM employee
WHERE manager_emp_id IS NOT NULL);
```

EMP_ID	LNAME	DEPT_ID	MANAGER_EMP_ID	SALARY	HIRE_DATE
7369	SMITH	20	7902	800	17-DEC-80
7499	ALLEN	30	7698	1600	20-FEB-81
7521	WARD	30	7698	1250	22-FEB-81
7654	MARTIN	30	7698	1250	28-SEP-81
7844	TURNER	30	7698	1500	08-SEP-81
7876	ADAMS	20	7788	1100	23-MAY-87
7900	JAMES	30	7698	950	03-DEC-81
7934	MILLER	10	7782	1300	23-JAN-82

8 rows selected.

In this example, the subquery returns the emp_id's of all the managers. The outer query then returns all the employees, except the ones returned by the subquery. This query can also be written as a correlated subquery using EXISTS instead of IN:

```
SELECT emp_id, lname, dept_id, manager_emp_id, salary, hire_date
FROM employee e
WHERE NOT EXISTS
(SELECT emp_id FROM employee e1 WHERE e.emp_id = e1.manager_emp_id);
```

EMP_ID	LNAME	DEPT_ID	MANAGER_EMP_ID	SALARY	HIRE_DATE
7369	SMITH	20	7902	800	17-DEC-80
7499	ALLEN	30	7698	1600	20-FEB-81
7521	WARD	30	7698	1250	22-FEB-81
7654	MARTIN	30	7698	1250	28-SEP-81
7844	TURNER	30	7698	1500	08-SEP-81
7876	ADAMS	20	7788	1100	23-MAY-87
7900	JAMES	30	7698	950	03-DEC-81
7934	MILLER	10	7782	1300	23-JAN-82

8 rows selected.

The correlated subquery checks each employee to see whether he is the manager of any other employee. If not, then that particular employee is included in the result set.

Oracle Database 10g introduces a pseudocolumn, CONNECT_BY_ISLEAF, which you can also use to identify leaf nodes. We discuss this pseudocolumn in the section "Enhancements in Oracle Database 10g."

Oracle SQL Extensions

In the previous section, you saw how to perform some operations on a hierarchical tree by using simple SQL techniques. Operations such as traversing a tree, finding levels, etc., require more complex SQL statements, and also require the use of features designed specifically for working with hierarchical data. Oracle provides some extensions to ANSI SQL to facilitate these operations. But before looking at the Oracle SQL extensions, let's look at how you can traverse a tree using ANSI SQL, and at the problems you'll encounter when doing that.

Tree Traversal Using ANSI SQL

Say you want to list each employee with his manager. Using regular Oracle SQL, you can perform self outer-joins on the employee table, as shown here:

```
SELECT e_top.lname, e_2.lname, e_3.lname, e_4.lname
FROM employee e_top LEFT OUTER JOIN employee e_2
                         ON e_top.emp_id = e_2.manager_emp_id
              LEFT OUTER JOIN employee e_3
                         ON e_2.emp_id = e_3.manager_emp_id
```

```
                    LEFT OUTER JOIN employee e_4
                              ON e_3.emp_id = e_4.manager_emp_id
        WHERE e_top.manager_emp_id IS NULL;

        LNAME                LNAME                LNAME                LNAME
        -------------------- -------------------- -------------------- ------
        KING                 JONES                FORD                 SMITH
        KING                 JONES                SCOTT                ADAMS
        KING                 BLAKE                TURNER
        KING                 BLAKE                ALLEN
        KING                 BLAKE                WARD
        KING                 CLARK                MILLER
        KING                 BLAKE                MARTIN
        KING                 BLAKE                JAMES

        8 rows selected.
```

The query returns eight rows, corresponding to the eight branches of the tree. To get those results, the query performs a self join on four instances of the employee table. Four employee table instances are needed in this statement because there are four levels to the hierarchy. Each level is represented by one copy of the employee table. The outer join is required because one employee (KING) has a NULL value in the manager_emp_id column.

This type of query has several drawbacks. First of all, you need to know the number of levels in an organization chart when you write the query, and it's not realistic to assume that you will know that information. It's even less realistic to think that the number of levels will remain stable over time. Moreover, you need to join four instances of the employee table together for a four-level hierarchy. Imagine an organization with 20 levels—you'd need to join 20 instances of the table! Such a join would cause a huge performance problem.

To circumvent problems such as these, Oracle has provided some extensions to ANSI SQL. Oracle provides the following three constructs to effectively and efficiently perform hierarchical queries:

- The START WITH...CONNECT BY clause
- The PRIOR operator
- The LEVEL pseudocolumn

The following sections discuss these three Oracle extensions in detail.

START WITH...CONNECT BY and PRIOR

You can extract information in hierarchical form from a table containing hierarchical data by using the SELECT statement's START WITH...CONNECT BY clause. The syntax for this clause is:

```
[[START WITH condition1]  CONNECT BY condition2]
```

The syntax elements are:

START WITH condition1
> Specifies the root row(s) of the hierarchy. All rows that satisfy condition1 are considered root rows. If you don't specify the START WITH clause, all rows are considered root rows, which is usually not desirable. You can include a sub-query in condition1.

CONNECT BY condition2
> Specifies the relationship between parent rows and child rows in the hierarchy. The relationship is expressed as a comparison expression, where columns from the current row are compared to corresponding parent columns. condition2 must contain the PRIOR operator, which is used to identify columns from the parent row. condition2 cannot contain a subquery.

PRIOR is a built-in Oracle SQL operator that is used with hierarchical queries only. In a hierarchical query, the CONNECT BY clause specifies the relationship between parent and child rows. When you use the PRIOR operator in an expression in the CONNECT BY condition, the expression following the PRIOR keyword is evaluated for the parent row of the current row in the query. In the following example, PRIOR is used to connect each row to its parent by connecting manager_emp_id in the child to emp_id in the parent:

```
SELECT lname, emp_id, manager_emp_id
FROM employee
START WITH manager_emp_id IS NULL
CONNECT BY PRIOR emp_id = manager_emp_id;
```

LNAME	EMP_ID	MANAGER_EMP_ID
KING	7839	
JONES	7566	7839
SCOTT	7788	7566
ADAMS	7876	7788
FORD	7902	7566
SMITH	7369	7902
BLAKE	7698	7839
ALLEN	7499	7698
WARD	7521	7698
MARTIN	7654	7698
TURNER	7844	7698
JAMES	7900	7698
CLARK	7782	7839
MILLER	7934	7782

```
14 rows selected.
```

The PRIOR column does not need to be listed first. The previous query could be restated as:

```
SELECT lname, emp_id, manager_emp_id
FROM employee
```

```
START WITH manager_emp_id IS NULL
CONNECT BY manager_emp_id = PRIOR emp_id;
```

The preceding two PRIOR examples list all the employees in the organization, because each query uses the START WITH clause to begin with the top-most employee (with NULL manager_emp_id). Instead of reporting out the whole organization chart, you may want to list only the subtree under a given employee, JONES for example. To do this, you can modify the START WITH condition so that it specifies JONES as the root of the query. For example:

```
SELECT lname, emp_id, manager_emp_id
FROM employee
START WITH lname = 'JONES'
CONNECT BY manager_emp_id = PRIOR emp_id;

LNAME                   EMP_ID MANAGER_EMP_ID
-------------------- ---------- --------------
JONES                      7566           7839
SCOTT                      7788           7566
ADAMS                      7876           7788
FORD                       7902           7566
SMITH                      7369           7902
```

Since this query considers JONES as the root of the hierarchy, only the employees that belong to the organization tree under JONES (including JONES himself) are returned by the query. Be careful while using conditions such as lname = 'JONES' in hierarchical queries. In this case, if we have two JONES in our organization, the result returned by the hierarchy may be wrong. It is better to use primary or unique key columns, such as emp_id, as the condition in such situations.

In the previous example, we listed the portion of our organization chart headed by the specific employee named "JONES." There can be situations when you may need to print the organization chart headed by any employee that meets a specific condition. For example, you may want to list all employees under the employee who has been working in the company for the longest time. In this case, the starting point of the query (the root) is dependent on a condition. Therefore, you have to use a subquery to generate the information needed to evaluate the condition and pass that information to the main query, as in the following example:

```
SELECT lname, emp_id, manager_emp_id
FROM employee
START WITH hire_date = (SELECT MIN(hire_date) FROM employee)
CONNECT BY manager_emp_id = PRIOR emp_id;

LNAME                   EMP_ID MANAGER_EMP_ID
-------------------- ---------- --------------
BLAKE                      7698           7839
ALLEN                      7499           7698
WARD                       7521           7698
MARTIN                     7654           7698
```

```
TURNER                  7844        7698
JAMES                   7900        7698
```

6 rows selected.

Note the START WITH clause in this example. The subquery in the START WITH clause returns the minimum hire_date in the table, which represents the hire_date of the employee with the longest service. The main query uses this information as the starting point of the hierarchy and lists the organization structure under this employee.

While using a subquery in the START WITH clause, be aware of how many rows will be returned by the subquery. If more than one row is returned when you are expecting just one row (indicated by the = sign), the query will generate an error. You can get around this by replacing = with the IN operator, but be warned that the hierarchical query may then end up dealing with multiple roots.

Since the CONNECT BY condition specifies the parent-child relationship, it cannot contain a loop (also known as a cycle). If a row is both parent (direct ancestor) and child (direct descendent) of another row, then you have a loop. For example, if the employee table had the following two rows, they would represent a loop:

```
EMP_ID LNAME         DEPT_ID MANAGER_EMP_ID   SALARY HIRE_DATE
------ ----------- --------- --------------- --------- ---------
  9001 SMITH            20            9002     1800 15-NOV-61
  9002 ALLEN            30            9001    11600 16-NOV-61
```

 The pseudocolumn CONNECT_BY_ISCYCLE and the keyword NOCYCLE, both introduced in Oracle Database 10g, help identify and ignore cycles. These are discussed later in the chapter.

When a parent-child relationship involves two or more columns, you need to use the PRIOR operator before each parent column. Let's take as an example an assembly in a manufacturing plant. An assembly may consist of several subassemblies, and a given subassembly may further contain one or more subassemblies. All of these are stored in a table, assembly:

DESC assembly

```
Name                      Null?    Type
------------------------- -------- --------------
assembly_type             NOT NULL VARCHAR2(4)
assembly_id               NOT NULL NUMBER(6)
description               NOT NULL VARCHAR2(20)
parent_assembly_type               VARCHAR2(4)
parent_assembly_id                 NUMBER(6)
```

Column assembly_type and assembly_id constitute the primary key of this table, and the columns parent_assembly_type and parent_assembly_id together constitute the self-referential foreign key. Therefore, if you want to perform a hierarchical query on this table, you need to include both columns in the START WITH and the CON-NECT BY clauses. You also need to use the PRIOR operator before each parent column, as shown in the following example:

```
SELECT * FROM assembly
START WITH parent_assembly_type IS NULL
AND parent_assembly_id IS NULL
CONNECT BY parent_assembly_type = PRIOR assembly_type
AND parent_assembly_id = PRIOR assembly_id;
```

```
ASSE ASSEMBLY_ID DESCRIPTION          PARE PARENT_ASSEMBLY_ID
---- ----------- -------------------- ---- ------------------
A           1234 Assembly A#1234
A           1256 Assembly A#1256      A                  1234
B           6543 Part Unit#6543       A                  1234
A           1675 Part Unit#1675       B                  6543
X           9943 Repair Zone 1
X           5438 Repair Unit #5438    X                  9943
X           1675 Readymade Unit #1675 X                  5438

7 rows selected.
```

The LEVEL Pseudocolumn

As we explained earlier, the term level refers to one layer of nodes. For example, in Figure 8-1, the root node (consisting of employee KING) is level 1. The next layer (employees JONES, BLAKE, CLARK) is level 2, and so forth. Oracle provides a pseudocolumn, LEVEL, to represent these levels in a hierarchy tree. Whenever you use the START WITH…CONNECT BY clauses in a hierarchical query, you can use the pseudocolumn LEVEL to return the level number for each row returned by the query. The following example illustrates the use of the LEVEL pseudocolumn:

```
SELECT level, lname, emp_id, manager_emp_id
FROM employee
START WITH manager_emp_id IS NULL
CONNECT BY manager_emp_id = PRIOR emp_id;
```

```
     LEVEL LNAME                    EMP_ID MANAGER_EMP_ID
---------- -------------------- ---------- --------------
         1 KING                       7839
         2 JONES                      7566           7839
         3 SCOTT                      7788           7566
         4 ADAMS                      7876           7788
         3 FORD                       7902           7566
         4 SMITH                      7369           7902
         2 BLAKE                      7698           7839
         3 ALLEN                      7499           7698
         3 WARD                       7521           7698
         3 MARTIN                     7654           7698
         3 TURNER                     7844           7698
         3 JAMES                      7900           7698
```

```
        2 CLARK                  7782            7839
        3 MILLER                 7934            7782

14 rows selected.
```

Note that each employee is now associated with a number, represented by the pseudocolumn LEVEL, that corresponds to that employee's level in the organization chart (see Figure 8-1).

Complex Hierarchy Operations

Using Oracle's hierarchical SQL extensions, you can perform complex, hierarchical queries much more easily than you would be able to do using standard, ANSI SQL.

Finding the Number of Levels

Previously we showed how the LEVEL pseudocolumn generates a level number for each record when we use the START WITH...CONNECT BY clause. You can use the following query to determine the number of levels in the hierarchy by finding the maximum level number returned by the LEVEL pseudocolumn:

```
SELECT MAX(LEVEL)
FROM employee
START WITH manager_emp_id IS NULL
CONNECT BY PRIOR emp_id = manager_emp_id;

MAX(LEVEL)
----------
         4
```

To determine the number of employees at each level, group the results by LEVEL and count the number of employees in each distinct group. For example:

```
SELECT LEVEL, COUNT(emp_id)
FROM employee
START WITH manager_emp_id IS NULL
CONNECT BY PRIOR emp_id = manager_emp_id
GROUP BY LEVEL;

    LEVEL COUNT(EMP_ID)
--------- -------------
        1             1
        2             3
        3             8
        4             2
```

Listing Records in Hierarchical Order

One of the very common programming challenges SQL programmers face is to list records in a hierarchy in their proper hierarchical order. For example, you might wish to list employees with their subordinates underneath them, as in the following query:

```
SELECT LEVEL, LPAD(' ',2*(LEVEL - 1)) || lname "Employee",
       emp_id, manager_emp_id
FROM employee
START WITH manager_emp_id IS NULL
CONNECT BY PRIOR emp_id = manager_emp_id;
```

LEVEL	Employee	EMP_ID	MANAGER_EMP_ID
1	KING	7839	
2	JONES	7566	7839
3	SCOTT	7788	7566
4	ADAMS	7876	7788
3	FORD	7902	7566
4	SMITH	7369	7902
2	BLAKE	7698	7839
3	ALLEN	7499	7698
3	WARD	7521	7698
3	MARTIN	7654	7698
3	TURNER	7844	7698
3	JAMES	7900	7698
2	CLARK	7782	7839
3	MILLER	7934	7782

```
14 rows selected.
```

Notice that by using the expression LPAD(' ',2*(LEVEL - 1)), we are able to align employee names in a manner that corresponds to their level. As the level number increases, the number of spaces returned by the expression increases, and the employee name is further indented.

The previous query lists all the employees in the employee table. If you want to filter out certain employees based on some condition, then you can use a WHERE clause in your hierarchical query. Here is an example:

```
SELECT LEVEL, LPAD(' ',2*(LEVEL - 1)) || lname "Employee",
       emp_id, manager_emp_id, salary
FROM employee
WHERE salary > 2000
START WITH manager_emp_id IS NULL
CONNECT BY manager_emp_id = PRIOR emp_id;
```

LEVEL	Employee	EMP_ID	MANAGER_EMP_ID	SALARY
1	KING	7839		5000
3	SCOTT	7788	7566	3000
3	FORD	7902	7566	3000
2	BLAKE	7698	7839	2850
2	CLARK	7782	7839	2450

This query lists records with `salary` > 2000. The WHERE clause restricts the rows returned by the query without affecting other rows in the hierarchy. In our example, the WHERE condition filtered JONES out of the result, but the employees below JONES in the hierarchy (SCOTT and FORD) are not filtered out, and are still indented as they were when JONES was present. The WHERE clause must come before the START WITH…CONNECT BY clause in a hierarchical query; otherwise, you'll get a syntax error.

 Though the WHERE clause comes before the START WITH…CONNECT BY construct, the filtering happens after the complete hierarchy tree is built.

As discussed earlier, the START WITH clause is optional—i.e., you can have a CONNECT BY without a START WITH. When the START WITH clause is missing, effectively the query doesn't specify where to start building the hierarchy. In that situation, each row of the table is considered a root, and a hierarchy is built for each row. For example:

```
SELECT LEVEL, LPAD(' ',2*(LEVEL - 1)) || lname "Employee",
       emp_id, manager_emp_id, salary
FROM employee
CONNECT BY manager_emp_id = PRIOR emp_id;
```

LEVEL	Employee	EMP_ID	MANAGER_EMP_ID	SALARY
1	SCOTT	7788	7566	3000
2	ADAMS	7876	7788	1100
1	FORD	7902	7566	3000
2	SMITH	7369	7902	800
1	ALLEN	7499	7698	1600
1	WARD	7521	7698	1250
1	JAMES	7900	7698	950
1	TURNER	7844	7698	1500
1	MARTIN	7654	7698	1250
1	MILLER	7934	7782	1300
1	ADAMS	7876	7788	1100
1	JONES	7566	7839	2000
2	SCOTT	7788	7566	3000
3	ADAMS	7876	7788	1100
2	FORD	7902	7566	3000
3	SMITH	7369	7902	800
1	CLARK	7782	7839	2450
2	MILLER	7934	7782	1300
1	BLAKE	7698	7839	2850
2	ALLEN	7499	7698	1600
2	WARD	7521	7698	1250
2	JAMES	7900	7698	950
2	TURNER	7844	7698	1500
2	MARTIN	7654	7698	1250
1	SMITH	7369	7902	800

```
1 KING              7839              5000
2    JONES          7566      7839    2000
3      SCOTT        7788      7566    3000
4        ADAMS      7876      7788    1100
3      FORD         7902      7566    3000
4        SMITH      7369      7902     800
2    CLARK          7782      7839    2450
3      MILLER       7934      7782    1300
2    BLAKE          7698      7839    2850
3      ALLEN        7499      7698    1600
3      WARD         7521      7698    1250
3      JAMES        7900      7698     950
3      TURNER       7844      7698    1500
3      MARTIN       7654      7698    1250
```

```
39 rows selected.
```

This example returns the hierarchy tree for each row in the table. In the organization tree under KING, SCOTT is at level 3; however, in the organization tree under JONES, SCOTT is at level 2, and under the organization tree headed by himself, SCOTT is at level 1.

Checking for Ascendancy

Another common operation on hierarchical data is to check for ascendancy. In an organization chart, you may ask whether one employee has authority over another. For example: "Does JONES have any authority over BLAKE?" To find out, you need to search for BLAKE in the subtree headed by JONES. If you find BLAKE in the subtree, then you know that BLAKE either directly or indirectly reports to JONES. If you don't find BLAKE in the subtree, then you know that JONES doesn't have any authority over BLAKE. The following query searches for BLAKE in the subtree headed by JONES:

```
SELECT *
FROM employee
WHERE lname = 'BLAKE'
START WITH lname = 'JONES'
CONNECT BY manager_emp_id = PRIOR emp_id;
```

```
no rows selected
```

The START WITH…CONNECT BY clause in this example generates the subtree headed by JONES, and the WHERE clause filters this subtree to find BLAKE. As you can see, no rows are returned. This means that BLAKE was not found in JONES's subtree, so you know that JONES has no authority over BLAKE. Let's take a look at another example that produces positive results. This time we'll check to see whether JONES has any authority over SMITH:

```
SELECT emp_id, lname, dept_id, manager_emp_id, salary, hire_date
FROM employee
WHERE lname = 'SMITH'
```

```
START WITH lname = 'JONES'
CONNECT BY manager_emp_id = PRIOR emp_id;

   EMP_ID LNAME          DEPT_ID MANAGER_EMP_ID    SALARY HIRE_DATE
---------- ---------- ---------- -------------- ---------- ---------
      7369 SMITH              20           7902        800 17-DEC-80
```

This time, SMITH was found in the list of employees in JONES's subtree, so you know that at some level JONES has management authority over SMITH.

Deleting a Subtree

Let's assume that the organization we are dealing with splits, and JONES and all his subordinates form a new company. Therefore, we don't need to maintain JONES and his subordinates in our employee table. Furthermore, we need to delete the entire subtree headed by JONES, as shown in Figure 8-1, from our table. We can do this by using a subquery as in the following example:

```
DELETE FROM employee
WHERE emp_id IN
(SELECT emp_id FROM employee
START WITH lname = 'JONES'
CONNECT BY manager_emp_id = PRIOR emp_id);

5 rows deleted.
```

In this example, the subquery generates the subtree headed by JONES, and returns the emp_ids of the employees in that subtree, including JONES's. The outer query then deletes the records with these emp_id values from the employee table.

Listing Multiple Root Nodes

An interesting variation on the problem of listing the root node of a hierarchy is to find and list the root nodes from several hierarchies that are all stored in the same table. For example, you might consider department managers to represent root nodes, and you might further wish to list all department managers found in the employee table.

There are no constraints on the employees belonging to any department. However, you can assume that if A reports to B and B reports to C, and A and C belong to the same department, then B also belongs to the same department. If an employee's manager belongs to another department, then that employee is the uppermost employee, or manager, of his department.

Therefore, to find the uppermost employee in each department, you need to search the tree for those employees whose managers belong to a different department than their own. You can do that using the following query:

```
SELECT emp_id, lname, dept_id, manager_emp_id, salary, hire_date
FROM employee
```

```
START WITH manager_emp_id IS NULL
CONNECT BY manager_emp_id = PRIOR emp_id
AND dept_id != PRIOR dept_id;

EMP_ID LNAME      DEPT_ID MANAGER_EMP_ID SALARY HIRE_DATE
------ --------   -------- -------------- ------ ---------
  7839 KING           10                   5000 17-NOV-81
  7566 JONES          20           7839    2000 02-APR-81
  7698 BLAKE          30           7839    2850 01-MAY-80
```

In this example, the extra condition (dept_id != PRIOR dept_id) added to the CON-NECT BY clause restricts the output to only those employees whose managers belong to a different department than their own.

Listing the Top Few Levels of a Hierarchy

Another common task in dealing with hierarchical data is listing the top few levels of a hierarchy tree. For example, you may want to list top management employees in an organization. Let's assume that the top two levels in our organization chart constitute top management. You can then use the LEVEL pseudocolumn to identify those employees, as in the following example:

```
SELECT emp_id, lname, dept_id, manager_emp_id, salary, hire_date
FROM employee
WHERE LEVEL <= 2
START WITH manager_emp_id IS NULL
CONNECT BY manager_emp_id = PRIOR emp_id;

EMP_ID LNAME      DEPT_ID MANAGER_EMP_ID SALARY HIRE_DATE
------ --------   -------- -------------- ------ ---------
  7839 KING           10                   5000 17-NOV-81
  7566 JONES          20           7839    2000 02-APR-81
  7698 BLAKE          30           7839    2850 01-MAY-80
  7782 CLARK          10           7839    2450 09-JUN-81
```

In this example, the LEVEL <= 2 condition in the WHERE clause restricts the results to only those employees in the top two levels of the organization chart.

Aggregating a Hierarchy

Another challenging requirement is to aggregate a hierarchy. For example, you may want to sum the salaries of all employees reporting to a specific employee. Or, you may want to consider each employee as a root, and for each employee print out the sum of the salaries of all subordinate employees.

The first problem is relatively simple. Earlier we described how to select a subtree headed by an employee. You can easily sum the salaries of all employees in such a subtree. For example:

```
SELECT SUM(salary)
FROM employee
```

```
START WITH lname = 'JONES'
CONNECT BY manager_emp_id = PRIOR emp_id;

SUM(SALARY)
-----------
       9900
```

The START WITH lname = 'JONES' clause generates the subtree headed by JONES, and the SUM(salary) expression sums the salary of employees in this subtree.

The second problem, a seemingly simple extension of the first, is relatively complex. You want to consider each employee as a root, and for each employee you want to sum the salaries of all employees in its subtree. In essence, you want to repeat the previous query for each employee in the table. The following SQL uses an inline view to achieve this:

```
SELECT t2.lname, t2.salary,
(SELECT SUM(t1.salary) FROM employee t1
START WITH t1.lname = t2.lname
CONNECT BY t1.manager_emp_id = PRIOR t1.emp_id) sum_salary
FROM employee t2;

LNAME                    SALARY SUM_SALARY
-------------------- ---------- ----------
SMITH                       800        800
ALLEN                      1600       1600
WARD                       1250       1250
JONES                      2000       9900
MARTIN                     1250       1250
BLAKE                      2850       9400
CLARK                      2450       3750
SCOTT                      3000       4100
KING                       5000      28050
TURNER                     1500       1500
ADAMS                      1100       1100
JAMES                       950        950
FORD                       3000       3800
MILLER                     1300       1300

14 rows selected.
```

In this example, the START WITH...CONNECT BY clause in the inline view generates a subtree for each employee. The inline view executes once for every row in the outer employee table. For each row in the outer employee table, the inline view generates a subtree headed by this employee, and returns the sum of salaries for all the employees in this subtree to the main query.

The result set provides two numbers for each employee. The first number, salary, is the employee's own salary. The second number, sum_salary, is the sum of the salaries of all employees under him (including himself/herself). Often programmers resort to PL/SQL to solve this type of problem. However, this query, which combines the power of hierarchical queries with that of inline views, solves the problem in a much more concise and elegant way.

Ordering Hierarchical Data

Sorting the results from a hierarchical query is a more interesting problem than it first may sound. A hierarchical query with a START WITH...CONNECT BY... construct displays the results in an arbitrary order, as shown in the following example:

```
SELECT LEVEL, LPAD(' ',2*(LEVEL - 1)) || lname "EMPLOYEE",
       emp_id, manager_emp_id
FROM employee
START WITH manager_emp_id IS NULL
CONNECT BY PRIOR emp_id = manager_emp_id;
```

```
    LEVEL EMPLOYEE                  EMP_ID MANAGER_EMP_ID
---------- --------------------  ---------- ---------------
        1 KING                     7839
        2   JONES                  7566          7839
        3     SCOTT                7788          7566
        4       ADAMS              7876          7788
        3     FORD                 7902          7566
        4       SMITH              7369          7902
        2   BLAKE                  7698          7839
        3     ALLEN                7499          7698
        3     WARD                 7521          7698
        3     MARTIN               7654          7698
        3     TURNER               7844          7698
        3     JAMES                7900          7698
        2   CLARK                  7782          7839
        3     MILLER               7934          7782
```

As always, you can use an ORDER BY clause to order the result rows in the way you want. However, in the case of a hierarchical query, an ORDER BY clause can destroy the hierarchical nature of the data returned by the query. This is shown in the following example, which orders the results by last name:

```
SELECT LEVEL, LPAD(' ',2*(LEVEL - 1)) || lname "EMPLOYEE",
       emp_id, manager_emp_id
FROM employee
START WITH manager_emp_id IS NULL
CONNECT BY PRIOR emp_id = manager_emp_id
ORDER BY lname;
```

```
    LEVEL EMPLOYEE                  EMP_ID MANAGER_EMP_ID
---------- --------------------  ---------- ---------------
        4       ADAMS              7876          7788
        3     ALLEN                7499          7698
        2   BLAKE                  7698          7839
        2   CLARK                  7782          7839
        3     FORD                 7902          7566
        3     JAMES                7900          7698
```

```
        2   JONES              7566           7839
        1 KING                 7839
        3     MARTIN           7654           7698
        3     MILLER           7934           7782
        3     SCOTT            7788           7566
        4       SMITH          7369           7902
        3     TURNER           7844           7698
        3     WARD             7521           7698
```

As you can see from this output, it is impossible to identify the hierarchical relation-ship between the rows. To resolve this problem, you can use the SIBLINGS (in Oracle9*i* and later) keyword in the ORDER BY clause, to order the hierarchical data while at the same time preserving the hierarchy. Oracle does this by sorting at each level while ensuring that child nodes remain underneath their parents. For example:

```
SELECT LEVEL, LPAD(' ',2*(LEVEL - 1)) || lname "EMPLOYEE",
       emp_id, manager_emp_id
FROM employee
START WITH manager_emp_id IS NULL
CONNECT BY PRIOR emp_id = manager_emp_id
ORDER SIBLINGS BY lname;
```

```
     LEVEL EMPLOYEE                 EMP_ID MANAGER_EMP_ID
---------- -------------------- ---------- --------------
         1 KING                   7839
         2   BLAKE                7698           7839
         3     ALLEN              7499           7698
         3     JAMES              7900           7698
         3     MARTIN             7654           7698
         3     TURNER             7844           7698
         3     WARD               7521           7698
         2   CLARK                7782           7839
         3     MILLER             7934           7782
         2   JONES                7566           7839
         3     FORD               7902           7566
         4       SMITH            7369           7902
         3     SCOTT              7788           7566
         4       ADAMS            7876           7788
```

In this example's output, BLAKE, CLARK, and JONES are siblings, and they are dis-played in ascending order. So are BLAKE's children: ALLEN, JAMES, MARTIN, TURNER, and WARD.

Finding the Path to a Node

You can list the entire path of a given node starting from the root node using the SYS_CONNECT_BY_PATH function (in Oracle9*i* and later). This function takes two arguments: a column name and a character string. The function then returns a list containing each value of the column from the root node to the current node, sep-arating values by the character string you provide. For example:

```
SELECT SYS_CONNECT_BY_PATH(lname, '#')
FROM employee
```

```
START WITH manager_emp_id IS NULL
CONNECT BY PRIOR emp_id = manager_emp_id;

SYS_CONNECT_BY_PATH(LNAME,'#')
---------------------------------
#KING
#KING#JONES
#KING#JONES#SCOTT
#KING#JONES#SCOTT#ADAMS
#KING#JONES#FORD
#KING#JONES#FORD#SMITH
#KING#BLAKE
#KING#BLAKE#ALLEN
#KING#BLAKE#WARD
#KING#BLAKE#MARTIN
#KING#BLAKE#TURNER
#KING#BLAKE#JAMES
#KING#CLARK
#KING#CLARK#MILLER
```

The preceding query lists the full organizational path for each employee starting at the top. For example, #KING#JONES#FORD#SMITH shows the complete reporting relation of SMITH in the organization.

To understand the usefulness of the SYS_CONNECT_BY_PATH function, think of a trail in a park. The branches of such a trail are illustrated in Figure 8-3.

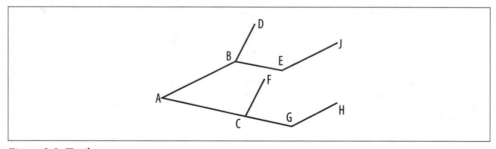

Figure 8-3. Trails

The various points in the trail, and the distance between them is stored in a table, trail:

```
CREATE TABLE trail (
  start_point CHAR,
  end_point   CHAR,
  distance    NUMBER
);

INSERT INTO trail VALUES ('A','B', 3);
INSERT INTO trail VALUES ('A','C', 2.5);
INSERT INTO trail VALUES ('B','D', 2);
INSERT INTO trail VALUES ('B','E', 1.5);
INSERT INTO trail VALUES ('C','F', 2.5);
```

```
INSERT INTO trail VALUES ('C','G', 2.5);
INSERT INTO trail VALUES ('G','H', 3.5);
INSERT INTO trail VALUES ('E','J', 1.5);
COMMIT;
```

You need to find the total distance of each point in the trail from the starting point "A." The following query uses SYS_CONNECT_BY_PATH to print the distance of each point concatenated with the distances of each of its ancestors in the tree:

```
SELECT end_point,
       SUBSTR(SYS_CONNECT_BY_PATH(distance,'+'),2) total_distance
FROM trail
START WITH start_point = 'A'
CONNECT BY start_point = PRIOR end_point;

E TOTAL_DISTANCE
- --------------------
B 3
D 3+2
E 3+1.5
J 3+1.5+1.5
C 2.5
F 2.5+2.5
G 2.5+2.5
H 2.5+2.5+3.5
```

The SUBSTR function takes out the first "+" in the query's output. Now, each of the total_distance expressions, one for each point, can be evaluated to compute the total distance. One way to evaluate such expressions is to write an eval function, as shown in the following code:

```
CREATE OR REPLACE FUNCTION eval (exp IN VARCHAR2) RETURN NUMBER IS
    result NUMBER;
BEGIN
    EXECUTE IMMEDIATE 'SELECT ' || exp || ' FROM DUAL' INTO result;
    RETURN result;
EXCEPTION
    WHEN OTHERS THEN
    RETURN NULL;
END;
/
```

The following example uses the eval function to compute the total distance of each point in the trail from the starting point A:

```
SELECT end_point,
       eval(SUBSTR(SYS_CONNECT_BY_PATH(distance,'+'),2)) total_distance
FROM trail
START WITH start_point = 'A'
CONNECT BY start_point = PRIOR end_point;

E TOTAL_DISTANCE
- --------------
B              3
D              5
```

```
E        4.5
J        6
C        2.5
F        5
G        5
H        8.5
```

From this output, it is easy to figure out how far each point is in the trail from the starting point "A."

Restrictions on Hierarchical Queries

Through Oracle8*i*, the following restrictions apply to hierarchical queries.

- A hierarchical query can't use a join.
- A hierarchical query cannot select data from a view that involves a join.

These restrictions were removed with the release of Oracle9*i*.

Enhancements in Oracle Database 10g

Oracle Database 10g introduces some new features for hierarchical queries. The new features include the CONNECT_BY_ROOT operator, the new CONNECT_BY_ISCYCLE and CONNECT_BY_ISLEAF pseudocolumns, and the NOCYCLE keyword. We will discuss each of these enhancements in the following sections.

Getting Data from the Root Row

Remember how you can use the PRIOR operator to retrieve a value from a node's parent row? You can now use the CONNECT_BY_ROOT operator to retrieve a value from a node's root. For example:

```
SELECT lname "Employee", CONNECT_BY_ROOT lname "Top Manager"
FROM employee
START WITH manager_emp_id = 7839
CONNECT BY PRIOR emp_id = manager_emp_id;

Employee             Top Manager
-------------------- -----------
JONES                JONES
SCOTT                JONES
ADAMS                JONES
FORD                 JONES
SMITH                JONES
BLAKE                BLAKE
ALLEN                BLAKE
WARD                 BLAKE
MARTIN               BLAKE
TURNER               BLAKE
```

```
JAMES          BLAKE
CLARK          CLARK
MILLER         CLARK
```

In this example, the hierarchy is built by starting with the rows that meet the condition `manager_emp_id = 7839`. This means that anyone whose manager is 7839 will be considered a root for this query. Those employees will be listed in the result set of the query along with the name of the top-most manager in their tree. The CONNECT_BY_ROOT operator returns that top-most manager name by accessing the root row for each row returned by the query.

Ignoring Cycles

Cycles are not allowed in a true tree structure. But life is not perfect, and someday you're bound to encounter hierarchical data containing cycles in which a node's child is also its parent. Such cycles are usually not good, need to be fixed, but can be frustratingly difficult to identify. You can try to find cycles by issuing a START WITH…CONNECT BY query, but such a query will report an error if there is a cycle (also known as a loop) in the data. In Oracle Database 10g, all this changes.

To allow the START WITH…CONNECT BY construct to work properly even if cycles are present in the data, Oracle Database 10g provides the new NOCYCLE keyword. If there are cycles in your data, you can use the NOCYCLE keyword in the CONNECT BY clause, and you will not get an error when hierarchically querying that data.

The test data we have in the employee table doesn't have a cycle. To test the NOCYCLE feature, you can introduce a cycle into the existing employee data by updating the `manager_emp_id` column of the top-most employee (KING with emp_id=7839) with the `manager_emp_id` of one of the lowest level employees (MARTIN with emp_id = 7654):

```
UPDATE employee
SET manager_emp_id = 7654
WHERE manager_emp_id IS NULL;
```

Now, if you perform the following hierarchical query, you will get an ORA-01436 error:

```
SELECT LEVEL, LPAD(' ',2*(LEVEL - 1)) || lname "EMPLOYEE",
       emp_id, manager_emp_id
FROM employee
START WITH emp_id = 7839
CONNECT BY PRIOR emp_id = manager_emp_id;
```

```
  LEVEL EMPLOYEE                 EMP_ID MANAGER_EMP_ID
---------- -------------------- ---------- --------------
      1 KING                       7839           7654
      2   JONES                    7566           7839
      3     SCOTT                  7788           7566
      4       ADAMS                7876           7788
```

```
3       FORD                    7902        7566
4         SMITH                 7369        7902
2     BLAKE                     7698        7839
3       ALLEN                   7499        7698
3       WARD                    7521        7698
3       MARTIN                  7654        7698
4         KING                  7839        7654
5           JONES               7566        7839
6             SCOTT             7788        7566
7               ADAMS           7876        7788
6             FORD              7902        7566
```
ERROR:
ORA-01436: CONNECT BY loop in user data

15 rows selected.

Other than the error, notice that the whole tree starting with KING starts repeating under MARTIN. This is erroneous and confusing. Use the NOCYCLE keyword in the CONNECT BY clause to get rid of the error message, and to prevent the listing of erroneously cyclic data:

```
SELECT LEVEL, LPAD(' ',2*(LEVEL - 1)) || lname "EMPLOYEE",
       emp_id, manager_emp_id
FROM employee
START WITH emp_id = 7839
CONNECT BY NOCYCLE PRIOR emp_id = manager_emp_id;
```

```
     LEVEL EMPLOYEE             EMP_ID MANAGER_EMP_ID
---------- -------------------- ---------- --------------
         1 KING                   7839        7654
         2   JONES                7566        7839
         3     SCOTT              7788        7566
         4       ADAMS            7876        7788
         3     FORD               7902        7566
         4       SMITH            7369        7902
         2   BLAKE                7698        7839
         3     ALLEN              7499        7698
         3     WARD               7521        7698
         3     MARTIN             7654        7698
         3     TURNER             7844        7698
         3     JAMES              7900        7698
         2   CLARK                7782        7839
         3     MILLER             7934        7782
```

This query recognizes that there is a cycle, ignores the cycle (as an impact of the NOCYCLE keyword), and returns the rows as if there were no cycles. Having the ability to query data containing cycles, your next problem is to identify those cycles.

You can use the NOCYCLE keyword regardless of whether you have a cycle in your data.

Identifying Cycles

It is sometimes difficult to identify cycles in hierarchical data. Oracle Database 10g's new pseudocolumn, CONNECT_BY_ISCYCLE, can help you identify the cycles in the data easily. CONNECT_BY_ISCYCLE can be used only in conjunction with the NOCYCLE keyword in a hierarchical query. The CONNECT_BY_ISCYCLE pseudocolumn returns 1 if the current row has a child that is also its ancestor; otherwise, it returns 0. For example:

```
SELECT lname, CONNECT_BY_ISCYCLE
FROM employee
START WITH emp_id = 7839
CONNECT BY NOCYCLE PRIOR emp_id = manager_emp_id;
```

LNAME	CONNECT_BY_ISCYCLE
KING	0
JONES	0
SCOTT	0
ADAMS	0
FORD	0
SMITH	0
BLAKE	0
ALLEN	0
WARD	0
MARTIN	1
TURNER	0
JAMES	0
CLARK	0
MILLER	0

Since MARTIN is KING's manager in this data set, and MARTIN also comes under KING in the organization tree, the row for MARTIN has the value 1 for CONNECT_BY_ISCYCLE.

 For correct results in subsequent queries, you should revert our example data back to its original state by rolling back the earlier change that forced a cycle in the data. If you have already committed the previous UPDATE, you should update the employee table again to set the manager_emp_id column to NULL for KING.

Identifying Leaf Nodes

In a tree structure, the nodes at the lowest level of the tree are referred to as leaf nodes. Leaf nodes have no children. CONNECT_BY_ISLEAF is a pseudocolumn that returns 1 if the current row is a leaf, and returns 0 if the current row is not a leaf. For example:

```
SELECT lname, CONNECT_BY_ISLEAF
FROM employee
START WITH manager_emp_id IS NULL
CONNECT BY PRIOR emp_id = manager_emp_id;


LNAME           CONNECT_BY_ISLEAF
--------------- -----------------
KING                            0
JONES                           0
SCOTT                           0
ADAMS                           1
FORD                            0
SMITH                           1
BLAKE                           0
ALLEN                           1
WARD                            1
MARTIN                          1
TURNER                          1
JAMES                           1
CLARK                           0
MILLER                          1
```

This new feature can help simplify SQL statements that need to identify all the leaf nodes in a hierarchy. Without this pseudocolumn, to identify the leaf nodes, you would write a query like the following:

```
SELECT emp_id, lname, salary, hire_date
FROM employee e
WHERE NOT EXISTS
(SELECT emp_id FROM employee e1 WHERE e.emp_id = e1.manager_emp_id);


 EMP_ID LNAME               SALARY HIRE_DATE
------- --------------- ---------- ---------
   7369 SMITH                  800 17-DEC-80
   7499 ALLEN                 1600 20-FEB-81
   7521 WARD                  1250 22-FEB-81
   7654 MARTIN                1250 28-SEP-81
   7844 TURNER                1500 08-SEP-81
   7876 ADAMS                 1100 23-MAY-87
   7900 JAMES                  950 03-DEC-81
   7934 MILLER                1300 23-JAN-82
```

However, you can make this query much simpler by using the new pseudocolumn CONNECT_BY_ISLEAF, as shown here:

```
SELECT emp_id, lname, salary, hire_date
FROM employee e
WHERE CONNECT_BY_ISLEAF = 1
START WITH manager_emp_id IS NULL
CONNECT BY PRIOR emp_id = manager_emp_id;
```

```
EMP_ID LNAME               SALARY HIRE_DATE
------- ---------------- ---------- ---------
   7876 ADAMS              1100 23-MAY-87
   7369 SMITH               800 17-DEC-80
   7499 ALLEN              1600 20-FEB-81
   7521 WARD               1250 22-FEB-81
   7654 MARTIN             1250 28-SEP-81
   7844 TURNER             1500 08-SEP-81
   7900 JAMES               950 03-DEC-81
   7934 MILLER             1300 23-JAN-82
```

This query builds the complete organization tree, and filters out only the leaf nodes by performing the check CONNECT_BY_ISLEAF = 1.

CHAPTER 9

DECODE and CASE

Whether it is for user presentation, report formatting, or data feed extraction, data is seldom presented exactly as it is stored in the database. Instead, data is generally combined, translated, or formatted in some way. Although procedural languages such as PL/SQL and Java provide many tools for manipulating data, it is often desirable to perform these manipulations as the data is extracted from the database. Similarly, when updating data, it is far easier to modify the data in place rather than to extract it, modify it, and apply the modified data back to the database. This chapter will focus on two powerful features of Oracle SQL that facilitate various data manipulations: the CASE expression and the DECODE function. Along the way we'll also demonstrate the use of several other functions (such as NVL and NVL2).

DECODE, NULLIF, NVL, and NVL2

Most of Oracle's built-in functions are designed to solve a specific problem. If you need to find the last day of the month containing a particular date, for example, the LAST_DAY function is just the ticket. The DECODE, NULLIF, NVL, and NVL2 functions, however, do not solve a specific problem; rather, they are best described as inline if-then-else statements. These functions are used to make decisions based on data values within a SQL statement without resorting to a procedural language like PL/SQL. Table 9-1 shows the syntax and logic equivalent for each of the four functions.

Table 9-1. If-then-else function logic

Function syntax	Logic equivalent
DECODE(E1, E2, E3, E4)	IF E1 = E2 THEN E3 ELSE E4
NULLIF(E1, E2)	IF E1 = E2 THEN NULL ELSE E1
NVL(E1, E2)	IF E1 IS NULL THEN E2 ELSE E1
NVL2(E1, E2, E3)	IF E1 IS NULL THEN E3 ELSE E2

DECODE

The DECODE function can be thought of as an inline IF statement. DECODE takes three or more expressions as arguments. Each expression can be a column, a literal, a function, or even a subquery. Let's look at a simple example using DECODE:

```
SELECT lname,
  DECODE(manager_emp_id, NULL, 'HEAD HONCHO', 'WORKER BEE') emp_type
FROM employee;

LNAME                EMP_TYPE
-------------------- -----------
SMITH                WORKER BEE
ALLEN                WORKER BEE
WARD                 WORKER BEE
JONES                WORKER BEE
MARTIN               WORKER BEE
BLAKE                WORKER BEE
CLARK                WORKER BEE
SCOTT                WORKER BEE
KING                 HEAD HONCHO
TURNER               WORKER BEE
ADAMS                WORKER BEE
JAMES                WORKER BEE
FORD                 WORKER BEE
MILLER               WORKER BEE
```

In this example, the first expression is a column, the second is NULL, and the third and fourth expressions are character literals. The intent is to determine whether each employee has a manager by checking whether an employee's manager_emp_id column is NULL. The DECODE function in this example compares each row's manager_emp_id column (the first expression) to NULL (the second expression). If the result of the comparison is true, DECODE returns 'HEAD HONCHO' (the third expression); otherwise, 'WORKER BEE' (the last expression) is returned.

Since the DECODE function compares two expressions and returns one of two expressions to the caller, it is important that the expression types are identical or that they can at least be translated to be the same type. This example works because E1 can be compared to E2, and E3 and E4 have the same type. If this were not the case, Oracle would raise an exception, as illustrated by the following example:

```
SELECT lname,
  DECODE(manager_emp_id, SYSDATE, 'HEAD HONCHO', 'WORKER BEE') emp_type
FROM employee;

ERROR at line 1:
ORA-00932: inconsistent datatypes: expected DATE got NUMBER
```

Since the manager_emp_id column, which is numeric, cannot be converted to a DATE type, the Oracle server cannot perform the comparison and must throw an exception.

The same exception would be thrown if the two return expressions (E3 and E4) did not have comparable types.

The previous example demonstrates the use of a DECODE function with the minimum number of parameters (four). The next example demonstrates how additional sets of parameters may be utilized for more complex logic:

```
SELECT p.part_nbr part_nbr, p.name part_name, s.name supplier,
  DECODE(p.status,
    'INSTOCK', 'In Stock',
    'DISC', 'Discontinued',
    'BACKORD', 'Backordered',
    'ENROUTE', 'Arriving Shortly',
    'UNAVAIL', 'No Shipment Scheduled',
    'Unknown') part_status
FROM part p INNER JOIN supplier s
ON p.supplier_id = s.supplier_id;
```

PART_NBR	PART_NAME	SUPPLIER	PART_STATUS
AI5-4557	Acme Part AI5-4557	Acme Industries	In Stock
TZ50828	Tilton Part TZ50828	Tilton Enterprises	In Stock
EI-T5-001	Eastern Part EI-T5-001	Eastern Importers	In Stock

This example compares the value of a part's status column to each of five values, and, if a match is found, returns the corresponding string. If a match is not found, then the string 'Unknown' is returned. Although the 12 parameters in this example are a great deal more than the 4 parameters of the earlier example, we are still a long way from the maximum allowable parameters, which is 255.

NULLIF

The NULLIF function compares two expressions and returns NULL if the expressions are equivalent, or the first expression otherwise. The equivalent logic using DECODE looks as follows:

```
DECODE(E1, E2, NULL, E1)
```

NULLIF is useful if you want to substitute NULL for a column's value, as demonstrated by the next query, which shows salary information for only those employees making less than $2000:

```
SELECT fname, lname,
  NULLIF(salary, GREATEST(2000, salary)) salary
FROM employee;
```

FNAME	LNAME	SALARY
JOHN	SMITH	800
KEVIN	ALLEN	1600
CYNTHIA	WARD	1250
TERRY	JONES	

```
KENNETH          MARTIN                    1250
MARION           BLAKE
CAROL            CLARK
DONALD           SCOTT
FRANCIS          KING
MARY             TURNER                    1500
DIANE            ADAMS                     1100
FRED             JAMES                      950
JENNIFER         FORD
BARBARA          MILLER                    1300
```

In this example, the GREATEST function returns either the employee's salary or 2000, whichever is greater. The NULLIF function compares this value to the employee's salary and returns NULL if they are the same.

NVL and NVL2

The NVL and NVL2 functions allow you to test an expression to see whether it is NULL. If an expression is NULL, you can return an alternate, non-NULL value, to use in its place. Since any of the expressions in a DECODE statement can be NULL, the NVL and NVL2 functions are actually specialized versions of DECODE. The following example uses NVL2 to produce the same results as the DECODE example shown in a previous section:

```
SELECT lname,
    NVL2(manager_emp_id, 'WORKER BEE', 'HEAD HONCHO') emp_type
FROM employee;

LNAME                 EMP_TYPE
--------------------  -----------
SMITH                 WORKER BEE
ALLEN                 WORKER BEE
WARD                  WORKER BEE
JONES                 WORKER BEE
MARTIN                WORKER BEE
BLAKE                 WORKER BEE
CLARK                 WORKER BEE
SCOTT                 WORKER BEE
KING                  HEAD HONCHO
TURNER                WORKER BEE
ADAMS                 WORKER BEE
JAMES                 WORKER BEE
FORD                  WORKER BEE
MILLER                WORKER BEE
```

NVL2 looks at the first expression, manager_emp_id in this case. If that expression evaluates to NULL, NVL2 returns the third expression. If the first expression is not NULL, NVL2 returns the second expression. Use NVL2 when you wish to specify alternate values to be returned for the case when an expression is NULL, and also for the case when an expression is not NULL.

The NVL function is most commonly used to substitute a default value when a column is NULL. Otherwise, the column value itself is returned. The next example shows the ID of each employee's manager, but substitutes the word 'NONE' when no manager has been assigned (i.e., when manager_emp_id is NULL):

```
SELECT emp.lname employee,
  NVL(mgr.lname, 'NONE') manager
FROM employee emp LEFT OUTER JOIN employee mgr
ON emp.manager_emp_id = mgr.emp_id;
```

EMPLOYEE	MANAGER
FORD	JONES
SCOTT	JONES
JAMES	BLAKE
TURNER	BLAKE
MARTIN	BLAKE
WARD	BLAKE
ALLEN	BLAKE
MILLER	CLARK
ADAMS	SCOTT
CLARK	KING
BLAKE	KING
JONES	KING
SMITH	FORD
KING	NONE

Even though DECODE may be substituted for any NVL or NVL2 function, most people prefer to use NVL or NVL2 when checking to see if an expresssion is NULL, presumably because the intent is clearer. Hopefully, the next section will convince you to use CASE expressions whenever you are in need of if-then-else functionality. Then you won't need to worry about which built-in function to use.

The Case for CASE

The CASE expression made its SQL debut in the SQL-92 specification in 1992. Eight years later, Oracle included the CASE expression in the Oracle8*i* release. Like the DECODE function, the CASE expression enables conditional logic within a SQL statement, which might explain why Oracle took so much time implementing this particular feature. If you have been using Oracle for a number of years, you might wonder why you should care about the CASE expression, since DECODE does the job nicely. Here are several reasons why you should make the switch:

- CASE expressions can be used everywhere that DECODE functions are permitted.
- CASE expressions are more readable than DECODE expressions.

- CASE expressions execute faster than DECODE expressions.[*]
- CASE expressions handle complex logic more gracefully than DECODE expressions.
- CASE is ANSI-compliant, whereas DECODE is proprietary.

The only downside to using CASE over DECODE is that CASE expressions are not supported in Oracle8i's PL/SQL language. If you are using Oracle9i Database or Oracle Database 10g, however, any SQL statements executed from PL/SQL may include CASE expressions.

The SQL-92 specification defines two distinct flavors of the CASE expression: *searched* and *simple*. Searched CASE expressions are the only type supported in the Oracle8i release. If you are using a later release, you may also use simple CASE expressions.

Searched CASE Expressions

A searched CASE expression evaluates a number of conditions and returns a result determined by which condition is true. The syntax for the searched CASE expression is as follows:

```
CASE
   WHEN C1 THEN R1
   WHEN C2 THEN R2
   . . .
   WHEN CN THEN RN
   ELSE RD
END
```

In the syntax definition, C1, C2...Cn represent conditions, and R1, R2...RN represent results. You can use up to 127 WHEN clauses in each CASE expression, so the logic can be quite robust. Conditions are evaluated in order. When a condition is found that evaluates to TRUE, the corresponding result is returned, and execution of the CASE logic ends. Therefore, carefully order WHEN clauses to ensure that your desired results are achieved. The following example illustrates the use of the CASE statement by determining the proper string to show on an order status report:

```
SELECT co.order_nbr, co.cust_nbr,
   CASE WHEN co.expected_ship_dt IS NULL THEN 'NOT YET SCHEDULED'
     WHEN co.expected_ship_dt <= SYSDATE THEN 'SHIPPING DELAYED'
     WHEN co.expected_ship_dt <= SYSDATE + 2 THEN 'SHIPPING SOON'
     ELSE 'BACKORDERED'
   END ship_status
```

[*] Since CASE is built into Oracle's SQL grammar, there is no need to call a function in order to evaluate the if-then-else logic. Although the difference in execution time is miniscule for a single call, the aggregate time savings from not calling a function should become noticeable when working with large result sets.

```
FROM cust_order co
WHERE co.ship_dt IS NULL AND co.cancelled_dt IS NULL;

ORDER_NBR   CUST_NBR SHIP_STATUS
---------- ---------- -----------------
      1001          1 SHIPPING DELAYED
      1003          4 SHIPPING DELAYED
      1004          4 SHIPPING DELAYED
      1005          8 SHIPPING DELAYED
      1007          5 SHIPPING DELAYED
      1008          5 SHIPPING DELAYED
      1009          1 SHIPPING DELAYED
      1012          1 SHIPPING DELAYED
      1017          4 SHIPPING DELAYED
      1019          4 SHIPPING DELAYED
      1021          8 SHIPPING DELAYED
      1025          5 SHIPPING DELAYED
      1027          5 SHIPPING DELAYED
      1029          1 SHIPPING DELAYED
```

Similar to DECODE, all results in a CASE expression must have comparable types; otherwise, ORA-00932 will be thrown. Each condition in each WHEN clause is independent of the others, however, so your conditions can include various data types, as demonstrated in the next example:

```
SELECT co.order_nbr, co.cust_nbr,
  CASE
    WHEN co.sale_price > 10000 THEN 'BIG ORDER'
    WHEN co.cust_nbr IN
     (SELECT cust_nbr FROM customer WHERE tot_orders > 100)
      THEN 'ORDER FROM FREQUENT CUSTOMER'
    WHEN co.order_dt < TRUNC(SYSDATE) - 7 THEN 'OLD ORDER'
    ELSE 'UNINTERESTING ORDER'
  END order_type
FROM cust_order co
WHERE co.ship_dt IS NULL AND co.cancelled_dt IS NULL;

ORDER_NBR   CUST_NBR ORDER_TYPE
---------- ---------- ------------
      1001          1 OLD ORDER
      1003          4 OLD ORDER
      1004          4 OLD ORDER
      1005          8 OLD ORDER
      1007          5 OLD ORDER
      1008          5 OLD ORDER
      1009          1 OLD ORDER
      1012          1 OLD ORDER
      1017          4 OLD ORDER
      1019          4 OLD ORDER
      1021          8 OLD ORDER
      1025          5 OLD ORDER
      1027          5 OLD ORDER
      1029          1 OLD ORDER
```

Simple CASE Expressions

Simple CASE expressions are structured differently than searched CASE expressions in that the WHEN clauses contain expressions instead of conditions, and a single expression to be compared to the expressions in each WHEN clause is placed in the CASE clause. Here's the syntax:

```
CASE E0
   WHEN E1 THEN R1
   WHEN E2 THEN R2
   ...
   WHEN EN THEN RN
   ELSE RD
END
```

Each of the expressions E1...EN are compared to expression E0. If a match is found, the corresponding result is returned; otherwise, the default result (*RD*) is returned. All of the expressions must be of the same type, since they all must be compared to *E0*, making simple CASE expressions less flexible than searched CASE expressions. The next example illustrates the use of a simple CASE expression to translate the status code stored in the part table:

```
SELECT p.part_nbr part_nbr, p.name part_name, s.name supplier,
  CASE p.status
     WHEN 'INSTOCK' THEN 'In Stock'
     WHEN 'DISC' THEN 'Discontinued'
     WHEN 'BACKORD' THEN 'Backordered'
     WHEN 'ENROUTE' THEN 'Arriving Shortly'
     WHEN 'UNAVAIL' THEN 'No Shipment Scheduled'
     ELSE 'Unknown'
  END part_status
FROM part p INNER JOIN supplier s
ON p.supplier_id = s.supplier_id;
```

PART_NBR	PART_NAME	SUPPLIER	PART_STATUS
AI5-4557	Acme Part AI5-4557	Acme Industries	In Stock
TZ50828	Tilton Part TZ50828	Tilton Enterprises	In Stock
EI-T5-001	Eastern Part EI-T5-001	Eastern Importers	In Stock

A searched CASE can do everything that a simple CASE can do, which is probably the reason Oracle only implemented searched CASE expressions the first time around. For certain uses, such as translating values for a column, a simple expression may prove more efficient if the expression being evaluated is computed via a function call.

DECODE and CASE Examples

The following sections present a variety of examples illustrating the uses of conditional logic in SQL statements. Although we recommend that you use the CASE expression rather than the DECODE function, where feasible we provide both DECODE and CASE versions of each example to help illustrate the differences between the two approaches.

Result Set Transformations

You may have run into a situation where you are performing aggregations over a finite set of values, such as days of the week or months of the year, but you want the result set to contain one row with N columns rather than N rows with two columns. Consider the following query, which aggregates sales data for each day of the week:

```
SELECT TO_CHAR(order_dt, 'DAY') day_of_week,
  SUM(sale_price) tot_sales
FROM cust_order
WHERE sale_price IS NOT NULL
GROUP BY TO_CHAR(order_dt, 'DAY')
ORDER BY 2 DESC;

DAY_OF_WEEK  TOT_SALES
------------ ----------
SUNDAY             396
WEDNESDAY          180
MONDAY             112
FRIDAY              50
SATURDAY            50
```

In order to transform this result set into a single row with seven columns (one for each day in the week), you will need to fabricate a column for each day of the week and, within each column, sum only those records whose order date falls in the desired day. You can do that with DECODE:

```
SELECT
  SUM(DECODE(TO_CHAR (order_dt, 'DAY'), 'SUNDAY   ', sale_price, 0)) SUN,
  SUM(DECODE(TO_CHAR (order_dt, 'DAY'), 'MONDAY   ', sale_price, 0)) MON,
  SUM(DECODE(TO_CHAR (order_dt, 'DAY'), 'TUESDAY  ', sale_price, 0)) TUE,
  SUM(DECODE(TO_CHAR (order_dt, 'DAY'), 'WEDNESDAY', sale_price, 0)) WED,
  SUM(DECODE(TO_CHAR (order_dt, 'DAY'), 'THURSDAY ', sale_price, 0)) THU,
  SUM(DECODE(TO_CHAR (order_dt, 'DAY'), 'FRIDAY   ', sale_price, 0)) FRI,
  SUM(DECODE(TO_CHAR (order_dt, 'DAY'), 'SATURDAY ', sale_price, 0)) SAT
FROM cust_order
WHERE sale_price IS NOT NULL;

      SUN       MON       TUE       WED       THU       FRI       SAT
--------- --------- --------- --------- --------- --------- ---------
      396       112         0       180         0        50        50
```

Each of the seven columns in the previous query are identical, except for the day being checked by the DECODE function. For the SUN column, for example, a value of 0 is returned unless an order was booked on a Sunday, in which case the sale_price column is returned. When the values from all orders are summed, only Sunday orders are added to the total, which has the effect of summing all Sunday orders while ignoring orders for all other days of the week. The same logic is used for Monday, Tuesday, etc., to sum orders for each of the other days.

The CASE version of this query is as follows:

```
SELECT
  SUM(CASE WHEN TO_CHAR(order_dt, 'DAY') = 'SUNDAY   '
    THEN sale_price ELSE 0 END) SUN,
  SUM(CASE WHEN TO_CHAR(order_dt, 'DAY') = 'MONDAY   '
    THEN sale_price ELSE 0 END) MON,
  SUM(CASE WHEN TO_CHAR(order_dt, 'DAY') = 'TUESDAY  '
    THEN sale_price ELSE 0 END) TUE,
  SUM(CASE WHEN TO_CHAR(order_dt, 'DAY') = 'WEDNESDAY'
    THEN sale_price ELSE 0 END) WED,
  SUM(CASE WHEN TO_CHAR(order_dt, 'DAY') = 'THURSDAY '
    THEN sale_price ELSE 0 END) THU,
  SUM(CASE WHEN TO_CHAR(order_dt, 'DAY') = 'FRIDAY   '
    THEN sale_price ELSE 0 END) FRI,
  SUM(CASE WHEN TO_CHAR(order_dt, 'DAY') = 'SATURDAY '
    THEN sale_price ELSE 0 END) SAT
FROM cust_order
WHERE sale_price IS NOT NULL;
```

SUN	MON	TUE	WED	THU	FRI	SAT
396	112	0	180	0	50	50

Obviously, such transformations are only practical when the number of values is relatively small. Aggregating sales for each weekday or month works fine, but expanding the query to aggregate sales for each week, with a column for each week, would quickly become tedious.

Selective Function Execution

Imagine you're generating an inventory report. Most of the information resides in your local database, but a trip across a gateway to an external, non-Oracle database is required to gather information for parts supplied by Acme Industries. The round trip from your database through the gateway to the external server and back takes 1.5 seconds on average. There are 10,000 parts in your database, but only 100 require information via the gateway. You create a user-defined function called get_resupply_date to retrieve the resupply date for parts supplied by ACME, and include it in your query:

```
SELECT s.name supplier_name, p.name part_name, p.part_nbr part_number
  p.inventory_qty in_stock, p.resupply_date resupply_date,
  my_pkg.get_resupply_date(p.part_nbr) acme_resupply_date
FROM part p INNER JOIN supplier s
ON p.supplier_id = s.supplier_id;
```

You then include logic in your reporting tool to use the acme_resupply_date instead of the resupply_date column if the supplier's name is Acme Industries. You kick off the report, sit back, and wait for the results. And wait. And wait...

Unfortunately, the server is forced to make 10,000 trips across the gateway when only 100 are required. In these types of situations, it is far more efficient to call the function only when necessary, instead of always calling the function and discarding the results when not needed:

```
SELECT s.name supplier_name, p.name part_name, p.part_nbr part_number,
  p.inventory_qty in_stock,
  DECODE(s.name, 'Acme Industries',
    my_pkg.get_resupply_date(p.part_nbr),
    p.resupply_date) resupply_date
FROM part p INNER JOIN supplier s
ON p.supplier_id = s.supplier_id;
```

The DECODE function checks if the supplier name is 'Acme Industries'. If so, it calls the function to retrieve the resupply date via the gateway; otherwise, it returns the resupply date from the local part table. The CASE version of this query looks as follows:

```
SELECT s.name supplier_name, p.name part_name, p.part_nbr part_number,
  p.inventory_qty in_stock,
  CASE WHEN s.name = 'Acme Industries'
    THEN my_pkg.get_resupply_date(p.part_nbr)
    ELSE p.resupply_date
  END resupply_date
FROM part p INNER JOIN supplier s
ON p.supplier_id = s.supplier_id;
```

Now the user-defined function is only executed if the supplier is Acme, reducing the query's execution time drastically. For more information on calling user-defined functions from SQL, see Chapter 11.

Conditional Update

If your database design includes denormalizations, you may run nightly routines to populate the denormalized columns. For example, the part table contains the denormalized column status, the value for which is derived from the inventory_qty and resupply_date columns. To update the status column, you could run four separate UPDATE statements each night, one for each of the four possible values for the status column. For example:

```
UPDATE part SET status = 'INSTOCK'
WHERE inventory_qty > 0;

UPDATE part SET status = 'ENROUTE'
WHERE inventory_qty = 0 AND resupply_date < SYSDATE + 5;
```

```
UPDATE part SET status = 'BACKORD'
WHERE inventory_qty = 0 AND resupply_date > SYSDATE + 5;

UPDATE part SET status = 'UNAVAIL'
WHERE inventory_qty = 0 and resupply_date IS NULL;
```

Given that columns such as inventory_qty and resupply_date are unlikely to be indexed, each of the four UPDATE statements would require a full table-scan of the part table. By adding conditional expressions to the statement, however, the four UPDATE statements can be combined, resulting in a single scan of the part table:

```
UPDATE part SET status =
  DECODE(inventory_qty, 0,
    DECODE(resupply_date, NULL, 'UNAVAIL',
      DECODE(LEAST(resupply_date, SYSDATE + 5), resupply_date,
        'ENROUTE', 'BACKORD')),
    'INSTOCK');
```

The CASE version of this UPDATE is as follows:

```
UPDATE part SET status =
  CASE WHEN inventory_qty > 0 THEN 'INSTOCK'
    WHEN resupply_date IS NULL THEN 'UNAVAIL'
    WHEN resupply_date < SYSDATE + 5 THEN 'ENROUTE'
    WHEN resupply_date > SYSDATE + 5 THEN 'BACKORD'
    ELSE 'UNKNOWN' END;
```

The readability advantage of the CASE expression is especially apparent here, since the DECODE version requires three nested levels to implement the same conditional logic handled by a single CASE expression.

Optional Update

In some situations, you may need to modify data only if certain conditions exist. For example, you have a table that records information such as the total number of orders and the largest order booked during the current month. Here's the table definition:[*]

describe mtd_orders;

Name	Null?	Type
TOT_ORDERS	NOT NULL	NUMBER(7)
TOT_SALE_PRICE	NOT NULL	NUMBER(11,2)
MAX_SALE_PRICE	NOT NULL	NUMBER(9,2)
EUROPE_TOT_ORDERS	NOT NULL	NUMBER(7)
EUROPE_TOT_SALE_PRICE	NOT NULL	NUMBER(11,2)
EUROPE_MAX_SALE_PRICE	NOT NULL	NUMBER(9,2)
NORTHAMERICA_TOT_ORDERS	NOT NULL	NUMBER(7)
NORTHAMERICA_TOT_SALE_PRICE	NOT NULL	NUMBER(11,2)
NORTHAMERICA_MAX_SALE_PRICE	NOT NULL	NUMBER(9,2)

[*] For this example, we will ignore the European and North American totals.

Each night, the table is updated with that day's order information. While most of the columns will be modified each night, the column for the largest order, which is called max_sale_price, will only change if one of the day's orders exceeds the current value of the column. The following PL/SQL block shows how this might be accomplished using a procedural language:

```
DECLARE
   tot_ord NUMBER;
   tot_price NUMBER;
   max_price NUMBER;
   prev_max_price NUMBER;
BEGIN
   SELECT COUNT(*), SUM(sale_price), MAX(sale_price)
   INTO tot_ord, tot_price, max_price
   FROM cust_order
   WHERE cancelled_dt IS NULL
     AND order_dt >= TRUNC(SYSDATE);

   UPDATE mtd_orders
   SET tot_orders = tot_orders + tot_ord,
     tot_sale_price = tot_sale_price + tot_price
   RETURNING max_sale_price INTO prev_max_price;

   IF max_price > prev_max_price THEN
     UPDATE mtd_orders
     SET max_sale_price = max_price;
   END IF;
END;
```

After calculating the total number of orders, the aggregate order price, and the maximum order price for the current day, the tot_orders and tot_sale_price columns of the mtd_orders table are modified with today's sales data. After the update is complete, the maximum sale price is returned from mtd_orders so that it can be compared with today's maximum sale price. If today's max_sale_price exceeds that stored in the mtd_orders table, a second UPDATE statement is executed to update the field.

Using DECODE or CASE, however, you can update the tot_orders and tot_sale_price columns *and* optionally update the max_sale_price column in the same UPDATE statement. Additionally, since you now have a single UPDATE statement, you can aggregate the data from the cust_order table within a subquery and eliminate the need for PL/SQL:

```
UPDATE mtd_orders mtdo
SET (mtdo.tot_orders, mtdo.tot_sale_price, mtdo.max_sale_price) =
  (SELECT mtdo.tot_orders + day_tot.tot_orders,
     mtdo.tot_sale_price + NVL(day_tot.tot_sale_price, 0),
     DECODE(GREATEST(mtdo.max_sale_price,
       NVL(day_tot.max_sale_price, 0)), mtdo.max_sale_price,
         mtdo.max_sale_price, day_tot.max_sale_price)
   FROM
```

```
     (SELECT COUNT(*) tot_orders, SUM(sale_price) tot_sale_price,
       MAX(sale_price) max_sale_price
     FROM cust_order
     WHERE cancelled_dt IS NULL
       AND order_dt >= TRUNC(SYSDATE)) day_tot);
```

In this statement, the max_sale_price column is set equal to itself unless the value returned from the subquery is greater than the current column value, in which case the column is set to the value returned from the subquery. The next statement uses CASE to perform the same optional update:

```
UPDATE mtd_orders mtdo
SET (mtdo.tot_orders, mtdo.tot_sale_price, mtdo.max_sale_price) =
 (SELECT mtdo.tot_orders + day_tot.tot_orders,
    mtdo.tot_sale_price + day_tot.tot_sale_price,
    CASE WHEN day_tot.max_sale_price > mtdo.max_sale_price
      THEN day_tot.max_sale_price
      ELSE mtdo.max_sale_price END
  FROM
   (SELECT COUNT(*) tot_orders, SUM(sale_price) tot_sale_price,
      MAX(sale_price) max_sale_price
    FROM cust_order
    WHERE cancelled_dt IS NULL
      AND order_dt >= TRUNC(SYSDATE)) day_tot);
```

One thing to keep in mind when using this approach is that setting a value equal to itself is still seen as a modification by the database and may trigger an audit record, a new value for the last_modified_date column, etc.

Selective Aggregation

To expand on the mtd_orders example in the previous section, imagine that you also want to store total sales for particular regions such as Europe and North America. For the additional six columns, individual orders will affect one set of columns or the other, but not both. An order will either be for a European or North American customer, but not for both at the same time. To populate these columns, you could generate two more update statements, each targeted to a particular region, as in:

```
/* Europe buckets */
UPDATE mtd_orders mtdo
SET (mtdo.europe_tot_orders, mtdo.europe_tot_sale_price,
  mtdo.europe_max_sale_price) =
 (SELECT mtdo.europe_tot_orders + eur_day_tot.tot_orders,
    mtdo.europe_tot_sale_price + nvl(eur_day_tot.tot_sale_price, 0),
    CASE WHEN eur_day_tot.max_sale_price > mtdo.europe_max_sale_price
      THEN eur_day_tot.max_sale_price
      ELSE mtdo.europe_max_sale_price END
  FROM
   (SELECT COUNT(*) tot_orders, SUM(co.sale_price) tot_sale_price,
      MAX(co.sale_price) max_sale_price
    FROM cust_order co INNER JOIN customer c
    ON co.cust_nbr = c.cust_nbr
```

```
    WHERE co.cancelled_dt IS NULL
      AND co.order_dt >= TRUNC(SYSDATE)
      AND c.region_id IN
        (SELECT region_id FROM region
         START WITH name = 'Europe'
         CONNECT BY PRIOR region_id = super_region_id)) eur_day_tot);

/* North America buckets */
UPDATE mtd_orders mtdo
SET (mtdo.northamerica_tot_orders, mtdo.northamerica_tot_sale_price,
  mtdo.northamerica_max_sale_price) =
  (SELECT mtdo.northamerica_tot_orders + na_day_tot.tot_orders,
     mtdo.northamerica_tot_sale_price + nvl(na_day_tot.tot_sale_price, 0),
     CASE WHEN na_day_tot.max_sale_price > mtdo.northamerica_max_sale_price
       THEN na_day_tot.max_sale_price
       ELSE mtdo.northamerica_max_sale_price END
   FROM
    (SELECT COUNT(*) tot_orders, SUM(co.sale_price) tot_sale_price,
       MAX(co.sale_price) max_sale_price
     FROM cust_order co INNER JOIN customer c
     ON co.cust_nbr = c.cust_nbr
     WHERE co.cancelled_dt IS NULL
       AND co.order_dt >= TRUNC(SYSDATE) - 60
       AND c.region_id IN
        (SELECT region_id FROM region
         START WITH name = 'North America'
         CONNECT BY PRIOR region_id = super_region_id)) na_day_tot);
```

However, why not save yourself a trip through the cust_order table and aggregate the North American and European totals at the same time? The trick here is to put conditional logic within the aggregation functions so that only the appropriate rows influence each calculation. This approach is similar to the example from "Result Set Transformations," in that it selectively aggregates data based on data stored in the table:

```
UPDATE mtd_orders mtdo
SET (mtdo.northamerica_tot_orders, mtdo.northamerica_tot_sale_price,
  mtdo.northamerica_max_sale_price, mtdo.europe_tot_orders,
  mtdo.europe_tot_sale_price, mtdo.europe_max_sale_price) =
  (SELECT mtdo.northamerica_tot_orders + nvl(day_tot.na_tot_orders, 0),
     mtdo.northamerica_tot_sale_price + nvl(day_tot.na_tot_sale_price, 0),
     CASE WHEN day_tot.na_max_sale_price > mtdo.northamerica_max_sale_price
       THEN day_tot.na_max_sale_price
       ELSE mtdo.northamerica_max_sale_price END,
     mtdo.europe_tot_orders + nvl(day_tot.eur_tot_orders, 0),
     mtdo.europe_tot_sale_price + nvl(day_tot.eur_tot_sale_price, 0),
     CASE WHEN day_tot.eur_max_sale_price > mtdo.europe_max_sale_price
       THEN day_tot.eur_max_sale_price
       ELSE mtdo.europe_max_sale_price END
   FROM
    (SELECT SUM(CASE WHEN na_regions.region_id IS NOT NULL THEN 1
               ELSE 0 END) na_tot_orders,
       SUM(CASE WHEN na_regions.region_id IS NOT NULL THEN co.sale_price
           ELSE 0 END) na_tot_sale_price,
```

```
        MAX(CASE WHEN na_regions.region_id IS NOT NULL THEN co.sale_price
            ELSE 0 END) na_max_sale_price,
        SUM(CASE WHEN eur_regions.region_id IS NOT NULL THEN 1
            ELSE 0 END) eur_tot_orders,
        SUM(CASE WHEN eur_regions.region_id IS NOT NULL THEN co.sale_price
            ELSE 0 END) eur_tot_sale_price,
        MAX(CASE WHEN eur_regions.region_id IS NOT NULL THEN co.sale_price
            ELSE 0 END) eur_max_sale_price
    FROM cust_order co INNER JOIN customer c
      ON co.cust_nbr = c.cust_nbr
      LEFT OUTER JOIN (SELECT region_id FROM region
        START WITH name = 'North America'
        CONNECT BY PRIOR region_id = super_region_id) na_regions
      ON c.region_id = na_regions.region_id
      LEFT OUTER JOIN (SELECT region_id FROM region
        START WITH name = 'Europe'
        CONNECT BY PRIOR region_id = super_region_id) eur_regions
      ON c.region_id = eur_regions.region_id
    WHERE co.cancelled_dt IS NULL
      AND co.order_dt >= TRUNC(SYSDATE)) day_tot);
```

This is a fairly robust statement, so let's break it down. Within the day_tot inline view, you are joining the cust_order table to the customer table, and then outer-joining from customer.region_id to each of two inline views (na_regions and eur_regions) that perform hierarchical queries on the region table. Thus, orders from European customers will have a non-null value for eur_regions.region_id, since the outer join would find a matching row in the eur_regions inline view. Six aggregations are performed on this result set; three check for a join against the na_regions inline view (North American orders), and three check for a join against the eur_regions inline view (European orders). The six aggregations are then used to modify the six columns in mtd_orders.

This statement could (and should) be combined with the statement from the previous example (which updated the first three columns) to create an UPDATE statement that touches every column in the mtd_orders table via one pass through the cust_order table. For data warehouse applications, where large data sets must be manipulated each night within tight time constraints, such an approach can often make the difference between success and failure.

Checking for Existence

When evaluating optional one-to-many relationships, there are certain cases where you want to know whether the relationship is zero or greater than zero without regard for the actual data. For example, you want to write a report showing each customer along with a flag showing whether the customer has had any orders in the past five years. Using conditional logic, you can include a correlated subquery on the cust_order table, check to see if the number of orders exceeds zero, and then assign either a 'Y' or a 'N' to the column:

```
SELECT c.cust_nbr cust_nbr, c.name name,
  DECODE(0, (SELECT COUNT(*) FROM cust_order co
```

```
    WHERE co.cust_nbr = c.cust_nbr AND co.cancelled_dt IS NULL
      AND co.order_dt > TRUNC(SYSDATE) - (5 * 365)),
    'N', 'Y') has_recent_orders
FROM customer c;
```

```
  CUST_NBR NAME                             H
---------- ------------------------------   -
         1 Cooper Industries                Y
         2 Emblazon Corp.                   N
         3 Ditech Corp.                     N
         4 Flowtech Inc.                    Y
         5 Gentech Industries               Y
         6 Spartan Industries               N
         7 Wallace Labs                     N
         8 Zantech Inc.                     Y
         9 Cardinal Technologies            N
        10 Flowrite Corp.                   N
        11 Glaven Technologies              N
        12 Johnson Labs                     N
        13 Kimball Corp.                    N
        14 Madden Industries                N
        15 Turntech Inc.                    N
        16 Paulson Labs                     N
        17 Evans Supply Corp.               N
        18 Spalding Medical Inc.            N
        19 Kendall-Taylor Corp.             N
        20 Malden Labs                      N
        21 Crimson Medical Inc.             N
        22 Nichols Industries               N
        23 Owens-Baxter Corp.               N
        24 Jackson Medical Inc.             N
        25 Worcester Technologies           N
        26 Alpha Technologies               Y
        27 Phillips Labs                    N
        28 Jaztech Corp.                    N
        29 Madden-Taylor Inc.               N
        30 Wallace Industries               N
```

Here is the CASE version of the query:

```
SELECT c.cust_nbr cust_nbr, c.name name,
  CASE WHEN EXISTS (SELECT 1 FROM cust_order co
    WHERE co.cust_nbr = c.cust_nbr AND co.cancelled_dt IS NULL
      AND co.order_dt > TRUNC(SYSDATE) - (5 * 365))
    THEN 'Y' ELSE 'N' END has_recent_orders
FROM customer c;
```

Division by Zero Errors

As a general rule, you should write your code so that unexpected data values are handled gracefully. One of the more common arithmetic errors is ORA-01476: divisor is equal to zero. Whether the value is retrieved from a column, passed in via a bind variable, or returned by a function call, always wrap divisors with DECODE or CASE, as illustrated by the following example:

```
SELECT p.part_nbr, SYSDATE + (p.inventory_qty /
  DECODE(my_pkg.get_daily_part_usage(p.part_nbr), NULL, 1,
    0, 1, my_pkg.get_daily_part_usage(p.part_nbr))) anticipated_shortage_dt
FROM part p
WHERE p.inventory_qty > 0;
```

The DECODE function ensures that the divisor is something other than zero. Here is the CASE version of the statement:

```
SELECT p.part_nbr, SYSDATE + (p.inventory_qty /
  CASE WHEN my_pkg.get_daily_part_usage(p.part_nbr) > 0
    THEN my_pkg.get_daily_part_usage(p.part_nbr)
    ELSE 1 END) anticipated_shortage_dt
FROM part p
WHERE p.inventory_qty > 0;
```

Of course, if you are bothered by the fact that the get_daily_part_usage function is called a second time for each part that yields a positive response, simply wrap the function call in an inline view, as in:

```
SELECT parts.part_nbr, SYSDATE + (parts.inventory_qty /
  CASE WHEN parts.daily_part_usage > 0
    THEN parts.daily_part_usage
    ELSE 1 END) anticipated_shortage_dt
FROM
  (SELECT p.part_nbr part_nbr, p.inventory_qty inventory_qty,
    my_pkg.get_daily_part_usage(p.part_nbr) daily_part_usage
   FROM part p
   WHERE p.inventory_qty > 0) parts;
```

State Transitions

In certain cases, the order in which the values may be changed is constrained as well as the allowable values for a column. Consider the diagram shown in Figure 9-1, which shows the allowable state transitions for an order.

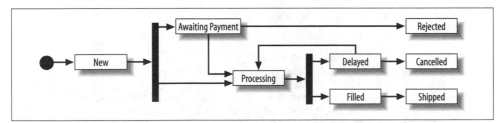

Figure 9-1. Order processing state transitions

As you can see, an order currently in the Processing state should only be allowed to move to either Delayed or Filled. Rather than allowing each application to implement logic to change the state of an order, write a user-defined function that returns the appropriate state depending on the current state of the order and the transition type. In this example, two transition types are defined: positive (POS) and negative (NEG). For example, an order in the Delayed state can make a positive transition to Processing or a negative transition to Cancelled. If an order is in one of the final states (Rejected, Cancelled, Shipped), the same state is returned. Here is the DECODE version of the PL/SQL function:

```
FUNCTION get_next_order_state(ord_nbr in NUMBER,
   trans_type in VARCHAR2 DEFAULT 'POS')
RETURN VARCHAR2 is
   next_state VARCHAR2(20) := 'UNKNOWN';
BEGIN
   SELECT DECODE(status,
      'REJECTED', status,
      'CANCELLED', status,
      'SHIPPED', status,
      'NEW', DECODE(trans_type, 'NEG', 'AWAIT_PAYMENT', 'PROCESSING'),
      'AWAIT_PAYMENT', DECODE(trans_type, 'NEG', 'REJECTED', 'PROCESSING'),
      'PROCESSING', DECODE(trans_type, 'NEG', 'DELAYED', 'FILLED'),
      'DELAYED', DECODE(trans_type, 'NEG', 'CANCELLED', 'PROCESSING'),
      'FILLED', DECODE(trans_type, 'POS', 'SHIPPED', 'UNKNOWN'),
      'UNKNOWN')
   INTO next_state
   FROM cust_order
   WHERE order_nbr = ord_nbr;

   RETURN next_state;
EXCEPTION
   WHEN NO_DATA_FOUND THEN
      RETURN next_state;
END get_next_order_state;
```

As of Oracle8i, the PL/SQL language does not include the CASE expression in its grammar, so you would need to be running Oracle9i or later to use the CASE version of the function:

```
FUNCTION get_next_order_state(ord_nbr in NUMBER,
   trans_type in VARCHAR2 DEFAULT 'POS')
RETURN VARCHAR2 is
   next_state VARCHAR2(20) := 'UNKNOWN';
BEGIN
   SELECT CASE
      WHEN status = 'REJECTED' THEN status
      WHEN status = 'CANCELLED' THEN status
      WHEN status = 'SHIPPED' THEN status
      WHEN status = 'NEW' AND trans_type = 'NEG' THEN 'AWAIT_PAYMENT'
      WHEN status = 'NEW' AND trans_type = 'POS' THEN 'PROCESSING'
      WHEN status = 'AWAIT_PAYMENT' AND trans_type = 'NEG' THEN 'REJECTED'
      WHEN status = 'AWAIT_PAYMENT' AND trans_type = 'POS' THEN 'PROCESSING'
      WHEN status = 'PROCESSING' AND trans_type = 'NEG' THEN 'DELAYED'
      WHEN status = 'PROCESSING' AND trans_type = 'POS' THEN 'FILLED'
      WHEN status = 'DELAYED' AND trans_type = 'NEG' THEN 'CANCELLED'
      WHEN status = 'DELAYED' AND trans_type = 'POS' THEN 'PROCESSING'
```

```
        WHEN status = 'FILLED' AND trans_type = 'POS' THEN 'SHIPPED'
        ELSE 'UNKNOWN'
    END
    INTO next_state
    FROM cust_order
    WHERE order_nbr = ord_nbr;

    RETURN next_state;
EXCEPTION
    WHEN NO_DATA_FOUND THEN
        RETURN next_state;
END get_next_order_state;
```

This example handles only the simple case in which there are just two paths out of each state, but it does demonstrate one strategy for managing state transitions in your database. To demonstrate how the previous function could be used, here is the UPDATE statement used to change the status of an order once it has made a successful state transition:

```
UPDATE cust_order
SET status = my_pkg.get_next_order_state(order_nbr, 'POS')
WHERE order_nbr = 1107;
```

CHAPTER 10

Partitioning

Over the past 15 years, hard disk capacities have evolved from around 10 MB to over 100 GB, and capacities are still growing. Disk arrays are fast approaching the 100 terabyte range. No matter how much storage is available, however, there is always a way to exhaust it. As databases grow in size, day-to-day operations become more and more challenging. For example, finding the time and resources to rebuild an index containing 100 million entries can prove quite demanding. Prior to Oracle8, database administrators would meet this challenge by manually breaking a large table into several smaller tables. Although the pieces could be hidden behind a special type of view (called a *partition view*) during a query, all DML statements had to be performed against the individual tables, thereby exposing the partitioning scheme to the database developers and users.

Starting with Version 8.0, Oracle provided a means for breaking a table into multiple pieces while preserving the look and feel of a single table. Each piece is called a *partition*, and, although every partition must share the same columns, constraints, indexes, and triggers, each partition can have its own unique storage parameters. While administrators generally deal with individual partitions when allocating storage and performing backups, developers may choose to deal with either the entire table or with individual partitions.

Partitioning Concepts

Database designers and administrators have been partitioning tables since long before Oracle8 hit the scene. Generally, table partitioning within a single database is done to improve performance and simplify administration tasks, while table partitioning between databases is meant to facilitate data distribution. For example, sales data might be partitioned by region and each partition hosted in a database housed at its respective regional sales office. Whereas a central data warehouse might gather sales data from each office for reporting and decision-support queries, it might be perfectly reasonable for the operational sales data to be distributed across multiple sites.

Partitioning by sets of rows such as in the sales data example, in which the value of the sales office column determines where the data resides, is known as *horizontal partitioning*. Partitioning may also be accomplished by splitting up sets of columns, in which case it is called *vertical partitioning*. For example, sensitive data such as salary information and social security numbers may be split off from the employee table into a separate table with restricted access. When partitioning vertically, primary key columns must be included in the set of columns for every partition. Therefore, unlike horizontal partitioning, where each partition contains nonoverlapping subsets of data, vertical partitioning mandates that some data be duplicated in each partition.

While both vertical and horizontal partitioning may be accomplished manually within and between Oracle databases, the Partitioning Option introduced in Oracle8 specifically deals with horizontal partitioning within a single database.

Partitioning Tables

When partitioning is employed, a table changes from a physical object to a virtual concept. There isn't really a table anymore, just a set of partitions. Since all of the partitions must share the same attribute and constraint definitions, however, it is possible to deal with the set of partitions as if they were a single table. The storage parameters, such as extent sizes and tablespace placement, are the only attributes that may differ among the partitions. This situation can facilitate some interesting storage scenarios, such as hosting infrequently accessed partitions on a CD jukebox while the heavily-hit data partitions reside on disk. You can also take advantage of Oracle's segmented buffer cache to keep the most active partitions in the *keep buffer* so they are always in memory, while the rest of the partitions can be targeted for the *recycle* or *default* buffers. Additionally, individual partitions may be taken offline without affecting the availability of the rest of the partitions, giving administrators a great deal of flexibility.

Depending on the partitioning scheme employed, you must choose one or more columns of a table to be the *partition key*. The values of the columns in the partition key determine the partition that hosts a particular row. Oracle also uses the partition key information in concert with your WHERE clauses to determine which partitions to search during SELECT, UPDATE, and DELETE operations (see "Partition Pruning" later in the chapter for more information).

Partitioning Indexes

So what, you may wonder, happens to the indexes on partitioned tables? The answer is that you have to choose whether each index will stay intact (referred to as a *global index*), or be split into pieces corresponding to the table partitions (referred to as a *local index*). Furthermore, with a global index, you can choose to partition the index in a different manner than the table was partitioned. When you throw the fact that you can partition both b-tree and bit-map indexes into the mix, things can become overwhelming. When you issue a SELECT, UPDATE, or DELETE statement against a partitioned table, the optimizer can take several routes to locate the target rows:

- Use a global index, if one is available and its columns are referenced in the SQL statement, to find the target rows across one or more partitions.
- Search a local index on every partition to identify whether any particular partition contains target rows.
- Define a subset of the partitions that might contain target rows, and then access local indexes on those partitions.

Although global indexes might seem to be the simplest solution, they can be problematic. Because global indexes span all of the partitions of a table, they are adversely affected by partition maintenance operations. For example, if a partition is split into multiple pieces, or if two partitions are merged into one, all global indexes on the partitioned table are marked as UNUSABLE and must be rebuilt before they can be used again. When modifying a partitioning scheme, you have your choice of rebuilding the global indexes manually, or of using the UPDATE GLOBAL INDEXES clause.

Partitioning Methods

To horizontally partition a table (or index), you must specify a set of rules so that Oracle can determine in which partition a given row should reside. The following sections explore the five types of partitioning available in Oracle Database 10*g*.

Range Partitioning

The first partitioning scheme, introduced in Oracle8 and known as *range partitioning*, allows a table to be partitioned over ranges of values for one or more columns of the table. The simplest and most widely implemented form of range partitioning is to partition using a single date column. Consider the following DDL statement:

```
CREATE TABLE cust_order (
  order_nbr NUMBER(7) NOT NULL,
  cust_nbr NUMBER(5) NOT NULL,
  order_dt DATE NOT NULL,
  sales_emp_id NUMBER(5) NOT NULL,
  sale_price NUMBER(9,2),
  expected_ship_dt DATE,
  cancelled_dt DATE,
  ship_dt DATE,
  status VARCHAR2(20)
  )
```

```
PARTITION BY RANGE (order_dt)
 (PARTITION orders_2000
    VALUES LESS THAN (TO_DATE('01-JAN-2001','DD-MON-YYYY'))
      TABLESPACE ord1,
  PARTITION orders_2001
    VALUES LESS THAN (TO_DATE('01-JAN-2002','DD-MON-YYYY'))
      TABLESPACE ord2,
  PARTITION orders_2002
    VALUES LESS THAN (TO_DATE('01-JAN-2003','DD-MON-YYYY'))
      TABLESPACE ord3);
```

Using this partitioning scheme, all orders prior to 2001 will reside in the orders_2000 partition; orders from 2001 will reside in the orders_2001 partition; and orders for the year 2002 will reside in the orders_2002 partition.

Hash Partitioning

In some cases, you may wish to partition a large table, but there are no columns for which range partitioning is suitable. Available in Oracle8i, *hash partitioning* allows you to specify the number of partitions and the partition columns (the partition key), but leaves the allocation of rows to partitions up to Oracle. As rows are inserted into the partitioned table, Oracle attempts to evenly spread the data across the partitions by applying a hashing function to the data in the partition key; the value returned by the hashing function determines the partition that hosts the row. If the partition columns are included in the WHERE clause of a SELECT, DELETE, or UPDATE statement, Oracle can apply the hash function to determine which partition to search. The following DDL statement demonstrates how the part table might be partitioned by hashing the part_nbr column:

```
CREATE TABLE part (
  part_nbr VARCHAR2(20) NOT NULL,
  name VARCHAR2(50) NOT NULL,
  supplier_id NUMBER(6) NOT NULL,
  inventory_qty NUMBER(6) NOT NULL,
  status VARCHAR2(10) NOT NULL,
  unit_cost NUMBER(8,2),
  resupply_date DATE
  )
PARTITION BY HASH (part_nbr)
 (PARTITION part1 TABLESPACE p1,
  PARTITION part2 TABLESPACE p2,
  PARTITION part3 TABLESPACE p3,
  PARTITION part4 TABLESPACE p4);
```

For the data to be evenly distributed across the partitions, it is important to choose columns with high cardinality as partition keys. A set of columns is said to have high cardinality if the number of distinct values is large compared to the size of the table. Choosing a high cardinality column for your partition key ensures an even distribution across your partitions; otherwise, the partitions can become unbalanced, causing performance to be unpredictable and making administration more difficult.

A unique key has the highest cardinality, since every row in the table has a distinct value. An example of a low cardinality column might be the country column in a customer table with millions of entries.

Composite Range-Hash Partitioning

If you are torn between whether to apply range or hash partitioning to your table, you can do some of each. *Composite partitioning*, also unveiled with Oracle8*i*, allows you to create multiple range partitions, each of which contains two or more hash *subpartitions*. There are two types of composite partitioning, *range-hash partitioning*, which was unveiled in Oracle8*i*, and *range-list partitioning*, which we'll talk about later in this chapter.

Composite partitioning is often useful when range partitioning is appropriate for the type of data stored in the table, but you want a finer granularity of partitioning than is practical using range partitioning alone. For example, it might make sense to partition your order table by year based on the types of queries against the table. If a year's worth of data proves too cumbersome for a single partition, however, you could subpartition each year by hashing the customer number across four buckets. The following example expands on the range-partitioning example shown earlier by generating subpartitions based on a hash of the customer number:

```
CREATE TABLE cust_order (
   order_nbr NUMBER(7) NOT NULL,
   cust_nbr NUMBER(5) NOT NULL,
   order_dt DATE NOT NULL,
   sales_emp_id NUMBER(5) NOT NULL,
   sale_price NUMBER(9,2),
   expected_ship_dt DATE,
   cancelled_dt DATE,
   ship_dt DATE,
   status VARCHAR2(20)
   )
PARTITION BY RANGE (order_dt)
SUBPARTITION BY HASH (cust_nbr) SUBPARTITIONS 4
STORE IN (order_sub1, order_sub2, order_sub3, order_sub4)
 (PARTITION orders_2000
    VALUES LESS THAN (TO_DATE('01-JAN-2000','DD-MON-YYYY'))
     (SUBPARTITION orders_2000_s1 TABLESPACE order_sub1,
      SUBPARTITION orders_2000_s2 TABLESPACE order_sub2,
      SUBPARTITION orders_2000_s3 TABLESPACE order_sub3,
      SUBPARTITION orders_2000_s4 TABLESPACE order_sub4),
   PARTITION orders_2001
    VALUES LESS THAN (TO_DATE('01-JAN-2001','DD-MON-YYYY'))
     (SUBPARTITION orders_2001_s1 TABLESPACE order_sub1,
      SUBPARTITION orders_2001_s2 TABLESPACE order_sub2,
      SUBPARTITION orders_2001_s3 TABLESPACE order_sub3,
      SUBPARTITION orders_2001_s4 TABLESPACE order_sub4),
   PARTITION orders_2002
```

```
VALUES LESS THAN (TO_DATE('01-JAN-2002','DD-MON-YYYY'))
 (SUBPARTITION orders_2002_s1 TABLESPACE order_sub1,
  SUBPARTITION orders_2002_s2 TABLESPACE order_sub2,
  SUBPARTITION orders_2002_s3 TABLESPACE order_sub3,
  SUBPARTITION orders_2002_s4 TABLESPACE order_sub4));
```

Interestingly, when composite partitioning is used, all of the data is physically stored in the subpartitions, while the partitions, just like the table, become virtual.

List Partitioning

Introduced in Oracle9i, *list partitioning* allows a table to be partitioned by one or more distinct values of a particular column. For example, a warehouse table containing sales summary data by product, state, and month/year could be partitioned into geographic regions, as in:

```
CREATE TABLE sales_fact (
  state_cd VARCHAR2(3) NOT NULL,
  month_cd NUMBER(2) NOT NULL,
  year_cd NUMBER(4) NOT NULL,
  product_cd VARCHAR2(10) NOT NULL,
  tot_sales NUMBER(9,2) NOT NULL
  )
PARTITION BY LIST (state_cd)
 (PARTITION sales_newengland VALUES ('CT','RI','MA','NH','ME','VT')
    TABLESPACE s1,
  PARTITION sales_northwest VALUES ('OR','WA','MT','ID','WY','AK')
    TABLESPACE s2,
  PARTITION sales_southwest VALUES ('NV','UT','AZ','NM','CO','HI')
    TABLESPACE s3,
  PARTITION sales_southeast VALUES ('FL','GA','AL','SC','NC','TN','WV')
    TABLESPACE s4,
  PARTITION sales_east VALUES ('PA','NY','NJ','MD','DE','VA','KY','OH')
    TABLESPACE s5,
  PARTITION sales_california VALUES ('CA')
    TABLESPACE s6,
  PARTITION sales_south VALUES ('TX','OK','LA','AR','MS')
    TABLESPACE s7,
  PARTITION sales_midwest VALUES ('ND','SD','NE','KS','MN','WI','IA',
    'IL','IN','MI','MO')
    TABLESPACE s8);
```

List partitioning is appropriate for low cardinality data in which the number of distinct values of a column is small relative to the number of rows. Unlike range and hash partitioning, where the partition key may contain several columns, list partitioning is limited to a single column.

Composite Range-List Partitioning

Available in the Oracle Database 10g release, range-list composite partitioning allows you to partition your data by range, and then subpartition via a list. This might be an excellent strategy for partitioning data in a sales warehouse so that you could partition your data both on sales periods (i.e., years, quarters, months) and on sales regions (i.e., states, countries, districts). The following example expands on the list partitioning example by adding yearly partitions:

```
CREATE TABLE sales_fact (
  state_cd VARCHAR2(3) NOT NULL,
  month_cd NUMBER(2) NOT NULL,
  year_cd NUMBER(4) NOT NULL,
  product_cd VARCHAR2(10) NOT NULL,
  tot_sales NUMBER(9,2) NOT NULL
  )
PARTITION BY RANGE (year_cd)
SUBPARTITION BY LIST (state_cd)
 (PARTITION sales_2000
    VALUES LESS THAN (2001)
    (SUBPARTITION sales_2000_newengland
       VALUES ('CT','RI','MA','NH','ME','VT') TABLESPACE s1,
    SUBPARTITION sales_2000_northwest
       VALUES ('OR','WA','MT','ID','WY','AK') TABLESPACE s2,
    SUBPARTITION sales_2000_southwest
       VALUES ('NV','UT','AZ','NM','CO','HI') TABLESPACE s3,
    SUBPARTITION sales_2000_southeast
       VALUES ('FL','GA','AL','SC','NC','TN','WV') TABLESPACE s4,
    SUBPARTITION sales_2000_east
       VALUES ('PA','NY','NJ','MD','DE','VA','KY','OH') TABLESPACE s5,
    SUBPARTITION sales_2000_california
       VALUES ('CA') TABLESPACE s6,
    SUBPARTITION sales_2000_south
       VALUES ('TX','OK','LA','AR','MS') TABLESPACE s7,
    SUBPARTITION sales_2000_midwest
       VALUES ('ND','SD','NE','KS','MN','WI','IA', 'IL','IN','MI','MO')
       TABLESPACE s8
    ),
  PARTITION sales_2001
    VALUES LESS THAN (2002)
    (SUBPARTITION sales_2001_newengland
       VALUES ('CT','RI','MA','NH','ME','VT') TABLESPACE s1,
    SUBPARTITION sales_2001_northwest
       VALUES ('OR','WA','MT','ID','WY','AK') TABLESPACE s2,
    SUBPARTITION sales_2001_southwest
       VALUES ('NV','UT','AZ','NM','CO','HI') TABLESPACE s3,
    SUBPARTITION sales_2001_southeast
       VALUES ('FL','GA','AL','SC','NC','TN','WV') TABLESPACE s4,
    SUBPARTITION sales_2001_east
       VALUES ('PA','NY','NJ','MD','DE','VA','KY','OH') TABLESPACE s5,
    SUBPARTITION sales_2001_california
       VALUES ('CA') TABLESPACE s6,
    SUBPARTITION sales_2001_south
       VALUES ('TX','OK','LA','AR','MS') TABLESPACE s7,
    SUBPARTITION sales_2001_midwest
       VALUES ('ND','SD','NE','KS','MN','WI','IA', 'IL','IN','MI','MO')
       TABLESPACE s8
    ),
```

```
PARTITION sales_2002
  VALUES LESS THAN (2003)
  (SUBPARTITION sales_2002_newengland
     VALUES ('CT','RI','MA','NH','ME','VT') TABLESPACE s1,
   SUBPARTITION sales_2002_northwest
     VALUES ('OR','WA','MT','ID','WY','AK') TABLESPACE s2,
   SUBPARTITION sales_2002_southwest
     VALUES ('NV','UT','AZ','NM','CO','HI') TABLESPACE s3,
   SUBPARTITION sales_2002_southeast
     VALUES ('FL','GA','AL','SC','NC','TN','WV') TABLESPACE s4,
   SUBPARTITION sales_2002_east
     VALUES ('PA','NY','NJ','MD','DE','VA','KY','OH') TABLESPACE s5,
   SUBPARTITION sales_2002_california
     VALUES ('CA') TABLESPACE s6,
   SUBPARTITION sales_2002_south
     VALUES ('TX','OK','LA','AR','MS') TABLESPACE s7,
   SUBPARTITION sales_2002_midwest
     VALUES ('ND','SD','NE','KS','MN','WI','IA', 'IL','IN','MI','MO')
     TABLESPACE s8
  ));
```

Rather than specifying the same list information over and over, Oracle Database 10g now allows the use of *subpartition templates* so that the subpartitioning scheme can be specified just once:

```
CREATE TABLE sales_fact (
  state_cd VARCHAR2(3) NOT NULL,
  month_cd NUMBER(2) NOT NULL,
  year_cd NUMBER(4) NOT NULL,
  product_cd VARCHAR2(10) NOT NULL,
  tot_sales NUMBER(9,2) NOT NULL
  )
PARTITION BY RANGE (year_cd)
SUBPARTITION BY LIST (state_cd)
SUBPARTITION TEMPLATE (
  SUBPARTITION newengland
    VALUES ('CT','RI','MA','NH','ME','VT') TABLESPACE s1,
  SUBPARTITION northwest
    VALUES ('OR','WA','MT','ID','WY','AK') TABLESPACE s2,
  SUBPARTITION southwest
    VALUES ('NV','UT','AZ','NM','CO','HI') TABLESPACE s3,
  SUBPARTITION southeast
    VALUES ('FL','GA','AL','SC','NC','TN','WV') TABLESPACE s4,
  SUBPARTITION east
    VALUES ('PA','NY','NJ','MD','DE','VA','KY','OH') TABLESPACE s5,
  SUBPARTITION california
    VALUES ('CA') TABLESPACE s6,
  SUBPARTITION south
    VALUES ('TX','OK','LA','AR','MS') TABLESPACE s7,
  SUBPARTITION midwest
    VALUES ('ND','SD','NE','KS','MN','WI','IA', 'IL','IN','MI','MO')
    TABLESPACE s8
  )
```

```
(PARTITION sales_2000
  VALUES LESS THAN (2001),
 PARTITION sales_2001
  VALUES LESS THAN (2002),
 PARTITION sales_2002
  VALUES LESS THAN (2003)
 );
```

Specifying Partitions

When you are writing SQL against partitioned tables, you have the option to treat the partitions as single, virtual tables, or to specify partition names within your SQL statements. If you write DML against a virtual table, the Oracle optimizer determines the partition or partitions that need to be involved. For an INSERT statement, the optimizer uses the values provided for the partition key to determine where to put each row. For UPDATE, DELETE, and SELECT statements, the optimizer uses the conditions from the WHERE clause along with information on local and global indexes to determine the partition or partitions that need to be searched.

If you know that your DML statement will utilize a single partition, and you know the name of the partition, you can use the PARTITION clause to tell the optimizer which partition to use. For example, if you want to summarize all orders for the year 2000, and you know that the cust_order table is range-partitioned by year, you could issue the following query:

```
SELECT COUNT(*) tot_orders, SUM(sale_price) tot_sales
FROM cust_order PARTITION (orders_2000)
WHERE cancelled_dt IS NULL;
```

This query's WHERE clause doesn't specify a date range, even though the table contains data spanning multiple years. Because you specified the orders_2000 partition, you know that the query will only summarize orders from 2000, so there is no need to check each order's date.

If your table is composite-partitioned, you can use the SUBPARTITION clause to focus on a single subpartition of the table. For example, the following statement deletes all rows from the orders_2000_s1 subpartition of the range-hash composite-partitioned version of the cust_order table:

```
DELETE FROM cust_order SUBPARTITION (orders_2000_s1);
```

You can also use the PARTITION clause to delete the entire set of subpartitions that fall within a given partition:

```
DELETE FROM cust_order PARTITION (orders_2000);
```

This statement would delete all rows from the orders_2000_s1, orders_2000_s2, orders_2000_s3, and orders_2000_s4 subpartitions of the cust_order table.

Here are a few additional things to consider when working with partitioned tables:

- If the optimizer determines that two or more partitions are needed to satisfy the WHERE clause of a SELECT, UPDATE, or DELETE statement, the table and/or index partitions may be scanned in parallel. Therefore, depending on the system resources available to Oracle, scanning every partition of a partitioned table could be much faster than scanning an entire unpartitioned table.

- Because hash partitioning spreads data randomly across the partitions,* we don't believe you would ever want to use the PARTITION clause for hash-partitioned tables or the SUBPARTITON clause for range-hash partitioned tables, since you don't know what data you are working on. The only reasonable scenario that comes to mind might be when you want to modify every row in the table, but you don't have enough rollback available to modify every row in a single transaction. In this case, you can perform an UPDATE or DELETE on each partition or subpartition and issue a COMMIT after each statement completes.

- Partitions can be merged, split, or dropped at any time by the DBA. Therefore, use caution when explicitly naming partitions in your DML statements. Otherwise, you may find your statements failing, or worse, your statements might work on the wrong set of data because partitions have been merged or split without your knowledge. You may want to check with your DBA to determine her policy concerning naming partitions in your DML statements.

If you need to access a single partition or subpartition but don't like having partition names sprinkled throughout your code, consider creating views to hide the partition names, as in the following:

```
CREATE VIEW cust_order_2000 AS
SELECT *
FROM cust_order PARTITION (orders_2000);
```

You can then issue your SQL statements against such views:

```
SELECT order_nbr, cust_nbr, sale_price, order_dt
FROM cust_order_2000
WHERE quantity > 100;
```

Partition Pruning

Even when you don't name a specific partition in a SQL statement, the fact that a table is partitioned might still influence the manner in which the statement accesses the table. When a SQL statement accesses one or more partitioned tables, the Oracle optimizer attempts to use the information in the WHERE clause to eliminate some of the partitions from consideration during statement execution. This process,

---

* It isn't actually random, but it will seem that way to you, since you don't have access to the hash function.

called *partition pruning*, speeds statement execution by ignoring any partitions that cannot satisfy the statement's WHERE clause. To do so, the optimizer uses information from the table definition combined with information from the statement's WHERE clause. For example, given the following table definition:

```
CREATE TABLE tab1 (
  col1 NUMBER(5) NOT NULL,
  col2 DATE NOT NULL,
  col3 VARCHAR2(10) NOT NULL)
PARTITION BY RANGE (col2)
 (PARTITION tab1_1998
   VALUES LESS THAN (TO_DATE('01-JAN-1999','DD-MON-YYYY'))
     TABLESPACE t1,
  PARTITION tab1_1999
   VALUES LESS THAN (TO_DATE('01-JAN-2000','DD-MON-YYYY'))
     TABLESPACE t1,
  PARTITION tab1_2000
   VALUES LESS THAN (TO_DATE('01-JAN-2001','DD-MON-YYYY'))
     TABLESPACE t3,
  PARTITION tab1_2001
   VALUES LESS THAN (TO_DATE('01-JAN-2002','DD-MON-YYYY'))
     TABLESPACE t4);
```

and the following query:

```
SELECT col1, col2, col3
FROM tab1
WHERE col2 > TO_DATE('01-OCT-2000','DD-MON-YYYY');
```

the optimizer would eliminate partitions `tab1_1998` and `tab1_1999` from consideration, since neither partition could contain rows with a value for `col2` greater than October 1, 2000.

 Partition pruning is sometimes referred to as *partition elimination*.

For the optimizer to make these types of decisions, the WHERE clause must reference at least one column from the set of columns that comprise the partition key. Although this might seem fairly straightforward, not all queries against a partitioned table naturally include the partition key. If a unique index exists on the `col1` column of the `tab1` table from the previous example, for instance, the following query would generally offer the most efficient access:

```
SELECT col1, col2, col3
FROM tab1
WHERE col1 = 1578;
```

If the index on col1 had been defined as a local index, however, Oracle would need to visit each partition's local index to find the one that holds the value 1578. If you also have information about the partition key (col2 in this case), you might want to consider including it in the query so that the optimizer can eliminate partitions, as in the following:

```
SELECT col1, col2, col3
FROM tab1
WHERE col1 = 1578
  AND col2 > TO_DATE('01-JAN-2001','DD-MON-YYYY');
```

With the additional condition, the optimizer can now eliminate the tab1_1998, tab1_1999, and tab1_2000 partitions from consideration. Oracle will now search a single unique index on the tab1_2001 partition instead of searching a unique index on each of the four table partitions. Of course, you would need to know that data pertaining to the value 1578 also had a value for col2 greater then January 1, 2001. If you can reliably provide additional information regarding the partition keys, than you should do so; otherwise, you'll just have to let the optimizer do its best. Running EXPLAIN PLAN on your DML statements against partitioned tables will allow you to see which partitions the optimizer decided to utilize.

When checking the results of EXPLAIN PLAN, there are a couple of partition specific columns that you should add to your query against plan_table to see which partitions are being considered by the optimizer. To demonstrate, we'll explain the following query against tab1:

```
EXPLAIN PLAN
SET STATEMENT_ID = 'qry1' FOR
SELECT col1, col2, col3
FROM tab1
WHERE col2 BETWEEN TO_DATE('01-JUL-1999','DD-MON-YYYY')
  AND TO_DATE('01-JUL-2000','DD-MON-YYYY');
```

When querying the plan_table table, you should include the partition_start and partition_end columns whenever the operation field starts with 'PARTITION':

```
SELECT lpad(' ',2 * level) || operation || ' ' ||
  options || ' ' || object_name ||
  DECODE(SUBSTR(operation, 1, 9), 'PARTITION',
    ' FROM ' || partition_start ||
    ' TO ' || partition_stop, ' ') "exec plan"
FROM plan_table
CONNECT BY PRIOR id = parent_id
START WITH id = 0 AND statement_id = 'qry1';

exec plan
-------------------------------------------------------
  SELECT STATEMENT
    PARTITION RANGE ITERATOR  FROM 2 TO 3
      TABLE ACCESS FULL TAB1
```

The value of PARTITION RANGE for the operation column along with the value of ITERATOR for the options column indicates that more than one partition will be involved in the execution plan.* The values of the partition_start and partition_end columns (2 and 3, respectively) indicate that the optimizer has decided to prune partitions 1 and 4, which correlate to the tab1_1998 and tab1_2001 partitions.† Given that the WHERE clause specifies a date range of July 1, 1999 to July 1, 2000, the optimizer has correctly pruned all partitions that cannot contribute to the result set.

---

* If the optimizer had pruned all but one partition, the options column would contain the value 'SINGLE'. If no partitions were pruned, the options column would contain the value 'ALL'.

† The number shown in the partition_start and partition_end columns correlates to the partition_position column in the user_tab_partitions table, so you can query this table to identify the names of the partitions that are included in the execution plan.

CHAPTER 11

PL/SQL

There are many fine books on the market that cover the PL/SQL language in great detail.[*] Because this is a book about Oracle SQL, the focus of this chapter is the use of PL/SQL within SQL statements as well as the use of SQL within PL/SQL programs.

What Is PL/SQL?

PL/SQL is a procedural programming language from Oracle that combines the following elements:

- Logical constructs such as IF-THEN-ELSE and WHILE
- SQL DML statements, built-in functions, and operators
- Transaction control statements such as COMMIT and ROLLBACK
- Cursor control statements
- Object and collection manipulation statements

Despite its humble origins as a scripting language in Version 6.0, PL/SQL became an integral part of the Oracle server with release 7.0. Because release 7.0 included the ability to compile and store PL/SQL programs within the server, Oracle began using the language to provide server functionality and to assist in database installation and configuration. With the 7.1 release of the server, Oracle added a new feature of particular use to SQL programmers: the ability to call PL/SQL stored functions from SQL statements (more on this later).

Along with the array of new features made available with each release of PL/SQL, Oracle began supplying prefabricated sets of PL/SQL functionality to allow programmers to tackle more sophisticated programming tasks and to help integrate with various

---

[*] For example, *Oracle PL/SQL Programming* by Steven Feuerstein (O'Reilly).

Oracle product offerings. These collections of stored procedures and functions, known as *Oracle Supplied Packages*, allow you to (among other things):

- Interface with and administer Oracle's Advanced Queueing feature
- Schedule database tasks for periodic execution
- Manipulate Oracle large objects (LOBs)
- Read from and write to external files
- Interface with Oracle's Advanced Replication features
- Issue dynamic SQL statements
- Generate and parse XML files
- Issue LDAP commands

The ever-expanding feature set of the PL/SQL language combined with the wide array of supplied packages has yielded a powerful database programming environment. Whether you are generating reports, writing data loading scripts, or writing custom applications, there's probably a place for PL/SQL in your project.

Procedures, Functions, and Packages

Although PL/SQL can still be used to write scripts, also known as *anonymous blocks*, the focus of this chapter is PL/SQL routines stored in the Oracle Database server. PL/SQL routines stored in the database may be one of two types: *stored procedures* or *stored functions*.* Stored functions and procedures are essentially identical except for the following:

- Stored functions have a return type, whereas procedures do not.
- Because stored functions return a value, they can be used in expressions, whereas procedures cannot.

Stored functions and procedures may be compiled individually, or they may be grouped together into *packages*. Along with being a convenient way to group related functionality together, packages are important for the following reasons:

- Packages are loaded into memory as a whole, increasing the likelihood that a procedure or function will be resident in memory when called.
- Packages can include private elements, allowing logic to be hidden from view.
- Placing functions and procedures inside packages eliminates the need to recompile all functions and procedures that reference a newly recompiled function/procedure.

---

* Database triggers are another type of stored PL/SQL, but they are outside the scope of this discussion.

- Function and procedure names may be overloaded within packages, whereas standalone functions and procedures cannot be overloaded.

- Functions and procedures inside packages can be checked for side effects at compile time rather than at execution time.

If these reasons haven't convinced you to place your stored functions and procedures inside packages, here's a bit of advice we can offer after working with PL/SQL since Version 7.0 of the Oracle Database server: you will never be sorry that you bundled your PL/SQL code into packages, but you will eventually be sorry if you don't.

Packages consist of two distinct parts: a *package specification*, which defines the signatures of the package's public procedures and functions, and a *package body*, which contains the code for the public procedures and functions and may also contain code for any private functions and procedures not included in the package specification. To give you an idea of what a package looks like, here is a simple example of a package specification:

```
CREATE OR REPLACE PACKAGE my_pkg AS
  PROCEDURE my_proc(arg1 IN VARCHAR2);

  FUNCTION my_func(arg1 IN NUMBER) RETURN VARCHAR2;
END my_pkg;
```

and its matching package body:

```
CREATE OR REPLACE PACKAGE BODY my_pkg AS
  FUNCTION my_private_func(arg1 IN NUMBER) RETURN VARCHAR2 IS
    return_val VARCHAR2(20);
  BEGIN
    SELECT col1 INTO return_val
    FROM tab2
    WHERE col2 = arg1;

    RETURN return_val;
  EXCEPTION
    WHEN NO_DATA_FOUND THEN
      RETURN 'NOT FOUND';
  END my_private_func;

  PROCEDURE my_proc(arg1 IN VARCHAR2) IS
  BEGIN
    UPDATE tab1 SET col1 = col1 + 1
    WHERE col2 = arg1;
  END my_proc;

  FUNCTION my_func(arg1 IN NUMBER) RETURN VARCHAR2 IS
  BEGIN
    RETURN my_private_func(arg1);
  END my_func;
END my_pkg;
```

As you can see, the my_pkg package includes one public procedure and one public function. The package specification includes the parameter names and types of the procedure and function, along with the return type of the function, but does not include any implementation code. The package body includes the implementation logic for the public function and procedure, and it also includes a private function (my_private_func) that is only accessible from inside the package body.

Calling Stored Functions from Queries

As mentioned earlier, stored functions may be called from within SQL statements. Since stored functions can in turn make calls to stored procedures, it can also be said that stored procedures may be called, albeit indirectly, from within SQL statements. Since stored functions may be used in expressions, they may be included wherever expressions are allowed in a query, including:

- The SELECT clause
- The WHERE clause
- The GROUP BY and HAVING clauses
- The ORDER BY clause
- The START WITH/CONNECT BY clauses (for hierarchical queries)
- The FROM clause (indirectly by using inline views or TABLE statements)

One of the most common uses of stored functions is to isolate commonly-used functionality to facilitate code reuse and simplify maintenance. For example, imagine that you are working with a large team to build a custom N-tier application. To simplify integration efforts between the various layers, it has been decided that all dates will be passed back and forth as the number of milliseconds since January 1, 1970. You could include the conversion logic in all of your queries, as in:

```
SELECT co.order_nbr, co.cust_nbr, co.sale_price,
  ROUND((co.order_dt - TO_DATE('01011970','MMDDYYYY')) * 86400 * 1000)
FROM cust_order co
WHERE ship_dt = TRUNC(SYSDATE);
```

However, this would become somewhat tedious and prove problematic should you wish to modify your logic in the future. Instead, build a utility package that includes functions for translating between Oracle's internal date format and the desired format:

```
CREATE OR REPLACE PACKAGE BODY pkg_util AS
  FUNCTION translate_date(dt IN DATE) RETURN NUMBER IS
  BEGIN
    RETURN ROUND((dt - TO_DATE('01011970','MMDDYYYY')) * 86400 * 1000);
  END translate_date;

  FUNCTION translate_date(dt IN NUMBER) RETURN DATE IS
  BEGIN
```

```
        RETURN TO_DATE('01011970','MMDDYYYY') + (dt / (86400 * 1000));
    END translate_date;
END pkg_util;
```

If you think you're seeing double, don't worry; the package contains two identically-named functions, one that requires a DATE parameter and returns a NUMBER, and another that requires a NUMBER parameter and returns a DATE. This strategy, called *overloading*, is only possible when your functions are contained in a package.

Your development team can now use these functions whenever they need to convert date formats, as in:

```
SELECT co.order_nbr, co.cust_nbr, co.sale_price,
  pkg_util.translate_date(co.order_dt) utc_order_dt
FROM cust_order co
WHERE co.ship_dt = TRUNC(SYSDATE);
```

Another common use of stored functions is to simplify and hide complex IF-THEN-ELSE logic from your SQL statements. Suppose you have to generate a report detailing all customer orders for the past month. You want to sort the orders using the ship_dt column if an order has been shipped, the expected_ship_dt column if a ship date has been assigned and is not in the past, the current day if the expected_ship_dt is in the past, or the order_dt column if the order hasn't been assigned a ship date. You could utilize a CASE statement in the ORDER BY clause:

```
SELECT co.order_nbr, co.cust_nbr, co.sale_price
FROM cust_order co
WHERE co.order_dt > TRUNC(SYSDATE, 'MONTH')
  AND co.cancelled_dt IS NULL
ORDER BY
  CASE
    WHEN co.ship_dt IS NOT NULL THEN co.ship_dt
    WHEN co.expected_ship_dt IS NOT NULL
      AND co.expected_ship_dt > SYSDATE
        THEN co.expected_ship_dt
    WHEN co.expected_ship_dt IS NOT NULL
      THEN GREATEST(SYSDATE, co.expected_ship_dt)
    ELSE co.order_dt
  END;
```

However, there are two problems with this approach:

- The resulting ORDER BY clause is fairly complex.
- You may wish to use this logic elsewhere, and duplicating it will create maintenance problems.

Instead, add a stored function to the pkg_util package that returns the appropriate date for a given order:

```
FUNCTION get_best_order_date(ord_dt IN DATE, exp_ship_dt IN DATE,
  ship_dt IN DATE) RETURN DATE IS
BEGIN
  IF ship_dt IS NOT NULL THEN
```

```
      RETURN ship_dt;
    ELSIF exp_ship_dt IS NOT NULL AND exp_ship_dt > SYSDATE THEN
      RETURN exp_ship_dt;
    ELSIF exp_ship_dt IS NOT NULL THEN
      RETURN SYSDATE;
    ELSE
      RETURN ord_dt;
    END IF;
  END get_best_order_date;
```

You may then call this function from both the SELECT and ORDER BY clauses:

```
SELECT co.order_nbr, co.cust_nbr, co.sale_price,
  pkg_util.get_best_order_date(co.order_dt, co.expected_ship_dt,
    co.ship_dt) best_date
FROM cust_order co
WHERE co.order_dt > TRUNC(SYSDATE, 'MONTH')
  AND co.cancelled_dt IS NULL
ORDER BY pkg_util.get_best_order_date(co.order_dt, co.expected_ship_dt,
    co.ship_dt);
```

If you are bothered by the fact that the stored function is called twice per row with the same parameters, you can always retrieve the data within an inline view and sort the results afterward, as in:

```
SELECT orders.order_nbr, orders.cust_nbr,
  orders.sale_price, orders.best_date
FROM
 (SELECT co.order_nbr order_nbr, co.cust_nbr cust_nbr,
    co.sale_price sale_price,
    pkg_util.get_best_order_date(co.order_dt, co.expected_ship_dt,
    co.ship_dt) best_date
  FROM cust_order co
  WHERE co.order_dt > TRUNC(SYSDATE, 'MONTH')
    AND co.cancelled_dt IS NULL) orders
ORDER BY orders.best_date;
```

Stored Functions and Views

Since a view is nothing more than a stored query and stored functions can be called from the SELECT clause of a query, columns of a view can map to stored function calls. This is an excellent way to shield your user community from complexity, and it has another interesting benefit as well. Consider the following view definition, which includes calls to several different stored functions:

```
CREATE OR REPLACE VIEW vw_example
  (col1, col2, col3, col4, col5, col6, col7, col8)
AS SELECT t1.col1,
  t1.col2,
  t2.col3,
  t2.col4,
  pkg_example.func1(t1.col1, t2.col3),
  pkg_example.func2(t1.col2, t2.col4),
```

```
    pkg_example.func3(t1.col1, t2.col3),
    pkg_example.func4(t1.col2, t2.col4)
FROM tab1 t1 INNER JOIN tab2 t2
    ON t1.col1 = t2.col3;
```

Whereas the first four columns of the view map to columns of the `tab1` and `tab2` tables, values for the remaining columns are generated by calling various functions in the `pkg_example` package. If one of your users executes the following query:

```
SELECT col2, col4, col7
FROM vw_example
WHERE col1 = 1001;
```

Only one stored function (`pkg_example.func3`) is actually executed even though the view contains four columns that map to stored function calls. This is because when a query is executed against a view, the Oracle server constructs a new query by combining the original query and the view definition. In this case, the query that is actually executed looks like:

```
SELECT t1.col2,
    t2.col4,
    pkg_example.func3(t1.col1, t2.col3)
FROM tab1 t1 INNER JOIN tab2 t2
    ON t1.col1 = t2.col3
WHERE t1.col1 = 1001;
```

Therefore, your view could contain dozens of stored function calls, but only those that are explicitly referenced by queries will be executed.[*]

Avoiding Table Joins

Imagine that you have deployed a set of views for your users to generate reports and ad-hoc queries against, and one of your users asks that a new column be added to one of the views. The column is from a table not yet included in the FROM clause, and the column is only needed for a single report issued once a month. You could add the table to the FROM clause, add the column to the SELECT clause, and add the join conditions to the ON clause. However, every query issued against the view would include the new table, even though most queries don't reference the new column.

An alternative strategy is to write a stored function that queries the new table and returns the desired column. The stored function can then be added to the SELECT clause without the need to add the new table to the FROM clause. To illustrate, let's

---

[*] This is one reason why you should never use SELECT * when working with a view. Always explicitly name the columns that you need so that the server doesn't waste time generating data that you never reference.

expand on the previous simple example. If the desired column is col6 in the tab3 table, you could add a new function to the pkg_example package such as:

```
FUNCTION func5(param1 IN NUMBER) RETURN VARCHAR2 IS
  ret_val VARCHAR2(20);
BEGIN
  SELECT col6 INTO ret_val
  FROM tab3
  WHERE col5 = param1;

  RETURN ret_val;
EXCEPTION
  WHEN NO_DATA_FOUND THEN
    RETURN null;
END func5;
```

You can now add a column to the view that maps to the new function, as in:

```
CREATE OR REPLACE VIEW vw_example
  (col1, col2, col3, col4, col5, col6, col7, col8, col9)
AS SELECT t1.col1,
  t1.col2,
  t2.col3,
  t2.col4,
  pkg_example.func1(t1.col1, t2.col3),
  pkg_example.func2(t1.col2, t2.col4),
  pkg_example.func3(t1.col1, t2.col3),
  pkg_example.func4(t1.col2, t2.col4),
  pkg_example.func5(t2.col3)
FROM tab1 t1 INNER JOIN tab2 t2
  ON t1.col1 = t2.col3;
```

Thus, you have provided your users access to column col6 of the tab3 table without adding the tab3 table to the view's FROM clause. Users who don't reference the new col9 column of the view will experience no changes to the performance of their queries against vw_example.

Even though the column was originally targeted for a single report, don't be surprised if other users decide to include the new column in their queries. As the column utilization increases, it may be advantageous to abandon the stored function strategy and include the tab3 table in the FROM clause. Since a view was employed, however, you would be able to make this change without the need for any of your users to modify their queries.

Deterministic Functions

Earlier in this section, we created a package containing two functions to be used for translating between a date and the number of milliseconds since January 1, 1970. Because these functions do not depend on data stored in the database or in package variables, they will always return the same result for any given input parameter. Any function having this property can be marked as DETERMINISTIC in the function declaration, as in:

```
CREATE OR REPLACE PACKAGE BODY pkg_util AS
  FUNCTION translate_date(dt IN DATE) RETURN NUMBER DETERMINISTIC;
  FUNCTION translate_date(dt IN NUMBER) RETURN DATE DETERMINISTIC;
END pkg_util;
```

Marking your functions as DETERMINISTIC allows the Oracle server to perform certain optimizations, such as storing a function's parameters and results in memory so that subsequent calls to the same function can be handled without the need to call the function again.

Restrictions on Calling PL/SQL from SQL

Although calling stored functions from SQL is a powerful feature, it is important to understand how doing so might have unintended consequences. For example, imagine that one of your co-workers has written a stored function that, given a part number, returns the number of times that part is included in all open orders. The function is contained in a utilities package, such as the following:

```
CREATE OR REPLACE PACKAGE pkg_util AS
  FUNCTION get_part_order_qty(pno IN VARCHAR2) RETURN NUMBER;
END pkg_util;
```

You have been tasked with generating a weekly inventory report, and you would like to make use of the function in one of your queries, as in:

```
SELECT p.part_nbr, p.name, s.name, p.inventory_qty,
  pkg_util.get_part_order_qty(p.part_nbr) open_order_qty
FROM part p INNER JOIN supplier s
  ON p.supplier_id = s.supplier_id
ORDER BY s.name, p.part_nbr;
```

When you run the query, however, you are surprised to see the following error:

```
ORA-14551: cannot perform a DML operation inside a query
```

Upon checking the package body, you find that the get_part_order_qty function, along with calculating the number of times a part is included in all open orders, generates a request to restock the part by inserting a record into the part_order table if the calculated value exceeds the number in inventory. Had Oracle allowed your statement to be executed, your query would have resulted in changes to the database without your knowledge or consent.

Purity Level

To determine whether a stored function might have unintended consequences when called from a SQL statement, Oracle assigns a *purity level* to the function that answers the following four questions:

1. Does the function read from database tables?
2. Does the function reference any global package variables?
3. Does the function write to any database tables?
4. Does the function modify any global package variables?

For each negative response to these questions, a designation is added to the purity level, as shown in Table 11-1.

Table 11-1. Purity level designations

Question #	Designation	Description
1	RNDS	Reads no database state
2	RNPS	Reads no package state
3	WNDS	Writes no database state
4	WNPS	Writes no package state

Therefore, a function with a purity level of {WNPS, WNDS} is guaranteed not to write to the database or modify package variables, but it may reference package variables and/or read from database tables. For a function to be called from a SQL statement, its purity level must at a minimum include the WNDS designation.

When using packaged functions in Oracle versions prior to release 8.1, it was required that the purity level be specified prior to calling a function from a SQL statement. This is accomplished by adding a *pragma*, or compiler directive, to the package specification. The RESTRICT_REFERENCES pragma follows the function declaration in the package specification, as demonstrated here:

```
CREATE OR REPLACE PACKAGE my_pkg AS
  FUNCTION my_func(arg1 IN NUMBER) RETURN VARCHAR2;
  PRAGMA RESTRICT_REFERENCES(my_func, RNPS, WNPS, WNDS);
END my_pkg;
```

When the package body is compiled, the code is checked against the designations listed in the RESTRICT_REFERENCES pragma. If the code does not meet the purity level asserted in the pragma, compilation fails with the following error:

```
PLS-00452: Subprogram 'MY_FUNC' violates its associated pragma
```

Therefore, you tell the compiler what your function will and won't do via the RESTRICT_REFERENCES pragma, and the compiler checks to see if you are telling it the truth.

Beginning with Oracle8*i*, you are no longer required to specify the purity level of functions in the package specification. All functions called from queries, whether stand-alone or within packages, are checked at runtime to ensure that there are no side effects. Nevertheless, you may want to consider using the RESTRICT_REFERENCES pragma so that you avoid any surprises later on.

Trust Me...

One of the reasons Oracle has relaxed the requirement that the purity level be asserted at compile time is that PL/SQL can make calls to functions written in C and Java, which have no mechanisms similar to PL/SQL's PRAGMA for asserting purity. To allow functions written in different languages to call each other, Oracle introduced the TRUST keyword in Oracle8*i*. Adding TRUST to the RESTRICT_REFERENCES pragma for a function causes Oracle to:

- Treat the function as if it satisfies the pragma without actually checking the code.
- Treat any functions or procedures called from the function that have the TRUST keyword as if they satisfy the pragma as well.

Thus, a stored function whose RESTRICT_REFERENCES pragma includes WNDS and TRUST could make calls to other PL/SQL functions that do not specify RESTRICT_REFERENCES pragmas and/or external C and Java functions and still be callable from SQL statements. In the case of external C or Java calls, you will need to include the TRUST designation in your function's RESTRICT_REFERENCES pragma if you want to call the function from SQL, since the C or Java source code is not available to the server for inspection.

To use TRUST, simply append it to the end of the purity designation list, as in:

```
CREATE OR REPLACE PACKAGE my_pkg AS
  FUNCTION my_func(arg1 IN NUMBER) RETURN VARCHAR2;
  PRAGMA RESTRICT_REFERENCES(my_func, RNPS, WNPS, WNDS, TRUST);
END my_pkg;
```

Other Restrictions

In addition to the WNDS requirement, Oracle checks that each function invoked from a SQL statement abides by the following rules:

- The function can't end the current transaction using COMMIT or ROLLBACK.
- The function can't alter a transaction by creating savepoints or rolling back to a previously defined savepoint.
- The function can't issue an ALTER SYSTEM or ALTER SESSION statement.

- All parameter types, including the return type, must be standard SQL types such as VARCHAR2, NUMBER, and DATE. PL/SQL types such as BOOLEAN and RECORD are not allowed.
- All parameters must be IN parameters. OUT and IN OUT parameters are not allowed.

The first three restrictions are designed to protect against changes that could alter the operational environment of the parent query. The fourth and fifth restrictions ensure that the data being returned from the PL/SQL function can be handled by the SQL statement.

Stored Functions in DML Statements

Stored functions may also be called from INSERT, UPDATE, and DELETE statements. Whereas most of the restrictions outlined earlier apply equally to stored functions called from DML statements, there is one major difference: since the parent DML statement is changing the state of the database, stored functions invoked from DML statements do not need to abide by the WNDS restriction. However, such stored functions may not read or modify the same table as the parent DML statement.

Like queries, DML statements may call stored functions where expressions are allowed, including:

- The VALUES clause of an INSERT statement
- The SET clause of an UPDATE statement
- The WHERE clause of an INSERT, UPDATE, or DELETE statement

Any subqueries called from a DML statement may also call stored functions as well under the same set of restrictions as the parent DML statement.

Often, sets of complementary stored functions are called from both queries and DML statements. For example, you saw earlier how the pkg_util.translate_date function could be called from a query to translate from the Oracle date format stored in the database to the format needed by a Java client. Similarly, the over-loaded pkg_util.translate_date function may be used within an update statement to perform the reverse translation, as in:

```
UPDATE cust_order
SET expected_ship_dt = pkg_util.translate_date(:1)
WHERE order_nbr = :2;
```

where :1 and :2 are placeholders for the UTC timedate and order number passed in by the Java client.

Stored functions may also be used in the WHERE clause in place of correlated subqueries, both to simplify the DML statement and to facilitate code reuse. For example, suppose you have been asked to push the expected ship date by five days for any order containing part number F34-17802. You could issue an UPDATE statement against the cust_order table using a correlated subquery, as in:

```
UPDATE cust_order co
SET co.expected_ship_dt = NVL(co.expected_ship_dt, SYSDATE) + 5
WHERE co.cancelled_dt IS NULL and co.ship_dt IS NULL
  AND EXISTS (SELECT 1 FROM line_item li
    WHERE li.order_nbr = co.order_nbr
      AND li.part_nbr = 'F34-17802');
```

After having written many subqueries against the line_item table, however, you feel it's time to write a multipurpose function and add it to the pkg_util package:

```
FUNCTION get_part_count(ordno IN NUMBER,
  partno IN VARCHAR2 DEFAULT NULL, max_cnt IN NUMBER DEFAULT 9999)
  RETURN NUMBER IS
  tot_cnt NUMBER(5) := 0;
  li_part_nbr VARCHAR2(20);
  CURSOR cur_li(c_ordno IN NUMBER) IS
    SELECT part_nbr
    FROM line_item
    WHERE order_nbr = c_ordno;
BEGIN
  OPEN cur_li(ordno);
  WHILE tot_cnt < max_cnt LOOP
    FETCH cur_li INTO li_part_nbr;
    EXIT WHEN cur_li%NOTFOUND;

    IF partno IS NULL OR
      (partno IS NOT NULL AND partno = li_part_nbr) THEN
      tot_cnt := tot_cnt + 1;
    END IF;
  END LOOP;
  CLOSE cur_li;

  RETURN tot_cnt;
END get_part_count;
```

The function may be used for multiple purposes, including:

- To count the number of line items in a given order
- To count the number of line items in a given order containing a given part
- To determine whether the given order has at least X occurrences of a given part

The UPDATE statement may now use the function to locate open orders that have at least one occurrence of part F34-17802:

```
UPDATE cust_order co
SET co.expected_ship_dt = NVL(co.expected_ship_dt, SYSDATE) + 5
WHERE co.cancelled_dt IS NULL and co.ship_dt IS NULL
  AND 1 = pkg_util.get_part_count(co.order_nbr, 'F34-17802', 1);
```

The SQL Inside Your PL/SQL

Now that we've explored calling PL/SQL from SQL, let's turn the tables and explore the use of SQL inside your PL/SQL code. SQL is great at manipulating large sets of data, but there are situations where you need to work with data at the row level. PL/SQL, with its looping and cursor control capabilities, allows the flexibility to work at the set level using SQL or at the row level using cursors. However, many PL/SQL programmers forego the power of SQL and do everything at the row level, even when it is unnecessary and time-consuming to do so.

As an analogy, imagine that you are working at a warehouse, and a large shipment of parts arrives on the loading dock. Your job is to separate the shipment by part type and distribute the pieces to different areas of the warehouse. To make your job easier, the warehouse owner has procured the best forklift money can buy. There are two possible strategies to employ:

- Pick up one box at a time, determine the type, and drive it to the appropriate destination.
- Spend some time analyzing the situation, determine that every box on a pallet is of the same type, and drive entire pallets to the appropriate destination.

Although this analogy might be overly simplistic, it does serve to illustrate the difference between set operations and row operations. Allowing the Oracle server to manipulate large sets in a single operation can often yield a performance improvement of several orders of magnitude over manipulating one row at a time, especially on systems with multiple CPUs.

When a procedural language is used for database access (whether it is PL/SQL, C with OCI calls, or Java using JDBC), there is a tendency to employ the first strategy. Perhaps programmers are accustomed to coding at a low level of granularity when using a procedural language and this spills over into their data access logic. This situation is especially prevalent in systems that need to process and load large amounts of data from external files, such as data warehouse load utilities.

Imagine that you are charged with building an infrastructure to accept files from multiple OLTP systems, perform various data cleaning operations, and aggregate the data into a data warehouse. Using PL/SQL (or C, Java, C++, Cobol, etc.), you could build functionality that:

1. Opens a given file.
2. Reads a line, verifies/cleans the data, and updates the appropriate row of the appropriate fact table in the data warehouse.
3. Repeats #2 until the file is exhausted.
4. Closes the file.

Although this approach might work for small files, it is not uncommon for large warehouses to receive feeds containing hundreds of thousands or millions of items. Even if your code is extremely efficient, processing a million-line file could take several hours.

Here's an alternate strategy that employs the power of the Oracle server to make quick work of large data feeds:

1. Create a staging table for each unique data feed file format.
2. At the start of the load process, truncate the staging tables.
3. Use SQL*Loader with the direct path option to quickly load the data file into the appropriate staging table.
4. Update all rows of the staging table to clean, verify, and transform data, marking rows as invalid if they fail verification. Perform the operation in parallel if possible.
5. Update the appropriate fact table using a subquery against the staging table. Again, perform in parallel if possible.

For this strategy to succeed, you need to have adequate disk space and sufficiently large rollback and temporary tablespaces. With adequate resources and properly constructed SQL statements, however, this strategy can yield a 10X improvement over the previous strategy.

So what role should PL/SQL play in such a scenario? In this case, PL/SQL would be an excellent vehicle for executing steps 4 and 5 of the previous list. Although the stored procedures might each contain only a single update statement, the SQL is likely to be complex and may contain optimizer hints and other advanced features. Therefore, it would be advisable to isolate the SQL from the rest of the application so that it may be independently monitored and tuned.

In general, when dealing with complex logic involving large data sets, it is advantageous to think in terms of data sets rather than programming steps. In other words, ask yourself where your data is, where it needs to move to, and what needs to happen to it during its journey instead of thinking in terms of what needs to happen with each piece of data to satisfy the business requirements. If you follow this strategy, you will find yourself writing substantial, efficient SQL statements that employ PL/SQL where appropriate, rather than writing complex PL/SQL routines that employ SQL when needed. In doing so, you will be providing the server with the opportunity to split large workloads into multiple pieces that run in parallel, which can greatly improve performance.

CHAPTER 12

Objects and Collections

Beginning with Version 8.0, Oracle has been adding object-oriented features to what had been a purely relational database server. *Object types* and *collections* were introduced in Oracle8, and both have been sufficiently refined in Oracle8*i*, Oracle9*i* Database, and Oracle Database 10*g* so that they may now be considered fully-functional.[*] Oracle now considers its database engine to be *object-relational*, in that a database may mix relational constructs such as tables and constraints with object-oriented constructs such as object types, collections, and references.

Object Types

An object type is a user-defined data type that combines data and related methods to model complex entities. In this regard, they are similar to class definitions in an object-oriented language such as C++ or Java. However, unlike Java and C++, Oracle object types have a built-in persistence mechanism, since a table can be defined to store an object type in the database. Thus, Oracle object types can be directly manipulated via SQL.

The best way to define the syntax and features of an object type is with an example. The following DDL statement creates an object type used to model an equity security such as a common stock:

```
CREATE TYPE equity AS OBJECT (
  issuer_id NUMBER,
  ticker VARCHAR2(6),
  outstanding_shares NUMBER,
  last_close_price NUMBER(9,2),
MEMBER PROCEDURE
  apply_split(split_ratio in VARCHAR2)
)
NOT FINAL;
```

---

[*] For example, in release 8.0, object types didn't support inheritance, and collections could not be nested (i.e., an array of arrays), resulting in a fairly cool reception to Oracle's early attempts at object orientation.

The equity object type has four attributes and a single member procedure. The NOT FINAL declaration at the end of the type definition allows for subtypes to be defined in the future (more on this later). The body of the `apply_split` procedure is defined within a CREATE TYPE BODY statement. The following example illustrates how the `apply_split` member procedure might be defined:

```
CREATE TYPE BODY equity AS
  MEMBER PROCEDURE apply_split(split_ratio in VARCHAR2) IS
    from_val NUMBER;
    to_val NUMBER;
  BEGIN
    /* parse the split ratio into its components */
    to_val := SUBSTR(split_ratio, 1, INSTR(split_ratio, ':') - 1);
    from_val := SUBSTR(split_ratio, INSTR(split_ratio, ':') + 1);

    /* apply the split ratio to the outstanding shares */
    SELF.outstanding_shares :=
      (SELF.outstanding_shares * to_val) / from_val;

    /* apply the split ratio to the last closing price */
    SELF.last_close_price :=
      (SELF.last_close_price * from_val) / to_val;
  END apply_split;
END;
```

In this example, the SELF keyword is used to identify the current instance of the equity object type. Although it is not required, we recommend using SELF in your code so that it is clear that you are referencing or modifying the current instance's data. We will explore how to call member functions and procedures a bit later in the chapter.

Instances of type equity are created using the default constructor, which has the same name as the object type and expects one parameter per attribute of the object type. The following PL/SQL block demonstrates how an instance of the equity object type can be created using the default constructor:

```
DECLARE
  eq equity := NULL;
BEGIN
  eq := equity(198, 'ACMW', 1000000, 13.97);
END;
```

Object type constructors may also be called from within DML statements. The next example queries the issuer table to find the issuer with the name 'ACME Wholesalers', and then uses the retrieved issuer_id field to construct an instance of the equity type:

```
DECLARE
  eq equity := NULL;
BEGIN
  SELECT equity(i.issuer_id, 'ACMW', 1000000, 13.97)
  INTO eq
```

```
   FROM issuer i
   WHERE i.name = 'ACME Wholesalers';
END;
```

Subtypes

Oracle9*i* introduced several notable features to the object-oriented toolset, including inheritance (release 1) and user-defined constructors (release 2). The following type definition demonstrates both of these features:

```
CREATE TYPE preferred_stock UNDER equity (
  last_dividend_date DATE,
  last_dividend_amount NUMBER(9,2),
  CONSTRUCTOR FUNCTION preferred_stock(last_div_dt DATE,
    last_div_amt NUMBER, eq equity) RETURN SELF AS RESULT
)
FINAL;
```

Because preferred stock is a special type of equity, you can create a subtype that includes all of the attributes and methods of the equity type along with additional attributes to hold dividend information. In this case, we have added two attributes to hold information about the last dividend payment, along with a user-defined constructor for the preferred_stock type, which is defined in the type body:

```
CREATE TYPE BODY preferred_stock AS
  CONSTRUCTOR FUNCTION preferred_stock(last_div_dt DATE,
    last_div_amt NUMBER, eq equity) RETURN SELF AS RESULT IS
  BEGIN
    SELF.last_dividend_date := last_div_dt;
    SELF.last_dividend_amount := last_div_amt;
    SELF.issuer_id := eq.issuer_id;
    SELF.ticker := eq.ticker;
    SELF.outstanding_shares := eq.outstanding_shares;
    SELF.last_close_price := eq.last_close_price;
    RETURN;
  END preferred_stock;
END;
```

For the constructor, we chose to pass in an instance of equity rather than pass in the four equity attributes individually. The next example shows how to create an instance of preferred_stock by creating an instance of equity and passing it into the user-defined constructor:

```
DECLARE
  eq equity := NULL;
  ps preferred_stock := NULL;
BEGIN
  eq := equity(198, 'ACMW', 1000000, 13.97);
  ps := preferred_stock(SYSDATE, 0.1, eq);
END;
```

Because preferred_stock is a subtype of equity, an instance of preferred_stock is also an instance of equity. The next example uses the IS OF function to demonstrate this:

```
SELECT equities.eq
FROM
 (SELECT equity(198, 'ACMW', 1000000, 13.97) eq FROM DUAL
  UNION ALL
  SELECT preferred_stock(SYSDATE, 0.1,
    equity(198, 'ACMW', 1000000, 13.97)) eq FROM DUAL
  ) equities
WHERE equities.eq IS OF (equity);

EQ(ISSUER_ID, TICKER, OUTSTANDING_SHARES, LAST_CLOSE_PRICE)
-----------------------------------------------------------------
EQUITY(198, 'ACMW', 1000000, 13.97)
PREFERRED_STOCK(198, 'ACMW', 1000000, 13.97, '03-DEC-03', .1)
```

The equities inline view constructs an instance of equity and an instance of preferred_stock, and the containing query returns those objects that are of type equity; as you can see, both instances, one of equity and one of preferred_stock, are returned. However, an instance of equity is *not* an instance of preferred_stock, as demonstrated in the next example:

```
SELECT equities.eq
FROM
 (SELECT equity(198, 'ACMW', 1000000, 13.97) eq FROM DUAL UNION ALL
  SELECT preferred_stock(SYSDATE, 0.1,
    equity(198, 'ACMW', 1000000, 13.97)) eq FROM DUAL
  ) equities
WHERE equities.eq IS OF (preferred_stock);

EQ(ISSUER_ID, TICKER, OUTSTANDING_SHARES, LAST_CLOSE_PRICE)
-----------------------------------------------------------------
PREFERRED_STOCK(198, 'ACMW', 1000000, 13.97, '03-DEC-03', .1)
```

In this case, the equity instance is *not* returned, since it is not of type preferred_stock. This distinction will be important when we look at collections later in the chapter.

Object Attributes

So far, we have created several object types and generated several non-persistent (not stored in a database) instances of those object types. If you want to store instances of your object types in a database, you have two choices: create a column in a table to store instances of your object type, or create a special type of table, called an *object table*, to store instances of your object type. This section will explore how to generate object-based columns, while the following section will explore object tables.

The following table definition shows how an equity object type may be used as an attribute of the fund_holding table:

```
CREATE TABLE fund_holding (
    fund_id VARCHAR2(10) NOT NULL,
    security equity NOT NULL,
    num_shares NUMBER NOT NULL);
```

While the fund_id and num_shares columns are defined using standard built-in data types, the security column is defined as type equity. When adding records to the table, you must utilize the object type constructor, as illustrated by the following INSERT statement:

```
INSERT INTO fund_holding (fund_id, security, num_shares)
VALUES ('101A', equity(198, 'ACMW', 1000000, 13.97), 20000);
```

To see the attributes of the equity object, you must provide an alias for the table and reference the alias, the name of the column containing the object type, and the object type's attribute. The next query retrieves the fund_id, which is a column in the fund_holding table, and the ticker, which is an attribute of the equity object within the fund_holding table:

```
SELECT fh.fund_id fund_id,
    fh.security.ticker ticker
FROM fund_holding fh;

FUND_ID    TICKER
---------- ------
101A       ACMW
```

Since preferred_stock is a subtype of equity, you can substitute an instance of preferred_stock:

```
UPDATE fund_holding fh
SET fh.security = preferred_stock(SYSDATE, 0.1,
    equity(198, 'ACMW', 1000000, 13.97));
```

 The ability to substitute a subtype for its parent type is turned on by default. If you do not want this behavior, you can turn it off when creating or altering your object table. For the fund_holding table, you would issue the following statement:

```
ALTER TABLE fund_holding MODIFY COLUMN
    security NOT SUBSTITUTABLE AT ALL LEVELS;
```

However, as shown in the next example, you will not be able to query attributes of the preferred_stock type explicitly, because the table definition specifies type equity:

```
SELECT fh.fund_id fund_id,
    fh.security.last_dividend_amount div_amt
FROM fund_holding fh;

ERROR at line 2:
ORA-00904: "FH"."SECURITY"."LAST_DIVIDEND_AMOUNT": invalid identifier
```

Even though you can substitute an instance of a subtype for an instance of a parent type, you are limited to using the attributes and methods defined for the parent type. In the most recent example, the SELECT statement "sees" a table of equity objects. That does not change just because one of those objects happens to be a specific subtype of equity.

Object Tables

In addition to creating object type columns, you can also build an object table specifically for holding instances of your object type. You create these tables by referencing the object type in the CREATE TABLE statement using the OF keyword:

```
CREATE TABLE equities OF equity;
```

You can populate the equities table using the constructor for the equity object type, or you may populate it from existing instances of the equity object type. For example, the next statement populates the equities table using the security column of the fund_holding table, which is defined as an equity type:

```
INSERT INTO equities
SELECT fh.security FROM fund_holding fh;
```

You can also store any subtype of the equity type in the table:

```
INSERT INTO equities
VALUES (preferred_stock(SYSDATE - 20, 0.05,
    equity(199, 'XYZ', 2000000, 8.87)));
```

When querying the equities table, you can reference the object type's attributes directly, just as you would an ordinary table:

```
SELECT issuer_id, ticker
FROM equities;

ISSUER_ID TICKER
---------- ------
      198 ACMW
      199 XYZ
```

If you want to retrieve the data in the equities table as an instance of an equity object rather than as a set of attributes, you can use the VALUE function to return an object. The following query retrieves the object having a ticker equal to 'ACMW' from the equities table:

```
SELECT VALUE(e)
FROM equities e
WHERE e.ticker = 'ACMW';


VALUE(E)(ISSUER_ID, TICKER, OUTSTANDING_SHARES, LAST_CLOSE_PRICE)
----------------------------------------------------------------
PREFERRED_STOCK(198, 'ACMW', 1000000, 13.97, '20-MAR-04', .1)
```

Since you can treat an object table as either a relational table or as a set of objects, object tables represent the best of both worlds.

 You *must* use a table alias with the VALUE function. You cannot pass a table name to VALUE.

Now that you have an object stored in the database, we can explore how to call the `apply_split` member procedure defined earlier. Before you call the procedure, you need to find the target object in the table and then tell the object to run its `apply_split` procedure. The following PL/SQL block expands on the previous example, which finds the object in the equities table with a `ticker` of `'ACMW'`, by finding an equity object, invoking its `apply_split` method, and saving it back to the table again:

```
DECLARE
   eq equity := NULL;
BEGIN
   SELECT VALUE(e)
   INTO eq
   FROM equities e
   WHERE ticker = 'ACMW'
   FOR UPDATE;

   /* apply a 2:1 stock split */
   eq.apply_split('2:1');

   /* store modified object */
   UPDATE equities e
   SET e = eq
   WHERE ticker = 'ACMW';
END;
```

It is important to realize that the `apply_split` procedure is not operating directly on the data in the equities table; rather, it is operating on a copy of the object held in memory. After the `apply_split` procedure has executed against the copy, the UPDATE statement overwrites the object in the equities table with the object referenced by the local variable eq, thus saving the modified version of the object.

 Specifying FOR UPDATE at the end of the SELECT statement signifies your intent to modify the data being selected at some point in the future, which causes Oracle to place a lock on the data on your behalf. If you do not specify FOR UPDATE in this case, it is possible for another user to modify or delete the data between when you first select the data and when you issue the UPDATE statement.

Object Parameters

Regardless of whether you decide to store object types persistently in the database, you can use them as vehicles for passing data within or between applications. Object types may be used as input parameters and return types for PL/SQL stored procedures and functions. Additionally, SELECT statements can instantiate and return object types even if none of the tables in the FROM clause contain object types. Therefore, object types may be used to graft an object-oriented veneer on top of a purely relational database design.

To illustrate how this might work, let's build an API for our example database that both accepts and returns object types to find and build customer orders. First, we'll identify the necessary object types:

```
CREATE TYPE customer_obj AS OBJECT
 (cust_nbr NUMBER,
  name VARCHAR2(30));

CREATE TYPE employee_obj AS OBJECT
 (emp_id NUMBER,
  name VARCHAR2(50));

CREATE TYPE order_obj AS OBJECT
 (order_nbr NUMBER,
  customer customer_obj,
  salesperson employee_obj,
  order_dt DATE,
  price NUMBER,
  status VARCHAR2(20));

CREATE TYPE line_item_obj AS OBJECT
 (part_nbr VARCHAR2(20),
  quantity NUMBER(8,2));
```

Using these object definitions, we can now define a PL/SQL package containing procedures and functions that support the lifecycle of a customer order:

```
CREATE PACKAGE order_lifecycle AS
  FUNCTION create_order(v_cust_nbr IN NUMBER, v_emp_id IN NUMBER)
    RETURN order_obj;
  PROCEDURE cancel_order(v_order_nbr IN NUMBER);
  FUNCTION get_order(v_order_nbr IN NUMBER) RETURN order_obj;
  PROCEDURE add_line_item(v_order_nbr IN NUMBER,
    v_line_item IN line_item_obj);
END order_lifecycle;

CREATE PACKAGE BODY order_lifecycle AS
  FUNCTION create_order(v_cust_nbr IN NUMBER, v_emp_id IN NUMBER)
    RETURN order_obj IS
    ord_nbr NUMBER;
  BEGIN
    SELECT seq_order_nbr.NEXTVAL INTO ord_nbr FROM DUAL;
```

```
    INSERT INTO cust_order (order_nbr, cust_nbr, sales_emp_id,
      order_dt, expected_ship_dt, status)
    SELECT ord_nbr, c.cust_nbr, e.emp_id,
      SYSDATE, SYSDATE + 7, 'NEW'
    FROM customer c CROSS JOIN employee e
    WHERE c.cust_nbr = v_cust_nbr
      AND e.emp_id = v_emp_id;

    RETURN order_lifecycle.get_order(ord_nbr);
  END create_order;

  PROCEDURE cancel_order(v_order_nbr IN NUMBER) IS
  BEGIN
    UPDATE cust_order SET cancelled_dt = SYSDATE,
      expected_ship_dt = NULL, status = 'CANCELED'
    WHERE order_nbr = v_order_nbr;
  END cancel_order;

  FUNCTION get_order(v_order_nbr IN NUMBER) RETURN order_obj IS
    ord order_obj := NULL;
  BEGIN
    SELECT order_obj(co.order_nbr,
      customer_obj(c.cust_nbr, c.name),
      employee_obj(e.emp_id, e.fname || ' ' || e.lname),
      co.order_dt, co.sale_price, co.status)
    INTO ord
    FROM cust_order co INNER JOIN customer c
      ON co.cust_nbr = c.cust_nbr
      INNER JOIN employee e
      ON co.sales_emp_id = e.emp_id
    WHERE co.order_nbr = v_order_nbr;

    RETURN ord;
  EXCEPTION
    WHEN NO_DATA_FOUND THEN
      RETURN ord;
  END get_order;

  PROCEDURE add_line_item(v_order_nbr IN NUMBER,
    V_line_item IN line_item_obj) IS
  BEGIN
    INSERT INTO line_item (order_nbr, part_nbr, qty)
    VALUES (v_order_nbr, v_line_item.part_nbr,
      v_line_item.quantity);
  END add_line_item;
END order_lifecycle;
```

From the API user's standpoint, objects are being stored and retrieved from the database, even though the database behind the API is purely relational. If you are squeamish about using object types in your database schema, this approach can be an attractive alternative to asking your Java coders to directly manipulate relational data.

Collection Types

During a traditional relational design process, one-to-many relationships, such as a department having many employees or an order consisting of many line items, are resolved as separate tables where the child table holds a foreign key to the parent table. In our example schema, each row in the line_item table knows which order it belongs to via a foreign key, but a row in the cust_order table does not directly know anything about line items. Beginning with Oracle8, such relationships can be internalized within the parent table using a *collection*. The two collection types available in Oracle8 and above are *variable arrays*, which are used for ordered, bounded sets of data, and *nested tables*, which are used for unordered, unbounded data sets.

Variable Arrays

Variable arrays, also called *varrays*, are arrays stored within a table. Elements of a varray must be of the same data type (although subtypes are permitted), are bounded by a maximum size, and are accessed positionally. Varrays may contain either a standard Oracle data type, such as DATE or VARCHAR2, or a user-defined object type. The following example illustrates the creation of a varray and its use as a column of a table:

```
CREATE TYPE resupply_dates AS VARRAY(100) OF DATE;

CREATE TABLE part_c (
  part_nbr VARCHAR2(20) NOT NULL,
  name VARCHAR2(50) NOT NULL,
  supplier_id NUMBER(6),
  unit_cost NUMBER(8,2),
  inventory_qty NUMBER(6),
  restocks resupply_dates);
```

Along with descriptive information about the part, each row in the part_c table can hold up to 100 dates corresponding to when a shipment was received from the supplier.

> Beginning with the Oracle Database 10g release, the maximum size of a varray can be modified after it has been defined, so you won't need to worry so much about how high to set the maximum size of your collections. To change the resupply_dates varray to hold 200 dates, you would issue the following:
>
> ```
> ALTER TYPE resupply_dates MODIFY LIMIT 200;
> ```

Nested Tables

Like varrays, all elements of a nested table must be of the same data type, either a built-in data type or a user-defined type. Unlike varrays, however, nested tables do not have a maximum size and are not accessed positionally. The following example defines a nested table type containing an object type:

```
CREATE TYPE line_item_obj AS OBJECT (
  part_nbr VARCHAR2(20),
  quantity NUMBER(8,2),
  MAP MEMBER FUNCTION to_string RETURN VARCHAR2);

CREATE TYPE line_item_tbl AS TABLE OF line_item_obj;
```

The to_string member function will be used later in the chapter for comparing instances of type line_item_obj.

Now that we have created a nested table type for line_item objects, we can choose to embed it into our cust_order table, as in the following:

```
CREATE TABLE cust_order_c (
  order_nbr NUMBER(8) NOT NULL,
  cust_nbr NUMBER(6) NOT NULL,
  sales_emp_id NUMBER(6) NOT NULL,
  order_dt DATE NOT NULL,
  sale_price NUMBER(9,2),
  order_items line_item_tbl)
NESTED TABLE order_items STORE AS order_items_table;
```

Using a nested table, we have absorbed an order's line items into the cust_order table, eliminating the need for the line_item table. Later in the chapter, you'll see how Oracle provides a way to detach the order_items collection when it is advantageous to do so.

Collection Instantiation

While the table definitions in the previous section look fairly straightforward, it isn't immediately obvious how you might go about populating the resulting tables. Whenever you want to create an instance of a collection, you need to use its constructor, which is a system-generated function with the same name as the collection. The constructor accepts one or more elements; for varrays, the number of elements cannot exceed the maximum size of the varray. For example, adding a row to the part_c table, which contains a varray column, can be done using the following:

```
INSERT INTO part_c (part_nbr, name, supplier_id, unit_cost,
  inventory_qty, restocks)
VALUES ('GX5-2786-A2', 'Spacely Sprocket', 157, 75, 22,
  resupply_dates(TO_DATE('03-SEP-1999','DD-MON-YYYY'),
    TO_DATE('22-APR-2000','DD-MON-YYYY'),
    TO_DATE('21-MAR-2001','DD-MON-YYYY')));
```

In this example, the resupply_dates constructor is called with three parameters, one for each time a shipment of parts was received. If you are using a collection-savvy query tool such as Oracle's SQL*Plus, you can query the collection directly, and the tool will format the results:

```
SELECT part_nbr, restocks
FROM part_c
WHERE name = 'Spacely Sprocket';

PART_NBR        RESTOCKS
--------------- -------------------------------------------------------
GX5-2786-A2     RESUPPLY_DATES('03-SEP-99', '22-APR-00', '21-MAR-01')
```

You deal with nested tables in a manner similar to varrays. The next example demonstrates how you would insert a new row into the cust_order_c table, which contains a nested table column:

```
INSERT INTO cust_order_c (order_nbr, cust_nbr, sales_emp_id,
  order_dt, sale_price, order_items)
VALUES (1000, 9568, 275, TO_DATE('21-MAR-2001','DD-MON-YYYY'), 15753,
  line_item_tbl(
    line_item_obj('A675-015', 25),
    line_item_obj('GX5-2786-A2', 1),
    line_item_obj('X378-9JT-2', 3)));
```

If you look carefully, you will notice that there are actually two different constructors called: one to create the nested table line_item_tbl, and the other to create each of three instances of the line_item_obj object type. Remember, the nested table is a table of line_item_obj objects. The end result is a single row in cust_order_c containing a collection of three line items.

Querying Collections

Now that you know how to get data into a collection, you need a way to get it out. Oracle provides a special TABLE expression just for this purpose.

 Prior to release 8*i*, the TABLE expression was called THE. Only the TABLE expression is used here.

The TABLE expression can be used in the FROM, WHERE, and HAVING clauses of a query to allow a nested table or varray column to be referenced as if it were a separate table. The following query extracts the resupply dates (from the restocks column) that were added previously to the part_c table:

```
SELECT *
FROM TABLE(SELECT restocks
  FROM part_c
  WHERE part_nbr = 'GX5-2786-A2');
```

```
COLUMN_VALUE
-----------
03-SEP-99
22-APR-00
21-MAR-01
```

To better illustrate the function of the TABLE expression, the next query retrieves the restocks varray directly from the part_c table:

```
SELECT restocks
FROM part_c
WHERE part_nbr = 'GX5-2786-A2';

RESTOCKS
--------------------------------------------------------
RESUPPLY_DATES('03-SEP-99', '22-APR-00', '21-MAR-01')
```

As you can see, the result set consists of a single row containing an array of dates, whereas the previous query unnests the varray so that each element is represented as a row with a single column.

Since the varray contains a built-in data type rather than an object type, it is necessary to give the varray name so that it may be explicitly referenced in SQL statements. Oracle assigns the varray's contents a default alias of column_value for this purpose. The next example makes use of the column_value alias.

Let's say that you wanted to find all parts resupplied on a particular date. Using the TABLE expression, you can perform a correlated subquery against the restocks varray to see if the desired date is found in the set:

```
SELECT p1.part_nbr, p1.name
FROM part_c p1
WHERE TO_DATE('03-SEP-1999','DD-MON-YYYY') IN
 (SELECT column_value FROM TABLE(SELECT restocks FROM part_c p2
  WHERE p2.part_nbr = p1.part_nbr));

PART_NBR             NAME
-------------------- ------------------------------
GX5-2786-A2          Spacely Sprocket
```

Collection Unnesting

Even if your developer community is comfortable manipulating collections within your database, it is often unrealistic to expect the various tools and applications accessing your data (data load and extraction utilities, reporting and ad-hoc query tools, etc.) to correctly handle them. Using a technique called *collection unnesting*, you can present the contents of the collection as if it were rows of an ordinary table.

For example, using the TABLE expression, you can write a query which unnests the order_items nested table from the cust_order_c table, as in:

```
SELECT co.order_nbr, co.cust_nbr, co.order_dt, li.part_nbr, li.quantity
FROM cust_order_c co,
  TABLE(co.order_items) li;

ORDER_NBR   CUST_NBR ORDER_DT  PART_NBR              QUANTITY
---------- ---------- --------- -------------------- ----------
      1000       9568 21-MAR-01 A675-015                    25
      1000       9568 21-MAR-01 GX5-2786-A2                  1
      1000       9568 21-MAR-01 X378-9JT-2                   3
```

Note that the two data sets do not need to be explicitly joined, since the collection members are already associated with a row in the cust_order_c table.

To make this unnested data set available to your users, you can wrap the previous query in a view:

```
CREATE VIEW cust_order_line_items AS
SELECT co.order_nbr, co.cust_nbr, co.order_dt, li.part_nbr, li.quantity
FROM cust_order_c co,
  TABLE(co.order_items) li;
```

Your users can now interact with the nested table via the view using standard SQL, as in the following:

```
SELECT *
FROM cust_order_line_items
WHERE part_nbr like 'X%';

ORDER_NBR   CUST_NBR ORDER_DT  PART_NBR              QUANTITY
---------- ---------- --------- -------------------- ----------
      1000       9568 21-MAR-01 X378-9JT-2                   3
```

Collection Functions

Oracle Database 10g supplies a number of functions that are useful when working with nested table collections. For example, if you are interested in the number of elements in a given collection, you can use the CARDINALITY function:

```
SELECT co.order_nbr, co.cust_nbr, co.order_dt,
  CARDINALITY(co.order_items) number_of_items
FROM cust_order_c co;

ORDER_NBR   CUST_NBR ORDER_DT  NUMBER_OF_ITEMS
---------- ---------- --------- ---------------
      1000       9568 21-MAR-01               3
```

Compare this with the following query, which obtains the same results without the benefit of the CARDINALITY function:

```
SELECT co.order_nbr, co.cust_nbr, co.order_dt,
  COUNT(*) number_of_items
```

```
FROM cust_order_c co, TABLE(co.order_items) oi
GROUP BY co.order_nbr, co.cust_nbr, co.order_dt;

ORDER_NBR   CUST_NBR ORDER_DT  NUMBER_OF_ITEMS
---------- ---------- --------- ---------------
      1000       9568 21-MAR-01               3
```

If you would like to perform set operations on multiple collections, there are functions that perform the equivalent of UNION, UNION ALL, MINUS, and INTERSECT. To illustrate these functions, we will add another row to the cust_order_c table and then perform set operations against the two rows in the table:

```
INSERT INTO cust_order_c (order_nbr, cust_nbr, sales_emp_id,
  order_dt, sale_price, order_items)
VALUES (1001, 9679, 275, TO_DATE('15-DEC-2003','DD-MON-YYYY'), 8645,
  line_item_tbl(
    line_item_obj('A675-015', 25),
    line_item_obj('TX-475-A2', 7)));
```

Here's a look at our two sets of line items:

```
ORDER_ITEMS(PART_NBR, QUANTITY)
-----------------------------------------------------------------------
LINE_ITEM_TBL(LINE_ITEM_OBJ('A675-015', 25),
              LINE_ITEM_OBJ('GX5-2786-A2', 1),
              LINE_ITEM_OBJ('X378-9JT-2', 3))

LINE_ITEM_TBL(LINE_ITEM_OBJ('A675-015', 25),
              LINE_ITEM_OBJ('TX-475-A2', 7))
```

As you can see, the two sets of line items share one common element (quantity 25 of part number A675-015). The next query demonstrates how the MULTISET UNION DISTINCT function can be used to build a new instance of line_item_tbl with the distinct set of line items:

```
SELECT co_1.order_items
  MULTISET UNION DISTINCT
  co_2.order_items distinct_items
FROM cust_order_c co_1, cust_order_c co_2
WHERE co_1.order_nbr = 1000 and co_2.order_nbr = 1001;

DISTINCT_ITEMS(PART_NBR, QUANTITY)
-----------------------------------------------------------------------
LINE_ITEM_TBL(LINE_ITEM_OBJ('A675-015', 25),
              LINE_ITEM_OBJ('GX5-2786-A2', 1),
              LINE_ITEM_OBJ('X378-9JT-2', 3),
              LINE_ITEM_OBJ('TX-475-A2', 7))
```

If you want the non-distinct union of line items from the two sets, simply replace the keyword DISTINCT with ALL:

```
SELECT co_1.order_items
  MULTISET UNION ALL
  co_2.order_items all_items
FROM cust_order_c co_1, cust_order_c co_2
WHERE co_1.order_nbr = 1000 and co_2.order_nbr = 1001;
```

```
ALL_ITEMS(PART_NBR, QUANTITY)
-------------------------------------------------------------------------
LINE_ITEM_TBL(LINE_ITEM_OBJ('A675-015', 25),
              LINE_ITEM_OBJ('GX5-2786-A2', 1),
              LINE_ITEM_OBJ('X378-9JT-2', 3),
              LINE_ITEM_OBJ('A675-015', 25),
              LINE_ITEM_OBJ('TX-475-A2', 7))
```

As you would expect, the common line item now appears twice in the all_items collection.

If you want the functionality of the MINUS set operator, you can use the MULTISET EXCEPT function. The keyword EXCEPT is used rather than MINUS, to conform to the ANSI/ISO SQL standard:

```
SELECT co_1.order_items
  MULTISET EXCEPT
  co_2.order_items diff_items
FROM cust_order_c co_1, cust_order_c co_2
WHERE co_1.order_nbr = 1000 and co_2.order_nbr = 1001;

DIFF_ITEMS(PART_NBR, QUANTITY)
-------------------------------------------------------------------------
LINE_ITEM_TBL(LINE_ITEM_OBJ('GX5-2786-A2', 1),
              LINE_ITEM_OBJ('X378-9JT-2', 3))
```

Finally, if you desire to generate the intersection between the two sets, you can use the MULTISET INTERSECT function:

```
SELECT co_1.order_items
  MULTISET INTERSECT
  co_2.order_items common_items
FROM cust_order_c co_1, cust_order_c co_2
WHERE co_1.order_nbr = 1000 and co_2.order_nbr = 1001;

COMMON_ITEMS(PART_NBR, QUANTITY)
-------------------------------------------------------------------------
LINE_ITEM_TBL(LINE_ITEM_OBJ('A675-015', 25))
```

Comparing Collections

If you are using nested tables, you can compare the structure and content of one collection to another. If the nested tables being compared contain a built-in data type such as NUMBER or VARCHAR2, the Oracle server will do the comparison for you; if the nested tables contain an object type, however, you will need to write a MAP method to tell the server how to compare multiple instance of your object type. The following code fragment demonstrates a simple mapping function for the line_item_obj type:

```
CREATE TYPE BODY line_item_obj AS
  MAP MEMBER FUNCTION to_string RETURN VARCHAR2 IS
  BEGIN
```

```
        RETURN part_nbr || ':' || to_char(quantity, '00009');
    END to_string;
END;
```

The to_string mapping function simply returns the part number concatenated to the quantity with a colon between. Oracle will call this function (there can only be one mapping function defined for each of your object types) whenever two instances of the type are being compared.

Now that the mapping function is in place, you can begin comparing different collections of line_item_obj. For example, if you want to find a customer order containing a certain set of line items, you can use the equality operator:

```
SELECT co.order_nbr, co.cust_nbr, co.order_dt
FROM cust_order_c co
WHERE co.order_items =
  line_item_tbl(
    line_item_obj('A675-015', 25),
    line_item_obj('GX5-2786-A2', 1),
    line_item_obj('X378-9JT-2', 3));

ORDER_NBR    CUST_NBR ORDER_DT
---------- ---------- ---------
      1000       9568 21-MAR-01
```

This query finds all customer orders containing the three part number/quantity pairs listed above.

Although it is useful to use the equality operator to look for an exact match, you are more likely to need only a partial match, especially if you are working with large collections. It might seem intuitive to use the IN operator to look for partial matches, as in:

```
SELECT co.order_nbr, co.cust_nbr, co.order_dt
FROM cust_order_c co
WHERE line_item_tbl(line_item_obj('GX5-2786-A2', 1))
  IN co.order_items

no rows selected
```

When working with nested tables, however, you will need to use the SUBMULTISET operator instead of using IN. The next example uses SUBMULTISET to find all customer orders that include one quantity of part number GX5-2786-A2:

```
SELECT co.order_nbr, co.cust_nbr, co.order_dt
FROM cust_order_c co
WHERE line_item_tbl(line_item_obj('GX5-2786-A2', 1))
  SUBMULTISET OF co.order_items;

ORDER_NBR    CUST_NBR ORDER_DT
---------- ---------- ---------
      1000       9568 21-MAR-01
```

Since the collection in the preceding example contains a single object, you can instead use the MEMBER OF operator to check to see if the co.order_items collection contains a given instance of line_item_obj:

```
SELECT co.order_nbr, co.cust_nbr, co.order_dt
FROM cust_order_c co
WHERE line_item_obj('GX5-2786-A2', 1)
  MEMBER OF co.order_items;


ORDER_NBR   CUST_NBR ORDER_DT
---------- ---------- ---------
      1000       9568 21-MAR-01
```

Because MEMBER OF checks individual elements of a collection rather than the collection as a whole, you only need to instantiate a line_item_obj instead of a collection of line_item_obj types as you did when using SUBMULTISET.

You will need Oracle Database 10g to use the SUBMULTISET and MEMBER OF operators.

Manipulating Collections

If you want to modify a collection's contents, you have two choices: replace the entire collection or modify individual elements of the collection. If the collection is a varray, you have no choice but to replace the entire collection. You can accomplish this by retrieving the contents of the varray, modifying the data, and then updating the table with the new varray. The following statement changes the restock dates for part number "GX5-2786-A2." Note that the varray is entirely recreated:

```
UPDATE part_c
SET restocks = resupply_dates(TO_DATE('03-SEP-1999','DD-MON-YYYY'),
    TO_DATE('25-APR-2000','DD-MON-YYYY'),
    TO_DATE('21-MAR-2001','DD-MON-YYYY'))
WHERE part_nbr = 'GX5-2786-A2';
```

If you are using nested tables, however, you can perform DML against individual elements of a collection. For example, the following statement adds an additional line item to the nested cust_order_c table for order number 1000:

```
INSERT INTO TABLE(SELECT order_items FROM cust_order_c
  WHERE order_nbr = 1000)
VALUES (line_item_obj('T25-ASM', 1));
```

To update data in the same nested table, use the TABLE expression to create a data set consisting of part numbers from order number 1000, and then modify the element with a specified part number:

```
UPDATE TABLE(SELECT order_items FROM cust_order_c
  WHERE order_nbr = 1000) oi
SET oi.quantity = 2
WHERE oi.part_nbr = 'T25-ASM';
```

Similarly, you can use the same data set to remove elements from the collection:

```
DELETE FROM TABLE(SELECT order_items FROM cust_order_c
  WHERE order_nbr = 1000) oi
WHERE oi.part_nbr = 'T25-ASM';
```

Multilevel Collections

If you are using Oracle9i release 2 or later, you will be able to nest a collection inside of another collection. Earlier in the chapter, we used a table called cust_order_c that contained a collection of line items. To illustrate multilevel collections, the cust_order_c table will be converted to a type definition and added to the customer table, so that each customer record contains a collection of orders, and each order contains a collection of line items:

```
CREATE TYPE line_item_obj AS OBJECT (
  part_nbr VARCHAR2(20),
  quantity NUMBER(8,2));

CREATE TYPE line_item_tbl AS TABLE OF line_item_obj;

CREATE TYPE cust_order_obj AS OBJECT (
  order_nbr NUMBER(8),
  sales_emp_id NUMBER(6),
  order_dt DATE,
  sale_price NUMBER(9,2),
  order_items line_item_tbl);

CREATE TYPE cust_order_tbl AS TABLE OF cust_order_obj;

CREATE TABLE customer_c (
  cust_nbr NUMBER(5) NOT NULL,
  name VARCHAR2(30) NOT NULL,
  region_id NUMBER(5),
  inactive_dt DATE,
  inactive_ind CHAR(1),
  orders cust_order_tbl)
NESTED TABLE orders STORE AS orders_c
  (NESTED TABLE order_items STORE AS order_items_c);
```

Now that the schema is in place, let's add some data:

```
INSERT INTO customer_c (cust_nbr, name, region_id,
  inactive_dt, inactive_ind, orders)
VALUES (1, 'Cooper Industries', 5, NULL, 'N',
  cust_order_tbl(
    cust_order_obj(9568, 275,
      TO_DATE('21-MAR-2001','DD-MON-YYYY'), 15753,
      line_item_tbl(
        line_item_obj('A675-015', 25),
        line_item_obj('GX5-2786-A2', 1),
        line_item_obj('X378-9JT-2', 3))),
    cust_order_obj(9867, 275,
```

```
       TO_DATE('08-DEC-2003','DD-MON-YYYY'), 22575,
       line_item_tbl(
         line_item_obj('A675-015', 43),
         line_item_obj('GX5-2786-A2', 1),
         line_item_obj('X378-9JT-2', 6))))));
```

While the INSERT statement above creates a single row, the statement has actually created a customer entry, two orders, and three line-items per order.

Querying Multilevel Collections

When querying multilevel collections, you can use the TABLE function to unnest your collections to make the data appear relational. For instance, you can look at all of the line items associated with Cooper Industries:

```
SELECT li.*
FROM customer_c c, TABLE(c.orders) o, TABLE(o.order_items) li
WHERE c.name = 'Cooper Industries';
```

```
PART_NBR               QUANTITY
-------------------- ----------
A675-015                     25
GX5-2786-A2                   1
X378-9JT-2                    3
A675-015                     43
GX5-2786-A2                   1
X378-9JT-2                    6
```

Since the unnested data is treated like a normal relational table, you are free to use the full array of available functionality in your queries. For example, you can use GROUP BY and aggregate functions, as demonstrated by the following:

```
SELECT o.order_nbr, SUM(li.quantity)
FROM customer_c c, TABLE(c.orders) o, TABLE(o.order_items) li
WHERE c.name = 'Cooper Industries'
GROUP BY o.order_nbr;
```

```
ORDER_NBR SUM(LI.QUANTITY)
---------- ----------------
      9568               29
      9867               50
```

DML Operations on Multilevel Collections

To perform DML operations on a multilevel collection, you need to isolate the collection to be modified via the TABLE function. For example, the next statement adds 1 to the quantity field of each line item for order number 9867 under Cooper Industries:

```
UPDATE TABLE(
    SELECT o.order_items
    FROM TABLE(
      SELECT c.orders
```

```
      FROM customer_c c
     WHERE c.name = 'Cooper Industries') o
   WHERE o.order_nbr = 9867) li
 SET li.quantity = li.quantity + 1;
```

The target of this update is the table returned by the outermost TABLE function.

CHAPTER 13

Advanced Group Operations

Group operations aggregate data over multiple rows. We discussed the GROUP BY clause and basic group operations in Chapter 4. Decision-support systems require more complex group operations. Data warehousing applications involve aggregation over multiple dimensions of data. To enable effective decision support, you need to summarize transaction data at various levels. We discuss advanced group operations used by decision-support systems in this chapter.

Oracle provides several handy SQL features to summarize data. These include the following:

- A ROLLUP function to generate totals and subtotals in the summarized results.
- A CUBE function to generate subtotals for all possible combinations of grouped columns.
- A GROUPING SETS function to generate summary information at the level you choose without including all the rows produced by the regular GROUP BY operation.
- The GROUPING, GROUPING_ID and GROUP_ID functions to help you correctly interpret results generated using ROLLUP, CUBE, and GROUPING SETS.

Multiple Summary Levels

In Chapter 4, you saw how the GROUP BY clause, along with the aggregate functions, can be used to produce summary results. For example, if you want to print the monthly total sales for each region, you would probably execute the following query:

```
SELECT r.name region,
       TO_CHAR(TO_DATE(o.month, 'MM'), 'Month') month, SUM(o.tot_sales)
FROM all_orders o JOIN region r
ON r.region_id = o.region_id
GROUP BY r.name, o.month;
```

```
REGION                MONTH       SUM(O.TOT_SALES)
--------------------  ----------  ----------------
New England           January              1527645
New England           February             1847238
New England           March                1699449
New England           April                1792866
New England           May                  1698855
New England           June                 1510062
New England           July                 1678002
New England           August               1642968
New England           September            1726767
New England           October              1648944
New England           November             1384185
New England           December             1599942
Mid-Atlantic          January              1832091
Mid-Atlantic          February             1286028
Mid-Atlantic          March                1911093
Mid-Atlantic          April                1623438
Mid-Atlantic          May                  1778805
Mid-Atlantic          June                 1504455
Mid-Atlantic          July                 1820742
Mid-Atlantic          August               1381560
Mid-Atlantic          September            1178694
Mid-Atlantic          October              1530351
Mid-Atlantic          November             1598667
Mid-Atlantic          December             1477374
Southeast US          January              1137063
Southeast US          February             1855269
Southeast US          March                1967979
Southeast US          April                1830051
Southeast US          May                  1983282
Southeast US          June                 1705716
Southeast US          July                 1670976
Southeast US          August               1436295
Southeast US          September            1905633
Southeast US          October              1610523
Southeast US          November             1661598
Southeast US          December             1841100

36 rows selected.
```

As expected, this report prints the total sales for each region and month combination. However, in a more complex application, you may also want to have the subtotal for each region over all months, along with the total for all regions, or you may want the subtotal for each month over all regions, along with the total for all months. In short, you may need to generate subtotals and totals at more than one level.

UNION

In data warehouse applications, you frequently need to generate summary information over various dimensions, and subtotal and total across those dimensions. Generating and retrieving this type of summary information is a core goal of almost all data warehouse applications.

By this time, you have realized that a simple GROUP BY query is not sufficient to generate the subtotals and totals described in this section. To illustrate the complexity of the problem, let's attempt to write a query that would return the following in a single output:

- Sales for each month for every region
- Subtotals over all months for every region
- Total sales for all regions over all months

One way to generate multiple levels of summary (the only way prior to Oracle8i) is to write a UNION query. For example, the following UNION query will give us the desired three levels of subtotals:

```
SELECT r.name region,
       TO_CHAR(TO_DATE(o.month, 'MM'), 'Month') month, SUM(o.tot_sales)
FROM all_orders o JOIN region r
ON r.region_id = o.region_id
GROUP BY r.name, o.month
UNION ALL
SELECT r.name region, NULL, SUM(o.tot_sales)
FROM all_orders o JOIN region r
ON r.region_id = o.region_id
GROUP BY r.name
UNION ALL
SELECT NULL, NULL, SUM(o.tot_sales)
FROM all_orders o JOIN region r
ON r.region_id = o.region_id;
```

REGION	MONTH	SUM(O.TOT_SALES)
New England	January	1527645
New England	February	1847238
New England	March	1699449
New England	April	1792866
New England	May	1698855
New England	June	1510062
New England	July	1678002
New England	August	1642968
New England	September	1726767
New England	October	1648944
New England	November	1384185
New England	December	1599942
Mid-Atlantic	January	1832091
Mid-Atlantic	February	1286028
Mid-Atlantic	March	1911093
Mid-Atlantic	April	1623438
Mid-Atlantic	May	1778805
Mid-Atlantic	June	1504455
Mid-Atlantic	July	1820742

Mid-Atlantic	August	1381560
Mid-Atlantic	September	1178694
Mid-Atlantic	October	1530351
Mid-Atlantic	November	1598667
Mid-Atlantic	December	1477374
Southeast US	January	1137063
Southeast US	February	1855269
Southeast US	March	1967979
Southeast US	April	1830051
Southeast US	May	1983282
Southeast US	June	1705716
Southeast US	July	1670976
Southeast US	August	1436295
Southeast US	September	1905633
Southeast US	October	1610523
Southeast US	November	1661598
Southeast US	December	1841100
Mid-Atlantic		18923298
New England		19756923
Southeast US		20605485
		59285706

```
40 rows selected.
```

This query produced 40 rows of output, 36 of which are the sales for each month for every region. The last four rows are the subtotals and the total. The three rows with region names and NULL values for the month are the subtotals for each region over all the months, and the last row with NULL values for both the region and month is the total sales for all the regions over all the months.

Now that you have the desired result, try to analyze the query a bit. You have a very small all_orders table with only 1440 rows in this example. You wanted to have summary information over just two dimensions—region and month. You have 3 regions and 12 months. To get the desired summary information from this table, you have to write a query consisting of three SELECT statements combined together using UNION ALL. The execution plan for this query is:

```
PLAN_TABLE_OUTPUT
--------------------------------------------------------

--------------------------------------------------------
| Id | Operation                    | Name       |
--------------------------------------------------------
|  0 | SELECT STATEMENT             |            |
|  1 | UNION-ALL                    |            |
|  2 | SORT GROUP BY                |            |
|  3 | MERGE JOIN                   |            |
|  4 | TABLE ACCESS BY INDEX ROWID  | REGION     |
|  5 | INDEX FULL SCAN              | REGION_PK  |
|* 6 | SORT JOIN                    |            |
|  7 | TABLE ACCESS FULL            | ALL_ORDERS |
|  8 | SORT GROUP BY                |            |
```

```
|   9 | MERGE JOIN                 |           |
|  10 | TABLE ACCESS BY INDEX ROWID| REGION    |
|  11 | INDEX FULL SCAN            | REGION_PK |
|* 12 | SORT JOIN                  |           |
|  13 | TABLE ACCESS FULL          | ALL_ORDERS|
|  14 | SORT AGGREGATE             |           |
|  15 | NESTED LOOPS               |           |
|  16 | TABLE ACCESS FULL          | ALL_ORDERS|
|* 17 | INDEX UNIQUE SCAN          | REGION_PK |
-------------------------------------------------------
```

As indicated by the execution plan output, Oracle needs to perform the following operations to get the results:

> Three FULL TABLE scans on `all_orders`
> Three INDEX scan on `region_pk` (Primary key of table `region`)
> Two Sort-Merge Joins
> One NESTED LOOPS JOIN
> Two SORT GROUP BY operations
> One SORT AGGREGATE operation
> One UNION ALL

In any practical application the `all_orders` table will consist of millions of rows, and performing all these operations would be time-consuming. Even worse, if you have more dimensions for which to prepare summary information than the two shown in this example, you have to write an even more complex query. The bottom line is that such a query badly hurts performance.

ROLLUP

Oracle8*i* introduced several new features for generating multiple levels of summary information with one query. One such feature is a set of extensions to the GROUP BY clause. In Oracle8*i*, the GROUP BY clause comes with two extensions: ROLLUP and CUBE. Oracle9*i* introduced another extension: GROUPING SETS. We discuss ROLLUP in this section. CUBE and GROUPING SETS are discussed later in this chapter.

ROLLUP is an extension to the GROUP BY clause, and therefore can only appear in a query with a GROUP BY clause. The ROLLUP operation groups the selected rows based on the expressions in the GROUP BY clause, and prepares a summary row for each group. The syntax of ROLLUP is:

```
SELECT ...
FROM ...
GROUP BY ROLLUP (ordered list of grouping columns)
```

Using ROLLUP, you can generate the summary information discussed in the previous section in a much easier way than in our UNION ALL query. For example:

```
SELECT r.name region,
       TO_CHAR(TO_DATE(o.month, 'MM'), 'Month') month, SUM(o.tot_sales)
FROM all_orders o JOIN region r
```

```
ON r.region_id = o.region_id
GROUP BY ROLLUP (r.name, o.month);
```

REGION	MONTH	SUM(O.TOT_SALES)
New England	January	1527645
New England	February	1847238
New England	March	1699449
New England	April	1792866
New England	May	1698855
New England	June	1510062
New England	July	1678002
New England	August	1642968
New England	September	1726767
New England	October	1648944
New England	November	1384185
New England	December	1599942
New England		19756923
Mid-Atlantic	January	1832091
Mid-Atlantic	February	1286028
Mid-Atlantic	March	1911093
Mid-Atlantic	April	1623438
Mid-Atlantic	May	1778805
Mid-Atlantic	June	1504455
Mid-Atlantic	July	1820742
Mid-Atlantic	August	1381560
Mid-Atlantic	September	1178694
Mid-Atlantic	October	1530351
Mid-Atlantic	November	1598667
Mid-Atlantic	December	1477374
Mid-Atlantic		18923298
Southeast US	January	1137063
Southeast US	February	1855269
Southeast US	March	1967979
Southeast US	April	1830051
Southeast US	May	1983282
Southeast US	June	1705716
Southeast US	July	1670976
Southeast US	August	1436295
Southeast US	September	1905633
Southeast US	October	1610523
Southeast US	November	1661598
Southeast US	December	1841100
Southeast US		20605485
		59285706

```
40 rows selected.
```

As you can see in this output, the ROLLUP operation produced subtotals across the
specified dimensions and a grand total. The argument to the ROLLUP operation is
an ordered list of grouping columns. Since the ROLLUP operation is used in conjunction with the GROUP BY clause, it first generates aggregate values based on the
GROUP BY operation on the ordered list of columns. It then generates higher-level

subtotals and finally a grand total. ROLLUP not only simplifies the query, it results in more efficient execution. The execution plan for this ROLLUP query is as follows:

```
PLAN_TABLE_OUTPUT
-----------------------------------------------------

-----------------------------------------------------
| Id  | Operation                     | Name       |
-----------------------------------------------------
|   0 | SELECT STATEMENT              |            |
|   1 |  SORT GROUP BY ROLLUP         |            |
|   2 |   MERGE JOIN                  |            |
|   3 |    TABLE ACCESS BY INDEX ROWID| REGION     |
|   4 |     INDEX FULL SCAN           | REGION_PK  |
|*  5 |    SORT JOIN                  |            |
|   6 |     TABLE ACCESS FULL         | ALL_ORDERS |
-----------------------------------------------------
```

Rather than the multiple table scans, joins, and other operations required by the UNION ALL version of the query, the ROLLUP query needs just one index scan on region_pk, one full table scan on all_orders, and one join to generate the required output.

If you want to generate subtotals for each month instead of for each region, all you need to do is change the order of columns in the ROLLUP operation, as in the following example:

```
SELECT r.name region,
TO_CHAR(TO_DATE(o.month, 'MM'), 'Month') month, SUM(o.tot_sales)
FROM all_orders o JOIN region r
ON r.region_id = o.region_id
GROUP BY ROLLUP (o.month, r.name);

REGION               MONTH      SUM(O.TOT_SALES)
-------------------- ---------  ----------------
New England          January           1527645
Mid-Atlantic         January           1832091
Southeast US         January           1137063
                     January           4496799
New England          February          1847238
Mid-Atlantic         February          1286028
Southeast US         February          1855269
                     February          4988535
New England          March             1699449
Mid-Atlantic         March             1911093
Southeast US         March             1967979
                     March             5578521
New England          April             1792866
Mid-Atlantic         April             1623438
Southeast US         April             1830051
                     April             5246355
New England          May               1698855
Mid-Atlantic         May               1778805
```

```
Southeast US        May             1983282
                    May             5460942
New England         June            1510062
Mid-Atlantic        June            1504455
Southeast US        June            1705716
                    June            4720233
New England         July            1678002
Mid-Atlantic        July            1820742
Southeast US        July            1670976
                    July            5169720
New England         August          1642968
Mid-Atlantic        August          1381560
Southeast US        August          1436295
                    August          4460823
New England         September       1726767
Mid-Atlantic        September       1178694
Southeast US        September       1905633
                    September       4811094
New England         October         1648944
Mid-Atlantic        October         1530351
Southeast US        October         1610523
                    October         4789818
New England         November        1384185
Mid-Atlantic        November        1598667
Southeast US        November        1661598
                    November        4644450
New England         December        1599942
Mid-Atlantic        December        1477374
Southeast US        December        1841100
                    December        4918416
                                    59285706
```

49 rows selected.

Adding dimensions does not result in additional complexity. The following query rolls up subtotals for the region, the month, and the year for the first quarter:

```
SELECT o.year, TO_CHAR(TO_DATE(o.month, 'MM'), 'Month') month,
r.name region, SUM(o.tot_sales)
FROM all_orders o JOIN region r
ON r.region_id = o.region_id
WHERE o.month BETWEEN 1 AND 3
GROUP BY ROLLUP (o.year, o.month, r.name);
```

```
      YEAR MONTH     REGION                SUM(O.TOT_SALES)
---------- --------- -------------------- ----------------
      2000 January   New England                  1018430
      2000 January   Mid-Atlantic                 1221394
      2000 January   Southeast US                  758042
      2000 January                                2997866
      2000 February  New England                  1231492
      2000 February  Mid-Atlantic                  857352
      2000 February  Southeast US                 1236846
      2000 February                               3325690
```

2000	March	New England	1132966
2000	March	Mid-Atlantic	1274062
2000	March	Southeast US	1311986
2000	March		3719014
2000			10042570
2001	January	New England	509215
2001	January	Mid-Atlantic	610697
2001	January	Southeast US	379021
2001	January		1498933
2001	February	New England	615746
2001	February	Mid-Atlantic	428676
2001	February	Southeast US	618423
2001	February		1662845
2001	March	New England	566483
2001	March	Mid-Atlantic	637031
2001	March	Southeast US	655993
2001	March		1859507
2001			5021285
			15063855

```
27 rows selected.
```

Partial ROLLUPs

In a ROLLUP query with N dimensions, the grand total is considered the top level. The various subtotal rows of N-1 dimensions constitute the next lower level, the subtotal rows of N-2 dimensions constitute yet another level down, and so on. In the most recent example, you have three dimensions (year, month, and region), and the total row is the top level. The subtotal rows for the year represent the next lower level, because these rows are subtotals across two dimensions (month and region). The subtotal rows for the year and month combination are one level lower, because these rows are subtotals across one dimension (region). The rest of the rows are the result of the regular GROUP BY operation (without ROLLUP), and form the lowest level.

If you want to exclude some subtotals and totals from the ROLLUP output, you can only move top to bottom, i.e., exclude the top-level total first, then progressively go down to the next level subtotals, and so on. To do this, you have to take out one or more columns from the ROLLUP operation, and put them in the GROUP BY clause. This is called a *partial ROLLUP*.

As an example of a partial ROLLUP, let's see what happens when you take out the first column, which is o.year, from the previous ROLLUP operation and move it into the GROUP BY clause.

```
SELECT o.year, TO_CHAR(TO_DATE(o.month, 'MM'), 'Month') month,
r.name region, SUM(o.tot_sales)
FROM all_orders o JOIN region r
ON r.region_id = o.region_id
WHERE o.month BETWEEN 1 AND 3
GROUP BY o.year, ROLLUP (o.month, r.name);
```

```
     YEAR MONTH     REGION                  SUM(O.TOT_SALES)
---------- --------- --------------------- ----------------
     2000 January   New England                   1018430
     2000 January   Mid-Atlantic                  1221394
     2000 January   Southeast US                   758042
     2000 January                                 2997866
     2000 February  New England                   1231492
     2000 February  Mid-Atlantic                   857352
     2000 February  Southeast US                  1236846
     2000 February                                3325690
     2000 March     New England                   1132966
     2000 March     Mid-Atlantic                  1274062
     2000 March     Southeast US                  1311986
     2000 March                                   3719014
     2000                                        10042570
     2001 January   New England                    509215
     2001 January   Mid-Atlantic                   610697
     2001 January   Southeast US                   379021
     2001 January                                 1498933
     2001 February  New England                    615746
     2001 February  Mid-Atlantic                   428676
     2001 February  Southeast US                   618423
     2001 February                                1662845
     2001 March     New England                    566483
     2001 March     Mid-Atlantic                   637031
     2001 March     Southeast US                   655993
     2001 March                                   1859507
     2001                                         5021285
```

26 rows selected.

The query in this example excludes the grand-total row from the output. By taking out o.year from the ROLLUP operation, you are asking the database not to roll up summary information over the years. Therefore, the database rolls up summary information on region and month. When you proceed to remove o.month from the ROLLUP operation, the query will not generate the roll up summary for the month dimension, and only the region-level subtotals will be printed in the output. For example:

```
SELECT o.year, TO_CHAR(TO_DATE(o.month, 'MM'), 'Month') month,
r.name region, SUM(o.tot_sales)
FROM all_orders o JOIN region r
ON r.region_id = o.region_id
WHERE o.month BETWEEN 1 AND 3
GROUP BY o.year, o.month, ROLLUP (r.name);
```

```
     YEAR MONTH     REGION                  SUM(O.TOT_SALES)
---------- --------- --------------------- ----------------
     2000 January   New England                   1018430
     2000 January   Mid-Atlantic                  1221394
     2000 January   Southeast US                   758042
     2000 January                                 2997866
     2000 February  New England                   1231492
```

```
2000 February   Mid-Atlantic       857352
2000 February   Southeast US      1236846
2000 February                     3325690
2000 March      New England       1132966
2000 March      Mid-Atlantic      1274062
2000 March      Southeast US      1311986
2000 March                        3719014
2001 January    New England        509215
2001 January    Mid-Atlantic       610697
2001 January    Southeast US       379021
2001 January                      1498933
2001 February   New England        615746
2001 February   Mid-Atlantic       428676
2001 February   Southeast US       618423
2001 February                     1662845
2001 March      New England        566483
2001 March      Mid-Atlantic       637031
2001 March      Southeast US       655993
2001 March                        1859507
```

```
24 rows selected.
```

CUBE

The CUBE extension of the GROUP BY clause takes aggregation one step further than ROLLUP. The CUBE operation generates subtotals for all possible combinations of the grouping columns. Therefore, output of a CUBE operation will contain all subtotals produced by an equivalent ROLLUP operation and also some additional subtotals. For example, if you are performing ROLLUP on columns region and month, you will get subtotals for all months for each region, and a grand total. However, if you perform the corresponding CUBE, you will get:

- The regular rows produced by the GROUP BY clause
- Subtotals for all months on each region
- A subtotal for all regions on each month
- A grand total

Like ROLLUP, CUBE is an extension of the GROUP BY clause, and can appear in a query only along with a GROUP BY clause. The syntax of CUBE is:

```
SELECT ...
FROM ...
GROUP BY CUBE (list of grouping columns)
```

For example, the following query returns subtotals for all combinations of regions and months in the all_orders table:

```
SELECT r.name region, TO_CHAR(TO_DATE(o.month, 'MM'), 'Month') month,
SUM(o.tot_sales)
FROM all_orders o JOIN region r
```

```
ON r.region_id = o.region_id
GROUP BY CUBE(r.name, o.month);
```

REGION	MONTH	SUM(O.TOT_SALES)
		59285706
	January	4496799
	February	4988535
	March	5578521
	April	5246355
	May	5460942
	June	4720233
	July	5169720
	August	4460823
	September	4811094
	October	4789818
	November	4644450
	December	4918416
New England		19756923
New England	January	1527645
New England	February	1847238
New England	March	1699449
New England	April	1792866
New England	May	1698855
New England	June	1510062
New England	July	1678002
New England	August	1642968
New England	September	1726767
New England	October	1648944
New England	November	1384185
New England	December	1599942
Mid-Atlantic		18923298
Mid-Atlantic	January	1832091
Mid-Atlantic	February	1286028
Mid-Atlantic	March	1911093
Mid-Atlantic	April	1623438
Mid-Atlantic	May	1778805
Mid-Atlantic	June	1504455
Mid-Atlantic	July	1820742
Mid-Atlantic	August	1381560
Mid-Atlantic	September	1178694
Mid-Atlantic	October	1530351
Mid-Atlantic	November	1598667
Mid-Atlantic	December	1477374
Southeast US		20605485
Southeast US	January	1137063
Southeast US	February	1855269
Southeast US	March	1967979
Southeast US	April	1830051
Southeast US	May	1983282
Southeast US	June	1705716
Southeast US	July	1670976
Southeast US	August	1436295
Southeast US	September	1905633

```
Southeast US        October        1610523
Southeast US        November       1661598
Southeast US        December       1841100
```

52 rows selected.

Note that the output contains not only the subtotals for each region, but also the subtotals for each month. You can get the same result from a query without the CUBE operation. However, that query would be lengthy and complex and, of course, very inefficient. Such a query would look like:

```
SELECT NULL region, NULL month, SUM(o.tot_sales)
FROM all_orders o JOIN region r
ON r.region_id = o.region_id
UNION ALL
SELECT NULL, TO_CHAR(TO_DATE(o.month, 'MM'), 'Month') month, SUM(o.tot_sales)
FROM all_orders o JOIN region r
ON r.region_id = o.region_id
GROUP BY o.month
UNION ALL
SELECT r.name region, NULL, SUM(o.tot_sales)
FROM all_orders o JOIN region r
ON r.region_id = o.region_id
GROUP BY r.name
UNION ALL
SELECT r.name region, TO_CHAR(TO_DATE(o.month, 'MM'), 'Month') month,
SUM(o.tot_sales)
FROM all_orders o JOIN region r
ON r.region_id = o.region_id
GROUP BY r.name, o.month;
```

```
REGION               MONTH     SUM(O.TOT_SALES)
-------------------- --------- ----------------
                               59285706
                     January    4496799
                     February   4988535
                     March      5578521
                     April      5246355
                     May        5460942
                     June       4720233
                     July       5169720
                     August     4460823
                     September  4811094
                     October    4789818
                     November   4644450
                     December   4918416
Mid-Atlantic                   18923298
New England                    19756923
Southeast US                   20605485
New England          January    1527645
New England          February   1847238
New England          March      1699449
New England          April      1792866
New England          May        1698855
```

```
New England      June         1510062
New England      July         1678002
New England      August       1642968
New England      September     1726767
New England      October       1648944
New England      November      1384185
New England      December      1599942
Mid-Atlantic     January      1832091
Mid-Atlantic     February     1286028
Mid-Atlantic     March        1911093
Mid-Atlantic     April        1623438
Mid-Atlantic     May          1778805
Mid-Atlantic     June         1504455
Mid-Atlantic     July         1820742
Mid-Atlantic     August       1381560
Mid-Atlantic     September     1178694
Mid-Atlantic     October       1530351
Mid-Atlantic     November      1598667
Mid-Atlantic     December      1477374
Southeast US     January      1137063
Southeast US     February     1855269
Southeast US     March        1967979
Southeast US     April        1830051
Southeast US     May          1983282
Southeast US     June         1705716
Southeast US     July         1670976
Southeast US     August       1436295
Southeast US     September     1905633
Southeast US     October       1610523
Southeast US     November      1661598
Southeast US     December      1841100

52 rows selected.
```

Since a CUBE produces aggregate results for all possible combinations of the grouping columns, the output of a query using CUBE is independent of the order of columns in the CUBE operation, if everything else remains the same. This is not the case with ROLLUP. If everything else in the query remains the same, ROLLUP(a,b) will produce a slightly different result set than ROLLUP(b,a). However, the result set of CUBE(a,b) will be the same as that of CUBE(b,a). The following example illustrates this by taking the example at the beginning of this section and reversing the order of columns in the CUBE operation:

```
SELECT r.name region, TO_CHAR(TO_DATE(o.month, 'MM'), 'Month') month,
SUM(o.tot_sales)
FROM all_orders o JOIN region r
ON r.region_id = o.region_id
GROUP BY CUBE(o.month, r.name);

REGION              MONTH     SUM(O.TOT_SALES)
------------------- --------- ----------------
                                      59285706
New England                           19756923
```

```
Mid-Atlantic                          18923298
Southeast US                          20605485
                    January            4496799
New England         January            1527645
Mid-Atlantic        January            1832091
Southeast US        January            1137063
                    February           4988535
New England         February           1847238
Mid-Atlantic        February           1286028
Southeast US        February           1855269
                    March              5578521
New England         March              1699449
Mid-Atlantic        March              1911093
Southeast US        March              1967979
                    April              5246355
New England         April              1792866
Mid-Atlantic        April              1623438
Southeast US        April              1830051
                    May                5460942
New England         May                1698855
Mid-Atlantic        May                1778805
Southeast US        May                1983282
                    June               4720233
New England         June               1510062
Mid-Atlantic        June               1504455
Southeast US        June               1705716
                    July               5169720
New England         July               1678002
Mid-Atlantic        July               1820742
Southeast US        July               1670976
                    August             4460823
New England         August             1642968
Mid-Atlantic        August             1381560
Southeast US        August             1436295
                    September          4811094
New England         September          1726767
Mid-Atlantic        September          1178694
Southeast US        September          1905633
                    October            4789818
New England         October            1648944
Mid-Atlantic        October            1530351
Southeast US        October            1610523
                    November           4644450
New England         November           1384185
Mid-Atlantic        November           1598667
Southeast US        November           1661598
                    December           4918416
New England         December           1599942
Mid-Atlantic        December           1477374
Southeast US        December           1841100

52 rows selected.
```

This query produced the same results as the earlier query; only the order of the rows happens to be different.

Partial CUBE

To exclude some subtotals from the output, you can do a *partial CUBE*, (similar to a partial ROLLUP) by taking out column(s) from the CUBE operation and putting them into the GROUP BY clause. Here's an example:

```
SELECT r.name region, TO_CHAR(TO_DATE(o.month, 'MM'), 'Month') month,
SUM(o.tot_sales)
FROM all_orders o JOIN region r
ON r.region_id = o.region_id
GROUP BY r.name, CUBE(o.month);
```

```
REGION               MONTH     SUM(O.TOT_SALES)
-------------------- --------- ----------------
New England                            19756923
New England          January           1527645
New England          February          1847238
New England          March             1699449
New England          April             1792866
New England          May               1698855
New England          June              1510062
New England          July              1678002
New England          August            1642968
New England          September         1726767
New England          October           1648944
New England          November          1384185
New England          December          1599942
Mid-Atlantic                           18923298
Mid-Atlantic         January           1832091
Mid-Atlantic         February          1286028
Mid-Atlantic         March             1911093
Mid-Atlantic         April             1623438
Mid-Atlantic         May               1778805
Mid-Atlantic         June              1504455
Mid-Atlantic         July              1820742
Mid-Atlantic         August            1381560
Mid-Atlantic         September         1178694
Mid-Atlantic         October           1530351
Mid-Atlantic         November          1598667
Mid-Atlantic         December          1477374
Southeast US                           20605485
Southeast US         January           1137063
Southeast US         February          1855269
Southeast US         March             1967979
Southeast US         April             1830051
Southeast US         May               1983282
Southeast US         June              1705716
Southeast US         July              1670976
Southeast US         August            1436295
```

```
Southeast US          September          1905633
Southeast US          October            1610523
Southeast US          November           1661598
Southeast US          December           1841100

39 rows selected.
```

If you compare the results of the partial CUBE operation with that of the full CUBE operation, discussed at the beginning of this section, you will notice that the partial CUBE has excluded the subtotals for each month and the grand total from the output. If you want to retain the subtotals for each month, but want to exclude the subtotals for each region, you can swap the position of r.name and o.month in the GROUP BY…CUBE clause, as shown here:

```
SELECT r.name region, TO_CHAR(TO_DATE(o.month, 'MM'), 'Month') month,
SUM(o.tot_sales)
FROM all_orders o JOIN region r
ON r.region_id = o.region_id
GROUP BY o.month, CUBE(r.name);
```

One interesting thing to note is that if you have one column in the CUBE operation, it produces the same result as the ROLLUP operation. Therefore, the following two queries produce identical results:

```
SELECT r.name region, TO_CHAR(TO_DATE(o.month, 'MM'), 'Month') month,
SUM(o.tot_sales)
FROM all_orders o JOIN region r
ON r.region_id = o.region_id
GROUP BY r.name, CUBE(o.month);

SELECT r.name region, TO_CHAR(TO_DATE(o.month, 'MM'), 'Month') month,
SUM(o.tot_sales)
FROM all_orders o JOIN region r
ON r.region_id = o.region_id
GROUP BY r.name, ROLLUP(o.month);
```

The GROUPING Function

ROLLUP and CUBE produce extra rows in the output that contain subtotals and totals. When a row represents a summary over a given column or set of columns, those columns will contain NULL values. Output containing NULLs and indicating subtotals doesn't make sense to an ordinary person who is unaware of the behavior of ROLLUP and CUBE operations. Does your corporate vice president (VP) care about whether you used ROLLUP or CUBE or any other operation to get him the monthly total sales for each region? Obviously, he doesn't. That's exactly why you are reading this page and not your VP.

If you know your way around the NVL function, you would probably attempt to translate each NULL value from CUBE and ROLLUP to some descriptive value, as in the following example:

```
SELECT NVL(TO_CHAR(o.year), 'All Years') year,
NVL(TO_CHAR(TO_DATE(o.month, 'MM'), 'Month'), 'First Quarter') month,
NVL(r.name, 'All Regions') region, SUM(o.tot_sales)
FROM all_orders o JOIN region r
ON r.region_id = o.region_id
WHERE o.month BETWEEN 1 AND 3
GROUP BY ROLLUP (o.year, o.month, r.name);
```

```
YEAR          MONTH          REGION          SUM(O.TOT_SALES)
------------  -------------  --------------  ----------------
2000          January        New England            1018430
2000          January        Mid-Atlantic           1221394
2000          January        Southeast US            758042
2000          January        All Regions            2997866
2000          February       New England            1231492
2000          February       Mid-Atlantic            857352
2000          February       Southeast US           1236846
2000          February       All Regions            3325690
2000          March          New England            1132966
2000          March          Mid-Atlantic           1274062
2000          March          Southeast US           1311986
2000          March          All Regions            3719014
2000          First Quarter  All Regions           10042570
2001          January        New England             509215
2001          January        Mid-Atlantic            610697
2001          January        Southeast US            379021
2001          January        All Regions            1498933
2001          February       New England             615746
2001          February       Mid-Atlantic            428676
2001          February       Southeast US            618423
2001          February       All Regions            1662845
2001          March          New England             566483
2001          March          Mid-Atlantic            637031
2001          March          Southeast US            655993
2001          March          All Regions            1859507
2001          First Quarter  All Regions            5021285
All Years     First Quarter  All Regions           15063855

27 rows selected.
```

The NVL function works pretty well for this example. However, if the data itself contains some NULL values, it becomes impossible to distinguish whether a NULL value represents unavailable data or a subtotal row. The NVL function will cause a problem in such a case. The following data can be used to illustrate this problem:

```
SELECT * FROM disputed_orders;

ORDER_NBR   CUST_NBR  SALES_EMP_ID  SALE_PRICE  ORDER_DT   EXPECTED_  STATUS
----------  --------  ------------  ----------  ---------  ---------  ---------
      1001         1          7354          99  22-JUL-01  23-JUL-01  DELIVERED
      1000         1          7354              19-JUL-01  24-JUL-01
```

```
1002      5      7368          12-JUL-01 25-JUL-01
1003      4      7654       56 16-JUL-01 26-JUL-01 DELIVERED
1004      4      7654       34 18-JUL-01 27-JUL-01 PENDING
1005      8      7654       99 22-JUL-01 24-JUL-01 DELIVERED
1006      1      7354          22-JUL-01 28-JUL-01
1007      5      7368       25 20-JUL-01 22-JUL-01 PENDING
1008      5      7368       25 21-JUL-01 23-JUL-01 PENDING
1009      1      7354       56 18-JUL-01 22-JUL-01 DELIVERED
1012      1      7354       99 22-JUL-01 23-JUL-01 DELIVERED
1011      1      7354          19-JUL-01 24-JUL-01
1015      5      7368          12-JUL-01 25-JUL-01
1017      4      7654       56 16-JUL-01 26-JUL-01 DELIVERED
1019      4      7654       34 18-JUL-01 27-JUL-01 PENDING
1021      8      7654       99 22-JUL-01 24-JUL-01 DELIVERED
1023      1      7354          22-JUL-01 28-JUL-01
1025      5      7368       25 20-JUL-01 22-JUL-01 PENDING
1027      5      7368       25 21-JUL-01 23-JUL-01 PENDING
1029      1      7354       56 18-JUL-01 22-JUL-01 DELIVERED
```

```
20 rows selected.
```

Note that the column status contains NULL values. If you want the summary status of orders for each customer, and you executed the following query (note the application of NVL to the status column), the output might surprise you.

```
SELECT NVL(TO_CHAR(cust_nbr), 'All Customers') customer,
NVL(status, 'All Status') status,
COUNT(*) FROM disputed_orders
GROUP BY CUBE(cust_nbr, status);
```

```
CUSTOMER                                  STATUS                COUNT(*)
----------------------------------------  --------------------  ----------
All Customers                             All Status                   6
All Customers                             All Status                  20
All Customers                             PENDING                      6
All Customers                             DELIVERED                    8
1                                         All Status                   4
1                                         All Status                   8
1                                         DELIVERED                    4
4                                         All Status                   4
4                                         PENDING                      2
4                                         DELIVERED                    2
5                                         All Status                   2
5                                         All Status                   6
5                                         PENDING                      4
8                                         All Status                   2
8                                         DELIVERED                    2
```

```
15 rows selected.
```

This output doesn't make any sense. The problem is that any time the status column legitimately contains a NULL value, the NVL function returns the string "All

Status." Obviously, NVL isn't useful in this situation. However, don't worry—Oracle provides a solution to this problem through the GROUPING function.

The GROUPING function is meant to be used in conjunction with either a ROLLUP or a CUBE operation. The GROUPING function takes a grouping column name as input and returns either 1 or 0. A 1 is returned if the column's value is NULL as the result of aggregation (ROLLUP or CUBE); otherwise, 0 is returned. The general syntax of the GROUPING function is:

```
SELECT ... [GROUPING(grouping_column_name)] ...
FROM ...
GROUP BY ... {ROLLUP | CUBE} (grouping_column_name)
```

The following example illustrates the use of GROUPING function in a simple way by returning the GROUPING function results for the three columns passed to ROLLUP:

```
SELECT o.year, TO_CHAR(TO_DATE(o.month, 'MM'), 'Month') month,
r.name region, SUM(o.tot_sales),
GROUPING(o.year) y, GROUPING(o.month) m, GROUPING(r.name) r
FROM all_orders o JOIN region r
ON r.region_id = o.region_id
WHERE o.month BETWEEN 1 AND 3
GROUP BY ROLLUP (o.year, o.month, r.name);
```

YEAR	MONTH	REGION	SUM(O.TOT_SALES)	Y	M	R
2000	January	New England	1018430	0	0	0
2000	January	Mid-Atlantic	1221394	0	0	0
2000	January	Southeast US	758042	0	0	0
2000	January		2997866	0	0	1
2000	February	New England	1231492	0	0	0
2000	February	Mid-Atlantic	857352	0	0	0
2000	February	Southeast US	1236846	0	0	0
2000	February		3325690	0	0	1
2000	March	New England	1132966	0	0	0
2000	March	Mid-Atlantic	1274062	0	0	0
2000	March	Southeast US	1311986	0	0	0
2000	March		3719014	0	0	1
2000			10042570	0	1	1
2001	January	New England	509215	0	0	0
2001	January	Mid-Atlantic	610697	0	0	0
2001	January	Southeast US	379021	0	0	0
2001	January		1498933	0	0	1
2001	February	New England	615746	0	0	0
2001	February	Mid-Atlantic	428676	0	0	0
2001	February	Southeast US	618423	0	0	0
2001	February		1662845	0	0	1
2001	March	New England	566483	0	0	0
2001	March	Mid-Atlantic	637031	0	0	0
2001	March	Southeast US	655993	0	0	0
2001	March		1859507	0	0	1
2001			5021285	0	1	1
			15063855	1	1	1

27 rows selected.

Look at the y, m, and r columns in this output. Row 4 is a region-level subtotal for a particular month and year, and therefore, the GROUPING function results in a value of 1 for the region and a value 0 for the month and year. Row 26 (the second to last) is a subtotal for all regions and months for a particular year, and therefore, the GROUPING function prints 1 for the month and the region and 0 for the year. Row 27 (the grand total) contains 1 for all the GROUPING columns.

With a combination of GROUPING and DECODE (or CASE), you can produce more readable query output when using CUBE and ROLLUP, as in the following example:

```
SELECT DECODE(GROUPING(o.year), 1, 'All Years', o.year) Year,
DECODE(GROUPING(o.month), 1, 'All Months',
TO_CHAR(TO_DATE(o.month, 'MM'), 'Month')) Month,
DECODE(GROUPING(r.name), 1, 'All Regions', r.name) Region, SUM(o.tot_sales)
FROM all_orders o JOIN region r
ON r.region_id = o.region_id
WHERE o.month BETWEEN 1 AND 3
GROUP BY ROLLUP (o.year, o.month, r.name);
```

YEAR	MONTH	REGION	SUM(O.TOT_SALES)
2000	January	New England	1018430
2000	January	Mid-Atlantic	1221394
2000	January	Southeast US	758042
2000	January	All Regions	2997866
2000	February	New England	1231492
2000	February	Mid-Atlantic	857352
2000	February	Southeast US	1236846
2000	February	All Regions	3325690
2000	March	New England	1132966
2000	March	Mid-Atlantic	1274062
2000	March	Southeast US	1311986
2000	March	All Regions	3719014
2000	All Months	All Regions	10042570
2001	January	New England	509215
2001	January	Mid-Atlantic	610697
2001	January	Southeast US	379021
2001	January	All Regions	1498933
2001	February	New England	615746
2001	February	Mid-Atlantic	428676
2001	February	Southeast US	618423
2001	February	All Regions	1662845
2001	March	New England	566483
2001	March	Mid-Atlantic	637031
2001	March	Southeast US	655993
2001	March	All Regions	1859507
2001	All Months	All Regions	5021285
All Years	All Months	All Regions	15063855

```
27 rows selected.
```

By using DECODE with GROUPING, we produced the same result that was produced by using NVL at the beginning of the section. However, the risk of mistreating a NULL data value as a summary row is eliminated by using GROUPING and DECODE. You will notice this in the following example, in which NULL data values in subtotal and total rows are treated differently by the GROUPING function than the NULL values in the summary rows:

```
SELECT DECODE(GROUPING(cust_nbr), 1, 'All Customers', cust_nbr) customer,
DECODE(GROUPING(status), 1, 'All Status', status) status, COUNT(*)
FROM disputed_orders
GROUP BY CUBE(cust_nbr, status);
```

CUSTOMER	STATUS	COUNT(*)
All Customers		6
All Customers	All Status	20
All Customers	PENDING	6
All Customers	DELIVERED	8
1		4
1	All Status	8
1	DELIVERED	4
4	All Status	4
4	PENDING	2
4	DELIVERED	2
5		2
5	All Status	6
5	PENDING	4
8	All Status	2
8	DELIVERED	2

```
15 rows selected.
```

GROUPING SETS

Earlier in this chapter, you saw how to generate summary information using ROLLUP and CUBE. However, the output of ROLLUP and CUBE include the rows produced by the regular GROUP BY operation along with the summary rows. Oracle9*i* introduced another extension to the GROUP BY clause called GROUPING SETS that you can use to generate summary information at the level you choose without including all the rows produced by the regular GROUP BY operation.

Like ROLLUP and CUBE, GROUPING SETS is also an extension of the GROUP BY clause, and can appear in a query only along with a GROUP BY clause. The syntax of GROUPING SETS is:

```
SELECT ...
FROM ...
GROUP BY GROUPING SETS (list of grouping columns)
```

Let's take an example to understand the GROUPING SETS operation further:

```
SELECT o.year, TO_CHAR(TO_DATE(o.month, 'MM'), 'Month') month,
r.name region, SUM(o.tot_sales)
FROM all_orders o JOIN region r
ON r.region_id = o.region_id
WHERE o.month BETWEEN 1 AND 3
GROUP BY GROUPING SETS (o.year, o.month, r.name);
```

```
      YEAR MONTH     REGION               SUM(O.TOT_SALES)
---------- --------- -------------------- ----------------
                     Mid-Atlantic                  5029212
                     New England                   5074332
                     Southeast US                  4960311
           January                                 4496799
           February                                4988535
           March                                   5578521
      2000                                        10042570
      2001                                         5021285

8 rows selected.
```

This output contains only the subtotals at the region, month, and year levels, but that none of the normal, more detailed, GROUP BY data is included. The order of columns in the GROUPING SETS operation is not critical. The operation produces the same output regardless of the order of the columns. For example:

```
SELECT o.year, TO_CHAR(TO_DATE(o.month, 'MM'), 'Month') month,
r.name region, SUM(o.tot_sales)
FROM all_orders o JOIN region r
ON r.region_id = o.region_id
WHERE o.month BETWEEN 1 AND 3
GROUP BY GROUPING SETS (o.month, r.name, o.year);
```

```
      YEAR MONTH     REGION               SUM(O.TOT_SALES)
---------- --------- -------------------- ----------------
                     Mid-Atlantic                  5029212
                     New England                   5074332
                     Southeast US                  4960311
           January                                 4496799
           February                                4988535
           March                                   5578521
      2000                                        10042570
      2001                                         5021285

8 rows selected.
```

Pushing the GROUPING Envelope

The grouping examples you have seen so far represent simple ways of aggregating data using Oracle's extensions of the GROUP BY clause. These simple mechanisms were introduced in Oracle8*i*. In Oracle9*i* Database, Oracle enhanced this new functionality in some interesting and useful ways. Oracle now allows for:

- Repeating column names in the GROUP BY clause
- Grouping on composite columns
- Concatenated groupings

Repeated Column Names in the GROUP BY Clause

In Oracle8*i*, repeating column names are not allowed in a GROUP BY clause. If the GROUP BY clause contains an extension (i.e., ROLLUP or CUBE), you cannot use the same column inside the extension as well as outside the extension. The following SQL is invalid in Oracle8*i*:

```
SELECT o.year, TO_CHAR(TO_DATE(o.month, 'MM'), 'Month') month,
r.name region, SUM(o.tot_sales) total
FROM all_orders o JOIN region r
ON r.region_id = o.region_id
WHERE o.month BETWEEN 1 AND 3
GROUP BY o.year, ROLLUP (o.year, o.month, r.name);
                            *
ERROR at line 6:
ORA-30490: Ambiguous expression in GROUP BY ROLLUP or CUBE list
```

However, the same query works in Oracle9*i* Database and later:

```
SELECT o.year, TO_CHAR(TO_DATE(o.month, 'MM'), 'Month') month,
r.name region, SUM(o.tot_sales) total
FROM all_orders o JOIN region r
ON r.region_id = o.region_id
WHERE o.month BETWEEN 1 AND 3
GROUP BY o.year, ROLLUP (o.year, o.month, r.name);
```

YEAR	MONTH	REGION	TOTAL
2000	January	Mid-Atlantic	1221394
2000	January	New England	1018430
2000	January	Southeast US	758042
2000	January		2997866
2000	February	Mid-Atlantic	857352
2000	February	New England	1231492
2000	February	Southeast US	1236846
2000	February		3325690
2000	March	Mid-Atlantic	1274062
2000	March	New England	1132966
2000	March	Southeast US	1311986
2000	March		3719014
2001	January	Mid-Atlantic	610697
2001	January	New England	509215
2001	January	Southeast US	379021
2001	January		1498933
2001	February	Mid-Atlantic	428676

```
2001 February  New England      615746
2001 February  Southeast US     618423
2001 February                  1662845
2001 March     Mid-Atlantic     637031
2001 March     New England      566483
2001 March     Southeast US     655993
2001 March                     1859507
2000                          10042570
2001                           5021285
2000                          10042570
2001                           5021285
```

```
28 rows selected.
```

Repetition of o.year in the GROUP BY clause as well as in the ROLLUP operation repeats the summary rows of each year in the output and suppresses the grand total. Repetition of column names in a GROUP BY clause isn't very useful, but it's worth knowing that such constructs are allowed in Oracle9*i* and later.

Grouping on Composite Columns

Oracle8*i* supports grouping on individual columns only. Oracle9*i* extends the grouping operations to include grouping on composite columns. A *composite column* is a collection of two or more columns, but their values are treated as one for the grouping computation. Oracle8*i* allows group operations of the form ROLLUP (a,b,c), while, Oracle9*i* allows group operations of the form ROLLUP (a,(b,c)) as well. In this case, (b,c) is treated as one column for the purpose of the grouping computation. For example:

```
SELECT o.year, TO_CHAR(TO_DATE(o.month, 'MM'), 'Month') month,
r.name region, SUM(o.tot_sales) total
FROM all_orders o JOIN region r
ON r.region_id = o.region_id
WHERE o.month BETWEEN 1 AND 3
GROUP BY ROLLUP ((o.year, o.month),r.name);
```

```
      YEAR MONTH     REGION                     TOTAL
---------- --------- -------------------- ----------
      2000 January   Mid-Atlantic            1221394
      2000 January   New England             1018430
      2000 January   Southeast US             758042
      2000 January                           2997866
      2000 February  Mid-Atlantic             857352
      2000 February  New England             1231492
      2000 February  Southeast US            1236846
      2000 February                          3325690
      2000 March     Mid-Atlantic            1274062
      2000 March     New England             1132966
      2000 March     Southeast US            1311986
      2000 March                             3719014
      2001 January   Mid-Atlantic             610697
```

```
2001 January   New England           509215
2001 January   Southeast US          379021
2001 January                         1498933
2001 February  Mid-Atlantic          428676
2001 February  New England           615746
2001 February  Southeast US          618423
2001 February                        1662845
2001 March     Mid-Atlantic          637031
2001 March     New England           566483
2001 March     Southeast US          655993
2001 March                           1859507
                                     15063855
```

25 rows selected.

In this example, two columns (o.year, o.month) are treated as one composite column. This causes Oracle to treat the combination of year and month as one dimension, and the summary rows are computed accordingly. Although this query is not allowed in Oracle8*i*, you can fake composite column groupings in Oracle8*i* by using the concatenation operator (||) to combine two columns and treat the result as one composite column. Oracle8*i* can then produce the same result as the previous query in Oracle 9*i*. For example:

```
SELECT TO_CHAR(o.year)||' '||TO_CHAR(TO_DATE(o.month,'MM'),'Month')
       Year_Month,
       r.name region, SUM(o.tot_sales)
FROM all_orders o JOIN region r
ON r.region_id = o.region_id
WHERE o.month BETWEEN 1 AND 3
GROUP BY
ROLLUP (TO_CHAR(o.year)||' '||
        TO_CHAR(TO_DATE(o.month,'MM'),'Month'), r.name);
```

```
YEAR_MONTH           REGION                SUM(O.TOT_SALES)
-------------------- --------------------- ----------------
2001 February        Mid-Atlantic                   857352
2001 February        New England                   1231492
2001 February        Southeast US                  1236846
2001 February                                       3325690
2000 January         Mid-Atlantic                  1221394
2000 January         New England                   1018430
2000 January         Southeast US                   758042
2000 January                                        2997866
2000 March           Mid-Atlantic                  1274062
2000 March           New England                   1132966
2000 March           Southeast US                  1311986
2000 March                                          3719014
2001 February        Mid-Atlantic                   428676
2001 February        New England                    615746
2001 February        Southeast US                   618423
2001 February                                       1662845
2001 January         Mid-Atlantic                   610697
2001 January         New England                    509215
```

```
2001 January       Southeast US            379021
2001 January                              1498933
2001 March         Mid-Atlantic            637031
2001 March         New England             566483
2001 March         Southeast US            655993
2001 March                                1859507
                                          15063855
```

25 rows selected.

This query converts the numeric month into the string expression of the name of the month and concatenates it with the string representation of the year. The same expression has to be used in the SELECT list and the ROLLUP clause. The expression TO_CHAR(o.year)||' '||TO_CHAR(TO_DATE(o.month,'MM'),'Month') is treated as one composite column.

Concatenated Groupings

With Oracle9*i* and later, you can have multiple ROLLUP, CUBE, or GROUPING SETS operations, or a combination of these under the GROUP BY clause in a query. This is not allowed in Oracle8*i*. You will get an error message if you attempt the following query in Oracle8*i*:

```
SELECT o.year, TO_CHAR(TO_DATE(o.month, 'MM'), 'Month') month,
r.name region, SUM(o.tot_sales) total
FROM all_orders o JOIN region r
ON r.region_id = o.region_id
WHERE o.month BETWEEN 1 AND 3
GROUP BY ROLLUP (o.year, o.month), ROLLUP(r.name);
                                   *
ERROR at line 6:
ORA-30489: Cannot have more than one rollup/cube expression list
```

However, the same query works in Oracle9*i* and later:

```
SELECT o.year, TO_CHAR(TO_DATE(o.month, 'MM'), 'Month') month,
r.name region, SUM(o.tot_sales) total
FROM all_orders o JOIN region r
ON r.region_id = o.region_id
WHERE o.month BETWEEN 1 AND 3
GROUP BY ROLLUP (o.year, o.month), ROLLUP(r.name);

      YEAR MONTH     REGION                    TOTAL
---------- --------- -------------------- ----------
      2000 January   Mid-Atlantic            1221394
      2000 January   New England             1018430
      2000 January   Southeast US             758042
      2000 January                           2997866
      2000 February  Mid-Atlantic             857352
      2000 February  New England             1231492
      2000 February  Southeast US            1236846
      2000 February                          3325690
      2000 March     Mid-Atlantic            1274062
```

```
2000 March      New England          1132966
2000 March      Southeast US         1311986
2000 March                           3719014
2000            Mid-Atlantic         3352808
2000            New England          3382888
2000            Southeast US         3306874
2000                                10042570
2001 January    Mid-Atlantic          610697
2001 January    New England           509215
2001 January    Southeast US          379021
2001 January                         1498933
2001 February   Mid-Atlantic          428676
2001 February   New England           615746
2001 February   Southeast US          618423
2001 February                        1662845
2001 March      Mid-Atlantic          637031
2001 March      New England           566483
2001 March      Southeast US          655993
2001 March                           1859507
2001            Mid-Atlantic         1676404
2001            New England          1691444
2001            Southeast US         1653437
2001                                 5021285
                Mid-Atlantic         5029212
                New England          5074332
                Southeast US         4960311
                                    15063855
```

36 rows selected.

When you have multiple grouping operations (ROLLUP, CUBE, or GROUPING SETS) in a GROUP BY clause, what you have is called a *concatenated grouping*. The result of the concatenated grouping is to produce a cross-product of groupings from each grouping operation. Therefore, the query:

```
SELECT o.year, TO_CHAR(TO_DATE(o.month, 'MM'), 'Month') month,
r.name region, SUM(o.tot_sales) total
FROM all_orders o JOIN region r
ON r.region_id = o.region_id
WHERE o.month BETWEEN 1 AND 3
GROUP BY ROLLUP(o.year),  ROLLUP (o.month), ROLLUP (r.name);
```

behaves as a CUBE and produces the same result as the query:

```
SELECT o.year, TO_CHAR(TO_DATE(o.month, 'MM'), 'Month') month,
r.name region, SUM(o.tot_sales) total
FROM all_orders o JOIN region r
ON r.region_id = o.region_id
WHERE o.month BETWEEN 1 AND 3
GROUP BY CUBE (o.year, o.month, r.name);
```

Since a CUBE contains aggregates for all possible combinations of the grouping columns, the concatenated grouping of CUBES is no different from a regular CUBE, and all the following queries return the same result as the query shown previously:

```
SELECT o.year, TO_CHAR(TO_DATE(o.month, 'MM'), 'Month') month,
r.name region, SUM(o.tot_sales) total
FROM all_orders o JOIN region r
ON r.region_id = o.region_id
WHERE o.month BETWEEN 1 AND 3
GROUP BY CUBE (o.year, o.month), CUBE (r.name);

SELECT o.year, TO_CHAR(TO_DATE(o.month, 'MM'), 'Month') month,
r.name region, SUM(o.tot_sales) total
FROM all_orders o JOIN region r
ON r.region_id = o.region_id
WHERE o.month BETWEEN 1 AND 3
GROUP BY CUBE (o.year), CUBE (o.month, r.name);

SELECT o.year, TO_CHAR(TO_DATE(o.month, 'MM'), 'Month') month,
r.name region, SUM(o.tot_sales) total
FROM all_orders o JOIN region r
ON r.region_id = o.region_id
WHERE o.month BETWEEN 1 AND 3
GROUP BY CUBE (o.year), CUBE (o.month), CUBE (r.name);
```

Concatenated groupings with GROUPING SETS

Concatenated groupings come in handy while using GROUPING SETS. Since GROUPING SETS produces only the subtotal rows, you can specify just the aggregation levels you want in your output by using a concatenated grouping of GROUPING SETS. The concatenated grouping of GROUPING SETS (a,b) and GROUPING SETS (c,d) will produce aggregate rows for the aggregation levels (a,c), (a,d), (b,c), and (b,d). The concatenated grouping of GROUPING SETS (a,b) and GROUPING SETS (c) will produce aggregate rows for the aggregation levels (a,c) and (b,c). For example:

```
SELECT o.year, TO_CHAR(TO_DATE(o.month, 'MM'), 'Month') month,
r.name region, SUM(o.tot_sales) total
FROM all_orders o JOIN region r
ON r.region_id = o.region_id
WHERE o.month BETWEEN 1 AND 3
GROUP BY GROUPING SETS (o.year, o.month), GROUPING SETS (r.name);
```

```
YEAR MONTH      REGION                TOTAL
---------- --------- -------------------- ----------
      2000            Mid-Atlantic          3352808
      2000            New England           3382888
      2000            Southeast US          3306874
      2001            Mid-Atlantic          1676404
      2001            New England           1691444
      2001            Southeast US          1653437
           January    Mid-Atlantic          1832091
           January    New England           1527645
```

```
January    Southeast US          1137063
February   Mid-Atlantic          1286028
February   New England           1847238
February   Southeast US          1855269
March      Mid-Atlantic          1911093
March      New England           1699449
March      Southeast US          1967979
```

15 rows selected.

The concatenated grouping GROUP BY GROUPING SETS (O.YEAR, O.MONTH), GROUPING SETS (R.NAME) in this example produces rows for aggregate levels (O.YEAR, R.NAME) and (O.MONTH, R.NAME). Therefore, you see aggregate rows for (Year, Region) and (Month, Region) combinations in the output. The following example extends the previous query:

```
SELECT o.year, TO_CHAR(TO_DATE(o.month, 'MM'), 'Month') month,
r.name region, SUM(o.tot_sales) total
FROM all_orders o JOIN region r
ON r.region_id = o.region_id
WHERE o.month BETWEEN 1 AND 3
GROUP BY GROUPING SETS (o.year, o.month), GROUPING SETS (o.year, r. name);
```

```
     YEAR MONTH     REGION                    TOTAL
     ---------- ---------  -------------------- ----------
 1:  2000                                     10042570
 2:  2001                                      5021285
 3:  2000 January                             2997866
 4:  2000 February                            3325690
 5:  2000 March                               3719014
 6:  2001 January                             1498933
 7:  2001 February                            1662845
 8:  2001 March                               1859507
 9:  2000           Mid-Atlantic              3352808
10:  2000           New England               3382888
11:  2000           Southeast US              3306874
12:  2001           Mid-Atlantic              1676404
13:  2001           New England               1691444
14:  2001           Southeast US              1653437
15:       January   Mid-Atlantic              1832091
16:       January   New England               1527645
17:       January   Southeast US              1137063
18:       February  Mid-Atlantic              1286028
19:       February  New England               1847238
20:       February  Southeast US              1855269
21:       March     Mid-Atlantic              1911093
22:       March     New England               1699449
23:       March     Southeast US              1967979
```

23 rows selected.

This example produces four grouping combinations. Table 13-1 describes the various grouping combinations produced by this query and references their corresponding row numbers in the output.

Table 13-1. Grouping combinations

Grouping combination	Corresponding rows
(o.year, o.year)	1–2
(o.year, r.name)	9–14
(o.month, o.year)	3–8
(o.month, r.name)	15–23

The GROUPING SETS operation is independent of the order of columns. Therefore, the following two queries will produce the same results as shown previously:

```
SELECT o.year, TO_CHAR(TO_DATE(o.month, 'MM'), 'Month') month,
r.name region, SUM(o.tot_sales) total
FROM all_orders o JOIN region r
ON r.region_id = o.region_id
WHERE o.month BETWEEN 1 AND 3
GROUP BY GROUPING SETS (o.year, r.name), GROUPING SETS (o.year, o.month);

SELECT o.year, TO_CHAR(TO_DATE(o.month, 'MM'), 'Month') month,
r.name region, SUM(o.tot_sales) total
FROM all_orders o JOIN region r
ON r.region_id = o.region_id
WHERE o.month BETWEEN 1 AND 3
GROUP BY GROUPING SETS (o.month, o.year), GROUPING SETS (r.name, o.year);
```

It is permissible to have a combination of ROLLUP, CUBE, and GROUPING SETS in a single GROUP BY clause, as in the following example:

```
SELECT o.year, TO_CHAR(TO_DATE(o.month, 'MM'), 'Month') month,
r.name region, SUM(o.tot_sales) total
FROM all_orders o JOIN region r
ON r.region_id = o.region_id
WHERE o.month BETWEEN 1 AND 3
GROUP BY GROUPING SETS (o.month, o.year), ROLLUP(r.name), CUBE (o.year);
```

However, the output from such queries seldom makes any sense. You should carefully evaluate the need for such a query if you intend to write one.

ROLLUP and CUBE as arguments to GROUPING SETS

Unlike the ROLLUP and CUBE operations, the GROUPING SETS operation can take a ROLLUP or a CUBE as its argument. As you have seen earlier, GROUPING SETS produces only subtotal rows. However, there are times when you may need to print the grand total along with the subtotals. In such situations, you can perform the GROUPING SETS operation on ROLLUP operations, as in the following example:

```
SELECT o.year, TO_CHAR(TO_DATE(o.month, 'MM'), 'Month') month,
r.name region, SUM(o.tot_sales) total
```

```
FROM all_orders o JOIN region r
ON r.region_id = o.region_id
WHERE o.month BETWEEN 1 AND 3
GROUP BY GROUPING SETS (ROLLUP (o.year),
                        ROLLUP (o.month),
                        ROLLUP (r. name));
```

YEAR	MONTH	REGION	TOTAL
		Mid-Atlantic	5029212
		New England	5074332
		Southeast US	4960311
	January		4496799
	February		4988535
	March		5578521
2000			10042570
2001			5021285
			15063855
			15063855
			15063855

```
11 rows selected.
```

This example produces the subtotals for each dimension, as expected from the regular GROUPING SETS operations. Also, it produces the grand total across all the
dimensions. However, you get three identical grand-total rows. The grand-total rows
are repeated because they are produced by each ROLLUP operation inside the
GROUPING SETS. If you insist on only one grand-total row, you may use the DIS-
TINCT keyword in the SELECT clause:

```
SELECT Distinct o.year,
               TO_CHAR(TO_DATE(o.month, 'MM'), 'Month') month,
               r.name region, SUM(o.tot_sales) total
FROM all_orders o JOIN region r ON r.region_id = o.region_id
WHERE o.month BETWEEN 1 AND 3
GROUP BY GROUPING SETS (ROLLUP (o.year), ROLLUP (o.month),
                        ROLLUP (r. name));
```

YEAR	MONTH	REGION	TOTAL
2000			10042570
2001			5021285
	February		4988535
	January		4496799
	March		5578521
		Mid-Atlantic	5029212
		New England	5074332
		Southeast US	4960311
			15063855

```
9 rows selected.
```

In this example, the DISTINCT keyword eliminated the duplicate grand-total rows. You can also eliminate duplicate rows by using the GROUP_ID function, as discussed later in this chapter.

If you are interested in subtotals and totals on composite dimensions, you can use composite or concatenated ROLLUP operations within GROUPING SETS, as in the following example:

```
SELECT o.year, TO_CHAR(TO_DATE(o.month, 'MM'), 'Month') month,
r.name region, SUM(o.tot_sales) total
FROM all_orders o JOIN region r
ON r.region_id = o.region_id
WHERE o.month BETWEEN 1 AND 3
GROUP BY GROUPING SETS (ROLLUP (o.year, o.month), ROLLUP(r.name));
```

```
 YEAR MONTH     REGION                    TOTAL
--------- --------- -------------------- ----------
                    Mid-Atlantic          5029212
                    New England           5074332
                    Southeast US          4960311
      2000 January                        2997866
      2000 February                       3325690
      2000 March                          3719014
      2000                               10042570
      2001 January                        1498933
      2001 February                       1662845
      2001 March                          1859507
      2001                                5021285
                                         15063855
                                         15063855
```

```
13 rows selected.
```

This query generates subtotals for (year, month) combinations, subtotals for the region, subtotals for the year, and the grand total. Note that there are duplicate grand-total rows because of the multiple ROLLUP operations within the GROUPING SETS operation.

The GROUPING_ID and GROUP_ID Functions

Earlier in this chapter, you saw how to use the GROUPING function to distinguish between the regular GROUP BY rows and the summary rows produced by the GROUP BY extensions. Oracle9*i* extended the concept of the GROUPING function and introduced two more functions that you can use with a GROUP BY clause:

- GROUPING_ID
- GROUP_ID

These functions can be used only with a GROUP BY clause. However, unlike the GROUPING function that can only be used with a GROUP BY extension, the

GROUPING_ID and GROUP_ID functions can be used in a query, even without a GROUP BY extension.

 Although it is legal to use these two functions without a GROUP BY extension, using GROUPING_ID and GROUP_ID without ROLLUP, CUBE, or GROUPING SETS doesn't produce any meaningful output, because GROUPING_ID and GROUP_ID are 0 for all regular GROUP BY rows.

The following sections discuss these two functions in detail.

GROUPING_ID

The syntax of the GROUPING_ID function is as follows:

```
SELECT ... , GROUPING_ID(ordered_list_of_grouping_columns)
FROM ...
GROUP BY ...
```

The GROUPING_ID function takes an ordered list of grouping columns as input, and computes the output by working through the following steps:

1. It generates the results of the GROUPING function as applied to each of the individual columns in the list. The result of this step is a set of ones and zeros.

2. It puts these ones and zeros in the same order as the order of the columns in its argument list to produce a bit vector.

3. Treating this bit vector (a series of ones and zeros) as a binary number, it converts the bit vector into a decimal (base 10) number.

4. The decimal number computed in Step 3 is returned as the GROUPING_ID function's output.

The following example illustrates this process and compares the results from GROUPING_ID with those from GROUPING:

```
SELECT o.year, TO_CHAR(TO_DATE(o.month, 'MM'), 'Month') month,
r.name region, SUM(o.tot_sales) total,
GROUPING(o.year) y, GROUPING(o.month) m, GROUPING(r.name) r,
GROUPING_ID (o.year, o.month, r.name) gid
FROM all_orders o JOIN region r
ON r.region_id = o.region_id
WHERE o.month BETWEEN 1 AND 3
GROUP BY CUBE (o.year, o.month, r.name);
```

YEAR	MONTH	REGION	TOTAL	Y	M	R	GID
2000	January	Mid-Atlantic	1221394	0	0	0	0
2000	January	New England	1018430	0	0	0	0
2000	January	Southeast US	758042	0	0	0	0
2000	January		2997866	0	0	1	1

2000	February	Mid-Atlantic	857352	0	0	0	0
2000	February	New England	1231492	0	0	0	0
2000	February	Southeast US	1236846	0	0	0	0
2000	February		3325690	0	0	1	1
2000	March	Mid-Atlantic	1274062	0	0	0	0
2000	March	New England	1132966	0	0	0	0
2000	March	Southeast US	1311986	0	0	0	0
2000	March		3719014	0	0	1	1
2000		Mid-Atlantic	3352808	0	1	0	2
2000		New England	3382888	0	1	0	2
2000		Southeast US	3306874	0	1	0	2
2000			10042570	0	1	1	3
2001	January	Mid-Atlantic	610697	0	0	0	0
2001	January	New England	509215	0	0	0	0
2001	January	Southeast US	379021	0	0	0	0
2001	January		1498933	0	0	1	1
2001	February	Mid-Atlantic	428676	0	0	0	0
2001	February	New England	615746	0	0	0	0
2001	February	Southeast US	618423	0	0	0	0
2001	February		1662845	0	0	1	1
2001	March	Mid-Atlantic	637031	0	0	0	0
2001	March	New England	566483	0	0	0	0
2001	March	Southeast US	655993	0	0	0	0
2001	March		1859507	0	0	1	1
2001		Mid-Atlantic	1676404	0	1	0	2
2001		New England	1691444	0	1	0	2
2001		Southeast US	1653437	0	1	0	2
2001			5021285	0	1	1	3
	January	Mid-Atlantic	1832091	1	0	0	4
	January	New England	1527645	1	0	0	4
	January	Southeast US	1137063	1	0	0	4
	January		4496799	1	0	1	5
	February	Mid-Atlantic	1286028	1	0	0	4
	February	New England	1847238	1	0	0	4
	February	Southeast US	1855269	1	0	0	4
	February		4988535	1	0	1	5
	March	Mid-Atlantic	1911093	1	0	0	4
	March	New England	1699449	1	0	0	4
	March	Southeast US	1967979	1	0	0	4
	March		5578521	1	0	1	5
		Mid-Atlantic	5029212	1	1	0	6
		New England	5074332	1	1	0	6
		Southeast US	4960311	1	1	0	6
			15063855	1	1	1	7

```
48 rows selected.
```

Note that the GROUPING_ID is the decimal equivalent of the bit vector generated by the individual GROUPING functions. In this output, the GROUPING_ID has values 0, 1, 2, 3, 4, 5, 6, and 7. Table 13-2 describes these aggregation levels.

Table 13-2. Result of GROUPING_ID(o.year, o.month, r.name)

Aggregation level	Bit vector	GROUPING_ID
Regular GROUP BY rows	0 0 0	0
Subtotal for Year-Month, aggregated at (Region)	0 0 1	1
Subtotal for Year-Region, aggregated at (Month)	0 1 0	2
Subtotal for Year, aggregated at (Month, Region)	0 1 1	3
Subtotal for Month-Region, aggregated at (Year)	1 0 0	4
Subtotal for Month, aggregated at (Year, Region)	1 0 1	5
Subtotal for Region, aggregated at (Year, Month)	1 1 0	6
Grand total for all levels, aggregated at (Year, Month, Region)	1 1 1	7

The GROUPING_ID function can be used effectively in a query to filter rows according to your requirement. Let's say you want only the summary rows to be displayed in the output, and not the regular GROUP BY rows. You can use the GROUPING_ID function in the HAVING clause to do this by restricting output to only those rows that contain totals and subtotals (i.e., for which GROUPING_ID > 0):

```
SELECT o.year, TO_CHAR(TO_DATE(o.month, 'MM'), 'Month') month,
r.name region, SUM(o.tot_sales) total
FROM all_orders o JOIN region r
ON r.region_id = o.region_id
WHERE o.month BETWEEN 1 AND 3
GROUP BY CUBE (o.year, o.month, r.name)
HAVING GROUPING_ID (o.year, o.month, r.name) > 0;

    YEAR MONTH     REGION                   TOTAL
--------- --------- -------------------- ----------
                                          15063855
                    New England           5074332
                    Mid-Atlantic          5029212
                    Southeast US          4960311
          January                         4496799
          January   New England           1527645
          January   Mid-Atlantic          1832091
          January   Southeast US          1137063
          February                        4988535
          February  New England           1847238
          February  Mid-Atlantic          1286028
          February  Southeast US          1855269
          March                           5578521
          March     New England           1699449
          March     Mid-Atlantic          1911093
          March     Southeast US          1967979
     2000                                10042570
     2000           New England           3382888
     2000           Mid-Atlantic          3352808
     2000           Southeast US          3306874
     2000 January                         2997866
     2000 February                        3325690
```

```
2000 March                           3719014
2001                                 5021285
2001          New England           1691444
2001          Mid-Atlantic          1676404
2001          Southeast US          1653437
2001 January                        1498933
2001 February                       1662845
2001 March                          1859507
```

30 rows selected.

As you can see, GROUPING_ID makes it easier to filter the output of aggregation operations. Without the GROUPING_ID function, you have to write a more complex query using the GROUPING function to achieve the same result. For example, the following query uses GROUPING rather than GROUPING_ID to display only totals and subtotals. Note the added complexity in the HAVING clause.

```sql
SELECT o.year, TO_CHAR(TO_DATE(o.month, 'MM'), 'Month') month,
r.name region, SUM(o.tot_sales) total
FROM all_orders o JOIN region r
ON r.region_id = o.region_id
WHERE o.month BETWEEN 1 AND 3
GROUP BY CUBE (o.year, o.month, r.name)
HAVING GROUPING(o.year) > 0
OR GROUPING(o.month) > 0
OR GROUPING(r.name) > 0;
```

```
YEAR MONTH      REGION                   TOTAL
----- --------- -------------------- ----------
                                       15063855
                New England            5074332
                Mid-Atlantic           5029212
                Southeast US           4960311
      January                          4496799
      January   New England            1527645
      January   Mid-Atlantic           1832091
      January   Southeast US           1137063
      February                         4988535
      February  New England            1847238
      February  Mid-Atlantic           1286028
      February  Southeast US           1855269
      March                            5578521
      March     New England            1699449
      March     Mid-Atlantic           1911093
      March     Southeast US           1967979
2000                                  10042570
2000            New England            3382888
2000            Mid-Atlantic           3352808
2000            Southeast US           3306874
2000  January                          2997866
2000  February                         3325690
2000  March                            3719014
2001                                   5021285
```

```
2001        New England        1691444
2001        Mid-Atlantic       1676404
2001        Southeast US       1653437
2001 January                   1498933
2001 February                  1662845
2001 March                     1859507
```

30 rows selected.

GROUPING and GROUPING_ID in ORDER BY

The GROUPING and GROUPING_ID functions not only help you filter rows returned from queries using CUBE and ROLLUP, they can also help you to order those rows in a meaningful way. The order of the rows in a query's output is not guaranteed unless you use an ORDER BY clause in the query. However, if you order the results of a CUBE or ROLLUP query by one dimension, the order of the results may not be meaningful with respect to other dimensions. In such an aggregate query, you may prefer to order the results based on the number of dimensions involved rather than by individual dimensions. For example, when executing the previous section's query, you may prefer to see the output rows in the following order:

1. Those rows representing an aggregate in one dimension
2. Those rows representing an aggregate in two dimensions
3. Those rows representing an aggregate in three dimensions

To achieve this ordering of rows, you need to use an ORDER BY clause that uses a combination of GROUPING and GROUPING_ID functions, as shown in the following example:

```
SELECT o.year, TO_CHAR(TO_DATE(o.month, 'MM'), 'Month') month,
r.name region, SUM(o.tot_sales) total,
GROUPING_ID (o.year, o.month, r.name) gid,
GROUPING(o.year) + GROUPING(o.month) + GROUPING(r.name) sum_grouping
FROM all_orders o JOIN region r
ON r.region_id = o.region_id
WHERE o.month BETWEEN 1 AND 3
GROUP BY CUBE (o.year, o.month, r.name)
HAVING GROUPING(o.year) > 0
OR GROUPING(o.month) > 0
OR GROUPING(r.name) > 0
ORDER BY (GROUPING(o.year) + GROUPING(o.month) + GROUPING(r.name)),
GROUPING_ID (o.year, o.month, r.name);

  YEAR MONTH     REGION              TOTAL   GID SUM_GROUPING
------ --------- -------------- ---------- ----- ------------
  2000 January                     2997866     1            1
  2000 February                    3325690     1            1
  2000 March                       3719014     1            1
  2001 March                       1859507     1            1
  2001 February                    1662845     1            1
```

2001	January		1498933	1	1
2000		New England	3382888	2	1
2001		Mid-Atlantic	1676404	2	1
2001		Southeast US	1653437	2	1
2001		New England	1691444	2	1
2000		Mid-Atlantic	3352808	2	1
2000		Southeast US	3306874	2	1
	January	New England	1527645	4	1
	January	Mid-Atlantic	1832091	4	1
	January	Southeast US	1137063	4	1
	February	Southeast US	1855269	4	1
	March	Mid-Atlantic	1911093	4	1
	March	New England	1699449	4	1
	February	Mid-Atlantic	1286028	4	1
	February	New England	1847238	4	1
	March	Southeast US	1967979	4	1
2000			10042570	3	2
2001			5021285	3	2
	January		4496799	5	2
	March		5578521	5	2
	February		4988535	5	2
		New England	5074332	6	2
		Mid-Atlantic	5029212	6	2
		Southeast US	4960311	6	2
			15063855	7	3

In this output, the aggegate rows for individual dimensions, region, month, and year are shown first. These are followed by the aggregate rows for two dimensions: month and region, year and region, and year and month, respectively. The last row is the one aggregated over all three dimensions.

GROUP_ID

As you saw in previous sections, Oracle9i Database allows you to have repeating grouping columns and multiple grouping operations in a GROUP BY clause. Some combinations could result in duplicate rows in the output. The GROUP_ID distinguishes between otherwise duplicate result rows.

The syntax of the GROUP_ID function is:

```
SELECT ... , GROUP_ID( )
FROM ...
GROUP BY ...
```

The GROUP_ID function takes no argument, and returns 0 through n − 1, where n is the occurrence count for duplicates. The first occurrence of a given row in the output of a query will have a GROUP_ID of 0, the second occurrence of a given row will have a GROUP_ID of 1, and so forth. The following example illustrates the use of the GROUP_ID function:

```
SELECT o.year, TO_CHAR(TO_DATE(o.month, 'MM'), 'Month') month,
r.name region, SUM(o.tot_sales) total, GROUP_ID( )
```

```
FROM all_orders o JOIN region r
ON r.region_id = o.region_id
WHERE o.month BETWEEN 1 AND 3
GROUP BY o.year, ROLLUP (o.year, o.month, r.name);
```

```
YEAR MONTH      REGION                 TOTAL GROUP_ID( )
---------- --------- -------------------- ---------- ----------
  2000 January   Mid-Atlantic         1221394          0
  2000 January   New England          1018430          0
  2000 January   Southeast US          758042          0
  2000 January                        2997866          0
  2000 February  Mid-Atlantic          857352          0
  2000 February  New England          1231492          0
  2000 February  Southeast US         1236846          0
  2000 February                       3325690          0
  2000 March     Mid-Atlantic         1274062          0
  2000 March     New England          1132966          0
  2000 March     Southeast US         1311986          0
  2000 March                          3719014          0
  2001 January   Mid-Atlantic          610697          0
  2001 January   New England           509215          0
  2001 January   Southeast US          379021          0
  2001 January                        1498933          0
  2001 February  Mid-Atlantic          428676          0
  2001 February  New England           615746          0
  2001 February  Southeast US          618423          0
  2001 February                       1662845          0
  2001 March     Mid-Atlantic          637031          0
  2001 March     New England           566483          0
  2001 March     Southeast US          655993          0
  2001 March                          1859507          0
  2000                               10042570          0
  2001                                5021285          0
  2000                               10042570          1
  2001                                5021285          1
```

28 rows selected.

Note that the value 1 is returned by the GROUP_ID function for the last two rows. These rows are indeed duplicates of the previous two rows. If you don't want to see the duplicates in your result set, restrict your query's results to GROUP_ID 0:

```
SELECT o.year, TO_CHAR(TO_DATE(o.month, 'MM'), 'Month') month,
r.name region, SUM(o.tot_sales) total
FROM all_orders o JOIN region r
ON r.region_id = o.region_id
WHERE o.month BETWEEN 1 AND 3
GROUP BY o.year, ROLLUP (o.year, o.month, r.name)
HAVING GROUP_ID( ) = 0;
```

```
YEAR MONTH      REGION                 TOTAL
---------- --------- -------------------- ----------
  2000 January   New England          1018430
  2000 January   Mid-Atlantic         1221394
```

```
2000 January    Southeast US            758042
2000 January                           2997866
2000 February   New England            1231492
2000 February   Mid-Atlantic            857352
2000 February   Southeast US           1236846
2000 February                          3325690
2000 March      New England            1132966
2000 March      Mid-Atlantic           1274062
2000 March      Southeast US           1311986
2000 March                             3719014
2001 January    New England             509215
2001 January    Mid-Atlantic            610697
2001 January    Southeast US            379021
2001 January                           1498933
2001 February   New England             615746
2001 February   Mid-Atlantic            428676
2001 February   Southeast US            618423
2001 February                          1662845
2001 March      New England             566483
2001 March      Mid-Atlantic            637031
2001 March      Southeast US            655993
2001 March                             1859507
2000                                   10042570
2001                                    5021285

26 rows selected.
```

This version of the query uses HAVING GROUP_ID() = 0 to eliminate the two duplicate totals from the result set. GROUP_ID is only meaningful in the HAVING clause, because it applies to summarized data. You can't use GROUP_ID in a WHERE clause, and it wouldn't make sense to try.

CHAPTER 14

Advanced Analytic SQL

For years, SQL has been criticized for its inability to handle routine decision support queries. With a host of new analytic functions introduced in Oracle8*i*, Oracle9*i*, Database, and Oracle Database 10*g*, Oracle has taken giant strides toward eliminating this deficiency. In doing so, Oracle has further blurred the distinction between its multipurpose relational database server and other, special-purpose data warehouse and statistical analysis servers.

Analytic SQL Overview

The types of queries issued by Decision Support Systems (DSS) differ from those issued against OLTP systems. Consider the following business queries:

- Find the top 10 salespeople in each sales district last year.

- Find all customers whose total orders last year exceeded 20% of the aggregate sales for their geographic region.

- Identify the region that suffered the worst quarter-to-quarter sales decline last year.

- Find the best and worst selling menu items by state for each quarter last year.

Queries such as these are staples of DSS, and are used by managers, analysts, marketing executives, etc., to spot trends, identify outliers, uncover business opportunities, and predict future business performance. DSS systems typically sit atop data warehouses, in which large quantities of scrubbed, aggregated data provide fertile grounds for researching and formulating business decisions.

Although all of the previous queries can be easily expressed in English, they have historically been difficult to formulate using SQL for the following reasons:

- They may require different levels of aggregation of the same data.

- They may involve intratable comparisons (comparing one or more rows in a table with other rows in the same table).

- They may require an extra filtering step after the result set has been sorted (i.e., finding the top 10 and bottom 10 salespeople last month).

Although it is possible to generate the desired results using such SQL features as self joins, inline views, and user-defined functions, the resulting queries can be difficult to understand and might yield unacceptably long execution times. To illustrate the difficulty in formulating such queries, we will walk through the construction of this query: "Find all customers whose total orders in 2001 exceeded 20% of the aggregate sales for their geographic region."

For this and other examples in this chapter, we use a simple star schema consisting of a single fact table (called orders) containing aggregated sales information across the following dimensions: region, salesperson, customer, and month. There are two main facets to this query, each requiring a different level of aggregation of the same data:

- Sum all sales per region last year.
- Sum all sales per customer last year.

After these two intermediate result sets have been constructed, each customer's total can be compared to the total for their region to see if it exceeds 20%. The final result set will show the customer names along with their total sales, region name, and the percentage of their region's sales.

The query to aggregate sales by region looks as follows:

```
SELECT o.region_id region_id, SUM(o.tot_sales) tot_sales
FROM orders o
WHERE o.year = 2001
GROUP BY o.region_id;


REGION_ID  TOT_SALES
---------- ----------
        5    6585641
        6    6307766
        7    6868495
        8    6854731
        9    6739374
       10    6238901
```

The query to aggregate sales by customer would be:

```
SELECT o.cust_nbr cust_nbr, o.region_id region_id,
  SUM(o.tot_sales) tot_sales
FROM orders o
WHERE o.year = 2001
GROUP BY o.cust_nbr, o.region_id;


  CUST_NBR  REGION_ID  TOT_SALES
---------- ---------- ----------
         1          5    1151162
         2          5    1224992
```

3	5	1161286
4	5	1878275
5	5	1169926
6	6	1788836
7	6	971585
8	6	1141638
9	6	1208959
10	6	1196748
11	7	1190421
12	7	1182275
13	7	1310434
14	7	1929774
15	7	1255591
16	8	1068467
17	8	1944281
18	8	1253840
19	8	1174421
20	8	1413722
21	9	1020541
22	9	1036146
23	9	1224992
24	9	1224992
25	9	2232703
26	10	1808949
27	10	1322747
28	10	986964
29	10	903383
30	10	1216858

By placing each of the two queries in an inline view and joining them on region_id, you can identify those customers whose total sales exceeds 20% of their region, as in:

```
SELECT cust_sales.cust_nbr cust_nbr, cust_sales.region_id region_id,
  cust_sales.tot_sales cust_sales, region_sales.tot_sales region_sales
FROM
 (SELECT o.region_id region_id, SUM(o.tot_sales) tot_sales
  FROM orders o
  WHERE o.year = 2001
  GROUP BY o.region_id) region_sales INNER JOIN
 (SELECT o.cust_nbr cust_nbr, o.region_id region_id,
    SUM(o.tot_sales) tot_sales
  FROM orders o
  WHERE o.year = 2001
  GROUP BY o.cust_nbr, o.region_id) cust_sales
  ON cust_sales.region_id = region_sales.region_id
WHERE cust_sales.tot_sales > (region_sales.tot_sales * .2);
```

```
  CUST_NBR  REGION_ID CUST_SALES REGION_SALES
---------- ---------- ---------- ------------
        4          5    1878275      6585641
        6          6    1788836      6307766
       14          7    1929774      6868495
       17          8    1944281      6854731
       20          8    1413722      6854731
```

25	9	2232703	6739374
26	10	1808949	6238901
27	10	1322747	6238901

The final step is to join the region and customer dimensions to include the customer and region names in the result set:

```
SELECT c.name cust_name,
  big_custs.cust_sales cust_sales, r.name region_name,
  100 * ROUND(big_custs.cust_sales /
    big_custs.region_sales, 2)  percent_of_region
FROM
 (SELECT cust_sales.cust_nbr cust_nbr, cust_sales.region_id region_id,
    cust_sales.tot_sales cust_sales,
    region_sales.tot_sales region_sales
  FROM
   (SELECT o.region_id region_id, SUM(o.tot_sales) tot_sales
    FROM orders o
    WHERE o.year = 2001
    GROUP BY o.region_id) region_sales INNER JOIN
   (SELECT o.cust_nbr cust_nbr, o.region_id region_id,
      SUM(o.tot_sales) tot_sales
    FROM orders o
    WHERE o.year = 2001
    GROUP BY o.cust_nbr, o.region_id) cust_sales
    ON cust_sales.region_id = region_sales.region_id
  WHERE cust_sales.tot_sales > (region_sales.tot_sales * .2)) big_custs INNER JOIN
customer c
  ON big_custs.cust_nbr = c.cust_nbr
  INNER JOIN region r
  ON big_custs.region_id = r.region_id;
```

CUST_NAME	CUST_SALES	REGION_NAME	PERCENT_OF_REGION
Flowtech Inc.	1878275	New England	29
Spartan Industries	1788836	Mid-Atlantic	28
Madden Industries	1929774	Southeast US	28
Evans Supply Corp.	1944281	Southwest US	28
Malden Labs	1413722	Southwest US	21
Worcester Technologies	2232703	Northwest US	33
Alpha Technologies	1808949	Central US	29
Phillips Labs	1322747	Central US	21

Using nothing more exotic than inline views, therefore, it is possible to construct a single query that generates the desired results. Such a solution, however, has the following shortcomings:

- The query is fairly complex.
- Two passes through the same rows of the orders table are required to generate the different aggregation levels needed by the query.

Let's see how we can both simplify the query and perform the same work in a single pass through the orders table using one of the new analytic functions. Rather than issuing two separate queries to aggregate sales per region and per customer, we will create a single query that aggregates sales over both region and customer, and then call an analytic function that performs a second level of aggregation to generate total sales per region:

```
1  SELECT o.region_id region_id, o.cust_nbr cust_nbr,
2    SUM(o.tot_sales) tot_sales,
3    SUM(SUM(o.tot_sales)) OVER (PARTITION BY o.region_id) region_sales
4  FROM orders o
5  WHERE o.year = 2001
6  GROUP BY o.region_id, o.cust_nbr;
```

REGION_ID	CUST_NBR	TOT_SALES	REGION_SALES
5	1	1151162	6585641
5	2	1224992	6585641
5	3	1161286	6585641
5	4	1878275	6585641
5	5	1169926	6585641
6	6	1788836	6307766
6	7	971585	6307766
6	8	1141638	6307766
6	9	1208959	6307766
6	10	1196748	6307766
7	11	1190421	6868495
7	12	1182275	6868495
7	13	1310434	6868495
7	14	1929774	6868495
7	15	1255591	6868495
8	16	1068467	6854731
8	17	1944281	6854731
8	18	1253840	6854731
8	19	1174421	6854731
8	20	1413722	6854731
9	21	1020541	6739374
9	22	1036146	6739374
9	23	1224992	6739374
9	24	1224992	6739374
9	25	2232703	6739374
10	26	1808949	6238901
10	27	1322747	6238901
10	28	986964	6238901
10	29	903383	6238901
10	30	1216858	6238901

The analytic function can be found in line 3 of the previous query and the result has the alias region_sales. The aggregate function (SUM(o.tot_sales)) in line 2 generates the total sales per customer and region as directed by the GROUP BY clause, and the analytic function in line 3 aggregates these sums for each region, thereby computing the aggregate sales per region. The value for the region_sales column is identical for all customers within the same region and is equal to the sum of all customer sales within that region. We can then wrap the query in an inline view, filter out those customers with less than 20% of their region's total sales, and join the region and customer tables to generate the desired result set:

```
SELECT c.name cust_name,
  cust_sales.tot_sales cust_sales, r.name region_name,
  100 * ROUND(cust_sales.tot_sales /
    cust_sales.region_sales, 2)  percent_of_region
FROM
 (SELECT o.region_id region_id, o.cust_nbr cust_nbr,
    SUM(o.tot_sales) tot_sales,
    SUM(SUM(o.tot_sales)) OVER (PARTITION BY o.region_id) region_sales
  FROM orders o
  WHERE o.year = 2001
  GROUP BY o.region_id, o.cust_nbr) cust_sales INNER JOIN region r
  ON cust_sales.region_id = r.region_id
  INNER JOIN customer c
  ON cust_sales.cust_nbr = c.cust_nbr
WHERE cust_sales.tot_sales > (cust_sales.region_sales * .2);
```

```
CUST_NAME               CUST_SALES REGION_NAME          PERCENT_OF_REGION
--------------------- ---------- -------------------- -----------------
Flowtech Inc.            1878275 New England                         29
Spartan Industries       1788836 Mid-Atlantic                        28
Madden Industries        1929774 Southeast US                        28
Evans Supply Corp.       1944281 Southwest US                        28
Malden Labs              1413722 Southwest US                        21
Worcester Technologies   2232703 Northwest US                        33
Alpha Technologies       1808949 Central US                          29
Phillips Labs            1322747 Central US                          21
```

Using an inline view saves us from having to join the region and customer tables to the orders table; otherwise, we would have to include columns from the region and customer tables in the GROUP BY clause.

Later in this chapter, under "Reporting Functions," we'll get into the details of how the SUM...OVER function works. For now, you can see that Oracle is performing an aggregation of an aggregation rather than revisiting the detail rows twice. Thus, the query runs faster and should also prove easier to understand and maintain once the syntax is familiar.

Unlike built-in functions such as DECODE, GREATEST, and SUBSTR, Oracle's suite of analytic functions can only be used in the SELECT and ORDER BY clauses of a query. This is because analytic functions are only executed *after* the FROM, WHERE, GROUP BY, and HAVING clauses have been evaluated. After the analytic functions have executed, the query's ORDER BY clause is evaluated to sort the final result set, and the ORDER BY clause is allowed to reference columns in the SELECT clause generated via analytic functions as well as specify analytic functions not found in the SELECT clause.

The remainder of this chapter introduces the Oracle8*i* Database and Oracle9*i* Database analytic functions, grouped by functionality.

Ranking Functions

Determining the performance of a particular business entity compared to its peers is central to a wide variety of business decisions. Examples include:

- Identifying assets with the highest utilization
- Determining the worst selling products by region
- Finding the best performing salespeople

Prior to the release of Oracle8*i* Database, you could use the ORDER BY clause to sort a result set on one or more columns, but any further processing to calculate rankings or percentiles had to be performed using a procedural language. Beginning with Oracle8*i* Database, however, you can take advantage of several new functions to either generate rankings for each row in a result set or to group rows into buckets for percentile calculations.

RANK, DENSE_RANK, and ROW_NUMBER

The RANK, DENSE_RANK, and ROW_NUMBER functions generate an integer value from 1 to N for each row, where N is less than or equal to the number of rows in the result set. The differences in the values returned by these functions revolves around how each one handles ties:

ROW_NUMBER
> Returns a unique number for each row starting with 1. For rows that have duplicate values, numbers are arbitrarily assigned.

DENSE_RANK
> Assigns a unique number for each row starting with 1, except for rows that have duplicate values, in which case the same ranking is assigned.

RANK
> Assigns a unique number for each row starting with 1, except for rows that have duplicate values, in which case the same ranking is assigned and a gap appears in the sequence for each duplicate ranking.

An example will best illustrate the differences. First, here is the query to generate the aggregate sales data by region and customer for the year 2001:

```
SELECT region_id, cust_nbr,
  SUM(tot_sales) cust_sales
FROM orders
WHERE year = 2001
```

```
GROUP BY region_id, cust_nbr
ORDER BY region_id, cust_nbr;

REGION_ID   CUST_NBR CUST_SALES
---------- ---------- ----------
         5          1    1151162
         5          2    1224992
         5          3    1161286
         5          4    1878275
         5          5    1169926
         6          6    1788836
         6          7     971585
         6          8    1141638
         6          9    1208959
         6         10    1196748
         7         11    1190421
         7         12    1182275
         7         13    1310434
         7         14    1929774
         7         15    1255591
         8         16    1068467
         8         17    1944281
         8         18    1253840
         8         19    1174421
         8         20    1413722
         9         21    1020541
         9         22    1036146
         9         23    1224992
         9         24    1224992
         9         25    2232703
        10         26    1808949
        10         27    1322747
        10         28     986964
        10         29     903383
        10         30    1216858
```

Notice that three of the customers (2, 23, and 24) have the same value for total sales ($1,224,992). In the next query, three function calls are added to generate rankings for each customer across all regions, and the results are then ordered by the ROW_NUMBER function to make the difference in rankings easier to observe:

```
SELECT region_id, cust_nbr,
  SUM(tot_sales) cust_sales,
  RANK( ) OVER (ORDER BY SUM(tot_sales) DESC) sales_rank,
  DENSE_RANK( ) OVER (ORDER BY SUM(tot_sales) DESC) sales_dense_rank,
  ROW_NUMBER( ) OVER (ORDER BY SUM(tot_sales) DESC) sales_number
FROM orders
WHERE year = 2001
GROUP BY region_id, cust_nbr
ORDER BY sales_number;
```

REGION_ID	CUST_NBR	CUST_SALES	SALES_RANK	SALES_DENSE_RANK	SALES_NUMBER
9	25	2232703	1	1	1
8	17	1944281	2	2	2
7	14	1929774	3	3	3
5	4	1878275	4	4	4
10	26	1808949	5	5	5
6	6	1788836	6	6	6
8	20	1413722	7	7	7
10	27	1322747	8	8	8
7	13	1310434	9	9	9
7	15	1255591	10	10	10
8	18	1253840	11	11	11
5	2	1224992	12	12	12
9	23	1224992	12	12	13
9	24	1224992	12	12	14
10	30	1216858	15	13	15
6	9	1208959	16	14	16
6	10	1196748	17	15	17
7	11	1190421	18	16	18
7	12	1182275	19	17	19
8	19	1174421	20	18	20
5	5	1169926	21	19	21
5	3	1161286	22	20	22
5	1	1151162	23	21	23
6	8	1141638	24	22	24
8	16	1068467	25	23	25
9	22	1036146	26	24	26
9	21	1020541	27	25	27
10	28	986964	28	26	28
6	7	971585	29	27	29
10	29	903383	30	28	30

Don't be confused by the ORDER BY clause at the end of the query and the ORDER BY clauses within each function call; the functions use their ORDER BY clauses internally to sort their results for the purpose of applying a ranking. Thus, each of the three functions applies its ranking algorithm to the sum of each customer's sales in descending order. The final ORDER BY clause specifies the results of the ROW_NUMBER function as the sort key for the final result set, but we could have picked any of the six columns as our sort key.

Both the RANK and DENSE_RANK functions assign the rank of 12 to the three rows with total sales of $1,224,992, while the ROW_NUMBER function assigns the ranks 12, 13, and 14 to the same rows. The difference between the RANK and DENSE_RANK functions manifests itself in the ranking assigned to the next-lowest sales total; the RANK function leaves a gap in the ranking sequence and assigns a rank of 15 to customer number 30, while the DENSE_RANK function continues the sequence with a ranking of 13.

Deciding which of the three functions to use depends on the desired outcome. If you want to identify the top 13 customers from this result set, you would use:

ROW_NUMBER

If you want exactly 13 rows without regard to ties. In this case, one of the customers who might otherwise be included in the list will be excluded from the final set.

RANK

If you want at least 13 rows but don't want to include rows that would have been excluded had there been no ties. In this case, you would retrieve 14 rows.

DENSE_RANK

If you want all customers with a ranking of 13 or less, including all duplicates. In this case, you would retrieve 15 rows.

While the previous query generates rankings across the entire result set, it is also possible to generate independent sets of rankings across multiple partitions of the result set. The following query generates rankings for customer sales within each region rather than across all regions. Note the addition of the PARTITION BY clause:

```
SELECT region_id, cust_nbr, SUM(tot_sales) cust_sales,
  RANK( ) OVER (PARTITION BY region_id
    ORDER BY SUM(tot_sales) DESC) sales_rank,
  DENSE_RANK( ) OVER (PARTITION BY region_id
    ORDER BY SUM(tot_sales) DESC) sales_dense_rank,
  ROW_NUMBER( ) OVER (PARTITION BY region_id
    ORDER BY SUM(tot_sales) DESC) sales_number
FROM orders
WHERE year = 2001
GROUP BY region_id, cust_nbr
ORDER BY region_id, sales_number;
```

REGION_ID	CUST_NBR	CUST_SALES	SALES_RANK	SALES_DENSE_RANK	SALES_NUMBER
5	4	1878275	1	1	1
5	2	1224992	2	2	2
5	5	1169926	3	3	3
5	3	1161286	4	4	4
5	1	1151162	5	5	5
6	6	1788836	1	1	1
6	9	1208959	2	2	2
6	10	1196748	3	3	3
6	8	1141638	4	4	4
6	7	971585	5	5	5
7	14	1929774	1	1	1
7	13	1310434	2	2	2
7	15	1255591	3	3	3
7	11	1190421	4	4	4
7	12	1182275	5	5	5
8	17	1944281	1	1	1
8	20	1413722	2	2	2
8	18	1253840	3	3	3

8	19	1174421	4	4	4
8	16	1068467	5	5	5
9	25	2232703	1	1	1
9	23	1224992	2	2	2
9	24	1224992	2	2	3
9	22	1036146	4	3	4
9	21	1020541	5	4	5
10	26	1808949	1	1	1
10	27	1322747	2	2	2
10	30	1216858	3	3	3
10	28	986964	4	4	4
10	29	903383	5	5	5

Each customer receives a ranking between one and five depending on their relation to other customers in the same region. Of the three customers with duplicate total sales, two of them are in region 9; as before, the RANK and DENSE_RANK functions generate identical rankings for both customers.

> The PARTITION BY clause used in ranking functions is used to divide a result set into pieces so that rankings can be applied within each subset. This is completely different from the PARTITION BY RANGE/HASH/LIST clauses introduced in Chapter 10 for breaking a table or index into multiple pieces.

Handling NULLs

All ranking functions allow you to specify where in the ranking order NULL values should appear. This is accomplished by appending either NULLS FIRST or NULLS LAST after the ORDER BY clause of the function, as in:

```
SELECT region_id, cust_nbr, SUM(tot_sales) cust_sales,
  RANK( ) OVER (ORDER BY SUM(tot_sales) DESC NULLS LAST) sales_rank
FROM orders
WHERE year = 2001
GROUP BY region_id, cust_nbr;
```

If omitted, NULL values will either appear last in ascending rankings or first in descending rankings.

Top/bottom N queries

One of the most common uses of a ranked data set is to identify the top N or bottom N performers. Since you can't call analytic functions from the WHERE or HAVING clauses, you are forced to generate the rankings for all the rows and then use an outer query to filter out the unwanted rankings. For example, the following query uses an inline view to identify the top five salespersons for 2001:

```
SELECT s.name, sp.sp_sales total_sales
FROM
  (SELECT salesperson_id, SUM(tot_sales) sp_sales,
    RANK( ) OVER (ORDER BY SUM(tot_sales) DESC) sales_rank
```

```
    FROM orders
    WHERE year = 2001
    GROUP BY salesperson_id) sp INNER JOIN salesperson s
    ON sp.salesperson_id = s.salesperson_id
  WHERE sp.sales_rank <= 5
  ORDER BY sp.sales_rank;

  NAME                                              TOTAL_SALES
  ------------------------------------------------- -----------
  Jeff Blake                                            1927580
  Sam Houseman                                          1814327
  Mark Russell                                          1784596
  John Boorman                                          1768813
  Carl Isaacs                                           1761814
  Tim McGowan                                           1761814
```

FIRST/LAST

Although there is no function for returning only the top or bottom N from a ranked result set, Oracle provides functionality for identifying the first (top 1) or last (bottom 1) records in a ranked set. This is useful for queries such as the following: "Find the regions with the best and worst total sales last year." Unlike the top five salespeople example from the previous section, this query needs an additional piece of information—the size of the result set—to answer the question.

Oracle9*i* provides the ability to answer such queries efficiently using functions that rank the result set based on a specified ordering, identify the row with the top or bottom ranking, and report on any column available in the result set. These functions are composed of three parts:

- An ORDER BY clause that specifies how to rank the result set.
- The keywords FIRST and LAST to specify whether to use the top or bottom-ranked row.
- An aggregate function (i.e., MIN, MAX, AVG, COUNT) used as a tiebreaker in case more than one row of the result set tie for the FIRST or LAST spot in the ranking.

The following query uses the MIN aggregate function to find the regions that rank FIRST and LAST by total sales:

```
SELECT
  MIN(region_id)
    KEEP (DENSE_RANK FIRST ORDER BY SUM(tot_sales) DESC) best_region,
  MIN(region_id)
    KEEP (DENSE_RANK LAST ORDER BY SUM(tot_sales) DESC) worst_region
FROM orders
WHERE year = 2001
GROUP BY region_id;

BEST_REGION WORST_REGION
----------- ------------
          7           10
```

The use of the MIN function in the previous query is a bit confusing: it is used only if more than one region ties for either first or last place in the ranking. If there were a tie, the row with the minimum value for region_id would be chosen. To find out if a tie actually exists, you could call each function twice using MIN for the first and MAX for the second, and see if they return the same results:

```
SELECT
  MIN(region_id)
    KEEP (DENSE_RANK FIRST ORDER BY SUM(tot_sales) DESC) min_best_region,
  MAX(region_id)
    KEEP (DENSE_RANK FIRST ORDER BY SUM(tot_sales) DESC) max_best_region,
  MIN(region_id)
    KEEP (DENSE_RANK LAST ORDER BY SUM(tot_sales) DESC) min_worst_region,
  MAX(region_id)
    KEEP (DENSE_RANK LAST ORDER BY SUM(tot_sales) DESC) max_worst_region
FROM orders
WHERE year = 2001
GROUP BY region_id;

MIN_BEST_REGION MAX_BEST_REGION MIN_WORST_REGION MAX_WORST_REGION
--------------- --------------- ---------------- ----------------
              7               7               10               10
```

In this case, there are no ties for either first or last place. Depending on the type of data you are working with, using an aggregate function as a tiebreaker can be somewhat arbitrary.

NTILE

Another way rankings are commonly used is to generate buckets into which sets of rankings are grouped. For example, you may want to find those customers whose total sales ranked in the top 25%. The following query uses the NTILE function to group the customers into four buckets (or quartiles):

```
SELECT region_id, cust_nbr, SUM(tot_sales) cust_sales,
  NTILE(4) OVER (ORDER BY SUM(tot_sales) DESC) sales_quartile
FROM orders
WHERE year = 2001
GROUP BY region_id, cust_nbr
ORDER BY sales_quartile, cust_sales DESC;

REGION_ID   CUST_NBR CUST_SALES SALES_QUARTILE
---------- ---------- ---------- --------------
         9         25    2232703              1
         8         17    1944281              1
         7         14    1929774              1
         5          4    1878275              1
        10         26    1808949              1
         6          6    1788836              1
         8         20    1413722              1
        10         27    1322747              1
         7         13    1310434              2
```

7	15	1255591	2
8	18	1253840	2
5	2	1224992	2
9	23	1224992	2
9	24	1224992	2
10	30	1216858	2
6	9	1208959	2
6	10	1196748	3
7	11	1190421	3
7	12	1182275	3
8	19	1174421	3
5	5	1169926	3
5	3	1161286	3
5	1	1151162	3
6	8	1141638	4
8	16	1068467	4
9	22	1036146	4
9	21	1020541	4
10	28	986964	4
6	7	971585	4
10	29	903383	4

The sales_quartile column in this query specifies NTILE(4) to create four buckets. The NTILE function finds each row's place in the ranking, and then assigns each row to a bucket such that every bucket contains the same number of rows. If the number of rows is not evenly divisible by the number of buckets, then the extra rows are distributed so that the number of rows per bucket differs by one at most. In the previous example, there are four buckets allocated for 30 rows, with buckets one and two containing eight rows each, and buckets three and four containing seven rows each. This approach is referred to as *equiheight buckets* because each bucket contains (optimally) the same number of rows.

Just like in the top N query discussed earlier, you will need to wrap the query in an inline view if you want to filter on the NTILE result:

```
SELECT r.name region, c.name customer, cs.cust_sales
FROM
  (SELECT region_id, cust_nbr, SUM(tot_sales) cust_sales,
    NTILE(4) OVER (ORDER BY SUM(tot_sales) DESC) sales_quartile
  FROM orders
  WHERE year = 2001
  GROUP BY region_id, cust_nbr) cs INNER JOIN customer c
  ON cs.cust_nbr = c.cust_nbr
  INNER JOIN region r
  ON cs.region_id = r.region_id
WHERE cs.sales_quartile = 1

ORDER BY cs.cust_sales DESC;

REGION                CUSTOMER                          CUST_SALES
-------------------   ------------------------------    ----------
Northwest US          Worcester Technologies               2232703
Southwest US          Evans Supply Corp.                   1944281
```

Southeast US	Madden Industries	1929774
New England	Flowtech Inc.	1878275
Central US	Alpha Technologies	1808949
Mid-Atlantic	Spartan Industries	1788836
Southwest US	Malden Labs	1413722
Central US	Phillips Labs	1322747

The outer query filters on sales_quartile = 1, which removes all rows not in the top 25% of sales, and then joins the region and customer dimensions to generate the final results.

WIDTH_BUCKET

Similar to the NTILE function, the WIDTH_BUCKET function groups rows of the result set into buckets. Unlike NTILE, however, the WIDTH_BUCKET function attempts to create *equiwidth buckets*, meaning that the range of values is evenly distributed across the buckets. If your data were distributed across a bell curve, therefore, you could expect the buckets representing the low and high ranges of the bell curve to contain few records, whereas the buckets representing the middle ranges would contain many records.

WIDTH_BUCKET can operate on numeric or date types, and takes the following four parameters:

- The expression that generates the buckets
- The value used as the start of the range for bucket #1
- The value used as the end of the range for bucket #N
- The number of buckets to create (N)

WIDTH_BUCKET uses the values of the second, third, and fourth parameters to generate N buckets containing comparable ranges. If the expression yields values that fall outside the range specified by the second and third parameters, the WIDTH_BUCKET function will generate two additional buckets, numbered 0 and N + 1, into which the outliers are placed. If you want to work with the entire result set, you need to make sure your values for the second and third parameters completely enclose the range of values in the result set. However, if you only wish to work with a subset of the data, you can specify values for the second and third parameters that enclose the desired range, and any rows falling outside the range will be placed into buckets 0 and N + 1.

Here's an example that uses the NTILE example from earlier to generate three buckets for the total sales per customer:

```
SELECT region_id, cust_nbr,
  SUM(tot_sales) cust_sales,
  WIDTH_BUCKET(SUM(tot_sales), 1, 3000000, 3) sales_buckets
FROM orders
WHERE year = 2001
```

```
GROUP BY region_id, cust_nbr
ORDER BY cust_sales;

REGION_ID   CUST_NBR CUST_SALES SALES_BUCKETS
----------  ---------- ---------- -------------
       10         29     903383             1
        6          7     971585             1
       10         28     986964             1
        9         21    1020541             2
        9         22    1036146             2
        8         16    1068467             2
        6          8    1141638             2
        5          1    1151162             2
        5          3    1161286             2
        5          5    1169926             2
        8         19    1174421             2
        7         12    1182275             2
        7         11    1190421             2
        6         10    1196748             2
        6          9    1208959             2
       10         30    1216858             2
        5          2    1224992             2
        9         24    1224992             2
        9         23    1224992             2
        8         18    1253840             2
        7         15    1255591             2
        7         13    1310434             2
       10         27    1322747             2
        8         20    1413722             2
        6          6    1788836             2
       10         26    1808949             2
        5          4    1878275             2
        7         14    1929774             2
        8         17    1944281             2
        9         25    2232703             3
```

Based on these parameters, the WIDTH_BUCKET function generates three buckets; the first bucket starts at 1, and the third bucket has an upper range of 3,000,000. Since there are three buckets, the ranges for each bucket will be 1 to 1,000,000, 1,000,001 to 2,000,000, and 2,000,001 to 3,000,000. When the rows are placed in the appropriate bucket, there are three rows that fall into bucket #1, a single row that falls in bucket #3, and the remaining 26 rows that fall into the second bucket.

The values 1 and 3,000,000 were chosen to guarantee that all rows in the result set would be placed into one of the three buckets. If you want to generate buckets only for rows that have aggregate sales between $1,000,000 and $2,000,000, the WIDTH_BUCKET function will place the remaining rows in the 0th and 4th buckets:

```
SELECT region_id, cust_nbr,
  SUM(tot_sales) cust_sales,
  WIDTH_BUCKET(SUM(tot_sales), 1000000, 2000000, 3) sales_buckets
FROM orders
WHERE year = 2001
```

```
GROUP BY region_id, cust_nbr
ORDER BY cust_sales;
```

REGION_ID	CUST_NBR	CUST_SALES	SALES_BUCKETS
10	29	903383	0
6	7	971585	0
10	28	986964	0
9	21	1020541	1
9	22	1036146	1
8	16	1068467	1
6	8	1141638	1
5	1	1151162	1
5	3	1161286	1
5	5	1169926	1
8	19	1174421	1
7	12	1182275	1
7	11	1190421	1
6	10	1196748	1
6	9	1208959	1
10	30	1216858	1
5	2	1224992	1
9	24	1224992	1
9	23	1224992	1
8	18	1253840	1
7	15	1255591	1
7	13	1310434	1
10	27	1322747	1
8	20	1413722	2
6	6	1788836	3
10	26	1808949	3
5	4	1878275	3
7	14	1929774	3
8	17	1944281	3
9	25	2232703	4

Keep in mind that the WIDTH_BUCKET function does not remove rows from the result set that do not lie within the specified range; rather, they are placed into special buckets that your query can either utilize or ignore as needed.

CUME_DIST and PERCENT_RANK

The final two ranking functions, CUME_DIST and PERCENT_RANK, use the rank of a particular row to calculate additional information. The CUME_DIST function (short for Cumulative Distribution) calculates the ratio of the number of rows that have a lesser or equal ranking to the total number of rows in the partition. The PERCENT_RANK function calculates the ratio of a row's ranking to the number of rows in the partition using the formula:

$$(RRP - 1) / (NRP - 1)$$

where *RRP* is the "rank of row in partition," and *NRP* is the "number of rows in partition."

Both functions utilize DENSE_RANK for their rankings and can be specified to be in ascending or descending order. The following query demonstrates the use of these two functions (both specifying descending order) with the customer yearly sales query:

```
SELECT region_id, cust_nbr,
  SUM(tot_sales) cust_sales,
  CUME_DIST( ) OVER (ORDER BY SUM(tot_sales) DESC) sales_cume_dist,
  PERCENT_RANK( ) OVER (ORDER BY SUM(tot_sales) DESC) sales_percent_rank
FROM orders
WHERE year = 2001
GROUP BY region_id, cust_nbr
ORDER BY cust_sales DESC;
```

REGION_ID	CUST_NBR	CUST_SALES	SALES_CUME_DIST	SALES_PERCENT_RANK
9	25	2232703	.033333333	0
8	17	1944281	.066666667	.034482759
7	14	1929774	.1	.068965517
5	4	1878275	.133333333	.103448276
10	26	1808949	.166666667	.137931034
6	6	1788836	.2	.172413793
8	20	1413722	.233333333	.206896552
10	27	1322747	.266666667	.24137931
7	13	1310434	.3	.275862069
7	15	1255591	.333333333	.310344828
8	18	1253840	.366666667	.344827586
5	2	1224992	.466666667	.379310345
9	23	1224992	.466666667	.379310345
9	24	1224992	.466666667	.379310345
10	30	1216858	.5	.482758621
6	9	1208959	.533333333	.517241379
6	10	1196748	.566666667	.551724138
7	11	1190421	.6	.586206897
7	12	1182275	.633333333	.620689655
8	19	1174421	.666666667	.655172414
5	5	1169926	.7	.689655172
5	3	1161286	.733333333	.724137931
5	1	1151162	.766666667	.75862069
6	8	1141638	.8	.793103448
8	16	1068467	.833333333	.827586207
9	22	1036146	.866666667	.862068966
9	21	1020541	.9	.896551724
10	28	986964	.933333333	.931034483
6	7	971585	.966666667	.965517241
10	29	903383	1	1

Let's walk through a couple of calculations for customer number 1 in the previous result set. With total sales of $1,151,162, customer number 1 ranks 23rd in the set of 30 customers in descending order of sales. Since there are a total of 30 rows, the CUME_DIST is equal to 23/30, or .766666667. The PERCENT_RANK function yields (23 − 1) / (30 − 1) = .75862069. It should come as no surprise that each function returns identical values for the rows that have identical sales totals, since the calculations are based on rank, which is identical for all three rows.

Hypothetical Functions

For some types of analysis, determining what *might* have happened is more revealing than knowing what really happened. Oracle provides special versions of RANK, DENSE_RANK, CUME_DIST, and PERCENT_RANK that allow rankings and distributions to be calculated for hypothetical data, allowing the user to see what would have happened if a specific value (or set of values) was included in a data set.

To illustrate this concept, let's rank all customers by total sales for 2001, and then see where a hypothetical sales figure would fall in the ranking. Here is the query that generates the rankings and distributions:

```
SELECT cust_nbr, SUM(tot_sales) cust_sales,
  RANK( ) OVER (ORDER BY SUM(tot_sales) DESC) rank,
  DENSE_RANK( ) OVER (ORDER BY SUM(tot_sales) DESC) dense_rank,
  CUME_DIST( ) OVER (ORDER BY SUM(tot_sales) DESC) cume_dist,
  PERCENT_RANK( ) OVER (ORDER BY SUM(tot_sales) DESC) percent_rank
FROM orders
WHERE year = 2001
GROUP BY cust_nbr
ORDER BY rank;
```

CUST_NBR	CUST_SALES	RANK	DENSE_RANK	CUME_DIST	PERCENT_RANK
25	2232703	1	1	.033333333	0
17	1944281	2	2	.066666667	.034482759
14	1929774	3	3	.1	.068965517
4	1878275	4	4	.133333333	.103448276
26	1808949	5	5	.166666667	.137931034
6	1788836	6	6	.2	.172413793
20	1413722	7	7	.233333333	.206896552
27	1322747	8	8	.266666667	.24137931
13	1310434	9	9	.3	.275862069
15	1255591	10	10	.333333333	.310344828
18	1253840	11	11	.366666667	.344827586
2	1224992	12	12	.466666667	.379310345
23	1224992	12	12	.466666667	.379310345
24	1224992	12	12	.466666667	.379310345
30	1216858	15	13	.5	.482758621
9	1208959	16	14	.533333333	.517241379
10	1196748	17	15	.566666667	.551724138
11	1190421	18	16	.6	.586206897
12	1182275	19	17	.633333333	.620689655
19	1174421	20	18	.666666667	.655172414
5	1169926	21	19	.7	.689655172
3	1161286	22	20	.733333333	.724137931
1	1151162	23	21	.766666667	.75862069
8	1141638	24	22	.8	.793103448
16	1068467	25	23	.833333333	.827586207

22	1036146	26	24 .866666667	.862068966
21	1020541	27	25 .9	.896551724
28	986964	28	26 .933333333	.931034483
7	971585	29	27 .966666667	.965517241
29	903383	30	28 1	1

Now let's see where a customer with an even million dollars of sales would have ranked:

```
SELECT
  RANK(1000000) WITHIN GROUP
    (ORDER BY SUM(tot_sales) DESC) hyp_rank,
  DENSE_RANK(1000000) WITHIN GROUP
    (ORDER BY SUM(tot_sales) DESC) hyp_dense_rank,
  CUME_DIST(1000000) WITHIN GROUP
    (ORDER BY SUM(tot_sales) DESC) hyp_cume_dist,
  PERCENT_RANK(1000000) WITHIN GROUP
    (ORDER BY SUM(tot_sales) DESC) hyp_percent_rank
FROM orders
WHERE year = 2001
GROUP BY cust_nbr;


HYP_RANK HYP_DENSE_RANK HYP_CUME_DIST HYP_PERCENT_RANK
---------- -------------- ------------- ----------------
      28             26    .903225806               .9
```

The WITHIN GROUP clause has the effect of injecting a fictitious row into the result set before determining the rankings. One possible use of this functionality would be to see how actual sales compare to sales targets.

Windowing Functions

The ranking functions described thus far are quite useful when comparing items within a fixed window of time, such as "last year" or "second quarter." But what if you want to perform computations using a window that slides as you progress through the data set? Oracle's windowing functions allow aggregates to be calculated for each row in a result set based on a specified window. The aggregation window can be defined in one of three ways:

- By specifying a set of rows: "From the current row to the end of the partition"
- By specifying a time interval: "For the 30 days preceding the transaction date"
- By specifying a range of values: "All rows having a transaction amount within 5% of the current row's transaction amount"

The first set of examples will generate a window that fills the entire partition, and then show how the window can be detached from one or both ends of the partition so that it floats with the current row. All of the examples will be based on the following query, which calculates total monthly sales in 2001 for the Mid-Atlantic region:

```
SELECT month,
  SUM(tot_sales) monthly_sales
```

```
FROM orders
WHERE year = 2001
  AND region_id = 6
GROUP BY month
ORDER BY month;

    MONTH MONTHLY_SALES
---------- -------------
        1        610697
        2        428676
        3        637031
        4        541146
        5        592935
        6        501485
        7        606914
        8        460520
        9        392898
       10        510117
       11        532889
       12        492458
```

The first step is to sum the monthly sales for the entire result set by specifying an "unbounded" window. Note the ROWS BETWEEN clause in the following example:

```
SELECT month,
  SUM(tot_sales) monthly_sales,
  SUM(SUM(tot_sales)) OVER (ORDER BY month
    ROWS BETWEEN UNBOUNDED PRECEDING AND UNBOUNDED FOLLOWING) total_sales
FROM orders
WHERE year = 2001
  AND region_id = 6
GROUP BY month
ORDER BY month;

    MONTH MONTHLY_SALES TOTAL_SALES
---------- ------------- -----------
        1        610697     6307766
        2        428676     6307766
        3        637031     6307766
        4        541146     6307766
        5        592935     6307766
        6        501485     6307766
        7        606914     6307766
        8        460520     6307766
        9        392898     6307766
       10        510117     6307766
       11        532889     6307766
       12        492458     6307766
```

Each time the function executes, it sums the monthly sales from months 1 through 12; thus, the same calculation is being performed 12 times. This is a rather inefficient way to generate the yearly sales total (see "Reporting Functions" later in this chapter for a better method), but it should give you an idea of the syntax for building an aggregation window. The next query will create a window that spans from the top of the partition to the current row. The function identifies the month that has the maximum sales, up to and including the current month:

```
SELECT month,
  SUM(tot_sales) monthly_sales,
  MAX(SUM(tot_sales)) OVER (ORDER BY month
    ROWS BETWEEN UNBOUNDED PRECEEDING AND CURRENT ROW) max_preceeding
FROM orders
WHERE year = 2001
  AND region_id = 6
GROUP BY month
ORDER BY month;
```

```
   MONTH MONTHLY_SALES MAX_PRECEEDING
---------- -------------- --------------
        1         610697         610697
        2         428676         610697
        3         637031         637031
        4         541146         637031
        5         592935         637031
        6         501485         637031
        7         606914         637031
        8         460520         637031
        9         392898         637031
       10         510117         637031
       11         532889         637031
       12         492458         637031
```

Unlike the first query, which has a window size fixed at 12 rows, this query's aggregation window grows from a single row for month 1 to 12 rows for month 12. The keywords CURRENT ROW are used to indicate that the window should end at the current row being inspected by the function. If you replace MAX in the previous query with SUM, you can calculate a running total:

```
SELECT month,
  SUM(tot_sales) monthly_sales,
  SUM(SUM(tot_sales)) OVER (ORDER BY month
    ROWS BETWEEN UNBOUNDED PRECEEDING AND CURRENT ROW) running_total
FROM orders
WHERE year = 2001
  AND region_id = 6
GROUP BY month
ORDER BY month;
```

```
   MONTH MONTHLY_SALES RUNNING_TOTAL
---------- -------------- --------------
        1         610697         610697
        2         428676        1039373
        3         637031        1676404
        4         541146        2217550
        5         592935        2810485
        6         501485        3311970
```

7	606914	3918884
8	460520	4379404
9	392898	4772302
10	510117	5282419
11	532889	5815308
12	492458	6307766

You have now seen examples using windows that are fixed at one or both ends. The next query will define a window that floats freely with each row:

```
SELECT month,
  SUM(tot_sales) monthly_sales,
  AVG(SUM(tot_sales)) OVER (ORDER BY month
    ROWS BETWEEN 1 PRECEDING AND 1 FOLLOWING) rolling_avg
FROM orders
WHERE year = 2001
  AND region_id = 6
GROUP BY month
ORDER BY month;
```

```
    MONTH MONTHLY_SALES ROLLING_AVG
---------- ------------- -----------
        1        610697     519686.5
        2        428676   558801.333
        3        637031   535617.667
        4        541146   590370.667
        5        592935   545188.667
        6        501485   567111.333
        7        606914       522973
        8        460520   486777.333
        9        392898   454511.667
       10        510117   478634.667
       11        532889   511821.333
       12        492458     512673.5
```

For each of the 12 rows, the function calculates the average sales of the current month, the previous month, and the following month. The value of the ROLLING_AVG column is therefore the average sales within a three month floating window centered on the current month, with the exception that months 1 and 12 are calculated using a two-month window, since there is no previous month for month 1 or following month for month 12.

Working with Ranges

The previous windowing examples use the ROWS BETWEEN option to specify which rows to include in the aggregation. You may alternately specify a range and let Oracle determine which rows lie within the range. For example, the previous query used ROWS BETWEEN 1 PRECEDING AND 1 FOLLOWING to generate a three-month rolling average; the same results can be achieved by substituting RANGE for ROWS:

```
SELECT month,
  SUM(tot_sales) monthly_sales,
```

```
  AVG(SUM(tot_sales)) OVER (ORDER BY month
  RANGE BETWEEN 1 PRECEDING AND 1 FOLLOWING) rolling_avg
FROM orders
WHERE year = 2001
  AND region_id = 6
GROUP BY month
ORDER BY month;

    MONTH MONTHLY_SALES ROLLING_AVG
---------- ------------- -----------
         1        610697     519686.5
         2        428676   558801.333
         3        637031   535617.667
         4        541146   590370.667
         5        592935   545188.667
         6        501485   567111.333
         7        606914       522973
         8        460520   486777.333
         9        392898   454511.667
        10        510117   478634.667
        11        532889   511821.333
        12        492458     512673.5
```

This substitution works because the month column contains integer values, so adding and subtracting 1 from the current month yields a three-month range. The next variation achieves the same results but specifies a range of +/− 1.999:

```
SELECT month,
  SUM(tot_sales) monthly_sales,
  AVG(SUM(tot_sales)) OVER (ORDER BY month
  RANGE BETWEEN 1.999 PRECEDING AND 1.999 FOLLOWING) rolling_avg
FROM orders
WHERE year = 2001
  AND region_id = 6
GROUP BY month
ORDER BY month;

    MONTH MONTHLY_SALES ROLLING_AVG
---------- ------------- -----------
         1        610697     519686.5
         2        428676   558801.333
         3        637031   535617.667
         4        541146   590370.667
         5        592935   545188.667
         6        501485   567111.333
         7        606914       522973
         8        460520   486777.333
         9        392898   454511.667
        10        510117   478634.667
        11        532889   511821.333
        12        492458     512673.5
```

If you are generating a window based on a DATE column, you can specify a range in increments of days, months, or years. Since the orders table has no DATE columns, the next example shows how a date range can be specified against the order_dt column of the cust_order table:

```
SELECT TRUNC(order_dt) day,
  SUM(sale_price) daily_sales,
  AVG(SUM(sale_price)) OVER (ORDER BY TRUNC(order_dt)
  RANGE BETWEEN INTERVAL '2' DAY PRECEDING
    AND INTERVAL '2' DAY FOLLOWING) five_day_avg
FROM cust_order
WHERE sale_price IS NOT NULL
  AND order_dt BETWEEN TO_DATE('01-JUL-2001','DD-MON-YYYY')
  AND TO_DATE('31-JUL-2001','DD-MON-YYYY')
GROUP BY TRUNC(order_dt);

DAY       DAILY_SALES FIVE_DAY_AVG
--------- ----------- ------------
16-JUL-01         112          146
18-JUL-01         180          114
20-JUL-01          50          169
21-JUL-01          50    165.333333
22-JUL-01         396    165.333333
```

This query generates a five-day rolling window by specifying a range of +/– two days around the truncated order date.

FIRST_VALUE and LAST_VALUE

Oracle provides two additional aggregate functions, called FIRST_VALUE and LAST_VALUE, that can be used with windowing functions to identify the values of the first and last values in the window. In the case of the three-month rolling average query shown previously, you could display the values of all three months along with the average of the three, as in:

```
SELECT month,
  FIRST_VALUE(SUM(tot_sales)) OVER (ORDER BY month
    ROWS BETWEEN 1 PRECEDING AND 1 FOLLOWING) prev_month,
  SUM(tot_sales) monthly_sales,
  LAST_VALUE(SUM(tot_sales)) OVER (ORDER BY month
    ROWS BETWEEN 1 PRECEDING AND 1 FOLLOWING) next_month,
  AVG(SUM(tot_sales)) OVER (ORDER BY month
    ROWS BETWEEN 1 PRECEDING AND 1 FOLLOWING) rolling_avg
FROM orders
WHERE year = 2001
  AND region_id = 6
GROUP BY month
ORDER BY month;

    MONTH PREV_MONTH MONTHLY_SALES NEXT_MONTH ROLLING_AVG
---------- ---------- ------------- ---------- -----------
        1     610697        610697     428676    519686.5
        2     610697        428676     637031  558801.333
        3     428676        637031     541146  535617.667
```

4	637031	541146	592935	590370.667
5	541146	592935	501485	545188.667
6	592935	501485	606914	567111.333
7	501485	606914	460520	522973
8	606914	460520	392898	486777.333
9	460520	392898	510117	454511.667
10	392898	510117	532889	478634.667
11	510117	532889	492458	511821.333
12	532889	492458	492458	512673.5

These functions are useful for queries that compare each value to the first or last value in the period, such as: "How did each month's sales compare to the first month?"

LAG/LEAD Functions

Although not technically windowing functions, the LAG and LEAD functions are included here because they allow rows to be referenced by their position relative to the current row, much like the PRECEDING and FOLLOWING clauses within windowing functions. LAG and LEAD are useful for comparing one row of a result set with another row of the same result set. For example, the query "Compute the total sales per month for the Mid-Atlantic region, including the percent change from the previous month" requires data from both the current and preceding rows to calculate the answer. This is, in effect, a two-row window, but the offset from the current row can be specified as one or more rows, making LAG and LEAD act like specialized windowing functions where only the outer edges of the window are utilized.

Here is the SQL that uses the LAG function to generate the data needed to answer the question posed in the previous paragraph:

```
SELECT month,
  SUM(tot_sales) monthly_sales,
  LAG(SUM(tot_sales), 1) OVER (ORDER BY month) prev_month_sales
FROM orders
WHERE year = 2001
  AND region_id = 6
GROUP BY month
ORDER BY month;
```

MONTH	MONTHLY_SALES	PREV_MONTH_SALES
1	610697	
2	428676	610697
3	637031	428676
4	541146	637031
5	592935	541146
6	501485	592935
7	606914	501485
8	460520	606914
9	392898	460520

10	510117	392898
11	532889	510117
12	492458	532889

As you might expect, the LAG value for month 1 is NULL, since there is no preceding month. This would also be the case for the LEAD value for month 12. If you would like the LAG and LEAD functions to return a non-NULL value for these cases, you can specify a substitute value via the optional third parameter (see next example).

The next query utilizes the output from the previous query to generate the percentage difference from month to month. Note how a third parameter has been specified for the LAG function so that month 1 will use the current month's sales instead of a NULL value for the percentage change:

```
SELECT months.month month, months.monthly_sales monthly_sales,
  ROUND((months.monthly_sales - months.prev_month_sales) /
    months.prev_month_sales, 3) * 100 percent_change
FROM
 (SELECT month,
    SUM(tot_sales) monthly_sales,
    LAG(SUM(tot_sales), 1, SUM(tot_sales))
      OVER (ORDER BY month) prev_month_sales
  FROM orders
  WHERE year = 2001
    AND region_id = 6
  GROUP BY month) months
ORDER BY month;
```

MONTH	MONTHLY_SALES	PERCENT_CHANGE
1	610697	0
2	428676	-29.8
3	637031	48.6
4	541146	-15.1
5	592935	9.6
6	501485	-15.4
7	606914	21
8	460520	-24.1
9	392898	-14.7
10	510117	29.8
11	532889	4.5
12	492458	-7.6

Reporting Functions

Similar to the windowing functions described earlier, reporting functions allow the execution of various aggregate functions (MIN, MAX, SUM, COUNT, AVG, etc.) against a result set. Unlike windowing functions, however, the reporting functions cannot specify localized windows and thus generate the same result for each entire partition (or the entire result set, if no partitions are specified). Therefore, anything that can be accomplished using a reporting function can also be accomplished using a windowing function with an unbounded window, although it will generally be more efficient to use the reporting function.

Earlier in the chapter, we used a windowing function with an unbounded reporting window to generate the total sales for the 12 months of 2001:

```
SELECT month,
  SUM(tot_sales) monthly_sales,
  SUM(SUM(tot_sales)) OVER (ORDER BY month
    ROWS BETWEEN UNBOUNDED PRECEDING AND UNBOUNDED FOLLOWING) total_sales
FROM orders
WHERE year = 2001
  AND region_id = 6
GROUP BY month
ORDER BY month;

    MONTH MONTHLY_SALES TOTAL_SALES
---------- ------------- -----------
        1        610697     6307766
        2        428676     6307766
        3        637031     6307766
        4        541146     6307766
        5        592935     6307766
        6        501485     6307766
        7        606914     6307766
        8        460520     6307766
        9        392898     6307766
       10        510117     6307766
       11        532889     6307766
       12        492458     6307766
```

The next query adds a reporting function to generate the same results:

```
SELECT month,
  SUM(tot_sales) monthly_sales,
  SUM(SUM(tot_sales)) OVER (ORDER BY month
    ROWS BETWEEN UNBOUNDED PRECEDING AND UNBOUNDED FOLLOWING) window_sales,
  SUM(SUM(tot_sales)) OVER () reporting_sales
FROM orders
WHERE year = 2001
  AND region_id = 6
GROUP BY month
ORDER BY month;

    MONTH MONTHLY_SALES WINDOW_SALES REPORTING_SALES
---------- ------------- ------------ ---------------
        1        610697      6307766         6307766
        2        428676      6307766         6307766
        3        637031      6307766         6307766
        4        541146      6307766         6307766
        5        592935      6307766         6307766
        6        501485      6307766         6307766
        7        606914      6307766         6307766
```

8	460520	6307766	6307766
9	392898	6307766	6307766
10	510117	6307766	6307766
11	532889	6307766	6307766
12	492458	6307766	6307766

The empty parentheses after the OVER clause for the reporting_sales column indicate that the entire result set should be included in the sum, which has the same effect as using an unbounded window function. Hopefully, you will agree that the reporting function is easier to understand than the unbounded window function.

Reporting functions are useful when you need both detail and aggregate data (or different aggregation levels) to answer a business query. For example, the query "Show the monthly sales totals for 2001 along with each month's percentage of yearly sales" requires the detail rows to be aggregated first to the month level, and then to the year level to answer the question. Rather than computing both aggregations from the detail rows, you can use the SUM function with a GROUP BY clause to aggregate to the month level, and then use a reporting function to aggregate the monthly totals, as in:

```
SELECT month,
  SUM(tot_sales) monthly_sales,
  SUM(SUM(tot_sales)) OVER () yearly_sales
FROM orders
WHERE year = 2001
GROUP BY month
ORDER BY month;
```

MONTH	MONTHLY_SALES	YEARLY_SALES
1	3028325	39594908
2	3289336	39594908
3	3411024	39594908
4	3436482	39594908
5	3749264	39594908
6	3204730	39594908
7	3233532	39594908
8	3081290	39594908
9	3388292	39594908
10	3279637	39594908
11	3167858	39594908
12	3325138	39594908

You would then simply divide MONTHLY_SALES by YEARLY_SALES to compute the requested percentage (see the section "RATIO_TO_REPORT" later in the chapter).

Report Partitions

Like ranking functions, reporting functions can include PARTITION BY clauses to split the result set into multiple pieces, allowing multiple aggregations to be computed across different subsets of the result set. The following query generates total sales per salesperson per region along with the total regional sales for comparison:

```
SELECT region_id, salesperson_id,
  SUM(tot_sales) sp_sales,
  SUM(SUM(tot_sales)) OVER (PARTITION BY region_id) region_sales
FROM orders
WHERE year = 2001
GROUP BY region_id, salesperson_id
ORDER BY region_id, salesperson_id;
```

REGION_ID	SALESPERSON_ID	SP_SALES	REGION_SALES
5	1	1927580	6585641
5	2	1461898	6585641
5	3	1501039	6585641
5	4	1695124	6585641
6	5	1688252	6307766
6	6	1392648	6307766
6	7	1458053	6307766
6	8	1768813	6307766
7	9	1735575	6868495
7	10	1723305	6868495
7	11	1737093	6868495
7	12	1672522	6868495
8	13	1516776	6854731
8	14	1814327	6854731
8	15	1761814	6854731
8	16	1761814	6854731
9	17	1710831	6739374
9	18	1625456	6739374
9	19	1645204	6739374
9	20	1757883	6739374
10	21	1542152	6238901
10	22	1468316	6238901
10	23	1443837	6238901
10	24	1784596	6238901

The value for the REGION_SALES column is the same for all salespeople in the same region. In the next section, you will see two different approaches for using this information to generate percentage calculations.

RATIO_TO_REPORT

One of the more common uses of reporting functions is to generate the value of the denominator for performance calculations. With the query from the previous section, for example, the next logical step would be to divide each salesperson's total sales (SP_SALES) by the total region sales (REGION_SALES) to determine what ratio of the total region sales can be attributed to each salesperson. One option is to use the reporting function as the denominator in the percentage calculation, as in:

```
SELECT region_id, salesperson_id,
  SUM(tot_sales) sp_sales,
```

```
     ROUND(SUM(tot_sales) /
        SUM(SUM(tot_sales)) OVER (PARTITION BY region_id),
        2) percent_of_region
FROM orders
WHERE year = 2001
GROUP BY region_id, salesperson_id
ORDER BY region_id, salesperson_id;
```

REGION_ID	SALESPERSON_ID	SP_SALES	PERCENT_OF_REGION
5	1	1927580	.29
5	2	1461898	.22
5	3	1501039	.23
5	4	1695124	.26
6	5	1688252	.27
6	6	1392648	.22
6	7	1458053	.23
6	8	1768813	.28
7	9	1735575	.25
7	10	1723305	.25
7	11	1737093	.25
7	12	1672522	.24
8	13	1516776	.22
8	14	1814327	.26
8	15	1761814	.26
8	16	1761814	.26
9	17	1710831	.25
9	18	1625456	.24
9	19	1645204	.24
9	20	1757883	.26
10	21	1542152	.25
10	22	1468316	.24
10	23	1443837	.23
10	24	1784596	.29

Because this is such a common operation, however, Oracle has spared us the trouble by including the RATIO_TO_REPORT function. The RATIO_TO_REPORT function allows you to calculate each row's contribution to either the entire result set, or some subset of the result set if the PARTITION BY clause is included. The next query uses RATIO_TO_REPORT to generate the percentage contribution of each salesperson to her region's total sales:

```
SELECT region_id, salesperson_id,
   SUM(tot_sales) sp_sales,
   ROUND(RATIO_TO_REPORT(SUM(tot_sales))
      OVER (PARTITION BY region_id), 2) sp_ratio
FROM orders
WHERE year = 2001
GROUP BY region_id, salesperson_id
ORDER BY region_id, salesperson_id;
```

REGION_ID	SALESPERSON_ID	SP_SALES	SP_RATIO
5	1	1927580	.29
5	2	1461898	.22
5	3	1501039	.23
5	4	1695124	.26
6	5	1688252	.27
6	6	1392648	.22
6	7	1458053	.23
6	8	1768813	.28
7	9	1735575	.25
7	10	1723305	.25
7	11	1737093	.25
7	12	1672522	.24
8	13	1516776	.22
8	14	1814327	.26
8	15	1761814	.26
8	16	1761814	.26
9	17	1710831	.25
9	18	1625456	.24
9	19	1645204	.24
9	20	1757883	.26
10	21	1542152	.25
10	22	1468316	.24
10	23	1443837	.23
10	24	1784596	.29

Summary

We have covered a lot of ground in this chapter, so don't feel bad if it takes a couple of passes to get a feel for all of the different analytic functions and how they can be applied. You'll find the material easier to digest if you concentrate on one category at a time (Ranking, Windowing, Reporting). If you've been working with Oracle for many years, you are probably chomping at the bit to give these functions a try. Along with being compact and efficient, Oracle's analytic functions keep analytical calculations where they belong—in the database server—instead of relying on procedural languages or spreadsheet macros to finish the job.

CHAPTER 15

SQL Best Practices

Writing maintainable and efficient SQL statements requires a good deal of experience. You can write a SQL query in many different ways, each giving the same result, but one can be a hundred times slower than another, or one can be easier to understand and maintain than the other.

Know When to Use Specific Constructs

Depending on the circumstances, certain SQL constructs are preferable to others. For example, use of the EXISTS predicate is often preferable to DISTINCT. The next sections discuss the usage of such constructs.

EXISTS Is Preferable to DISTINCT

The DISTINCT keyword used in a SELECT clause eliminates duplicate rows in the result set. To eliminate those duplicates, Oracle performs a sort, and that sort requires time and disk space. Therefore, avoid using DISTINCT if you can tolerate having duplicate rows returned by a query. If you can't tolerate the duplicate rows, or your application can't handle them, use EXISTS in place of DISTINCT.

For example, assume you are trying to find the names of customers who have orders. Your query has to be based on two tables: `customer` and `cust_order`. Using DISTINCT, your query would be written as follows:

```
SELECT DISTINCT c.cust_nbr, c.name
FROM customer c JOIN cust_order o
ON c.cust_nbr = o.cust_nbr;
```

The corresponding execution plan for this query is as follows. Note the SORT operation, which is a result of DISTINCT being used.

```
Query Plan
-------------------------------------------
SELECT STATEMENT   Cost = 3056
  SORT UNIQUE
```

```
    MERGE JOIN
      INDEX FULL SCAN IND_ORD_CUST_NBR
      SORT JOIN
        TABLE ACCESS FULL CUSTOMER
```

To use EXISTS, the query needs to be rewritten as follows:

```
SELECT c.cust_nbr, c.name
FROM customer c
WHERE EXISTS (SELECT 1 FROM cust_order o WHERE c.cust_nbr = o.cust_nbr);
```

Here is the execution plan for the EXISTS version of the queries:

```
Query Plan
----------------------------------------
SELECT STATEMENT    Cost = 320
  FILTER
    TABLE ACCESS FULL CUSTOMER
    INDEX RANGE SCAN IND_ORD_CUST_NBR
```

Notice that the second query eliminates the overhead of the sort operation, and therefore runs faster.

WHERE Versus HAVING

We discussed the GROUP BY and HAVING clauses in Chapter 4. Sometimes, when writing a GROUP BY query, you have a condition that you can specify in either the WHERE or HAVING clause. In situations where you have a choice, you'll always get better performance if you specify the condition in the WHERE clause. The reason is that it's less expensive to eliminate rows before they are summarized than it is to eliminate results after summarization.

Let's look at an example illustrating the advantage of WHERE over HAVING. Here's a query with the HAVING clause that reports the number of orders in the year 2000:

```
SELECT year, COUNT(*)
FROM orders
GROUP BY year
HAVING year = 2001;

      YEAR   COUNT(*)
---------- ----------
      2001       1440
```

The execution plan for this query is as follows:

```
Query Plan
-------------------------------------------
SELECT STATEMENT    Cost = 6
  FILTER
    SORT GROUP BY
      INDEX FAST FULL SCAN ORDERS_PK
```

Now, look at that same query, but with the year restriction in the WHERE clause:

```
SELECT year, COUNT(*)
FROM orders
WHERE year = 2001
GROUP BY year;

     YEAR    COUNT(*)
--------- ----------
     2001        1440
```

The execution plan for this version of the query is:

```
Query Plan
-------------------------------------
SELECT STATEMENT    Cost = 2
  SORT GROUP BY NOSORT
    INDEX FAST FULL SCAN ORDERS_PK
```

With the HAVING clause, the query performs the group operation first, and then filters the groups for the condition specified. The WHERE clause version of the query filters the rows *before* performing the group operation. The result of filtering with the WHERE clause is that there are fewer rows to summarize, and consequently, the query performs better.

However, you should note that not all types of filtering can be achieved using the WHERE clause. Sometimes, you may need to summarize the data first and then filter the summarized data based on the summarized values. In such situations, you have to filter using the HAVING clause, because only the HAVING clause can "see" summarized values. Moreover, there are situations when you may need to use the WHERE clause and the HAVING clause together in a query to filter the results the way you want. For details, see Chapter 4.

UNION Versus UNION ALL

We discussed UNION and UNION ALL in Chapter 7. UNION ALL combines the results of two SELECT statements. UNION combines the results of two SELECT statements, and then returns only distinct rows from the combination; duplicates are eliminated. It is, therefore, obvious that to remove the duplicates, UNION performs one extra step than UNION ALL. This extra step is a sort, which is costly in terms of performance. Therefore, whenever your application can handle duplicates or you are certain that no duplicates will result, consider using UNION ALL instead of UNION.

Let's look an example to understand this issue better. The following query uses UNION to return a list of orders where the sale price exceeds $50.00 or where the customer is located in region 5:

```
SELECT order_nbr, cust_nbr
FROM cust_order
```

```
WHERE sale_price > 50
UNION
SELECT order_nbr, cust_nbr
FROM cust_order
WHERE cust_nbr IN
(SELECT cust_nbr FROM customer WHERE region_id = 5);

ORDER_NBR   CUST_NBR
---------- ----------
      1000          1
      1001          1
      1002          5
      1003          4
      1004          4
      1005          8
      1006          1
      1007          5
      1008          5
      1009          1
      1011          1
      1012          1
      1015          5
      1017          4
      1019          4
      1021          8
      1023          1
      1025          5
      1027          5
      1029          1

20 rows selected.
```

The execution plan for this UNION query is:

```
Query Plan
-------------------------------------------------------------------------
SELECT STATEMENT   Cost = 8
  SORT UNIQUE
    UNION-ALL
      TABLE ACCESS FULL CUST_ORDER
      HASH JOIN
        TABLE ACCESS FULL CUSTOMER
        TABLE ACCESS FULL CUST_ORDER
```

The following query uses UNION ALL instead of UNION to get the same information:

```
SELECT order_nbr, cust_nbr
FROM cust_order
WHERE sale_price > 50
UNION ALL
SELECT order_nbr, cust_nbr
FROM cust_order
WHERE cust_nbr IN
(SELECT cust_nbr FROM customer WHERE region_id = 5);
```

```
ORDER_NBR    CUST_NBR
----------   ----------
      1001           1
      1003           4
      1005           8
      1009           1
      1012           1
      1017           4
      1021           8
      1029           1
      1001           1
      1000           1
      1002           5
      1003           4
      1004           4
      1006           1
      1007           5
      1008           5
      1009           1
      1012           1
      1011           1
      1015           5
      1017           4
      1019           4
      1023           1
      1025           5
      1027           5
      1029           1

26 rows selected.
```

Note the duplicate rows in the output. However, note also that UNION ALL performs better than UNION, as you can see from the following execution plan:

```
Query Plan
-------------------------------------------------------------------------
SELECT STATEMENT   Cost = 4
  UNION-ALL
    TABLE ACCESS FULL CUST_ORDER
    HASH JOIN
      TABLE ACCESS FULL CUSTOMER
      TABLE ACCESS FULL CUST_ORDER
```

You can see that the extra operation (SORT UNIQUE) in the UNION makes it run slower than UNION ALL.

LEFT Versus RIGHT OUTER JOIN

As you have seen in Chapter 3, outer joins can be of type LEFT, RIGHT, or FULL. LEFT and RIGHT are really two ways of looking at the same operation. Mixing LEFT and RIGHT outer joins in the same application can cause confusion, as you and other programmers must constantly shift your point-of-view from one approach to the other. Use both LEFT and RIGHT outer joins in the *same query*, and you'll find your confusion greatly magnified. For example:

```
SELECT e.lname, j.function, d.name
FROM job j LEFT OUTER JOIN employee e ON e.job_id = j.job_id
          RIGHT OUTER JOIN department d ON e.dept_id = d.dept_id;
```

LNAME	FUNCTION	NAME
MILLER	CLERK	ACCOUNTING
CLARK	MANAGER	ACCOUNTING
KING	PRESIDENT	ACCOUNTING
SMITH	CLERK	RESEARCH
FORD	ANALYST	RESEARCH
JONES	MANAGER	RESEARCH
SCOTT	ANALYST	RESEARCH
JAMES	CLERK	SALES
BLAKE	MANAGER	SALES
MARTIN	SALESPERSON	SALES
TURNER	SALESPERSON	SALES
ALLEN	SALESPERSON	SALES
		OPERATIONS

Such confusion is unnecessary. Since both LEFT and RIGHT outer joins represent the same operation, but from differing points of view, you can simply pick one point of view and use it consistently. For example, many programmers write all outer joins as either FULL or LEFT, ignoring RIGHT.

The preceding query uses a LEFT and then a RIGHT outer join to do the following:

1. Connect an outer join from employee to job, with employee as the required table

2. Connect another outer join from department to the results from Step 1, with department as the required table

Using parentheses to explicitly state the above order of operations, you can rewrite the query using all LEFT outer joins, as follows:

```
SELECT e.lname, j.function, d.name
FROM department d LEFT OUTER JOIN
        (job j LEFT OUTER JOIN employee e
        ON e.job_id = j.job_id)
     ON e.dept_id = d.dept_id;
```

LNAME	FUNCTION	NAME
MILLER	CLERK	ACCOUNTING
CLARK	MANAGER	ACCOUNTING
KING	PRESIDENT	ACCOUNTING
SMITH	CLERK	RESEARCH
FORD	ANALYST	RESEARCH
JONES	MANAGER	RESEARCH
SCOTT	ANALYST	RESEARCH
JAMES	CLERK	SALES

```
BLAKE            MANAGER                SALES
MARTIN           SALESPERSON            SALES
TURNER           SALESPERSON            SALES
ALLEN            SALESPERSON            SALES
                                        OPERATIONS
```

The tradeoff here is between using parentheses and mixing RIGHT and LEFT outer joins. This second version of the query still joins employee to job, and then joins department to that result. The operations are exactly the same as in the previous version. This time, the parentheses make the order of operations clearer, and we personally find the second version of the query a bit easier to understand.

Avoid Unnecessary Parsing

Before your SQL can be executed by Oracle, it needs to be parsed. The importance of parsing when it comes to tuning SQL lies in the fact that no matter how many times a given SQL statement is executed, it needs to be parsed only once. During parsing, the following steps are performed (not necessarily in the sequence shown):

- The syntax of the SQL statement is verified.
- The data dictionary is searched to verify table and column definitions.
- The data dictionary is searched to verify security privileges on relevant objects.
- Parse locks are acquired on the relevant objects.
- The optimal execution plan is determined.
- The statement is loaded into the shared SQL area (also known as the library cache) in the shared pool of the system global area (SGA). The execution plan and parse information are saved here in case the same statement is executed once again.

If a SQL statement involves any remote objects (e.g., database links), then these steps are repeated for the remote objects. As you can see, lots of work is performed during the parsing of a SQL statement. However, a statement is parsed only if Oracle doesn't find an identical SQL statement already in the shared SQL area (library cache) of the SGA.

Before parsing a SQL statement, Oracle searches the library cache for an identical SQL statement. If Oracle finds an exact match, there is no need to parse the statement again. However, if an identical SQL statement is not found, Oracle goes through all the aforementioned steps to parse the statement.

The most important keyword in the previous paragraph is "identical." To share the same SQL area, two statements need to be truly identical. Two statements that look similar, or that return the same result, need not be identical. To be truly identical, the statements must:

- Have the same uppercase and lowercase characters
- Have the same whitespace and newline characters
- Reference the same objects using the same names, which must in turn have the same owners

If there is a possibility that your application executes the same (or similar) SQL statements multiple times, by all means try to avoid unnecessary parsing. This will improve the overall performance of your applications. The following techniques can help you reduce SQL parsing:

- Use bind variables.
- Use table aliases.

Using Bind Variables

When multiple users use an application, they actually execute the same set of SQL statements over and over, but with different data values. For example, one customer service representative may be executing the following statement:

```
SELECT * FROM customer WHERE cust_nbr = 121;
```

while another customer service representative will be executing:

```
SELECT * FROM customer WHERE cust_nbr = 328;
```

These two statements are similar, but not "identical"—the customer ID numbers are different; therefore, Oracle has to parse twice.

Because the only difference between these statements is the value used for the customer number, this application can be rewritten to use bind variables. In that case, the SQL statement in question can be as follows:

```
SELECT * FROM customer WHERE cust_nbr = :x;
```

Oracle needs to parse this statement only once. The actual customer numbers would be supplied after parsing for each execution of the statement. Multiple, concurrently executing programs could share the same copy of this SQL statement while at the same time supplying different customer number values.

In a multiuser application, situations such as the one described here are very common, and overall performance can be significantly improved by using bind variables, thereby reducing unnecessary parsing.

Using Table Aliases

The use of table aliases can help to improve the performance of your SQL statements. Before getting into the performance aspects of table aliases, let's quickly review what table aliases are and how they are used.

When you select data from two or more tables, you should specify which table each column belongs to. Otherwise, if the two tables have columns with the same name, you will end up with an error:

```
SELECT cust_nbr, name, order_nbr
FROM customer, cust_order;
SELECT cust_nbr, name, order_nbr
       *
ERROR at line 1:
ORA-00918: column ambiguously defined
```

The error in this case occurs because both the customer and cust_order tables have columns named cust_nbr. Oracle can't tell which cust_nbr column you are referring to. To fix this problem, you can rewrite this statement as follows:

```
SELECT customer.cust_nbr, customer.name, cust_order.order_nbr
FROM customer JOIN cust_order
ON customer.cust_nbr = cust_order.cust_nbr;
```

```
  CUST_NBR NAME                                  ORDER_NBR
---------- ------------------------------------ ----------
         1 Cooper Industries                         1001
         1 Cooper Industries                         1000
         5 Gentech Industries                        1002
         4 Flowtech Inc.                             1003
         4 Flowtech Inc.                             1004
         8 Zantech Inc.                              1005
         1 Cooper Industries                         1006
         5 Gentech Industries                        1007
         5 Gentech Industries                        1008
         1 Cooper Industries                         1009
         1 Cooper Industries                         1012
         1 Cooper Industries                         1011
         5 Gentech Industries                        1015
         4 Flowtech Inc.                             1017
         4 Flowtech Inc.                             1019
         8 Zantech Inc.                              1021
         1 Cooper Industries                         1023
         5 Gentech Industries                        1025
         5 Gentech Industries                        1027
         1 Cooper Industries                         1029

20 rows selected.
```

Note the use of the table name to qualify each column name. This eliminates any ambiguity as to which cust_nbr column the query is referring to.

Instead of qualifying column names with full table names, you can use table aliases, as in the following example:

```
SELECT c.cust_nbr, c.name, o.order_nbr
FROM customer c JOIN cust_order o
ON c.cust_nbr = o.cust_nbr;
```

```
CUST_NBR NAME                                    ORDER_NBR
-------- --------------------------------------- ---------
       1 Cooper Industries                            1001
       1 Cooper Industries                            1000
       5 Gentech Industries                           1002
       4 Flowtech Inc.                                1003
       4 Flowtech Inc.                                1004
       8 Zantech Inc.                                 1005
       1 Cooper Industries                            1006
       5 Gentech Industries                           1007
       5 Gentech Industries                           1008
       1 Cooper Industries                            1009
       1 Cooper Industries                            1012
       1 Cooper Industries                            1011
       5 Gentech Industries                           1015
       4 Flowtech Inc.                                1017
       4 Flowtech Inc.                                1019
       8 Zantech Inc.                                 1021
       1 Cooper Industries                            1023
       5 Gentech Industries                           1025
       5 Gentech Industries                           1027
       1 Cooper Industries                            1029
```

```
20 rows selected.
```

The letters "c" and "o" in this example are table aliases. You can specify these aliases following their respective table names in the FROM clause, and they can be used everywhere else in the query in place of the table name. Table aliases provide a convenient shorthand notation, allowing your queries to be more readable and concise.

 Table aliases are not limited to one character in length; they can be up to 30 characters in length.

An important thing to remember while using table aliases is that if you define aliases in the FROM clause, you must use only those aliases, and not the actual table names, in the rest of the query. If you alias a table, and then use the actual table name elsewhere in the query, you will encounter errors. For example:

```
SELECT c.cust_nbr, c.name, o.order_nbr
FROM customer c JOIN cust_order o
ON customer.cust_nbr = cust_order.cust_nbr;
WHERE customer.cust_nbr = cust_order.cust_nbr
                        *
```

```
ERROR at line 3:
ORA-00904: invalid column name
```

Many developers make the mistake of forgetting to use their table aliases while writing hints. Once you define an alias, you must specify the alias instead of the actual table name in any hints; otherwise, those hints will be silently ignored. Here's an example of this common mistake:

```
SELECT /*+ USE_HASH(customer cust_order) */ c.cust_nbr, c.name, o.order_nbr
FROM customer c JOIN cust_order o
ON c.cust_nbr = o.cust_nbr;
```

The USE_HASH hint specifies the customer and cust_order tables. However, the FROM clause provides aliases for both those tables. Because of the aliases, the table names have no meaning, and the hint is ignored, possibly to the detriment of performance. Following is the correct version of this query:

```
SELECT /*+ USE_HASH(c o) */ c.cust_nbr, c.name, o.order_nbr
FROM customer c JOIN cust_order o
ON c.cust_nbr = o.cust_nbr;
```

This time, the USE_HASH hint properly uses the table aliases that have been defined in the FROM clause. This hint will have the desired effect.

When selecting data from multiple tables, it makes sense to qualify each column name with its corresponding table alias. The column cust_nbr appears in both the customer and cust_order tables. Without proper qualification, this column is said to be "ambiguously defined" in the query. Therefore, you must qualify the cust_nbr column with a table alias (or a full table name, if you are not using aliases). However, the other two columns used in the query are not ambiguous. Therefore, the following statement, which only qualifies the cust_nbr column, is valid:

```
SELECT c.cust_nbr, name, order_nbr
FROM customer c, cust_order o
WHERE c.cust_nbr = o.cust_nbr;
```

```
  CUST_NBR NAME                                ORDER_NBR
---------- ----------------------------------- ----------
         1 Cooper Industries                        1001
         1 Cooper Industries                        1000
         5 Gentech Industries                       1002
         4 Flowtech Inc.                            1003
         4 Flowtech Inc.                            1004
         8 Zantech Inc.                             1005
         1 Cooper Industries                        1006
         5 Gentech Industries                       1007
         5 Gentech Industries                       1008
         1 Cooper Industries                        1009
         1 Cooper Industries                        1012
         1 Cooper Industries                        1011
         5 Gentech Industries                       1015
         4 Flowtech Inc.                            1017
         4 Flowtech Inc.                            1019
```

```
        8 Zantech Inc.                   1021
        1 Cooper Industries              1023
        5 Gentech Industries             1025
        5 Gentech Industries             1027
        1 Cooper Industries              1029
```

    20 rows selected.

This is where the performance aspect of using table aliases comes into play. Since the query doesn't qualify the columns NAME and ORDER_NBR, Oracle has to search both the CUSTOMER and CUST_ORDER tables while parsing this statement to find which table each of these columns belongs to. The time required for this search may be negligible for one query, but it does add up if you have a number of such queries to parse. It's good programming practice to qualify *all* columns in a query with table aliases, even those that are not ambiguous, so that Oracle can avoid this extra search when parsing the statement.

Consider Literal SQL for Decision-Support Systems

We discussed the benefits of using bind variables previously. The use of bind variables is often beneficial in terms of performance. However, there is a downside to consider. Bind variables hide actual values from the optimizer. This hiding of actual values can have negative performance implications, especially in decision-support systems. For example, consider the following statement:

```
SELECT * FROM customer WHERE region_id = :x
```

The optimizer can parse this statement, but it won't be able to take into account the specific region being selected. If 90% of your customers were in region 5, then a full table scan would likely be the most efficient approach when selecting those customers. An index scan would probably be more efficient when selecting customers in other regions. When you hardcode values into your SQL statements, the cost-based optimizer (CBO) can look at histograms (a type of statistic) and generate an execution plan that takes into account the specific values you are supplying. When you use bind variables, however, the optimizer generates an execution plan without having a complete picture of the SQL statement. Such an execution plan may or may not be the most efficient.

In Decision-Support Systems (DSS), it is very rare that multiple users use the same query over and over. More typically, a handful of users execute complex, different queries against a large database. Since it is very rare that the SQL statements will be repetitive, the parsing time saved by using bind variables will be negligible. At the same time, since DSS applications run complex queries against large databases, the time required to fetch the resulting data can be significant. Therefore, it is important that the optimizer generate the most efficient execution plan for the query. To help the optimizer generate the best possible plan, provide the optimizer as much information as you can, including the actual values of the columns or variables. Therefore, in DSS applications, use literal SQL statements with hardcoded values instead of bind variables.

Our earlier advice about using bind variables in Online Transaction Processing (OLTP) applications is still valid. In OLTP systems, multiple users all use the same programs, and thus issue the same queries. The amount of data returned per query is typically small. Thus, parse time is a more significant performance factor than in DSS systems. When developing OLTP applications, save parsing time and space in the shared SQL area by using bind variables.

CHAPTER 16

XML

Extensible Markup Language (XML) has become the standard mechanism for sharing data between applications. This chapter will explore how XML documents may be stored in an Oracle database, how the data within an XML document can be extracted and stored in relational tables, and how an XML document can be constructed from data in relational tables.

What Is XML?

XML is a close cousin to HTML, but while HTML is primarily concerned with formatting and displaying data, XML is concerned with the data itself. Unlike HTML, with XML you may create your own tags, which is why XML is perfectly suited for describing data. The easiest way to understand XML is through an example, so here is an XML document that represents a customer purchase order:

```
<?xml version="1.0"?>
<purchase_order>
  <customer_name>Alpha Technologies</customer_name>
  <po_number>11257</po_number>
  <po_date>2004-01-20</po_date>
  <po_items>
    <item>
      <part_number>AI5-4557</part_number>
      <quantity>20</quantity>
    </item>
    <item>
      <part_number>EI-T5-001</part_number>
      <quantity>12</quantity>
    </item>
  </po_items>
</purchase_order>
```

The first line defines that the text that follows is an XML document that adheres to Version 1.0 of the XML specification. The second line is the *root node* of the document and has the tag <purchase_order>. A valid XML document must contain exactly one root node. Other nodes of the document can appear more than once as necessary to describe the data, as illustrated by the multiple <item> tags under the <po_items> tag. This document describes that Alpha Technologies issued P.O. #11257 on January 20, 2004, in which 20 units of part number AI5-4557 and 12 units of EI-T5-001 were requested. Since this document will be the basis for every example in this chapter, it would be worthwhile to become comfortable with it before forging ahead.

XML Resources

Because this book is about SQL, the focus of this chapter is how to utilize SQL to interact with XML documents. Thus, the XML examples used in this chapter are rather simple so as not to needlessly complicate things. If you are interested in delving deeper into XML, here are a few excellent resources:

www.w3c.org
    The World Wide Web Consortium (W3C) site, useful for history of the XML specification, as well as the specification itself

www.xml.org
    Portal for everything XML, including tutorials, FAQs, white papers, news, etc.

XML in a Nutshell (O'Reilly)
    An excellent reference guide for XML and related technologies

Oracle and XML

Oracle first began adding support for XML in the Oracle8*i* Database release. This support, which consisted largely of XML parser toolkits for Java, PL/SQL, and C/C++, allowed users to manipulate XML data but did not offer any native support for XML within the database kernel. The Oracle 9*i* Database releases raised the bar significantly by adding a new data type called XMLType for storing XML documents in the database and by creating a mechanism for organizing, accessing, and versioning XML documents called *XML Repository*. Oracle branded this set of technologies as *Oracle XML DB*. Additionally, XML data can be loaded and unloaded from a database using Oracle's import/export utilities, read from external files using SQL*Loader, and published via Advanced Queuing, making it clear that Oracle has made the integration of XML technologies a high priority over the past few releases.

Storing XML Data

The XMLType data type, first introduced in Oracle9*i* Database, allows an XML document to be stored in a table. XMLType is actually an object type, so you have your choice of creating a column of type XMLType within a a table or creating an object table (i.e., CREATE TABLE purchase_order OF xmltype). Since we may want to store additional data about a purchase order along with the XML document itself, it might be best to create a table that contains a unique identifier, several attribute columns, and the XML document:

```
CREATE TABLE purchase_order
 (po_id NUMBER(5) NOT NULL,
  customer_po_nbr VARCHAR2(20),
  customer_inception_date DATE,
  order_nbr NUMBER(5),
  purchase_order_doc XMLTYPE,
  CONSTRAINT purchase_order_pk PRIMARY KEY (po_id)
);
```

By default, the purchase_order_doc column will be stored as a CLOB (Character Large Object). Later in the chapter, you will see how the XML document can be stored as a set of objects by defining an XML Schema for your XML documents, but we'll keep it simple now and move on to the more complicated case later in this chapter.

Storing XML as a CLOB

The XMLType object type includes constructors that accept many different data types, including VARCHAR2, CLOB, BFILE, and REF CURSOR. For example, here is the definition for the constructor used in the remainder of the chapter:

```
FINAL CONSTRUCTOR FUNCTION XMLTYPE RETURNS SELF AS RESULT
Argument Name               Type              In/Out Default?
--------------------------- ----------------- ------ --------
XMLDATA                     BINARY FILE LOB      IN
CSID                        NUMBER               IN
SCHEMA                      VARCHAR2             IN     DEFAULT
VALIDATED                   NUMBER               IN     DEFAULT
WELLFORMED                  NUMBER               IN     DEFAULT
```

As you can see, the first two parameters are required, and the next three parameters are optional. The following PL/SQL block uses this constructor without the optional parameters to instantiate an XMLType object and insert it into the purchase_order table:

```
/* create directory to point to where XML docs are stored */
CREATE DIRECTORY xml_data AS 'c:\\alan\\OReilly\\2nd_Edition';

DECLARE
  bfl BFILE;
BEGIN
  /* attach XML document purch_ord.xml to bfile locator */
  bfl := BFILENAME('XML_DATA', 'purch_ord.xml');

  /* add to purchase_order table */
  INSERT INTO purchase_order (po_id, purchase_order_doc)
```

```
    VALUES (1000,
      XMLTYPE(bfl, nls_charset_id('WE8MSWIN1252')));

    COMMIT;
  END;
```

The purchase_order table now contains a record with the contents of the *purch_ord. xml* file stored as a CLOB. At this point, the file is assumed to contain a valid XML document, but the contents have not been checked for validity (more on this later). If you would like to see the contents of the document, you can simply select the XML-Type column:

```
SELECT po.purchase_order_doc
FROM purchase_order po;

PURCHASE_ORDER_DOC
-----------------------------------------------------------------------
<?xml version="1.0"?>
<purchase_order>
  <customer_name>Alpha Technologies</customer_name>
  <po_number>11257</po_number>
  <po_date>2004-01-20</po_date>
  <po_items>
    <item>
      <part_number>AI5-4557</part_number>
      <quantity>20</quantity>
    </item>
    <item>
      <part_number>EI-T5-001</part_number>
      <quantity>12</quantity>
    </item>
  </po_items>
</purchase_order>
```

Inspecting the XML Document

Now that the XML document has been stored in the purchase_order table, what should you do with it? Unless your intent is to simply store the document for safekeeping, you will probably want to at least inspect the data inside the document, if not extract that data for storage in relational tables. The XMLType object contains numerous methods to help with this effort.

XPath

Before you can begin inspecting XML documents, you will need to have a method for identifying different parts of a document. Oracle has adopted the use of XPath expressions for this purpose. XPath is a W3C recommendation used for walking a tree of nodes. Before describing how to build an XPath expression, it might be helpful to view the purchase order document as a tree, as shown in Figure 16-1.

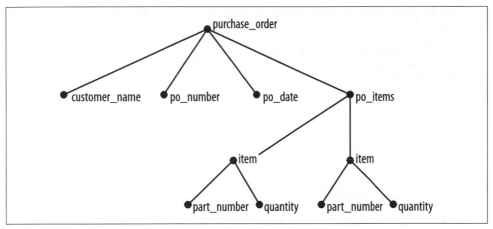

Figure 16-1. Tree view of purchase order

The root node has four children, one of which (po_items) has two children of its own. Each of these child nodes has two children nodes as well. XPath specifies a notation for describing a specific node or nodes in the tree, as shown in Table 16-1.

Table 16-1. Path notation elements

Element	Meaning
/	Used to separate nodes or to denote the root node if first character of expression.
//	Used to denote all children of a given node.
*	Wildcard character.
[]	Used to identify a specific child if a node has more than one child (i.e., [2]). May also contain one or more expressions used to identify nodes by their values (i.e., [customer_name="Acme"]).

Using this notation, the customer_name node in the purchase_order tree would be represented as /purchase_order/customer_name, and the second item node would be represented as /purchase_order/po_items/item[2]. To find all item nodes in the purchase order document, you could specify /purchase_order//item or /purchase_order/*/item. Along with finding nodes based on tag names, you may also search for nodes based on values, such as /purchase_order[po_number=11257]/po_items, which returns the po_items for the purchase order having a po_number of 11257. Now that you have a way of describing nodes in the XML document, you can begin extracting data.

The extract( ) member function

The extract( ) member function takes an XMLType instance and an XPath expression and returns an XMLType instance. The XMLType instance returned by the function represents some fragment of the original as resolved by the XPath expression, and it does not need to be a valid XML document. If the XPath expression does not resolve to a node of the XML document, a NULL is returned. Here's a simple example:

```
SELECT extract(po.purchase_order_doc,
       '/purchase_order/customer_name') xml_fragment
FROM purchase_order po
WHERE po.po_id = 1000;

XML_FRAGMENT
---------------------------------------------------
<customer_name>Alpha Technologies</customer_name>
```

The XML fragment being returned is a perfectly valid, albeit brief, XML document consisting of just a root node. Here's another example that returns all of the purchase order items:

```
SELECT extract(po.purchase_order_doc,
       '/purchase_order//item') xml_fragment
FROM purchase_order po
WHERE po.po_id = 1000;

XML_FRAGMENT
---------------------------------------------------
<item>
  <part_number>AI5-4557</part_number>
  <quantity>20</quantity>
</item>
<item>
  <part_number>EI-T5-001</part_number>
  <quantity>12</quantity>
</item>
```

The XML fragment returned from this query is not a valid XML document, since it contains two root nodes. If you are interested in retrieving only the first item, you can specify this using [1] in your XPath expression, as demonstrated by the following:

```
SELECT extract(po.purchase_order_doc,
       '/purchase_order/po_items/item[1]') xml_fragment
FROM purchase_order po
WHERE po.po_id = 1000;

XML_FRAGMENT
---------------------------------------------------
<item>
  <part_number>AI5-4557</part_number>
  <quantity>20</quantity>
</item>
```

The extractValue( ) member function

The extractValue( ) member function is similar to the extract( ) member function, except that it returns a string (VARCHAR2) instead of an instance of XMLType. For example, if you wanted to extract the customer name without the enclosing tags, you could do the following:

```
SELECT extractValue(po.purchase_order_doc,
    '/purchase_order/customer_name') cust_name
FROM purchase_order po
WHERE po.po_id = 1000;

CUST_NAME
--------------------------------------------------
Alpha Technologies
```

If you know that the value being returned is a number or date, you can wrap the call to extractValue( ) with to_number or to_date as needed. Keep in mind that you cannot substitute extractValue( ) for extract( ) in every situation; to use extractValue( ), the node resolved from the XPath expression must be a single child node. For example, the following statement generates an error because the node resolved by the XPath expression has child nodes beneath it:

```
SELECT extractValue(po.purchase_order_doc,
    '/purchase_order/po_items') cust_name
FROM purchase_order po
WHERE po.po_id = 1000;
    *
ERROR at line 3:
ORA-19025: EXTRACTVALUE returns value of only one node
```

The existsNode( ) member function

If you would like to determine whether a specific node exists in your document, you can use the existsNode( ) member function. existsNode( ) takes an XMLType instance and an XPath expression and returns 1 if one or more nodes are found and 0 otherwise. This method is most often used in the WHERE clause of a query, although it is also useful in the SELECT clause (generally within a CASE expression) or the FROM clause (generally within an inline view). The following example uses existsNode( ) in the WHERE clause to ensure that the specified node exists:

```
SELECT extract(po.purchase_order_doc,
    '/purchase_order/customer_name') xml_fragment
FROM purchase_order po
WHERE po.po_id = 1000
  AND 1 = existsNode(po.purchase_order_doc,
    '/purchase_order/customer_name');

XML_FRAGMENT
--------------------------------------------------
<customer_name>Alpha Technologies</customer_name>
```

The next example uses existsNode( ) in the SELECT clause to determine how many line items are in the purchase order:

```
SELECT CASE
  WHEN 1 = existsNode(po.purchase_order_doc,
    '/purchase_order/po_items/item[6]') THEN '>5'
  WHEN 1 = existsNode(po.purchase_order_doc,
    '/purchase_order/po_items/item[5]') THEN '5'
  WHEN 1 = existsNode(po.purchase_order_doc,
    '/purchase_order/po_items/item[4]') THEN '4'
  WHEN 1 = existsNode(po.purchase_order_doc,
    '/purchase_order/po_items/item[3]') THEN '3'
  WHEN 1 = existsNode(po.purchase_order_doc,
    '/purchase_order/po_items/item[2]') THEN '2'
  WHEN 1 = existsNode(po.purchase_order_doc,
    '/purchase_order/po_items/item[1]') THEN '1'
  END num
FROM purchase_order po
WHERE po.po_id = 1000;

NUM
--
2
```

Keep in mind that existsNode( ) will return 1 if a node exists, regardless of whether or not the node has a value. Let's say you received the following purchase order:

```
<?xml version="1.0"?>
<purchase_order>
  <customer_name>Alpha Technologies</customer_name>
  <po_number></po_number>
  <po_date>2004-01-20</po_date>
  <po_items>
    <item>
      <part_number>AI5-4557</part_number>
      <quantity>20</quantity>
    </item>
    <item>
      <part_number>EI-T5-001</part_number>
      <quantity>12</quantity>
    </item>
  </po_items>
</purchase_order>
```

If you search for the existence of the <po_number> node, the existsNode( ) function will return 1, even though no value has been supplied for this node. You will need to use the extractValue( ) function to determine whether a valid PO number has been provided.

Moving data to relational tables

Now that you know how to navigate through and extract fragments from your XML documents, you can build DML statements to move data from your XML documents to relational tables. The purchase_order table created earlier contains two columns that must be populated from data in the purchase order document. The next statement shows how this data can be populated via a single UPDATE statement:

```
UPDATE purchase_order po
SET po.customer_po_nbr = extractvalue(po.purchase_order_doc,
    '/purchase_order/po_number'),
  po.customer_inception_date = to_date(extractvalue(po.purchase_order_doc,
    '/purchase_order/po_date'),'YYYY-MM-DD'),
  po.order_nbr = 7101
WHERE po.po_id = 1000;
```

 For this set of examples, we've arbitrarily chosen to use 7101 as the primary key value for the cust_order table, for the purchase order we're working with. Normally, this value would be generated via a sequence.

Now that the purchase_order table has been completed, the next step is to generate data for the cust_order and line_item tables so that the customer's order can begin processing. Here is the INSERT statement for the cust_order table:

```
INSERT INTO cust_order
 (order_nbr, cust_nbr, sales_emp_id, order_dt,
  expected_ship_dt, status)
SELECT 7101,
 (SELECT c.cust_nbr FROM customer c
  WHERE c.name = ext.cust_name),
 0, SYSDATE, TRUNC(SYSDATE + 7), 'NEW'
FROM (SELECT extractValue(po.purchase_order_doc,
    '/purchase_order/customer_name') cust_name
  FROM purchase_order po
  WHERE po.po_id = 1000) ext;
```

```
1 row created.
```

The previous statement is fairly straightforward, in that it extracts the value of the customer_name node from the purchase order and uses the value to look up the appropriate cust_nbr value in the customer table. The statement for inserting the two line items, however, is a bit more complex because there are multiple item nodes, each with two child nodes underneath them: part_number and quantity. Before you can interact with the data in a SQL statement, you need to transform it from a single XML fragment containing two item nodes to a table of item nodes containing two rows. Fortunately, Oracle has included a built-in function called xmlSequence( ) specifically for this task. First, here are the two line items returned as a single XMLType instance using the extract( ) function:

```
SELECT extract(po.purchase_order_doc,
  '/purchase_order//item')
FROM purchase_order po
WHERE po.po_id = 1000;
```

```
EXTRACT(PO.PURCHASE_ORDER_DOC,'/PURCHASE_ORDER//ITEM')
----------------------------------------------------------
<item>
  <part_number>AI5-4557</part_number>
  <quantity>20</quantity>
</item>
<item>
  <part_number>EI-T5-001</part_number>
  <quantity>12</quantity>
</item>

1 row selected.
```

The next example uses xmlSequence( ) to generate a varray of two items from the XML fragment returned by the extract( ) method. You can then query the output of the xmlSequence( ) function by wrapping it in a TABLE expression and placing it in the FROM clause of a containing query:

```
SELECT itm.*
FROM TABLE(SELECT xmlSequence(extract(po.purchase_order_doc,
    '/purchase_order//item'))
  FROM purchase_order po
  WHERE po.po_id = 1000) itm;

COLUMN_VALUE
----------------------------------------------------------
<item>
  <part_number>AI5-4557</part_number>
  <quantity>20</quantity>
</item>

<item>
  <part_number>EI-T5-001</part_number>
  <quantity>12</quantity>
</item>

2 rows selected.
```

The result set now consists of two rows, each containing a single XMLType instance. You can then use this query to insert data into the line_item table by using the extractValue( ) method to extract the text from the part_number and quantity nodes:

```
INSERT INTO line_item
  (order_nbr, part_nbr, qty)
SELECT 7101, extractValue(itm.column_value, '/item/part_number'),
    extractvalue(itm.column_value, '/item/quantity')
FROM TABLE(SELECT xmlSequence(extract(po.purchase_order_doc,
    '/purchase_order//item'))
  FROM purchase_order po
  WHERE po.po_id = 1000) itm;

2 rows created.
```

Storing XML as a Set of Objects

All of the previous examples have one thing in common: the user understands how the XML document is organized, but Oracle just stores the document as a CLOB without any understanding of what the document contains. You have the option, however, of providing Oracle with a roadmap of the documents that will be stored in an XMLtype column by defining an XML Schema. Once a schema has been defined, the Oracle server can check the validity of the XML documents being stored, as well as add additional functionality to many of the member functions of the XMLType object type.

Defining a schema for your documents allows you to specify, among other things, what elements are required and what elements are optional, in what order your document elements must appear, and min/max and default values for attributes. Here's a simple schema for the purchase order documents:

```xml
<?xml version="1.0" encoding="UTF-8"?>
<xs:schema xmlns:xs="http://www.w3.org/2001/XMLSchema" version="1.0"
 elementFormDefault="unqualified">
   <xs:element name="purchase_order">
      <xs:complexType>
         <xs:sequence>
            <xs:element name="customer_name" type="xs:string"/>
            <xs:element name="po_number" type="xs:string"/>
            <xs:element name="po_date" type="xs:date"/>
            <xs:element name="po_items">
               <xs:complexType>
                  <xs:sequence>
                     <xs:element name="item" maxOccurs="9999">
                        <xs:complexType>
                           <xs:sequence>
                              <xs:element name="part_number" type="xs:string"/>
                              <xs:element name="quantity" type="xs:integer"/>
                           </xs:sequence>
                        </xs:complexType>
                     </xs:element>
                  </xs:sequence>
               </xs:complexType>
            </xs:element>
         </xs:sequence>
      </xs:complexType>
   </xs:element>
</xs:schema>
```

Without going into great detail on how to construct XML Schema definitions, here's a brief description of the above schema:

- The first element in the document is purchase_order.

- The purchase_order element contains an ordered set of elements: customer_name, po_number, po_date, and po_items.

- The po_items element can contain up to 9,999 item elements.

- The item element contains an ordered set of two elements: part_number and quantity.

This schema just brushes the surface of what can be done with XML Schema, but it is sufficient to illustrate how a schema is used by Oracle. If you would like to explore the full power of XML Schema, you might consider picking up *XML Schema* by Eric van der Vlist (O'Reilly).

Registering your schema

Now that you have defined a schema for your purchase order documents, you need to register it with Oracle before you can assign it to XMLType columns. To register the schema, you will need to call the dbms_xmlschema.registerSchema( ) built-in procedure, which requires an identifying URL and the schema definition. The schema definition, which is stored in the *purch_ord.xsd* file in the XML_DATA directory created earlier, will be loaded into a binary file variable and passed in as the second parameter to registerSchema( ):

```
DECLARE
  bfl BFILE;
BEGIN
  /* attach XSD document to bfile locator */
  bfl := BFILENAME('XML_DATA', 'purch_ord.xsd');

  /* register schema */
  dbms_xmlschema.registerSchema(
    'http://localhost:8080/home/xml/schemas/purch_ord.xsd',
    bfl);
END;
```

The registerSchema( ) procedure reads the schema definition and creates whatever database objects it deems appropriate for storing the data defined in the schema definition. Although it is beyond the scope of this book, you may annotate your schema definition to tell Oracle how to store the data and what to call the database objects. Because we didn't annotate the *purch_ord.xsd* file, Oracle created one table (purchase_order165_tab), three object types (purchase_order161_t, po_items162_t, and item163_t), and a collection type (item164_coll) to store the purchase order data. Keep in mind that these are Oracle-generated names, so your results will vary.

Assigning the schema to a column

Now that the Oracle server is aware of your schema, you can assign it to a column. The following DDL statement creates the purchase_order2 table and, at the end of the statement, specifies that the schema associated with the URL *http://localhost:8080/home/xml/schemas/purch_ord.xsd* is to be applied to the purchase_order_doc column:

```
CREATE TABLE purchase_order2
  (po_id NUMBER(5) NOT NULL,
```

```
    customer_po_nbr VARCHAR2(20),
    customer_inception_date DATE,
    order_nbr NUMBER(5),
    purchase_order_doc XMLTYPE,
    CONSTRAINT purchase_order2_pk PRIMARY KEY (po_id)
  )
XMLTYPE COLUMN purchase_order_doc
    XMLSCHEMA "http://localhost:8080/home/xml/schemas/purch_ord.xsd"
    ELEMENT "purchase_order";
```

Whenever a document is added to the purchase_order2 table, the data from the XML document will be extracted and stored in the table that was generated when you registered your schema using the registerSchema() procedure. Thus, the actual XML document will not be stored in the database, so keep this in mind if your business rules require that the document be stored intact. If you would like to assign a schema to your XMLType column, but you want to store the XML documents intact, you can specify that the documents be stored in a CLOB. The next example demonstrates how this is done by specifying the STORE AS CLOB phrase before naming the schema URL:

```
CREATE TABLE purchase_order3
  (po_id NUMBER(5) NOT NULL,
    customer_po_nbr VARCHAR2(20),
    customer_inception_date DATE,
    order_nbr NUMBER(5),
    purchase_order_doc XMLTYPE,
    CONSTRAINT purchase_order3_pk PRIMARY KEY (po_id)
  )
XMLTYPE COLUMN purchase_order_doc
    STORE AS CLOB
    XMLSCHEMA "http://localhost:8080/home/xml/schemas/purch_ord.xsd"
    ELEMENT "purchase_order";
```

Inserting data

To insert data into the schema-based table purchase_order2, you will use the same mechanism as you did for the non-schema-based purchase_order table. However, you will first need to alter the root node of your document to include the schema URL:

```
<purchase_order
  xmlns:xsi="http://www.w3.org/2001/XMLSchema-instance"
  xsi:noNamespaceSchemaLocation="http://localhost:8080/home/xml/schemas/purch_ord.
xsd">
```

With this change in place, you can insert your document as before:

```
DECLARE
  bfl BFILE;
BEGIN
  /* attach XML document to bfile locator */
  bfl := BFILENAME('XML_DATA', 'purch_ord.xml');
```

```
    /* add to purchase_order2 table */
    INSERT INTO purchase_order2 (po_id, purchase_order_doc)
    VALUES (2000, XMLTYPE(bfl, nls_charset_id('WE8MSWIN1252')));

    COMMIT;
END;
```

If the document matches the schema definition, then the data will be extracted from the document and stored. At this point, the document has been *partially validated* against the schema, meaning that Oracle has checked that all mandatory elements are present and that no undefined elements are present. If you need to fully validate your documents against the schema definition, you will need to call one of several XMLType member functions demonstrated in the next section.

To illustrate what happens if the document does not match the schema definition, assume we change the root node from <purchase_order> to <customer_invoice> and try to insert the document:

```
DECLARE
  bfl BFILE;
BEGIN
  /* attach XML document to bfile locator */
  bfl := BFILENAME('XML_DATA', 'purch_ord.xml');

  /* add to purchase_order2 table */
  INSERT INTO purchase_order2 (po_id, purchase_order_doc)
  VALUES (2001, XMLTYPE(bfl, nls_charset_id('WE8MSWIN1252')));

  COMMIT;
END;
/
DECLARE
*
ERROR at line 1:
ORA-31043: Element 'customer_invoice' not globally defined in schema
'http://localhost:8080/home/xml/schemas/purch_ord.xsd'
```

Upon changing the root node back to <purchase_order> but adding a new child node called <comments>, we would see the following error:

```
DECLARE
  bfl BFILE;
BEGIN
  /* attach XML document to bfile locator */
  bfl := BFILENAME('XML_DATA', 'purch_ord.xml');

  /* add to purchase_order2 table */
  INSERT INTO purchase_order2 (po_id, purchase_order_doc)
  VALUES (2001, XMLTYPE(bfl, nls_charset_id('WE8MSWIN1252')));

  COMMIT;
END;
/
```

```
DECLARE
*
ERROR at line 1:
ORA-30937: No schema definition for 'comments' (namespace '##local') in
parent 'purchase_order'
```

Depending on the needs of your application, you can make your schema fairly simple, like the purchase order schema used here, or you can make your schema much more restrictive. If you find yourself writing code to check the validity of an XML document, you might be better off creating a robust schema definition and letting Oracle do the work for you.

XMLType validity functions

If you are checking your XML documents against a schema, then you will be able to make use of several member functions of the XMLType object type. If you want to check to see if your documents are based on a schema, and get the schema's URL, you could do the following:

```
SELECT CASE WHEN 1 = po.purchase_order_doc.isSchemaBased( )
  THEN po.purchase_order_doc.getSchemaURL( )
  ELSE 'No Schema Defined'
  END schema_name
FROM purchase_order2 po
WHERE po.po_id = 2000;

SCHEMA_NAME
-------------------------------------------------------
http://localhost:8080/home/xml/schemas/purch_ord.xsd
```

This query uses two of XMLType's member functions: the isSchemaBased( ) function returns 1 if the XMLType column has been assigned a schema, and the getSchemaURL( ) function returns the schema's URL.

If you want to check to see if a particular XMLType instance has been fully validated, you can use the isSchemaValidated( ) member function:

```
SELECT CASE WHEN 1 = po.purchase_order_doc.isSchemaValidated( )
  THEN 'VALIDATED'
  ELSE 'NOT VALIDATED' END status
FROM purchase_order2 po
WHERE po.po_id = 2000;

STATUS
-------------
NOT VALIDATED
```

Since the document has not been fully validated, you have your choice of calling the member function isSchemaValid( ) to check for validity without changing the document's status, or calling the member procedure schemaValidate( ) to check for validity and change the status. Here's an example of calling the isSchemaValid( ) function:

```
SELECT CASE WHEN 1 = po.purchase_order_doc.isSchemaValid( )
  THEN 'VALID'
```

```
    ELSE 'NOT VALID' END validity
FROM purchase_order2 po
WHERE po.po_id = 2000;

VALIDITY
---------
VALID
```

Finally, here's an example of calling the member procedure schemaValidate( ):

```
DECLARE
  doc XMLTYPE;
BEGIN
  SELECT po.purchase_order_doc
  INTO doc
  FROM purchase_order2 po
  WHERE po.po_id = 2000;

  doc.schemaValidate( );
END;
```

Remember, isSchemaValid( ) returns the status without changing it, whereas schemaValidate( ) potentially changes the status without returning it.

Updating document content

If you want to modify the contents of an XML document, you will need to replace the XMLType instance stored in the table with another instance. If you would like to replace the entire document, you can simply generate a new XMLType instance and replace the existing one:

```
UPDATE purchase_order po
SET po.purchase_order_doc =
  XMLTYPE(BFILENAME('XML_DATA', 'other_purch_ord.xml'),
    nls_charset_id('WE8MSWIN1252'))
WHERE po.po_id = 2000;
```

However, if your intent is to modify the existing document, you can do so using the member function updateXML( ), which uses a find/replace mechanism to alter the document content and returns an XMLType instance. To specify the content to be replaced, you need to specify an XPath expression. For example, the following UPDATE statement replaces the value of the customer_name node with "Wallace Industries":

```
SELECT extract(po.purchase_order_doc,
       '/purchase_order/customer_name') xml_fragment
FROM purchase_order po
WHERE po_id = 1000;

XML_FRAGMENT
------------------------------------------------
<customer_name>Alpha Technologies</customer_name>
```

```
UPDATE purchase_order po
SET po.purchase_order_doc =
  updateXML(po.purchase_order_doc,
    '/purchase_order/customer_name/text()', 'Wallace Industries')
WHERE po.po_id = 1000;

SELECT extract(po.purchase_order_doc,
      '/purchase_order/customer_name') xml_fragment
FROM purchase_order po
WHERE po_id = 1000;

XML_FRAGMENT
---------------------------------------------------
<customer_name>Wallace Industries</customer_name>
```

The XPath expression used to update the customer name in this example includes a call to the text( ) function, which causes the value of the text node to be returned instead of the entire node. Thus, an XPATH expression of /purchase_order/customer_name resolves to the XML fragment <customer_name>Alpha Technologies</customer_name>, whereas the XPATH expression /purchase_order/customer_name/text( ) resolves to the string "Alpha Technologies". You can accomplish the same text substitution without the use of the text( ) function, but your third parameter to the updateXML( ) function would need to be an XML fragment rather than a string:

```
UPDATE purchase_order po
SET po.purchase_order_doc =
  updateXML(po.purchase_order_doc,
    '/purchase_order/customer_name',
    XMLTYPE('<customer_name>Wallace Industries</customer_name>'))
WHERE po.po_id = 1000;
```

If you need to make multiple changes to your document, you can specify multiple find/replace pairs, as in the following example:

```
UPDATE purchase_order po
SET po.purchase_order_doc =
  updateXML(po.purchase_order_doc,
    '/purchase_order/customer_name/text()', 'Wallace Industries',
    '/purchase_order/po_number/text()', '11359')
WHERE po.po_id = 1000;
```

Along with replacing individual text attributes, you can also use updateXML( ) to replace an item in a collection. To do so, you can use one of the XMLType constructors to generate an XML fragment and then substitute the fragment into the document. For example, the following example replaces the entire second line item of the purchase order:

```
SELECT extract(po.purchase_order_doc,
      '/purchase_order//item') xml_fragment
FROM purchase_order po
WHERE po.po_id = 1000;
```

```
XML_FRAGMENT
-----------------------------------------
<item>
  <part_number>AI5-4557</part_number>
  <quantity>20</quantity>
</item>
<item>
  <part_number>EI-T5-001</part_number>
  <quantity>12</quantity>
</item>

UPDATE purchase_order po
SET po.purchase_order_doc =
  updateXML(po.purchase_order_doc,
    '/purchase_order/po_items/item[2]',
    XMLTYPE('<item>
              <part_number>TZ50828</part_number>
              <quantity>12</quantity>
            </item>'))
WHERE po.po_id = 1000;

SELECT extract(po.purchase_order_doc,
       '/purchase_order//item') xml_fragment
FROM purchase_order po
WHERE po.po_id = 1000;

XML_FRAGMENT
-----------------------------------------
<item>
  <part_number>AI5-4557</part_number>
  <quantity>20</quantity>
</item>
<item>
  <part_number>TZ50828</part_number>
  <quantity>12</quantity>
</item>
```

Generating XML Documents

The first sections of this chapter focused on how to store, inspect, validate, and modify an XML document. While this is all well and good if someone has provided you with an XML document, what should you do if you need to construct an XML document from data in your database? For this purpose, Oracle has included a set of built-in SQL functions that conform to the emerging SQL/XML standard. After describing the functions individually, we will demonstrate how these functions can be used to generate a purchase order document from the data stored in the customer, cust_order, and line_item tables.

XMLElement( )

The `XMLElement( )` function is tasked with generating XML elements. It takes as arguments an element name, a value, and an optional set of attributes. The following example generates an XML fragment consisting of data from the supplier table:

```
SELECT XMLElement("supplier_id", s.supplier_id) ||
  XMLElement("name", s.name) xml_fragment
FROM supplier s;

XML_FRAGMENT
------------------------------------------------------------
<supplier_id>1</supplier_id><name>Acme Industries</name>
<supplier_id>2</supplier_id><name>Tilton Enterprises</name>
<supplier_id>3</supplier_id><name>Eastern Importers</name>
```

Calls to `XMLElement( )` can be nested to facilitate parent/child elements. The next example builds on the previous example by wrapping the two supplier elements in a parent element called `<supplier>`:

```
SELECT XMLElement("supplier",
  XMLElement("supplier_id", s.supplier_id) || XMLElement("name", s.name)
  ) xml_fragment
FROM supplier s;

XML_FRAGMENT
---------------------------------------------------------------------------
<supplier>
  <supplier_id>1</supplier_id><name>Acme Industries</name>
</supplier>
<supplier>
  <supplier_id>2</supplier_id><name>Tilton Enterprises</name>
</supplier>
<supplier>
  <supplier_id>3</supplier_id><name>Eastern Importers</name>
</supplier>
```

Please note that the three rows of output from the previous example would normally print as three lines; we have taken the liberty of adding line feeds and tabs for readability and will do so for the rest of the examples.

XMLAgg( )

The `XMLAgg( )` function groups together sets of elements so that they can all be children to the same parent. This function is useful for working with collections or for wrapping a set of elements under a parent element. The next example builds on the previous example by wrapping the supplier elements in a root element called `<supplier_list>`:

```
SELECT XMLElement("supplier_list",
  XMLAgg(XMLElement("supplier",
    XMLElement("supplier_id", s.supplier_id) || XMLElement("name", s.name)
```

```
    ))) xml_document
FROM supplier s;

XML_DOCUMENT
----------------------------------------------------------------------------
<supplier_list>
  <supplier>
    <supplier_id>1</supplier_id><name>Acme Industries</name>
  </supplier>
  <supplier>
    <supplier_id>2</supplier_id><name>Tilton Enterprises</name>
  </supplier>
  <supplier>
    <supplier_id>3</supplier_id><name>Eastern Importers</name>
  </supplier>
</supplier_list>
```

To spice things up a bit, the next example adds the part table to the FROM clause and adds a list of parts supplied by each supplier:

```
SELECT XMLElement("supplier_list",
  XMLAgg(XMLElement("supplier",
    XMLElement("supplier_id", s.supplier_id) || XMLElement("name", s.name)
      || XMLElement("part_list", XMLAgg(XMLElement("part",
         XMLElement("part_nbr", p.part_nbr) || XMLElement("name", p.name))))
  ))) xml_document
FROM supplier s INNER JOIN part p
  ON s.supplier_id = p.supplier_id
GROUP BY s.supplier_id, s.name;

XML_DOCUMENT
-----------------------------------------------------------------
<supplier_list>
  <supplier>
    <supplier_id>1</supplier_id><name>Acme Industries</name>
    <part_list>
      <part><part_nbr>AI5-4557</part_nbr><name>Acme Part AI5-4557</name></part>
    </part_list>
  </supplier>
  <supplier>
    <supplier_id>2</supplier_id><name>Tilton Enterprises</name>
    <part_list>
      <part><part_nbr>TZ50828</part_nbr><name>Tilton Part TZ50828</name><part>
    </part_list>
  </supplier>
  <supplier>
    <supplier_id>3</supplier_id><name>Eastern Importers</name>
    <part_list>
      <part><part_nbr>EI-T5-001</part_nbr><name>Eastern Part EI-T5-001</name></part>
    </part_list>
  </supplier>
</supplier_list>
```

XMLForest( )

The previous examples in this section have used concatenation (||) to append sibling elements together. The XMLForest( ) function takes a list of values, generates elements for each one, and concatenates them together for you:

```
SELECT XMLElement("supplier",
  XMLForest(s.supplier_id, s.name)
  ) xml_fragment
FROM supplier s;

XML_FRAGMENT
-------------------------------------------------------------------------
<supplier>
  <SUPPLIER_ID>1</SUPPLIER_ID><NAME>Acme Industries</NAME>
</supplier>
<supplier>
  <SUPPLIER_ID>2</SUPPLIER_ID><NAME>Tilton Enterprises</NAME>
</supplier>
<supplier>
  <SUPPLIER_ID>3</SUPPLIER_ID><NAME>Eastern Importers</NAME>
</supplier>
```

If you want to specify your own element names, you can optionally use the AS clause, as demonstrated by the following:

```
SELECT XMLElement("supplier",
  XMLForest(s.supplier_id AS "sup_id", s.name AS "sup_name")
  ) xml_fragment
FROM supplier s;

XML_FRAGMENT
-------------------------------------------------------------------------
<supplier>
  <sup_id>1</sup_id><sup_name>Acme Industries</sup_name>
</supplier>
<supplier>
  <sup_id>2</sup_id><sup_name>Tilton Enterprises</sup_name>
</supplier>
<supplier>
  <sup_id>3</sup_id><sup_name>Eastern Importers</sup_name>
</supplier>
```

Putting It All Together

Earlier in the chapter, you saw how data from the purchase order document could be extracted and stored in various tables. Using the three built-in SQL functions described above, we will demonstrate how to recreate the XML document from the purchase_order, cust_order, line_item, and customer tables. We'll start by generating the root element and basic purchase order data from the purchase_order, cust_order, and customer tables:

```
SELECT XMLElement("purchase_order",
  XMLForest(c.name AS "customer_name",
    po.customer_po_nbr AS "po_number",
    TO_CHAR(po.customer_inception_date, 'YYYY-MM-DD')
      AS "po_date")
) purchase_order
FROM purchase_order po INNER JOIN cust_order co
  ON po.order_nbr = co.order_nbr
  INNER JOIN customer c ON co.cust_nbr = c.cust_nbr
WHERE po.po_id = 1000;

PURCHASE_ORDER
---------------------------------------------------------------------
<purchase_order>
  <customer_name>Alpha Technologies</customer_name>
  <po_number>11257</po_number>
  <po_date>2004-01-20</po_date>
</purchase_order>
```

Next, we will aggregate the line item data from the line_item table:

```
SELECT XMLElement("purchase_order",
  XMLForest(c.name AS "customer_name",
    po.customer_po_nbr AS "po_number",
    TO_CHAR(po.customer_inception_date, 'YYYY-MM-DD') AS "po_date",
    XMLAgg(XMLElement("item",
      XMLForest(li.part_nbr AS "part_number", li.qty AS "quantity")))
      AS "po_items")
) purchase_order
FROM purchase_order po INNER JOIN cust_order co
  ON po.order_nbr = co.order_nbr
  INNER JOIN customer c ON co.cust_nbr = c.cust_nbr
  INNER JOIN line_item li ON co.order_nbr = li.order_nbr
WHERE po.po_id = 1000
GROUP BY po.customer_po_nbr, po.customer_inception_date, c.name;

PURCHASE_ORDER
---------------------------------------------------------------------
<purchase_order>
  <customer_name>Alpha Technologies</customer_name>
  <po_number>11257</po_number>
  <po_date>2004-01-20</po_date>
  <po_items>
    <item>
      <part_number>AI5-4557</part_number>
      <quantity>20</quantity>
    </item>
    <item>
```

```
        <part_number>EI-T5-001</part_number>
        <quantity>12</quantity>
      </item>
    </po_items>
  </purchase_order>
```

Hopefully, this looks familiar. Although the output is satisfactory, we find the number of joins and the GROUP BY clause to be a bit excessive, so the next version of the query uses subqueries to retrieve the customer name and line items:

```
SELECT XMLElement("purchase_order",
  XMLForest((SELECT c.name
    FROM customer c INNER JOIN cust_order co ON c.cust_nbr = co.cust_nbr
    WHERE co.order_nbr = po.order_nbr) AS "customer_name",
    po.customer_po_nbr AS "po_number",
    TO_CHAR(po.customer_inception_date, 'YYYY-MM-DD') AS "po_date",
    (SELECT XMLAgg(XMLElement("item",
      XMLForest(li.part_nbr AS "part_number", li.qty AS "quantity")))
     FROM line_item li
     WHERE li.order_nbr = po.order_nbr) AS "po_items")
) purchase_order
FROM purchase_order po
WHERE po.po_id = 1000;

PURCHASE_ORDER
-------------------------------------------------------------------------
<purchase_order>
  <customer_name>Alpha Technologies</customer_name>
  <po_number>11257</po_number>
  <po_date>2004-01-20</po_date>
  <po_items>
    <item>
      <part_number>AI5-4557</part_number>
      <quantity>20</quantity>
    </item>
    <item>
      <part_number>EI-T5-001</part_number>
      <quantity>12</quantity>
    </item>
  </po_items>
</purchase_order>
```

Summary

This chapter has covered quite a bit of ground as far as how SQL and XML interact, including the storage, validation, modification, and generation of XML documents, yet it has barely scratched the surface as far as XML is concerned. There is much more to XML than has been demonstrated here, and far more to XML Schema than was utilized in the schema definition for the purchase order documents. Additionally, there are a large number of related technologies, such as Document Object Model (DOM) and Extensible Stylesheet Language Transformations (XSLT), that have not been covered in this chapter, but which are available in Oracle XML DB. It is impossible to cover all of this territory in a single chapter, so we urge you to utilize the resources mentioned earlier in the chapter if you are new to XML.

CHAPTER 17

Regular Expressions

One of the most exciting SQL features in Oracle Database 10*g* is support for regular expressions. Open source databases such as MySQL and PostgreSQL have supported regular expressions for years. Frankly, we were tired of having that thrown in our faces, of feeling one-upped by the open source competition. In the Oracle Database 10*g* release, Oracle has implemented regular expression support with a vengeance. We were surprised and delighted at what we found. You will be, too.

Elementary Regular Expression Syntax

Regular expressions provide a syntax to describe patterns in text. Being able to describe a passage of text gives you power, the power to manipulate that text in ways that would otherwise be impossible. For example, regular expressions enable you to easily perform an operation such as the following:

> Find all apparent phone numbers in a free-text, comment column, and reformat those numbers, at least the U.S. and Canadian numbers, so that all appear in the form: (999) 999-9999.

By the end of this chapter, we'll have shown you exactly how to implement this directive. For now, we want to familiarize you with some elementary regular expression syntax.

Matching a Single Character

The most basic regular expression metacharacter is probably the period (.). Use it to match any single character, except for the newline (usually chr(10)). For example, assume that users of our book's example database have taken to entering employee address and phone number information into a free-form text column. Further suppose that you need to identify and extract the phone numbers from that column. All employees are in the States, so you can use the pattern ...-.... to search for the common phone number pattern of three digits, a hyphen, and four digits:

```
SELECT emp_id, text
FROM employee_comment
WHERE REGEXP_LIKE(text,'...-....');

    EMP_ID TEXT
---------- ------------------------------------------------------------
      7369 126 Varnum, Edmore MI 48829, 989 313-5351
      7499 1105 McConnell Court
           Cedar Lake MI 48812
           Home: 989-387-4321
           Cell: (237) 438-3333
      7521 Her address is: 12646 Bramell. Her city and state are Vestab
           urg, MI 48891
           Home phone is 387-1698
 ...
      7900 Cares for 100-year-old aunt during the day. Schedule only fo
           r evening and night shifts.
 ...
```

REGEXP_LIKE is the regular expression equivalent to the LIKE predicate. You'll notice that it looks like a function, and if you prefer to think of it that way, that's fine, because in PL/SQL, REGEXP_LIKE is, in fact, a function, a Boolean function. However, in SQL, Oracle refers to REGEXP_LIKE as a predicate.

Whatever you choose to call it, REGEXP_LIKE searches the target string to see whether it contains an occurrence of the pattern you specify. In our example, the predicate searches the text column for the phone number pattern, and evaluates to TRUE whenever that pattern is found.

As you can see from our query's output, our users have taken the words "free-form" to heart. Phone numbers have been entered using a variety of formats. The expression used in our query doesn't catch every phone number. It also matches at least one string that is not a phone number: "100-year-old" in the comment for #7900. We'll refine the expression as we present more of Oracle's regular expression syntax.

 Before running the examples in this chapter, we used the following SQL*Plus formatting commands: SET RECSEP OFF, COLUMN text FORMAT A60.

When using regular expressions in Oracle, you aren't limited to detecting occurrences of a pattern. After all, once you've determined that a string contains text matching a pattern, you're likely to want to do something with that text. For that Oracle provides the REGEXP_SUBSTR function. REGEXP_SUBSTR extracts text matching a regular expression:

```
SELECT emp_id, REGEXP_SUBSTR(text,'...-....') text
FROM employee_comment
WHERE REGEXP_LIKE(text,'...-....');
```

```
EMP_ID TEXT
---------- ---------------
      7369 313-5351
      7499 989-387-
      7521 387-1698
```

Hmm… What's up with 989-387-? We didn't ask for a trailing hyphen, or did we? In a way, we did. Our pattern used a period (.) to ask for any four characters following a hyphen, and a hyphen is itself a character. The string 989-387- comes from the combined area code and phone number 989-387-4321. Keep reading! We'll show you how to fix this.

Fuzziness

Fuzziness is a term some of us use to describe the fact that using regular expressions to identify data in free-form text is not an exact science. When you query the employee table, and you select values from the dept_id column, you can be certain of getting department ID numbers. After all, those are what the column is defined as holding, and you have database constraints and application logic to ensure that the column holds only the sort of values it is supposed to hold.

When using regular expressions to extract data elements from free-form text, you always run the risk of getting back something other than what you are looking for. Search for phone numbers using a pattern such as ...-...., and you might find a string such as '210-acre' instead. No matter how well you constrain your search pattern, you can never be certain that text matching your pattern has the meaning you expect.

Matching Any of a Set of Characters

Phone numbers are not made up of any characters; they are, well, numbers. Our previous regular expression is a bit too broad in this respect, as it allows for hyphens and other characters where we want to see only digits. Not to worry! There is a solution. You can use square-brackets to define a *matching-list* consisting of only the digits 0 through 9. The pattern [0123456789] will match any of the digits, 0 through 9, given in the list. Using this pattern, you can write a phone number expression that more narrowly focuses in on phone numbers:

```
[0123456789][0123456789][0123456789]-[0123456789][0123456789][0123456789][0123456789]
```

This pattern is rather awful though, in that it repeats the digits from 0 through 9 seven times. It's a good thing we aren't looking for area codes too. Maybe we *should* look for area codes, but for now we'll just tell you that you can use a hyphen within square-brackets as a short-hand for enumerating each character in a range. Rather than write [0123456789], you can use the much simpler [0-9] to represent the same set of values. You can now shorten the phone number expression to:

```
[0-9][0-9][0-9]-[0-9][0-9][0-9][0-9]
```

The following query shows the change in results from using this more refined expression:

```
SELECT emp_id,
    REGEXP_SUBSTR(text,'[0-9][0-9][0-9]-[0-9][0-9][0-9][0-9]') text
FROM employee_comment
WHERE REGEXP_LIKE(text,'[0-9][0-9][0-9]-[0-9][0-9][0-9][0-9]');

    EMP_ID TEXT
---------- -------------
      7369 313-5351
      7499 387-4321
      7521 387-1698
```

This query is much better. Notice 387-4321 in the second row of output. This is the correct phone number that was misrepresented as 989-387- by our query at the end of the preceding section.

You're not limited to specifying a single range within square-brackets. You can specify any combination of ranges and single characters. For example, you can generate the same matching set as from [0-9] using the following expression:

[01-3456-9]

The matching set in this expression is composed of:

- The single digit 0
- The range of digits from 1 through 3
- The single digits 4 and 5
- The range of digits 6 through 9

Be aware that, under the default NLS_SORT=BINARY setting, any ranges you specify depend on the underlying character set encoding. It so happens that most, if not all, ASCII- and Unicode-based encodings map the digits 0 through 9 to contiguous code points. However, you can run into problems in this area. For example, the range [A-Z] encompasses all the uppercase Latin characters used in American English, but that range does not encompass other uppercase Latin characters, such as the Croatian alphabet's *LJ*. You'll also find that, while the letters A–Z are contiguous in ASCII, they are *not* contiguous in EBCDIC (an encoding with roots in IBM operating systems). In EBCDIC, you'll find that the range [A-Z] encompasses not only the letters A through Z, but also the closing curly-brace (}), the backslash (\), and some unassigned code points.

In addition to defining a range, you can negate a matching set. Do this by writing a caret (^) as the first character following the opening square-bracket. For example, use the expression [^0-9] to match all characters but the digits 0 through 9. Use [^a-zA-Z] to match characters other than the 26 letters used in American English.

Within square-brackets, the hyphen (-), caret (^), and other characters take on a special meaning. Table 17-1 tells you a bit more about working with these characters.

Table 17-1. Characters with special meaning inside square brackets

Character	Usage and example
^	Negates a matching set. To include the actual ^ character in a set, place it in any position but the first. For example: [0-9^] includes the digits 0 through 9, plus the caret character.
-	Separates the first and last characters in a range. To include the hyphen as itself, use it in either the first or last position, where it can't possibly define a range. For example: [-0-9] and [0-9-] both include the digits 0–9 along with the hyphen. In a negation situation you can write the hyphen immediately following the caret. The expression [^-0-9] excludes the digits 0 through 9, as well as excluding the hyphen.
[	Within a square-bracket expression, an opening square-bracket simply represents itself. For example, [[0-9] includes the digits 0 through 9 as well as the [character.
]	Closes a matching set. To include] in a set, specify it as the first character following the opening square-bracket (e.g., []0-9]). When negating a set, you can specify] immediately following the caret, as in: [^]0-9].

Bracket expressions seem simple at first, but can get a bit tricky to write because of the special characters described in Table 17-1. The treatment of those characters may seem arbitrary at first, but there is a logic that will begin to sink in as you gain more experience writing regular expressions.

> In addition to the characters described in Table 17-1, the sequences [:. : :], [. .], and [= =] also have special meaning. We describe these in "Advanced Regular Expression Syntax."

REGEXP_LIKE Versus LIKE

There's a subtle difference in operation between REGEXP_LIKE and LIKE. The difference lies in whether the pattern you supply must match the entire target string. LIKE evaluates to TRUE only when a pattern matches the entire target string. Thus, to find strings containing a phone number using LIKE, you need to write a pattern such as '%___-____%'. The percent signs (%) on either end allow for other text on either side of the phone number.

REGEXP_LIKE is different from LIKE in this regard. REGEXP_LIKE evaluates to true whenever a pattern is found anywhere *within* a string. That's why you can use an expression like '...-....' to detect phone numbers without worrying about text that might precede or follow those numbers.

This subtle difference in operation between the two predicates is something you'll want to take into account should you ever translate a pattern from LIKE's syntax to the regular expression syntax used with REGEXP_LIKE.

Matching Repeating Sequences

The period (.) matches a single character in a target string. So does a bracket expression, which is why we had to repeat [0-9] three times, and then again four times, in our phone number expression. Wouldn't it be nice to more easily define elements of an expression that repeat? Sure it would, and to that end you have what are termed quantifiers. A *quantifier* is a special character, or sequence of characters that specify a valid range of occurrences for the immediately preceding element.

Getting back to our phone number example, rather than repeat each element in the phone number expression:

```
[0-9][0-9][0-9]-[0-9][0-9][0-9][0-9]
```

you can specify each element once followed by a quantifier giving the repeat count:

```
[0-9]{3}-[0-9]{4}
```

The first element, in this case, is the bracket expression [0-9]. The quantifier for the first element is {3}, which means that we want three repetitions of [0-9]. Similarly, the quantifier {4} for the third element specifies four repetitions of a digit. The second element is the hyphen, for which we didn't specify a quantifier, so the default is to look for a single occurrence. Plugging this shorter and simpler expression into our query from the previous section gives the following, equivalent query:

```
SELECT emp_id,
    REGEXP_SUBSTR(text,'[0-9]{3}-[0-9]{4}') text
FROM employee_comment
WHERE REGEXP_LIKE(text,'[0-9]{3}-[0-9]{4}');
```

Oracle's regular expression syntax supports the quantifiers shown in Table 17-2.

Table 17-2. Regular expression quantifiers

Quantifier	Description
*	Specifies that an element may occur zero or more times. For example, . * is the regular expression equivalent to the LIKE predicate's % metacharacter.
+	Specifies that an element may occur one or more times.
?	Specifies that an element may occur zero or one times, but no more.
{n}	Specifies that an element must occur n times.
{n,}	Specifies than an element must occur at least n times, but may occur more than n times.
{n,m}	Specifies that an element must occur anywhere between n and m times, inclusive.
{0,m}	Is the same case really, as {n,m}, but this is a way to specify that an element occurs up to, but not more than, m times.

Defining Alternate Possibilities

Our users have not been at all consistent in how they've entered data into our free-form comment column. Some phone numbers have area codes. Some do not. And when it comes to separating digit groups, our users show no end of creativity. They've used hyphens, periods, and spaces as separators, have mixed those in a single phone number, and you'll even find a few area codes enclosed within parentheses. What's a SQL programmer to do?

Dealing with alternate possibilities is an area in which regular expressions really shine when compared to the rather lame LIKE predicate. Let's begin with the problem of area codes. Some phone numbers have them, and others do not. One way to handle this is to simply write an expression for each case, and join those two expressions with the vertical-bar (|) operator:

```
[0-9]{3}-[0-9]{3}-[0-9]{4}|[0-9]{3}-[0-9]{4}
```

This regular expression will find phone numbers in the following two forms: 999-999-9999 and 999-9999. The vertical bar defines an *alternation*, or a choice between two possibilities: one with an area code and one without.

Alternation appears to take care of the area code problem. Let's turn to the issue of separators. You could try to take care of the different separators by adding even more alternations, with a different expression to cover each permutation of separators:

```
[0-9]{3}-[0-9]{3}-[0-9]{4}|[0-9]{3}.[0-9]{3}.[0-9]{4}|[0-9]{3} [0-9]{3} [0-9]{4}|[0-9]{3}-[0-9]{3}.[0-9]{4}|[0-9]{3}.[0-9]{3}-[0-9]{4}|[0-9]{3} [0-9]{3}.[0-9]{4}|...
```

This gets messy fast. A combined area code and phone number contains two separator characters, and with three possible characters to choose from in each position, the number of permutations gets quickly out of hand. Since we're dealing with single characters, a better approach might be to define a matching set of valid separators:

```
[0-9]{3}[-. ][0-9]{3}[-. ][0-9]{4}|[0-9]{3}[-. ][0-9]{4}
```

This is much better. We're back to a single alternation between two patterns. The matching set [-.] matches any of the three separator characters that we are recognizing as valid.

 Because the hyphen (-) comes first in the matching set [-.], that hyphen is treated as a character in the set. On the other hand, in the matching set [0-9], the hyphen, because it is neither first nor last, is treated as a delimiter between the first (0) and last (9) characters in a range.

The following query shows the results of using this improved expression:

```
SELECT emp_id,
    REGEXP_SUBSTR(
        text,
        '[0-9]{3}[-. ][0-9]{3}[-. ][0-9]{4}|[0-9]{3}[-. ][0-9]{4}')
        text
FROM employee_comment
WHERE REGEXP_LIKE(
    text,
    '[0-9]{3}[-. ][0-9]{3}[-. ][0-9]{4}|[0-9]{3}[-. ][0-9]{4}');
```

```
EMP_ID TEXT
---------- -------------
      7369 989 313-5351
      7499 989-387-4321
      7521 387-1698
      7566 989.387.4444
      7654 231-898-9823
      7698 388-1234
      7844 989-387.5359
      7876 453-9999
```

Order matters with alternation. Consider the following two regular expressions:

[0-9]{3}-[0-9]{3}|[0-9]{3}-[0-9]{3}-[0-9]{4}

[0-9]{3}-[0-9]{3}-[0-9]{4}|[0-9]{3}-[0-9]{3}

Both of these expressions look for either a 999-999 or a 999-999-9999 pattern. The 999-999 is a purposeful deviation from our phone number pattern. The difference between the expressions lies solely in the order in which the alternation is written. Look at the difference in output:

```
SELECT REGEXP_SUBSTR(text,'[0-9]{3}-[0-9]{3}|[0-9]{3}-[0-9]{3}-[0-9]{4}')
FROM employee_comment
WHERE emp_id = 7499;

REGEXP_SUBSTR
-------------
989-387

SELECT REGEXP_SUBSTR(text,'[0-9]{3}-[0-9]{3}-[0-9]{4}|[0-9]{3}-[0-9]{3}')
FROM employee_comment
WHERE emp_id = 7499;

REGEXP_SUBSTR
-------------
989-387-4321
```

Why the difference in results? It's because Oracle's regular expression engine looks at the alternates in left-to-right order. For reference, here's an example showing the target text:

```
SELECT text
FROM employee_comment
WHERE emp_id = 7499;

TEXT
--------------------
1105 McConnell Court
Cedar Lake MI 48812
Home: 989-387-4321
Cell: (237) 438-3333
```

Both alternates begin to match at the same point in the target text. Whenever that happens, the regular expression engine looks at the alternates from left-to-right. If the left-most alternate matches, the regular expression engine is satisfied, and that match is returned from REGEXP_SUBSTR. When writing alternations, if you have any preference as to which alternation takes precedence, be sure to write that alternation first.

Subexpressions

We're not quite done with phone numbers yet. One last issue to deal with is that of phone numbers with area codes enclosed in parentheses, in the form: (999) 999-9999. Here's one way to think about this problem:

- A phone number might have an area code:
  — The area code might be enclosed within parentheses.
  — The area code might not be enclosed within parentheses.
- The phone number might not have an area code.

Essentially, what you have here is an alternation within an alternation. Working from the inside out, you can write the following expression to accommodate both area code possibilities:

```
[0-9]{3}|\([0-9]{3}\)
```

The left side of this expression looks for three digits. The right side looks for three digits enclosed within parentheses. Why the backslash (\) characters? Those are there because otherwise the parentheses are treated as special characters, enclosing a subexpression.

A *subexpression* is a portion of a longer expression that you wish to treat as a discrete unit. For example, you might wish to apply a quantifier to a subexpression. Indeed, that's a good way to indicate that area codes are optional:

```
([0-9]{3}|\([0-9]{3}\))?
```

The parentheses, the ones not preceded by \ characters, define a subexpression defining two alternate representations of an area code. The ? quantifier specifies that the preceding subexpression, the area code, occurs either once or not at all.

There's one more housekeeping detail to take care of before filling out the nonoptional portion of the phone number expression. If there's an optional area code, it will be followed by some sort of separator. That separator will be a space if the area code is enclosed by parentheses, or it will be one of either a hyphen, period, or space:

```
([0-9]{3}[-. ]|\([0-9]{3}\) )?
```

Now, all that remains is to add the seven-digit phone number pattern onto the end of the preceding expression:

```
([0-9]{3}[-. ]|\([0-9]{3}\) )?[0-9]{3}[-. ][0-9]{4}
```

The following query shows the results of this latest iteration of the phone number pattern:

```
SELECT emp_id, REGEXP_SUBSTR(text,
  '([0-9]{3}[-. ]|\([0-9]{3}\) )?[0-9]{3}[-. ][0-9]{4}')
  text
FROM employee_comment;
```

```
    EMP_ID TEXT
---------- ---------------
      7369 989 313-5351
      7499 989-387-4321
      7521 387-1698
      7566 989.387.4444
      7654 231-898-9823
      7698 (989) 388-1234
      7782
      7788
      7839
      7844 989-387.5359
      7876 (231) 453-9999
      7900
```

In addition to dealing with tricky alternations, subexpressions are also essential when working with backreferences, something you'll read more about later in the section "Advanced Regular Expression Syntax."

Anchoring an Expression

Two metacharacters allow you to anchor an expression to either the beginning or end, or both, of the target string. When you anchor an expression to the beginning of the target string, you are specifying that no other characters may precede the expression. Likewise, when you anchor an expression to the end of a string, you are specifying that no characters are allowed to follow the expression.

Use a caret (^) to anchor an expression to the beginning of a string. Use a dollar sign ($) to anchor an expression to the end of a string. Here's an example, using REGEXP_INSTR, to illustrate. The REGEXP_INSTR function returns the character position where a match for an expression is found:

```
SELECT REGEXP_INSTR('123','[0-9]') unanchored,
       REGEXP_INSTR('123','[0-9]$') anchored_end
FROM dual;
```

```
UNANCHORED ANCHORED_END
---------- ------------
         1            3
```

Notice the difference in character positions returned by the two function calls. The expression in the second function call used a $ to search for a digit at the end of the string, and that's exactly what the function found.

Regular Expressions and Index Usage

Many of our examples in this chapter use REGEXP_LIKE in the WHERE clause of a SELECT statement to search for patterns of text. You might rightfully wonder about index usage when executing such queries. When you apply REGEXP_LIKE to a column, you have the same issue that you have when you apply any other SQL function to a column: you preclude the use of any index defined on that column.

If you always search for the same pattern, you can create a function-based index to help you locate that pattern. However, if you always search for the same pattern, we'd argue that you should redesign your database to store your target data in discrete columns. For example, if you are constantly searching for phone number patterns, you should extract phone numbers once, and place them into their own column.

If you must create a function-based index, you won't be able to base it on REGEXP_LIKE, because that function returns a Boolean value. SQL, and by extension indexes, do not support Boolean values. You can, however, use one of the other regular expression functions:

```
CREATE INDEX phone_number
ON employee_comment (
    REGEXP_SUBSTR(text,'...-....'));
```

You can use this index to support queries such as:

```
SELECT *
FROM employee_comment
WHERE REGEXP_SUBSTR(text,'...-....') = '313-5351';
```

Again though, we would argue that regular expressions are best reserved for ad-hoc queries. If you issue the same regular expression query often enough to want to index for it, we think you should consider modifying your database design to enable querying the target data without resorting to regular expressions. More importantly, realize that you can do a lot with regular expressions outside of the WHERE clause, where indexes, or the lack thereof, aren't a factor.

 The ^ and $ are anchor characters only when used outside of a bracket expression.

You can combine the use of ^ and $ to write an expression encompassing the entire target string. The following example searches for comments containing only a phone number:

```
SELECT emp_id, REGEXP_SUBSTR(text,
  '^([0-9]{3}[-. ]|\([0-9]{3}\) )?[0-9]{3}[-. ][0-9]{4}$')
  text
FROM employee_comment
WHERE REGEXP_LIKE(text,
  '^([0-9]{3}[-. ]|\([0-9]{3}\) )?[0-9]{3}[-. ][0-9]{4}$');
```

```
EMP_ID TEXT
---------- -------------
     7844 989-387.5359
```

There's one thing to be careful of when using the anchoring characters. It's possible to write expressions that can't possibly match anything in the target text. For example, you could write $[0-9], which anchors the *beginning* of the expression to the *end* of the target string. You won't find any digits after the string ends, so this expression will always fail. Watch for this sort of thing, and be careful about where you place your anchoring metacharacters.

Understanding Greediness

Greediness is an important concept to understand when writing regular expressions. We don't mean greed of the Enron sort, but rather that each quantifier in a regular expression will always match as much text as possible. The results from this rule can sometimes be surprising.

For example, consider the following quotation:

> Brighten the corner where you are.

Think about the problem of extracting the first word from this text. Many would look at the text, see that a word is a series of letters followed by a space, and would immediately translate that thought to an expression like '.* ', which matches any number of characters followed by space. That seems logical, doesn't it? Yet look at the results:

```
SELECT REGEXP_SUBSTR('Brighten the corner where you are',
                     '.* ')
FROM dual;

REGEXP_SUBSTR('BRIGHTENTHECORN
-------------------------------
Brighten the corner where you
```

Is this the result you expected? If it is, then go to the head of the class and take a gold star, because you're already way ahead of us. If this result surprises you, then think about what we asked for:

> We asked for a series of characters, of any length, followed by a space.

Faced with this requirement, how would you satisfy it? It turns out there are three possible approaches you can take:

- You could stop at the first space.
- You could stop at the last space.
- You could stop at some arbitrary space somewhere in between the first and the last.

Computers are not good at being arbitrary, and no one wants them to be arbitrary either, so that last option is out. Here's how Oracle's regular expression engine conceptually matches the expression '.* ' with our example text:

1. The first element of the expression is a period, representing any character. The quantifier allows any number of occurrences, so the engine finds all the characters that it can, stopping only when it reaches the letter e at the end of the string. At this point, the engine has matched the entire string: "Brighten the corner where you are".

2. The expression calls for a space. An e is not a space, so the engine backs up one character to the r.

3. An r is not a space, so the engine backs up another character to the a.

4. An a is not a space, so the engine backs up again, finds the space following "you", and returns "Brighten the corner where you", including the trailing-space, as the result from REGEXP_SUBSTR.

The key point to take away from this section is that the regular expression engine doesn't look at a pattern quite the same way you might. When you mentally apply the pattern '.* ' to a string, your tendency is probably going to be to stop the moment you have a match. You can do that easily, because your brain is a much better pattern-matching engine than a computer. You see the pattern as a whole, and you'll tend to gravitate toward the interpretation that you had in mind when you wrote the expression. Regular expression engines look at patterns and strings a character at a time, moving back and forth, finding the longest match for each regular expression element.

Advanced Function Options

By now we've introduced you to all but one of Oracle's regular expression functions. However, you've only seen them used in their simplest form. Their full syntax is:

```
REGEXP_INSTR(source_string, expression
            [, position [, occurrence
            [, return_option
            [, match_parameter]]]])

REGEXP_LIKE (source_string, expression
            [, match_parameter])

REGEXP_REPLACE(source_string, expression
            [, replace_string
            [, position [, occurrence
            [, match_parameter]]]])

REGEXP_SUBSTR(source_string, expression
            [, position [, occurrence
            [, match_parameter]]])
```

Matching a Single Word

In the section "Understanding Greediness," we used the expression '.* ' to match a word in a string. That expression actually matches more than just a word. It matches a word followed by a space, and it won't find the single word in the string 'Brighten', because there is no trailing space at the end of the string.

Although it worked well to illustrate greediness, the pattern '.* ' isn't at all the best way to define a word. For one thing, you don't want to define a word in terms of what it isn't (that trailing space), but rather in terms of what it is. Perhaps a better way to look at a word is as a sequence of non-space characters. You can use negation inside a bracket expression to accomplish that:

```
SELECT REGEXP_SUBSTR(
    'Brighten the corner where you are', '[^ ]*')
FROM dual;

REGEXP_S
--------
Brighten
```

However, non-space characters include punctuation as well, so you might want to narrow things down even more, by insisting that your word contain only alphabetic characters:

```
SELECT REGEXP_SUBSTR(
    'Brighten the corner where you are',
    '[A-Za-z]*')
FROM dual;
```

Depending on your application, you might or might not wish to allow for the possibility that a word might contain digits. A password, for example, might look like My8Secret. And then you have hyphenated words to think about. Is area-code one word or two? Sometimes the problem is not so much writing the expression as it is defining the thing you want that expression to match.

If you're familiar with Oracle's string-manipulation functions, you'll have no trouble discerning the purpose of the REGEXP functions:

REGEXP_INSTR
> Returns the character position at which text can be found matching a regular expression in a target string.

REGEXP_LIKE
> Discerns whether a given string contains text matching an expression. This is a Boolean function, returning TRUE or FALSE, or NULL.

REGEXP_REPLACE

Performs a regular expression search-and-replace operation, which you'll learn about in the section "Advanced Regular Expression Syntax."

REGEXP_SUBSTR

Extracts text matching a regular expression from a string.

The parameters to these functions are as follows:

source_string

The string to be searched.

expression

A regular expression describing the pattern of text that you seek.

replace_string

A string generating the replacement text to be used in a search-and-replace operation.

position

The character position within *source_string* at which to begin a search. This defaults to 1.

occurrence

The occurrence of the pattern you wish to locate. This defaults to 1, giving you the first possible match.

return_option

Valid only for REGEXP_INSTR, and determines whether the beginning or ending character position is returned for text matching a pattern. The default is 0, for the beginning. Use 1 to return the ending position.

match_parameter

A text string through which you may specify options to vary the behavior of the regular expression matching engine.

The `match_parameter` deserves a bit of explanation. It's a character string that you build using one or more of the following letters: i, c, n, m. One use is to specify whether matching is case-sensitive. By default, your NLS_SORT setting drives this aspect of regular expression behavior. You can override that default on a call-by-call basis, using i to get case-insensitive matching, and c to get case-sensitive matching. Following is a simple demonstration that works with our example data set. When the i option is used, the match succeeds, even though the case really does not match:

```
SELECT emp_id, text
FROM employee_comment
WHERE REGEXP_LIKE(text, 'CEDAR LAKE', 'c');

no rows selected

SELECT emp_id, text
FROM employee_comment
WHERE REGEXP_LIKE(text, 'CEDAR LAKE', 'i');
```

```
          EMP_ID TEXT
          ---------- --------------------------------------------------
            7499 1105 McConnell Court
                 Cedar Lake MI 48812
                 Home: (989) 387-4321
                 Cell: (237) 438-3333
            7782 Academy Apartments, #138, Cedar Lake MI 48812
            7788 #1 Water Tower Lane
                 Cedar Lake MI 48812
```

The n option is useful when working with data, such as ours, that contains embedded newline (usually chr(10)) characters. By default, the period (.) does not match newlines, which is why the following query brings back only the first line of comment text:

```
SELECT emp_id, REGEXP_SUBSTR(text, '.*') text
FROM employee_comment
WHERE emp_id = 7698;
```

```
          EMP_ID TEXT
          ---------- ----------------
            7698 Marion Blake
```

Using 'n' for the match parameter, you can have the period match newlines, which in the case of this query, results in the entire comment being returned:

```
SELECT emp_id, REGEXP_SUBSTR(text, '.*', 1, 1, 'n') text
FROM employee_comment
WHERE emp_id = 7698;
```

```
          EMP_ID TEXT
          ---------- ----------------------
            7698 Marion Blake
                 N1375 Lakeshore Drive
                 Vestaburg MI 48891
                 (989) 388-1234
```

This example also illustrates the important point that specifying a match parameter forces you to also specify any preceding, optional parameters that you would otherwise skip.

The final match option is m, which changes the definition of *line* with respect to the ^ and $ metacharacters. By default, line means *the entire target string*, so an expression such as ^.*$, together with the n option, will bring back all characters in the target string:

```
SELECT emp_id, REGEXP_SUBSTR(text, '^.*$', 1, 1, 'n') text
FROM employee_comment
WHERE emp_id = 7788;
```

```
          EMP_ID TEXT
          ---------- --------------------
            7788 #1 Water Tower Lane
                 Cedar Lake MI 48812
```

The n option is necessary here, because otherwise the period would not match the newline. If the period did not match the newline, the expression would fail to match at that point, and it would be impossible to match all characters between the beginning and end of the string.

However, using the m option causes the definition of line to change from *the entire target string*, to *any line within that string*, where lines are delimited by newline characters. The following example removes n, replacing it with m:

```
SELECT emp_id, REGEXP_SUBSTR(text, '^.*$', 1, 1, 'm') text
FROM employee_comment
WHERE emp_id = 7788;

    EMP_ID TEXT
---------- --------------------
      7788 #1 Water Tower Lane
```

You can specify multiple match parameters in any order. For example, 'in' means the same as 'ni'. If you specify conflicting options, such as 'ic', the last option, 'c' in this case, is the one that takes precedence.

 Try our last example in this section using 'mn' as the match parameter string. You'll get back the entire target string. Why? Because of the greediness rule. When 'mn' is used, the first line is a match, but the entire string is a longer match.

Advanced Regular Expression Syntax

As you delve more deeply into using regular expressions, and especially if you work with multilingual data, there are some advanced aspects to regular expressions that you'll find helpful.

Using Backreferences

You've already learned about subexpressions. A *backreference* is a way that you can reference the *value* of text matching a preceding subexpression. Think about the problem of searching specifically for 10-digit phone numbers that are inconsistent in their use of separator characters:

```
906.387-5359
989 313-5351
```

Each of these numbers uses a separator between the first two digit groups that differs from that used between the second two digit groups. What sort of expression would you write to detect this sort of mismatch? One with backreferences.

The key issue in the mismatched separator example we've just described is that to solve the problem, to identify phone-numbers with mismatched separators, you need the ability within an expression to refer to characters matched by earlier parts of that expression. In this case, you need the ability to refer to the first separator from the position of the second. Backreferences let you do this.

The following regular expression includes parentheses around the first bracket expression, which corresponds to the first separator. The parentheses define a subexpression:

```
[0-9]{3}([-. ])[0-9]{3}\1[0-9]{4}
```

The subexpression ([-.]) is the first subexpression, so you refer to it using the notation \1. Later in the expression, where you would otherwise expect to see a second occurrence of the bracket expression [-.], you see \1, which references the value *matched by* the first subexpression.

The words *matched by* are critical here. The backreference \1 is not equivalent to [-.]. Rather, the backreference is equivalent to that part of the text that is matched by [-.]. If the first separator is a hyphen, then \1 will be equivalent to a hyphen. A specific value for \1 won't be known until you execute a regular expression query, and even then it will change from row to row, as the regular expression is applied to one phone number after another.

The following query uses REGEXP_SUBSTR to extract the first phone number from the free-text, comment column. Only 10-digit phone numbers without parentheses around area codes are considered. That first phone number is then tested using NOT REGEXP_LIKE, to see whether both separators are the same.

```
SELECT emp_id, text
FROM employee_comment
WHERE NOT REGEXP_LIKE(
   REGEXP_SUBSTR(text, '[0-9]{3}[-. ][0-9]{3}[-. ][0-9]{4}'),
   '[0-9]{3}([-. ])[0-9]{3}\1[0-9]{4}');

    EMP_ID TEXT
---------- -------------------------------------------
      7369 126 Varnum, Edmore MI 48829, 989 313-5351
      7844 989-387.5359
```

If the separators in a given phone number differ, then REGEXP_LIKE returns FALSE, causing NOT REGEXP_LIKE to return TRUE, with the result that the row containing the phone number is included in the result set.

 If you try using WHERE NOT REGEXP_LIKE(text, '[0-9]{3}([-.])[0-9]{3}\1[0-9]{4}'), you'll find many comments without phone numbers in that format. However, not all of those comments will contain phone numbers with mismatched separators.

Oracle allows you up to nine backreferences, numbered \1 through \9. These refer to the first up-to-nine subexpressions, counting from left to right.

Backreferences are particularly important in performing regular expression search-and-replace operations. In fact, most of our own backreference usage falls into this category.

Remember all those phone number searches from our earlier examples in this chapter? Remember how creative our users were when it came to formatting phone numbers? Imagine for a moment that you want to unify the phone number format across all those free-form text entries. You want all phone numbers to be in the form 999-9999, with a hyphen separating digit groups. If there's an area code, you want that in parentheses, in the form (999) 999-9999. This is a hard problem, or it would be, if you had to write PL/SQL to solve it. Using regular expressions, it's not such a hard problem at all. You can solve it with one UPDATE statement using a nested call to Oracle's REGEXP_REPLACE function.

Begin by resurrecting the seven-digit portion of the phone number expression from our earlier section on "Subexpressions":

```
[0-9]{3}[-. ][0-9]{4}
```

Enclose the pattern for each digit group within parentheses, making two subexpressions:

```
([0-9]{3})[-. ]([0-9]{4})
```

You can now reference the first three digits as \1, and the last four digits as \2. What's more, you can use these two backreferences in the replacement text that you provide to REGEXP_REPLACE:

```
SELECT emp_id, REGEXP_REPLACE(
    text, '([0-9]{3})[-. ]([0-9]{4})', '\1-\2') text
FROM employee_comment;

    EMP_ID TEXT
---------- ------------------------------------------
      7369 126 Varnum, Edmore MI 48829, 989 313-5351
      7499 90 McConnell Court
           Cedar Lake MI 48812
           Home: 989-387-4321
           Cell: (237) 438-3333
...
```

The REGEXP_REPLACE function call in this statement finds each occurrence of the pattern matched by the second parameter, and replaces it with text from the third parameter. The backreferences are what make this operation truly exciting. Using backreferences, you can reference the text to be replaced from your replacement string, giving you great power to move and reformat text.

You're not done though. Now it's time to worry about that area code. Following is the area code pattern developed earlier in this chapter:

```
([0-9]{3}[-. ]|\([0-9]{3}\) )?
```

All the seven-digit phone numbers, whether following an area code or not, should fit the following pattern, which allows only a hyphen as a separator:

```
[0-9]{3}-[0-9]{4}
```

Put the two patterns together, and you have:

```
([0-9]{3}[-. ]|\([0-9]{3}\) )?[0-9]{3}-[0-9]{4}
```

For this particular replacement, you want to leave seven-digit phone numbers alone, because you've already fixed those. To this end, remove the ? to make the area code required:

```
([0-9]{3}[-. ]|\([0-9]{3}\) )[0-9]{3}-[0-9]{4}
```

Your next step is to put parentheses around each element of the phone number that you care about. There already are parentheses around the area code, but that subexpression also encompasses whatever separator character follows the area code. The following expression factors the separator out of the area code subexpression:

```
([0-9]{3}|\([0-9]{3}\))[-. ][0-9]{3}-[0-9]{4}
```

The semantics of this expression differ slightly from the previous. When the area code is enclosed in parentheses, this expression allows not only a space to follow, but also a period or a hyphen. We could work around this by approaching parenthetically enclosed area codes as a completely separate problem, to be solved using a separate UPDATE statement, but we've chosen to be flexible and loosen up our pattern just a bit to make our work easier. Sometimes you need to do that.

Next, put parentheses around the elements in the pattern that you wish to manipulate. The seven-digit phone number is ok as it is, so you can enclose that entire portion of the pattern, making it one subexpression:

```
([0-9]{3}|\([0-9]{3}\))[-. ]([0-9]{3}-[0-9]{4})
```

Dealing with the area code gets a bit tricky, and you'll see why in a moment. For now, look at the expression so far, and realize that \1 refers to the area code, and \2 to the remainder of the phone number. Following is a new SQL query that feeds the results of the earlier REGEXP_REPLACE function, the one to fix seven-digit numbers, into a second REGEXP_REPLACE call, this time to correctly format area codes:

```
SELECT emp_id,
   REGEXP_REPLACE(
      REGEXP_REPLACE(
         text, '([0-9]{3})[-. ]([0-9]{4})', '\1-\2'),
      '([0-9]{3}|\([0-9]{3}\))[-. ]([0-9]{3}-[0-9]{4})',
      '(\1) \2') text
FROM employee_comment;

   EMP_ID TEXT
---------- ------------------------------------------------
     7369 126 Varnum, Edmore MI 48829, (989) 313-5351
     7499 90 McConnell Court
          Cedar Lake MI 48812
```

```
Home: (989) 387-4321
Cell: ((237)) 438-3333
```
. . .

Finding an Anti-Pattern

Sometimes you need to find occurrences of text that match one pattern but not another. The problem of finding phone numbers with mismatched separators is an example of this requirement: first you need to find a phone number, and then you need to test it, to see whether it's properly formatted. Earlier, we showed a query that tested only the first phone number found in a comment. The following query illustrates a technique you can use to test *all* phone numbers in a comment:

```
SELECT emp_id, text
FROM employee_comment
WHERE REGEXP_LIKE(text,
  '[0-9]{3}[-. ][0-9]{3}[-. ][0-9]{4}')
AND REGEXP_LIKE(
  REGEXP_REPLACE(text,
    '[0-9]{3}([-. ])[0-9]{3}\1[0-9]{4}','***'),
  '[0-9]{3}[-. ][0-9]{3}[-. ][0-9]{4}');
```

The first REGEXP_LIKE identifies comments containing at least one occurrence of our phone number pattern, without regard to whether the separators match. The nested invocation of REGEXP_REPLACE then replaces all good phone numbers, those with matching separators, with a string of three asterisks. Any remaining phone number patterns found by the enclosing REGEXP_LIKE must, therefore, represent phone numbers with mismatched separators. In this way, you can find phone numbers with mismatched separators regardless of whether they come first in their respective comment field.

For more on this technique, which you can extend to similar problems, read Jonathan Gennick's article "Regular Expression Anti-Patterns" at *http://gennick.com/antiregex.htm*.

We realize this query is becoming difficult to follow. Please stick with us, and study this query until you understand it. Notice the output, in particular the cell-phone number, which now reads ((237)) 438-3333. Oops! Doubled parentheses are not at all what you wanted to see around an area code. What happened?

The reason you see doubled parentheses is because of what \1 refers to. If you carefully study the regular expression feeding into the outermost call to REGEXP_REPLACE, you'll see that the first subexpression *includes* any parentheses that may already be around an area code. The replacement text rebuilds the area code by using (\1) to enclose it within parentheses. Take an area code already within parentheses, enclose it again, and you end up with results such as ((237)).

We fell into the pit we've just described while writing this chapter. We're telling you the story now for a couple reasons. One, you wouldn't otherwise easily understand why we went with the solution we're about to show you. Two, we want you to know that the thought-process to a successful regular expression is rarely a straight line from problem to solution. You'll often go down a path only to encounter a problem, forcing you to backtrack a bit and try again. Indeed, we backtracked and changed course at least three times while developing this example. Don't be dissuaded if your first attempt at a regular expression solution doesn't quite have the effect you're after. Expect to do a certain amount of experimenting and testing whenever you write anything but the simplest of expressions.

The following expression is the key to resolving the doubled parentheses problem:

```
(([0-9]{3})|\(([0-9]{3})\)))[-. ]([0-9]{3}-[0-9]{4})
```

In this expression, we've made each of the two alternate area code possibilities into its own subexpression. Both those subexpressions are nested within a larger subexpression. Subexpressions are numbered, from left to right, beginning at \1, based on the order in which each opening parenthesis is encountered. In this expression, \1 will be the area code inclusive of any parentheses that might be present. \2 corresponds to the area code without parentheses, if one is found. Otherwise, \2 will be NULL. Likewise, \3 corresponds to an area code enclosed within parentheses, but does not include those parentheses. The following query uses (\2\3) to generate the area code in the correct format. It may seem odd to use both backreferences, but the technique works in this case, because one will always be NULL.

```
SELECT emp_id,
  REGEXP_REPLACE(
    REGEXP_REPLACE(
      text, '([0-9]{3})[-. ]([0-9]{4})', '\1-\2'),
      '(([0-9]{3})|\(([0-9]{3})\)))[-. ]([0-9]{3}-[0-9]{4})',
      '(\2\3) \4') text
FROM employee_comment;

    EMP_ID TEXT
---------- --------------------------------------------
      7369 126 Varnum, Edmore MI 48829, (989) 313-5351
      7499 90 McConnell Court
           Cedar Lake MI 48812
           Home: (989) 387-4321
           Cell: (237) 438-3333
...
```

Now that all the kinks have been worked out of the expression, it's a relatively simple matter to use it in an UPDATE statement:

```
UPDATE employee_comment
SET text =
  REGEXP_REPLACE(
    REGEXP_REPLACE(
      text, '([0-9]{3})[-. ]([0-9]{4})', '\1-\2'),
```

```
'((([0-9]{3})|\(([0-9]{3})\))[-. ]([0-9]{3}-[0-9]{4}))',
'(\2\3) \4');
```

And there you have it. With one statement, and a little bit of regular expression magic, you can consistently format all those randomly formatted phone numbers in a free-format comment column.

 Before unleashing a regular expression search-and-replace, follow our example from this section and test what you are doing by issuing a SELECT statement, and carefully verify that your regular expression is having the effect that you expected it to have. When everything looks good, then unleash your UPDATE.

Coming from Perl?

If you come to Oracle with experience writing regular expressions in Perl, we want to warn you that you won't necessarily be able to take a Perl regular expression and drop it into Oracle. There are many differences in how the two platforms support regular expressions.

Perl handles string literals differently than Oracle. Perl permits \x for embedding arbitrary byte codes into a string, supports character sequences such as \n for newline, and provides for the use of the $ to dereference variables from within a string. Regular expressions that depend on Perl's syntax for string literals won't translate directly to Oracle.

Perl also supports a great deal of Perl-specific regular expression syntax. You have lazy-quantifiers, for example, enabling non-greedy, regular expressions. Conversely, Perl does not support some of the Portable Operating System Interface (POSIX) syntax, such as the [= =] notation used to specify equivalence classes.

For a fuller discussion of these issues, including recommendations on Oracle equivalents to Perl-specific syntax, refer to the section "Differences Between Perl and Oracle" in Jonathan Gennick and Peter Linsley's *Oracle Regular Expressions Pocket Reference* (O'Reilly).

Using Named Character Classes

Earlier, in our phone number examples, we used bracket expressions such as [0123456789] and [0-9] to create matching sets to match any of the digits, zero through nine. Oracle also supports named, character classes, which provide you with a handy and reliable way to create commonly used matching sets. For example, you can use [:digit:] within a bracket expression to represent the set of all digits. Instead of using [0-9] in the following expression:

```
([0-9]{3}[-. ]|\([0-9]{3}\) )?[0-9]{3}[-. ][0-9]{4}
```

You can use [[:digit:]] to match any character defined as a digit:

```
([[:digit:]]{3}[-. ]|\([ [:digit:]]{3}\) )?[ [:digit:]]{3}[-. ][ [:digit:]]{4}
```

Table 17-3 gives a list of valid, character class names, which you must always enclose within a bracket expression. You can include other characters within the same bracket expression. For example, you can write [[:digit:]A-F] to create a matching set of all digits plus the letters A–F.

Table 17-3. Supported character classes

Class	Description
[:alnum:]	Alphanumeric characters (same as [:alpha:] + [:digit:])
[:alpha:]	Alphabetic characters only
[:blank:]	Blankspace characters, such as space and tab.
[:cntrl:]	Nonprinting, or control characters
[:digit:]	Numeric digits
[:graph:]	Graphical characters (same as [:punct:] + [:upper:] + [:lower:] + [:digit:])
[:lower:]	Lowercase letters
[:print:]	Printable characters
[:punct:]	Punctuation characters
[:space:]	Whitespace characters, such as space, form-feed, newline, carriage return, horizontal tab, and vertical tab
[:upper:]	Uppercase letters
[:xdigit:]	Hexadecimal characters

There are pros and cons to using named character classes, but mostly pros:

- You don't need to worry about the underlying code points used to represent characters in whatever character set you are using. A matching set defined as [A-Za-z] might include characters other than those letters. A matching set defined as [[:alpha:]] will contain only letters.

- You can easily accommodate characters from many languages. For example, [:digit:] matches not only the English 0–9, but also the Arabic-Indic ●–۹. This is important in multilingual environments.

- You don't need to worry about inadvertently omitting a character from a matching set. Quick! If I want to match all punctuation, and use [.,;:!], have I forgotten anything? That worry goes away when using [[:punct:]].

- You can more easily include characters that would otherwise be difficult to type from the keyboard. The [:cntrl:] class, for example, represents nonprinting, control characters.

The only downside we can think of to using named character classes, and you could argue that it's not even a downside, is that if you do use a class such as [:digit:], and you really do care only about 0–9, you may prefer the results from [0-9] instead. In practice though, we have yet to regret using a named character class whenever one fits the problem at hand.

Specifying Collation Elements

Oracle has always been strong in its support of multilingual data, and that strength now extends to regular expressions. When working with languages other than English, you'll sometimes encounter characters that appear to be two letters, because they are composed of two glyphs. For example, Spanish, at least old-Spanish, treats *ch* and *ll* as single letters.

Dealing with letters such as *ch* can sometimes be problematic. The following example shows one attempt to extract a word beginning with either the letter *ch* or *ll* from a string. We use the XSPANISH sort, because that sort works by the old rules under which *ch* and *ll* are each treated as one letter. We build our regular expression as follows:

(^|)
: A word is preceded by either the beginning of a line, or by a space.

[chll]
: We want our word to begin with either *ch* or *ll*. This bracket expression is our first attempt to define a matching set containing those two characters.

[^[:space:][:punct:]]+
: The first letter of our word must be followed by one or more non-space, non-punctuation characters. We could use * instead + to include one-letter words in our search.

Using the expression we've just described, we specify 'i' as the match parameter to get a case-insensitive search. Look carefully at the results:

```
ALTER SESSION SET NLS_SORT=XSPANISH;
SELECT TRIM(REGEXP_SUBSTR(
   'El caballo, Chico come la tortilla.',
   '(^| )[chll][^[:space:][:punct:]]+',1,1,'i'))
FROM dual;

caballo
```

This result isn't what we want at all. The problem here is that our use of [chll] results in a matching set composed of three letters, *c*, *h*, and *l*, any of which is deemed a valid match. Hence, our query found caballo rather than Chico. Collation element syntax lets you deal with this situation. To treat a multicharacter collation element as a single letter, enclose it within [. and .]. Then you must enclose that within a bracket expression. The result is that [.ch.] is recognized as the single letter *ch*, and [.ll.] is recognized as the single letter *ll*:

```
ALTER SESSION SET NLS_SORT=XSPANISH;
SELECT TRIM(REGEXP_SUBSTR(
   'El caballo, Chico come la tortilla.',
   '(^| )[[.ch.][.ll.]][^[:space:][:punct:]]+',1,1,'i'))
FROM dual;
```

```
Chico
```

Technically, any single character is a collation element. Thus, [a] and [[.a.]] are equivalent. In practice, you only need use collation element syntax when a collation element consists of multiple characters that linguistically represent one character.

> You cannot arbitrarily put any two letters in a collation. For example, you cannot write [.jg.], because those are two, separate letters, which you cannot arbitrarily treat as a single letter.

Table 17-4 provides a list of collation elements recognized by Oracle. The elements in the table are valid only for the specified NLS_SORT settings.

Table 17-4. Collation elements

NLS_SORT	Multicharacter collation elements
XDANISH	aa AA Aa oe OE Oe
XSPANISH	ch CH Ch ll LL Ll
XHUNGARIAN	cs CS Cs gy GY Gy ly LY Ly ny NY Ny sz SZ Sz ty TY Ty zs ZS Zs
XCZECH	ch CH Ch
XCZECH_PUNCTUATION	ch CH Ch
XSLOVAK	dz DZ Dz dž DŽ Dž ch CH Ch
XCROATIAN	dž DŽ Dž lj LJ Lj nj Nj NJ

Defining Equivalence Classes

An equivalence class is a set of characters that would all be the same except for their case or the way they are accented. You can create such a class by using [= and =] to surround a letter when you wish to match all accented and unaccented versions of that letter. The resulting equivalence class reference must always be within a bracket expression.

For example:

```
SELECT REGEXP_SUBSTR('eéëèÉËÈE' '[[=É=]]+')
FROM dual;

eéëèÉËÈE

SELECT REGEXP_SUBSTR('eéëèÉËÈE', '[[=e=]]+')
FROM dual;

eéëèÉËÈE
```

A Regular Expression Standard

Regular expressions are widely used, especially in the world of Unix and Linux. Perl, for example, has probably done more than any other tool or utility to popularize their use. Today, regular expressions are everywhere. They are supported by Perl, Python, Java, and other programming languages. You'll find regular expression support in database management systems such as Oracle and MySQL. You'll even find regular expression support in popular email clients such as *The Bat!*, or in programmer-oriented text editors such as *MultiEdit*.

As ubiquitous as regular expressions have become, you may be surprised to find that regular expression syntax is not well-standardized. The POSIX standard defines a regular expression syntax, which you can read about at:

> *http://www.opengroup.org/onlinepubs/007904975/basedefs/xbd_chap09.html*

Oracle follows the POSIX standard quite closely. However, other implementations may not. Perl's metacharacters and implementation is different from Python's, is different from Java's, is different from Oracle's, is different from MySQL's. Superficially, the syntax is very similar from one platform to the next. In practice though, you should not blindly port, say, a Perl regular expression to Oracle. Take the time to study, understand, and to thoroughly test any regular expression that you decide to port to Oracle.

If you're specifically interested in porting Perl regular expressions to Oracle, Jonathan Gennick and Peter Linsley's *Oracle Regular Expressions Pocket Reference* (O'Reilly) contains a good section describing some of the differences between those two platforms.

It doesn't matter which version of a letter you specify between the [= and =]. All equivalent accented and unaccented letters, whether uppercase or lowercase, will match.

 NLS_SORT determines which characters are considered to be equivalent. Thus, equivalence is determined appropriately for whatever language you are using.

CHAPTER 18

Model Queries

Some complex calculations are not easily amenable to SQL. Tasks such as forecasting sales, computing market share, solving simultaneous equations, analyzing time series, and so on involve iterative calculations, often referencing interdependent rows across multiple dimensions. It becomes extremely difficult to solve such problems in SQL, and the resultant SQL code becomes very difficult to understand and maintain. Such SQL often involves multiple levels of subqueries, joins, and UNIONs, and therefore performs inefficiently.

Rather than use SQL to solve problems such as we've just described, people usually download the data to a spreadsheet and perform the computations there. Some applications move data into specially created, external calculation engines that can perform the necessary computations efficiently. Downloading data into spreadsheets, or moving data into special-purpose engines, involves overhead and adversely impacts performance, scalability, manageability, and security of the system managing the data.

Oracle Database 10g introduces a new MODEL clause that allows you to treat relational data as a multidimensional array for the purpose of performing spreadsheet-like operations. Now you can more easily solve such problems as we've just described, in the database, using a single SQL statement.

Basic Elements of a Model Query

Let's take an example to understand the basic elements of a model query. The sales_ history table holds the sales data for three regions for each of the 12 months of the years 2000 and 2001. We want to forecast sales for the first three months of the year 2004, by using a simple formula: the sales for each region for each month of 2004 will be forecasted to be the average sales for that region and that month for years 2000 and 2001. Mathematically, our formula looks as follows:

```
sales_2004 = (sales_2000 + sales_2001) / 2
```

Using the MODEL clause introduced in Oracle Database 10*g*, this forecasting model can be written into a SQL query as follows:

```
SELECT r, y, m, s
FROM sales_history
WHERE month <= 3
MODEL
RETURN UPDATED ROWS
PARTITION BY (region_id r)
DIMENSION BY (year y, month m)
MEASURES (sales s)
RULES (s[2004, FOR m in (1,2,3)] = (s[2000,CV()] + s[2001,CV()]) / 2)
ORDER BY y, r, m;
```

```
         R          Y          M          S
---------- ---------- ---------- ----------
         5       2004          1   763822.5
         5       2004          2     923619
         5       2004          3   849724.5
         6       2004          1   916045.5
         6       2004          2     643014
         6       2004          3   955546.5
         7       2004          1   568531.5
         7       2004          2   927634.5
         7       2004          3   983989.5

9 rows selected.
```

The preceding query is called a *model query*, and introduces some new keywords: MODEL, PARTITION BY, DIMENSION BY, MEASURES, and RULES.

The keyword MODEL marks the start of the MODEL clause. The MODEL clause enables you to work with the relational data as a multidimensional array, which is referred to as a *model*. Once you've arranged your data into an array, you perform spreadsheet-like calculations.

The PARTITION BY clause defines logical blocks of the model. You can think of the PARTITION BY clause as separating the data into multiple models, each model being of the same structure, but containing a different subset of the data. This is very similar to the effect of the PARTITION BY clause used with the analytical functions discussed in Chapter 13. If you wish to apply the same calculations to multiple subsets of your data, and you wish each subset to be independent of the other, then partition your data such that each partition corresponds to one of those subsets.

The DIMENSION BY clause specifies the dimensions of the multidimensional array created by the MODEL clause. The columns in the DIMENSION BY clause uniquely identify a cell in a partition of the multidimensional array. The dimensions in a model query are equivalent to the dimensions in a star schema. In the example under discussion, the columns year and month are specified as the dimensions, which indicates that each partition will be a two-dimensional array, and a combination of year and the month values will identify each cell.

The columns specified in the MEASURES clause are the columns on which the spreadsheet calculations are performed. Measures in a model query are equivalent to the measures in the fact table of a star schema. In our example in this section, the sales column is identified as the measure, and the spreadsheet calculations (estimating future sales) are performed on that column.

 Each cell in the model contains the values specified by the MEASURES clause. Our example here uses one value per cell, but later you'll see examples with multiple values per cell.

The RULES keyword introduces the clause specifying the formulae for calculations that you wish to perform. We'll talk more about rules in the section "Rules."

When you execute a MODEL query, the MODEL clause is almost the last clause to be executed. Only SELECT and ORDER BY come later. Thus, to see the data feeding into a model, you need only remove the MODEL clause, execute the remaining query, and look at the output.

A discussion of aliases is in order. Look carefully at the preceding query, and you'll see that aliases are specified in both the SELECT and MODEL clauses. The SELECT and ORDER BY clauses "see" the data that is returned from the MODEL clause. Thus, when you give a column an alias in your MODEL clause, you must use that same alias to refer to the column in your SELECT and ORDER BY clauses. Your SELECT clause may provide yet another alias, which will become the column name "seen" by the user or application program executing the query.

Cell References

Referencing cells in a spreadsheet is one of the basic requirements of model queries. You reference a cell by qualifying all the dimensions in a partition. Cells in a spreadsheet can be referenced in one of the two ways—symbolic cell referencing and positional cell referencing.

Symbolic Cell References

In a symbolic cell reference, you specify each dimension using a boolean expression, such as:

```
s[y=2004, m=3]
```

An example query with a symbolic cell reference is:

```
SELECT r, y, m, s
FROM sales_history
WHERE month <= 10
MODEL
RETURN UPDATED ROWS
```

```
PARTITION BY (region_id r)
DIMENSION BY (year y, month m)
MEASURES (sales s)
RULES (s[y=2004,m=3] = 200000)
ORDER BY y, r, m;
```

Look at the RULES clause in this example, and see that each cell is referenced symbolically by specifying a value for each dimension. In the RULES clause, s refers to the measure sales declared in the MEASURES clause. This measure is structured in a two-dimensional array, as defined by the DIMENSION BY clause. The dimensions are year (y) and month (m). To reference any cell in the two-dimensional array, you need to specify both the dimensions. In the preceding example, the cell for March 2004 is referenced by specifying a value for the year dimension (y=2004) and the month dimension (m=3). You need to specify the dimensions in the same order as they appear in the DIMENSION BY clause.

Positional Cell References

In a positional cell reference, each dimension is implied by its position in the DIMENSION BY clause. The example from the previous section can be rewritten using positional cell reference as follows:

```
s[2004,3]
```

An example query with a positional cell reference is:

```
SELECT r, y, m, s
FROM sales_history
WHERE month <= 10
MODEL
RETURN UPDATED ROWS
PARTITION BY (region_id r)
DIMENSION BY (year y, month m)
MEASURES (sales s)
RULES (s[2004,3] = 200000)
ORDER BY y, r, m;
```

In this query's RULES clause each cell is referenced positionally by specifying a value corresponding to each column listed in the DIMENSION BY clause. Since the DIMENSION BY clause has two columns (year y, month m), the first value in s[2004,3] refers to the column year, and the second value refers to the column month.

Combined Positional and Symbolic References

You may write queries containing both positional and symbolic cell referencing. For example:

```
SELECT r, y, m, s
FROM sales_history
WHERE month <= 10
MODEL
```

```
RETURN UPDATED ROWS
PARTITION BY (region_id r)
DIMENSION BY (year y, month m)
MEASURES (sales s)
RULES (s[2004, m=3] = (s[2000,m=3] + s[2001,m=3]) / 2)
ORDER BY y, r, m;
```

In this query, the RULES clause, s[2004, m=3], contains both positional and symbolic cell referencing. The first dimension (year) is specified positionally, whereas the second dimension (month) is specified symbolically.

NULL Measures and Missing Cells

SQL models may involve two types of non-available value: existing cells with a NULL value, and non-existing cells. In the MODEL clause, any missing cells are treated as NULLs. Whether they are missing or existing cells with NULL values, the MODEL clause allows you to treat them in either of two ways—IGNORE or KEEP.

You can keep the NULL values by specifying KEEP NAV in the MODEL clause. KEEP NAV is the default behavior. Alternatively, you can specify IGNORE NAV in the MODEL clause to return the following values for NULL, depending on the data type of the measure:

- 0 for numeric data types
- 01-JAN-2000 for datetime (DATE, TIMESTAMP, etc.) data types
- An empty string for character (CHAR, VARCHAR2, etc.) data types
- NULL for all other data types

The following two examples illustrate the usage of KEEP NAV and IGNORE NAV. The sales history data in the table sales_history has NULL values for the month 12. Therefore, the following query returns NULL values for the measure s:

```
SELECT r, y, m, s
FROM sales_history
WHERE month = 12
MODEL
RETURN UPDATED ROWS
PARTITION BY (region_id r)
DIMENSION BY (year y, month m)
MEASURES (sales s)
RULES (s[2004,12] = (s[2000,12] + s[2001,12]) / 2)
ORDER BY y, r, m;
```

```
    R          Y          M          S
----- ---------- ---------- ----------
    5       2004         12
    6       2004         12
    7       2004         12
```

As you can see KEEP NAV is the default behavior. If you want zeros instead of the NULL values for the computed measure s, you can use the IGNORE NAV option in the MODEL clause, as shown in the following example:

```
SELECT r, y, m, s
FROM sales_history
WHERE month = 12
MODEL
IGNORE NAV
RETURN UPDATED ROWS
PARTITION BY (region_id r)
DIMENSION BY (year y, month m)
MEASURES (sales s)
RULES   (s[2004,12] = (s[2000,12] + s[2001,12]) / 2)
ORDER BY y, r, m;
```

```
    R        Y          M          S
----- ---------- ---------- ----------
    5      2004         12          0
    6      2004         12          0
    7      2004         12          0
```

Whether you choose to keep or ignore NULL values depends on your application.

UNIQUE DIMENSION/UNIQUE SINGLE REFERENCE

There are two ways to specify the uniqueness of the rows in a MODEL query. The default option is to use UNIQUE DIMENSION, which means that the combination of columns in the PARTITION BY and DIMENSION BY forms the unique key of the input data. When you don't specify any uniqueness condition, or when you specify UNIQUE DIMENSION, the database engine performs a check on the input data to ensure that each cell of the model has at most one row for each combination of PARTITION BY and DIMENSION BY columns. For example:

```
SELECT r, y, m, s
FROM sales_history
WHERE month <= 3
MODEL
UNIQUE DIMENSION
PARTITION BY (region_id r)
DIMENSION BY (year y, month m)
MEASURES (sales s)
RULES (s[2004, 3] = (s[2000,3] + s[2001,3]) / 2)
ORDER BY y, r, m;
```

```
    R        Y          M          S
----- ---------- ---------- ----------
    5      2000          1    1018430
    5      2000          2    1231492
    5      2000          3    1132966
    6      2000          1    1221394
    6      2000          2     857352
```

6	2000	3	1274062
7	2000	1	758042
7	2000	2	1236846
7	2000	3	1311986
5	2001	1	509215
5	2001	2	615746
5	2001	3	566483
6	2001	1	610697
6	2001	2	428676
6	2001	3	637031
7	2001	1	379021
7	2001	2	618423
7	2001	3	655993
5	2004	3	849724.5
6	2004	3	955546.5
7	2004	3	983989.5

If you are sure that your input data is keyed on the PARTITION BY and DIMEN-SION BY columns, you can specify UNIQUE SINGLE REFERENCE instead of UNIQUE DIMENSION. When you specify UNIQUE SINGLE REFERENCE, the database engine will not perform the uniqueness check on the entire input data. Rather it will check that all the cells referenced in the righthand side of the rules each correspond to just one row of input data. The reduced checking done by the UNIQUE SINGLE REFERENCE option may improve performance when querying large amounts of data. The following example illustrates the usage of the UNIQUE SINGLE REFERENCE option:

```
SELECT r, y, m, s
FROM sales_history
WHERE month <= 3
MODEL
UNIQUE SINGLE REFERENCE
PARTITION BY (region_id r)
DIMENSION BY (year y, month m)
MEASURES (sales s)
RULES (s[2004, 3] = (s[2000,3] + s[2001,3]) / 2)
ORDER BY y, r, m;
```

R	Y	M	S
5	2000	1	1018430
5	2000	2	1231492
5	2000	3	1132966
6	2000	1	1221394
6	2000	2	857352
6	2000	3	1274062
7	2000	1	758042
7	2000	2	1236846
7	2000	3	1311986
5	2001	1	509215
5	2001	2	615746
5	2001	3	566483

6	2001	1	610697
6	2001	2	428676
6	2001	3	637031
7	2001	1	379021
7	2001	2	618423
7	2001	3	655993
5	2004	3	849724.5
6	2004	3	955546.5
7	2004	3	983989.5

If you are using UNIQUE DIMENSION, and the input data doesn't satisfy the uniqueness condition of the PARTITION BY and DIMENSION BY columns, you will get an error, as illustrated in the following example:

```
SELECT r, y, m, s
FROM sales_history
WHERE month >= 10
MODEL
UNIQUE DIMENSION
PARTITION BY (region_id r)
DIMENSION BY (year y, month m)
MEASURES (sales s)
RULES (s[2004, 10] = (s[2000,10] + s[2001,10]) / 2)
ORDER BY y, r, m;
FROM sales_history
     *
ERROR at line 2:
ORA-32638: Non unique addressing in spreadsheet dimensions
```

This example returns an error because, in our example data, we have deliberately created duplicate rows for November 2000 and 2001. It doesn't matter that we aren't referencing data from that month in our rule. The duplication causes an error, because data for that month represents a cell somewhere in our model.

The same query with the UNIQUE SINGLE REFERENCE option will not cause any error, because the cells referenced in the righthand side of the rules satisfy the required uniqueness condition:

```
SELECT r, y, m, s
FROM sales_history
WHERE month >= 10
MODEL
UNIQUE SINGLE REFERENCE
PARTITION BY (region_id r)
DIMENSION BY (year y, month m)
MEASURES (sales s)
RULES (s[2004, 10] = (s[2000,10] + s[2001,10]) / 2)
ORDER BY y, r, m;
```

R	Y	M	S
5	2000	10	1099296
5	2000	11	922790
5	2000	11	922790

5	2000	12	
6	2000	10	1020234
6	2000	11	1065778
6	2000	11	1065778
6	2000	12	
7	2000	10	1073682
7	2000	11	1107732
7	2000	11	1107732
7	2000	12	
5	2001	10	549648
5	2001	11	461395
5	2001	11	461395
5	2001	12	
6	2001	10	510117
6	2001	11	532889
6	2001	11	532889
6	2001	12	
7	2001	10	536841
7	2001	11	553866
7	2001	11	553866
7	2001	12	
5	2004	10	824472
6	2004	10	765175.5
7	2004	10	805261.5

Notice the duplicate rows of data in the above output for month 11 in the years 2000 and 2001. If our rules referenced that data, the query would have caused an error. For example:

```
SELECT r, y, m, s
FROM sales_history
WHERE month >= 10
MODEL
UNIQUE SINGLE REFERENCE
PARTITION BY (region_id r)
DIMENSION BY (year y, month m)
MEASURES (sales s)
RULES (s[2004, 11] = (s[2000,11] + s[2001,11]) / 2)
ORDER BY y, r, m;
FROM sales_history
     *
ERROR at line 2:
ORA-32638: Non unique addressing in spreadsheet dimensions
```

This query fails, because there are multiple input rows for a single cell referenced by the rule. Which of the available rows for a given cell should the database choose to use? The answer is that the database doesn't know the answer. That's why the database throws an error. Without this checking for duplicate rows, the database would not be able to guarantee repeatable results.

Returning Rows

The objective of all SQL queries is to return a result set. With a model query, you have two options: you can choose to return all the rows represented in the model, or you can choose to return only those rows updated by the rules. Returning all the rows is the default behavior. Use the following clause to specify which behavior you desire:

```
RETURN [ALL | UPDATED] ROWS
```

The RETURN clause belongs immediately after the MODEL keyword, except when you are using any cell reference options such as IGNORE NAV, KEEP NAV, UNIQUE DIMENSION, or UNIQUE SINGLE REFERENCE. If you are using cell reference options, then those cell reference options need to come before the RETURN clause.

The following example illustrates the default behavior:

```
SELECT r, y, m, s
FROM sales_history
WHERE month = 3
MODEL
PARTITION BY (region_id r)
DIMENSION BY (year y, month m)
MEASURES (sales s)
RULES  (s[2004,3] = (s[2000,3] + s[2001,3]) / 2)
ORDER BY y, r, m;
```

R	Y	M	S
5	2000	3	1132966
6	2000	3	1274062
7	2000	3	1311986
5	2001	3	566483
6	2001	3	637031
7	2001	3	655993
5	2004	3	849724.5
6	2004	3	955546.5
7	2004	3	983989.5

The sales_history table has rows for the year 2000 and 2001. The rows for the year 2004 are computed based on the rules. Since the query didn't specify a RETURN clause, all the rows that satisfy the WHERE condition are returned.

To return only updated rows, use the RETURN UPDATED ROWS option, as in the following MODEL query:

```
SELECT r, y, m, s
FROM sales_history
WHERE month = 3
MODEL
RETURN UPDATED ROWS
PARTITION BY (region_id r)
```

```
DIMENSION BY (year y, month m)
MEASURES (sales s)
RULES  (s[2004,3] = (s[2000,3] + s[2001,3]) / 2)
ORDER BY y, r, m;

    R          Y          M          S
 -----  ---------- ---------- ----------
     5       2004          3   849724.5
     6       2004          3   955546.5
     7       2004          3   983989.5
```

This time, only the new rows generated by the query are returned. For the purpose of the RETURN clause, the newly generated rows are also considered "UPDATED ROWS." If the model query had updated some existing rows, those rows would also have been returned in the result set.

Rules

Rules are the core of a model query. Rules specify the formulae to compute values for the cells in the spreadsheet. Use the RULES clause to specify the rules for a model query. The RULES clause encloses all the rules in parentheses, and each rule is separated from the next by a comma.

Constructing a Rule

Each rule represents an assignment, and consists of a lefthand side and a righthand side. The RULES clause of one of the previous examples looks like the following:

```
RULES  (s[2004,3] = (s[2000,3] + s[2001,3]) / 2)
```

The lefthand side of a rule (s[2004,3] in this example) identifies the cells to be updated using values from the righthand side of the rule. The righthand side of a rule is an expression that represents the computation to be performed. You can use any valid SQL operator or function in an expression. There are also some additional constructs that you can use in rules, that are specific to the MODEL clause.

CV( )

You can use the CV( ) function in the righthand side of a rule. It returns the current value of a dimension column from the lefthand side of the rule. The following example illustrates:

```
SELECT r, y, m, s
FROM sales_history
WHERE month = 3
MODEL
RETURN UPDATED ROWS
PARTITION BY (region_id r)
```

```
DIMENSION BY (year y, month m)
MEASURES (sales s)
RULES   (s[2004,3] = (s[2000,CV()] + s[2001,CV()]) / 2)
ORDER BY y, r, m;
```

```
    R         Y          M          S
----- ---------- ---------- ----------
    5      2004          3   849724.5
    6      2004          3   955546.5
    7      2004          3   983989.5
```

The CV( ) function evaluates to the current value of the corresponding dimension. In this example, CV( ) evaluates to 3, corresponding to the month dimension specified on the lefthand side of the rule. The CV( ) function comes in handy when you need to evaluate a rule multiple times, and each time a dimension column takes a different value (such as in FOR loops, discussed later).

Optionally, the CV( ) function can take a dimension column as an argument. For example, we could have written CV(m) to access the current month value from the lefthand side of our rule. When no argument is specified, positional referencing is used, which means that the dimension column in the corresponding position is used.

ANY

ANY can be used as a wildcard in a rule written with positional referencing. It accepts any value for the corresponding column (including NULL). The following example illustrates the usage of ANY:

```
SELECT r, y, m, s
FROM sales_history
WHERE month <= 3
MODEL
RETURN UPDATED ROWS
PARTITION BY (region_id r)
DIMENSION BY (year y, month m)
MEASURES (sales s)
RULES   (s[ANY,3] = (s[CV(),1] + s[CV(),2]) / 2)
ORDER BY y, r, m;
```

```
    R         Y          M          S
----- ---------- ---------- ----------
    5      2000          3    1124961
    6      2000          3    1039373
    7      2000          3     997444
    5      2001          3   562480.5
    6      2001          3   519686.5
    7      2001          3     498722
```

In this example, ANY is used as a wildcard for the year dimension, which translates into "all the values for the column year in the sales_history table." This example also illustrates why CV( ) is so important. Our rule will update every cell for March (month = 3), regardless of the year. We use CV( ) on the righthand side to capture the current year, so that we can reference the values for January and February of that same year.

 The use of ANY wildcard prevents cell insertion. We talk more about cell insertion in the section "Creating and Updating Cells."

FOR loops

FOR loops allow you to write a "rule" that affects a number of cells, and acts like a FOR loop in a procedural language such as PL/SQL. FOR loops are expanded at compile-time, so what looks like one rule to you is really seen by the database as many rules. More on this in a bit.

FOR loops are allowed only in the lefthand side of a rule. FOR loops allow multiple cells to be inserted by a single rule. FOR loops can take one of the following three forms:

```
FOR d IN (subquery | list)
FOR d [LIKE pattern] FROM v1 TO v2 [INCREMENT | DECREMENT] n
FOR (d1, d2, ...) IN (multi_column_subquery | multi_column_list)
```

The syntax elements are:

d   A single-dimension column.

subquery
    A subquery returning value(s) for the dimension column.

list
    A list of value(s) for the dimension column.

pattern
    A string with a %. This pattern behaves slightly differently from the LIKE pattern used in a WHERE clause predicate. This pattern doesn't accept underscore. Values from *v1* through *v2* are substituted into the *pattern* at the position marked by %.

v1, v2
    Two literals specifying the upper and lower bound for the dimension *d*.

n   A number to increment or decrement by. The value *n* must be positive.

d1, d2, ...
    Multiple-dimension columns in a FOR loop.

multi_column_subquery
    A subquery returning values for the multiple-dimension columns.

multi_column_list
    A list of values for the multiple-dimension columns.

The following example illustrates a single-column FOR loop:

```
SELECT r, y, m, s
FROM sales_history
WHERE month <= 6
MODEL
RETURN UPDATED ROWS
PARTITION BY (region_id r)
DIMENSION BY (year y, month m)
MEASURES (sales s)
RULES
(
  s[2004,
    FOR m IN (SELECT DISTINCT month FROM sales_history WHERE month <= 6)]
  =  s[2000,CV()]
)
ORDER BY y, r, m;
```

R	Y	M	S
5	2004	1	1018430
5	2004	2	1231492
5	2004	3	1132966
5	2004	4	1195244
5	2004	5	1132570
5	2004	6	1006708
6	2004	1	1221394
6	2004	2	857352
6	2004	3	1274062
6	2004	4	1082292
6	2004	5	1185870
6	2004	6	1002970
7	2004	1	758042
7	2004	2	1236846
7	2004	3	1311986
7	2004	4	1220034
7	2004	5	1322188
7	2004	6	1137144

This query copies the sales history for the year 2000 to the year 2004, for each month, for the first six months. The following example does the same thing, but using a multiple column FOR loop:

```
SELECT r, y, m, s
FROM sales_history
WHERE month <= 6
MODEL
RETURN UPDATED ROWS
PARTITION BY (region_id r)
DIMENSION BY (year y, month m)
MEASURES (sales s)
RULES
(
  s[FOR (y,m)
```

```
    IN (SELECT DISTINCT 2004, month FROM sales_history WHERE month <= 6)]
  =  s[2000,CV()]
)
ORDER BY y, r, m;
```

R	Y	M	S
5	2004	1	1018430
5	2004	2	1231492
5	2004	3	1132966
5	2004	4	1195244
5	2004	5	1132570
5	2004	6	1006708
6	2004	1	1221394
6	2004	2	857352
6	2004	3	1274062
6	2004	4	1082292
6	2004	5	1185870
6	2004	6	1002970
7	2004	1	758042
7	2004	2	1236846
7	2004	3	1311986
7	2004	4	1220034
7	2004	5	1322188
7	2004	6	1137144

The following restrictions apply to subqueries used in FOR loops:

- They cannot be correlated.
- They cannot be defined using the WITH clause.
- They cannot return more than 10,000 rows.

The last restriction needs more explanation. The total number of rules you can specify in the RULES clause is 10,000. When you use a FOR loop, the RULES clause is expanded by unfolding the FOR loop at compile-time, with the database creating one rule for each value returned by the FOR loop. If the total number of rules, including those not generated from FOR loops, exceeds 10,000 for a given model query, you will get an error. The following example illustrates this error:

```
SELECT r, y, m, s
FROM sales_history
MODEL
RETURN UPDATED ROWS
PARTITION BY (region_id r)
DIMENSION BY (year y, month m)
MEASURES (sales s)
RULES
(
  s[2004, FOR m IN (SELECT ROWNUM
                    FROM orders o1 CROSS JOIN orders o2
                    WHERE ROWNUM <= 10001)]
  = s[2000,CV()]
)
```

```
ORDER BY y, r, m;
SELECT r, y, m, s
       *
ERROR at line 1:
ORA-32633: Spreadsheet subquery FOR cell index returns too many rows
```

In this example, the FOR loop is forced to execute 10,001 times, resulting in 10,001 rules being created, which exceeds the 10,000 rule limit. Even though the error message indicates that the limit is on the subquery of the FOR loop, the limit is actually on the *total number of rules* in the model. The subquery is simply the component of the model query that caused the limit to be exceeded. If a subquery returns less than 10,000 rows, but the total number of rules after unfolding all the FOR loops still exceeds 10,000, you will get an error, as illustrated in the following example:

```
SELECT r, y, m, s
FROM sales_history
MODEL
RETURN UPDATED ROWS
PARTITION BY (region_id r)
DIMENSION BY (year y, month m)
MEASURES (sales s)
RULES
(
    s[2004, FOR m IN (SELECT ROWNUM
                      FROM orders o1 CROSS JOIN orders o2
                      WHERE ROWNUM <= 5000)]
    = s[2000,CV()],
    s[2005, FOR m IN (SELECT ROWNUM
                      FROM orders o1 CROSS JOIN orders o2
                      WHERE ROWNUM <= 5001)]
    = s[2001,CV()]
)
ORDER BY y, r, m;
    s[2005, FOR m IN (SELECT ROWNUM
                  *
ERROR at line 14:
ORA-32636: Too many rules in spreadsheet
```

In this example, one FOR loop results in 5000 rules, and the other FOR loop results in 5001 rules, which make a total of 10001 rules. Therefore, you get the error message that indicates that you have too many rules.

IS ANY

IS ANY can be used as a wildcard in a rule when using symbolic referencing. It accepts any value for the corresponding column (including NULL), and returns TRUE always. This is the equivalent to the ANY wildcard used in positional referencing. IS ANY can be used only in the lefthand side of a rule. The following example illustrates the usage of IS ANY:

```
SELECT r, y, m, s
FROM sales_history
```

```
WHERE month = 3
MODEL
PARTITION BY (region_id r)
DIMENSION BY (year y, month m)
MEASURES (sales s)
RULES  (s[y IS ANY, m=3] = (s[CV(),m=3] + s[CV( ),m=3]) / 2)
ORDER BY y, r, m;
```

```
    R          Y          M          S
  -----  ----------  ----------  ----------
    5        2000         3        1132966
    6        2000         3        1274062
    7        2000         3        1311986
    5        2001         3         566483
    6        2001         3         637031
    7        2001         3         655993
```

In this example, IS ANY is used as a wildcard for the year dimension, which translates into "all the values for the column year in the sales_history table."

> The use of the IS ANY wildcard prevents cell insertion. We talk more about cell insertion in the section "Creating and Updating Cells."

IS PRESENT

IS PRESENT returns TRUE if the cell referenced existed prior to the execution of the MODEL clause. Otherwise, if the cell was created as a result of executing a rule, or does not exist at all, IS PRESENT returns FALSE. The following example illustrates the usage of the IS PRESENT condition:

```
SELECT r, y, m, s
FROM sales_history
WHERE month = 3
MODEL
PARTITION BY (region_id r)
DIMENSION BY (year y, month m)
MEASURES (sales s)
RULES (s[2004, 3] = CASE WHEN s[2003,3] IS PRESENT
                              THEN s[2003,3]
                         ELSE   0
                    END)
ORDER BY y, r, m;
```

```
    R          Y          M          S
  -----  ----------  ----------  ----------
    5        2000         3        1132966
    6        2000         3        1274062
    7        2000         3        1311986
    5        2001         3         566483
    6        2001         3         637031
    7        2001         3         655993
```

5	2004	3	0
6	2004	3	0
7	2004	3	0

In this example the IS PRESENT condition is used from within a CASE expression to test whether the cell s[2003,3] was present prior to execution of the MODEL clause. If the cell s[2003,3] was present, then the value of the cell s[2003,3] is assigned to the new cell s[2004,3]; if the cell s[2003,3] wasn't present, then the value 0 is assigned to s[2004,3]. As you can see from the result set, the referenced cell didn't satisfy the IS PRESENT condition. You can tell that this is the case, because each of the 2004 rows has been given a 0 value for estimated March (m=3) sales.

PRESENTV

The PRESENTV function returns a value based on the existence of a cell prior to the execution of the MODEL clause. PRESENTV can be used only on the righthand side of a rule and takes the following form:

```
PRESENTV(cell, exp1, exp2)
```

The syntax elements are:

cell
    A cell reference

exp1, exp2
    Expressions that resolve to a value for the cell referenced

PRESENTV returns exp1 if the referenced cell existed prior to the execution of the MODEL clause; otherwise, the function returns exp2. The following example does the same thing as the IS PRESENT example in the previous section, but using the PRESENTV function instead of a CASE and IS PRESENT:

```
SELECT r, y, m, s
FROM sales_history
WHERE month = 3
MODEL
PARTITION BY (region_id r)
DIMENSION BY (year y, month m)
MEASURES (sales s)
RULES (s[2004,3] = PRESENTV(s[2003,3], s[2003,3], 0))
ORDER BY y, r, m;
```

R	Y	M	S
5	2000	3	1132966
6	2000	3	1274062
7	2000	3	1311986
5	2001	3	566483
6	2001	3	637031
7	2001	3	655993
5	2004	3	0
6	2004	3	0
7	2004	3	0

In this example, the value for the cell s[2004,3] is determined based on whether the cell s[2003,3] existed before the execution of the MODEL clause. If the cell s[2003,3] existed, its value will be assigned to the cell s[2004,3]. If the cell s[2003,3] didn't exist, a value 0 will be assigned to the cell s[2004,3]. As it appears from the result set, the cell s[2003,3] didn't exist in any of the partitions prior to the execution of the MODEL clause. You can tell that this is the case, because each of the 2004 rows has been given a 0 value for estimated March (m=3) sales.

PRESENTNNV

The syntax of the PRESENTNNV function is of the same form as that of the PRESENTV function, and like PRESENTV, it can be used only on the righthand side of a rule. PRESENTNNV means "present not null value," and returns exp1 if a cell existed prior to the execution of the MODEL clause, *and* had a NOT NULL value; otherwise, the function returns exp2. The following example illustrates the usage of PRESENTNNV function:

```
SELECT r, y, m, s
FROM sales_history
MODEL
UNIQUE SINGLE REFERENCE
RETURN UPDATED ROWS
PARTITION BY (region_id r)
DIMENSION BY (year y, month m)
MEASURES (sales s)
RULES (s[2004,3] = PRESENTNNV(s[2000,3], s[2000,3], 0))
ORDER BY y, r, m;
```

R	Y	M	S
5	2004	3	1132966
6	2004	3	1274062
7	2004	3	1311986

The cell s[2000,3] existed prior to the execution of the MODEL clause, and had a NOT NULL value. You can know this, because all occurrences of s[2004,3] are nonzero in the result set.

Range References on the Righthand Side

In most of the examples you have seen so far in this chapter, one cell in the righthand side of a rule has been used to assign a value for one cell in the lefthand side. Or, if more than one cell has been used, each cell has been explicitly referenced. However, there are situations in which you want to use a set of cells on the righthand side to assign one value to a cell on the lefthand side. You can do that by using an aggregate function, such as AVG, COUNT, SUM, MAX, MIN, applied to the multiple cells on the righthand side. This is illustrated in the following example:

```
SELECT r, y, m, s
FROM sales_history
MODEL
UNIQUE SINGLE REFERENCE
RETURN UPDATED ROWS
PARTITION BY (region_id r)
DIMENSION BY (year y, month m)
MEASURES (sales s)
RULES (s[2004, 3] = AVG(s)[y BETWEEN 1995 AND 2003,3])
ORDER BY y, r, m;
```

```
    R         Y          M         S
----- ---------- ---------- ----------
    5      2004          3   849724.5
    6      2004          3   955546.5
    7      2004          3   983989.5
```

This example uses the syntax AVG(s)[y BETWEEN 1995 AND 2003,3] to generate the average of all March sales (month 3) between 1995 and 2003 inclusive. In our data, this range encompasses: s[1995,3], s[1996,3], s[1997,3], s[1998,3], s[1999,3], s[2000,3], s[2001,3], s[2002,3], and s[2003,3]. When you invoke an aggregate function, be sure to place only the measure name within the parentheses. All the dimensions go outside the parentheses.

Order of Evaluation of Rules

A MODEL clause usually consists of multiple rules. Quite often, those rules are interdependent. Cells computed by one rule are often used as input to other rules. In such cases, it is very important that rules are evaluated in a proper order. To influence the order of rule evaluation, you can qualify the RULES clause using two options: SEQUENTIAL ORDER and AUTOMATIC ORDER. The syntax to use is:

```
RULES [ [SEQUENTIAL | AUTOMATIC] ORDER ]
```

The following sections describe the difference between these two approaches to the order in which rules are evaluated.

SEQUENTIAL ORDER

If you don't specify the ordering option in the RULES clause, SEQUENTIAL ORDER is enforced. The rules are evaluated in the order they appear in the RULES clause (also known as, lexical order). The following example illustrates evaluation of the rules in sequential order:

```
SELECT r, y, m, s
FROM sales_history
WHERE month = 3
```

```
MODEL
  RETURN UPDATED ROWS
  PARTITION BY (region_id r)
  DIMENSION BY (year y, month m)
  MEASURES (sales s)
  RULES SEQUENTIAL ORDER
  (
    s[2002,3] = (s[2000,3] + s[2001,3])/2,
    s[2003,3] = s[2002,3] * 1.1
  )
ORDER BY y, r, m;
```

```
         R          Y          M          S
---------- ---------- ---------- ----------
         5       2002          3    849724.5
         6       2002          3    955546.5
         7       2002          3    983989.5
         5       2003          3   934696.95
         6       2003          3  1051101.15
         7       2003          3  1082388.45
```

In this query, the first rule computes the cell s[2002,3], and the second rule uses the resulting value to compute the cell s[2003,3]. If you reverse the order of the rules, you won't get the same results:

```
SELECT r, y, m, s
FROM sales_history
WHERE month = 3
MODEL
  UNIQUE SINGLE REFERENCE
  RETURN UPDATED ROWS
  PARTITION BY (region_id r)
  DIMENSION BY (year y, month m)
  MEASURES (sales s)
  RULES SEQUENTIAL ORDER
  (
    s[2003,3] = s[2002,3] * 1.1,
    s[2002,3] = (s[2000,3] + s[2001,3])/2
  )
ORDER BY y, r, m;
```

```
         R          Y          M          S
---------- ---------- ---------- ----------
         5       2002          3    849724.5
         6       2002          3    955546.5
         7       2002          3    983989.5
         5       2003          3
         6       2003          3
         7       2003          3
```

Notice the NULL values returned by the cell s[2003,3] in all the partitions, in this example's output. We asked for sequential ordering of the rules, and the rule to compute s[2003,3] appears before the rule to compute s[2002,3]. The rule to compute s[2003,3] uses s[2002,3]. Since the cell s[2002,3] doesn't exist before the second rule is evaluated, it's value is NULL, and the value for s[2003,3] ends up being NULL as well.

AUTOMATIC ORDER

With AUTOMATIC ORDER, the evaluation order of the rules is determined using a dependency graph. This is done automatically in a way that ensures that a rule computing a new value for a cell is executed prior to that cell being used to supply a value to another rule. All you need to do to get this behavior is to specify AUTOMATIC ORDER after the RULE keyword. The NULL output of the previous example can be avoided by automatic ordering of the rules, as illustrated in the following example:

```
SELECT r, y, m, s
FROM sales_history
WHERE month = 3
MODEL
  UNIQUE SINGLE REFERENCE
  RETURN UPDATED ROWS
  PARTITION BY (region_id r)
  DIMENSION BY (year y, month m)
  MEASURES (sales s)
  RULES AUTOMATIC ORDER
  (
    s[2003,3] = s[2002,3] * 1.1,
    s[2002,3] = (s[2000,3] + s[2001,3])/2
  )
ORDER BY y, r, m;
```

```
         R          Y          M           S
--------- ---------- ---------- ----------
        5       2002          3    849724.5
        6       2002          3    955546.5
        7       2002          3    983989.5
        5       2003          3   934696.95
        6       2003          3  1051101.15
        7       2003          3  1082388.45
```

In this version of the query, the automatic ordering of the rules ensures that the second rule is evaluated before the first rule.

A model with automatic ordering of rules is referred to as an *automatic order model*, whereas a model with sequential ordering of rules is referred to as a *sequential order model*. In an automatic order model, a cell can be assigned a value only once, because if a cell is assigned a value more than once, the dependency graph will involve a cycle, and rule evaluation will go into an infinite loop. If you attempt to assign a value to a given cell more than once, you will get an error, as in the following example:

```
SELECT r, y, m, s
FROM sales_history
WHERE month = 3
```

```
MODEL
  RETURN UPDATED ROWS
  PARTITION BY (region_id r)
  DIMENSION BY (year y, month m)
  MEASURES (sales s)
  RULES AUTOMATIC ORDER
  (
    s[2002,3] = (s[2000,3] + s[2001,3])/2,
    s[2002,3] = 20000
  )
ORDER BY y, r, m;


    s[2002,3] = 20000
    *
ERROR at line 11:
ORA-32630: multiple assignment in automatic order SPREADSHEET
```

However, in a sequential order spreadsheet, you can assign a value to a cell more than once. When you do that, you should remember that the last assignment will be reflected in the final outcome of the query, as illustrated in the following example:

```
SELECT r, y, m, s
FROM sales_history
WHERE month = 3
MODEL
  UNIQUE SINGLE REFERENCE
  RETURN UPDATED ROWS
  PARTITION BY (region_id r)
  DIMENSION BY (year y, month m)
  MEASURES (sales s)
  RULES
  (
    s[2002,3] = (s[2000,3] + s[2001,3])/2,
    s[2002,3] = 20000
  )
ORDER BY y, r, m;


        R          Y          M          S
--------- ---------- ---------- ----------
        5       2002          3      20000
        6       2002          3      20000
        7       2002          3      20000
```

In this example, the initial assignment of the cell s[2002,3] is overwritten by the value 20000 assigned by the last rule in the list. One more thing to notice about this query is that it doesn't specify an ordering option for the rules. Thus, SEQUENTIAL ORDER is used by default.

Why not use AUTOMATIC ORDER all the time? Whenever you are sure about the sequence of rules, you should use SEQUENTIAL ORDER. By doing so, you are saving the database from the overhead of building the dependency graph and determining the rule order every time the query is executed. There are also cases, such as when you must assign a value to a cell, and then later assign another value to the same cell, that preclude automatic ordering.

Creating and Updating Cells

The rules in the RULES clause allow you to update existing cells, and to create new cells in a model. If the cell specified by the lefthand side of a rule is present in your model, the value for that cell is updated. If the cell doesn't exist, a new row, corresponding to that cell, is inserted into the result set of your model query. The necessary values for the columns other than the measure columns in any newly inserted row will be derived from its partition and dimension values. This is the default semantics, and is known as *UPSERT* (update or insert) *semantics*.

The alternative to UPSERT semantics is to use UPDATE semantics. You can specify which to use in the RULES clause:

```
RULES [UPSERT | UPDATE] [SEQUENTIAL ORDER | AUTOMATIC ORDER]
```

In UPDATE semantics, if the cell specified by the lefthand side of a rule is present in the model, it is updated. If the cell doesn't exist, the assignment is ignored.

The following example illustrates UPDATE semantics, in which existing cells are updated, and updates to non-existent cells are ignored:

```
SELECT r, y, m, s
FROM sales_history
MODEL
  UNIQUE SINGLE REFERENCE
  RETURN UPDATED ROWS
  PARTITION BY (region_id r)
  DIMENSION BY (year y, month m)
  MEASURES (sales s)
  RULES UPDATE
  (
    s[2001,3] = 20000,
    s[2002,3] = 20000
  )
ORDER BY y, r, m;

    R         Y          M          S
----- ---------- ---------- ----------
    5      2001          3      20000
    6      2001          3      20000
    7      2001          3      20000
```

In this example, the model has the cell s[2001,3], and for each of three partitions, for the regions numbered 5, 6, and 7. The first rule arbitrarily stores the value 20000 into the s[2001,3] cell for each region. The second rule attempts to do the same for the cell s[2002,3], but since that cell doesn't already exist in the spreadsheet, the second rule is ignored. This is how UPDATE semantics work.

However, with UPSERT semantics, new cells *will* be inserted for s[2002,3], as illustrated by the following example:

```
SELECT r, y, m, s
FROM sales_history
MODEL
   UNIQUE SINGLE REFERENCE
   RETURN UPDATED ROWS
   PARTITION BY (region_id r)
   DIMENSION BY (year y, month m)
   MEASURES (sales s)
   RULES UPSERT
   (
     s[2001,3] = 20000,
     s[2002,3] = 20000
   )
ORDER BY y, r, m;
```

R	Y	M	S
5	2001	3	20000
6	2001	3	20000
7	2001	3	20000
5	2002	3	20000
6	2002	3	20000
7	2002	3	20000

With UPSERT semantics, when you specify a previously non-existent cell and assign a value to that cell, the database inserts a new row into the result set by combining the dimension, measure, and partition information.

New cells cannot be inserted in the following situations:

- As a result of using the ANY wildcard on the lefthand side
- As a result of using symbolic referencing on the lefthand side

The ANY wildcard is essentially a predicate that filters selected rows from the population of currently existing rows. When you use a predicate in the WHERE clause of a SELECT statement, that predicate can never generate new rows. Likewise, you can't use a predicate to generate new rows in a model.

Symbolic referencing is also a predicate, and this is a subtle, but important point to understand. For example, the cell reference s[y=2003, m=3] is loosely equivalent to a WHERE clause such as WHERE y=2003 AND m=3. Such a WHERE clause can never generate new rows, and neither can such a cell reference.

 Whether using UPDATE or UPSERT semantics, realize that any insert or update takes place only in the result set operated on by the MODEL clause, and not in the actual data in the underlying table(s).

Iterative Models

Iteration is a powerful tool in mathematical modeling. Some applications involving approximate calculations involve iterative computation. Usually developers resort to procedural languages to implement iteration. The MODEL clause provides a way to write iterate code using SQL.

At times, you may need to evaluate the rules of a model repeatedly, until some sort of condition is met. MODEL's ITERATE subclause provides the required functionality to iterate rules. The syntax of the ITERATE subclause, which is a part of the RULES clause, is:

```
RULES [UPSERT | UPDATE] [SEQUENTIAL ORDER | AUTOMATIC ORDER]
ITERATE (n) [UNTIL (condition)]
```

The syntax elements are:

n   A positive number specifying the number of iterations.

condition
    An early-termination condition.

The early-termination condition is optional. If specified, the condition is evaluated at the end of every iteration. If you specify an early-termination condition, iteration ends when that condition is satisfied, regardless of whatever value you specify for n.

The following example illustrates iteration of rules:

```
SELECT r, y, m, s
FROM sales_history
MODEL
  UNIQUE SINGLE REFERENCE
  RETURN UPDATED ROWS
  PARTITION BY (region_id r)
  DIMENSION BY (year y, month m)
  MEASURES (sales s)
  RULES ITERATE (4)
  (
    s[2001,3] = s[2001,3] / 2
  )
ORDER BY y, r, m;
```

R	Y	M	S
5	2001	3	35405.1875
6	2001	3	39814.4375
7	2001	3	40999.5625

In this query, the cell s[2001,3] is computed by dividing s[2001,3] by 2 four times. You can stop the iteration before all four iterations are executed, by using the UNTIL option, as illustrated in the following example:

```
SELECT r, y, m, s
FROM sales_history
```

```
MODEL
  UNIQUE SINGLE REFERENCE
  RETURN UPDATED ROWS
  PARTITION BY (region_id r)
  DIMENSION BY (year y, month m)
  MEASURES (sales s)
  RULES ITERATE (4) UNTIL (s[2001,3] < 100000)
  (
    s[2001,3] = s[2001,3] / 2
  )
ORDER BY y, r, m;

    R          Y          M          S
----- ---------- ---------- ----------
    5       2001          3 70810.375
    6       2001          3 79628.875
    7       2001          3 81999.125
```

In this latest example, after every iteration, the condition in the UNTIL clause is evaluated. If the condition is false, the next iteration starts; if the condition is true, the iterative evaluation stops. In this case, once the value of the cell s[2001,3] drops below 100,000, the iteration stops. Compare the two preceding examples, and you will find that the second query didn't perform all four iterations.

Knowing how many iterations have occurred

Sometimes it's useful to know how many iterations have occurred. Oracle provides a useful function (also referred to as a system variable) called ITERATION_NUMBER to keep a count of the number of iterations through a set of rules. The function returns the current iteration number. It starts with 0 for the first iteration, and increments by 1 for every subsequent iteration. So, after a query has completed four iterations, ITERATION_NUMBER will return 3 (iterations 0, 1, 2, and 3). The following example illustrates how you can get the iteration number from a query:

```
SELECT r, y, m, s, i
FROM sales_history
MODEL
  UNIQUE SINGLE REFERENCE
  RETURN UPDATED ROWS
  PARTITION BY (region_id r)
  DIMENSION BY (year y, month m)
  MEASURES (sales s, 0 i)
  RULES ITERATE (4) UNTIL (s[2001,3] < 100000)
  (
    s[2001,3] = s[2001,3] / 2,
    i[2001,3] = ITERATION_NUMBER
  )
ORDER BY y, r, m;

    R          Y          M          S          I
----- ---------- ---------- ---------- ----------
    5       2001          3 70810.375          2
```

6	2001	3	79628.875	2
7	2001	3	81999.125	2

Returning the iteration number takes a bit of innovative coding. In the preceding example, a new measure called i has been introduced to capture the iteration number. This measure is updated by the output of the function ITERATION_NUMBER at every iteration. Since i doesn't correspond to any column of the table, we initialized the measure i to the constant 0; we did that in the MEASURES clause. We could have used any constant value to initialize i, and the output would still be the same. This is because the initial value of the measure i is updated to 0 during the first iteration, and then incremented by 1 each iteration thereafter.

Referencing values from the previous iteration

Another useful feature when using iterations is the PREVIOUS function. The PREVI-OUS function takes a single cell reference as input, and returns the value of the cell as it existed after the previous iteration, just before the current iteration began. The following example illustrates how you can use the PREVIOUS function to get the value of a cell as it existed after the previous iteration:

```
SELECT r, y, m, s, i
FROM sales_history
MODEL
  UNIQUE SINGLE REFERENCE
  RETURN UPDATED ROWS
  PARTITION BY (region_id r)
  DIMENSION BY (year y, month m)
  MEASURES (sales s, 'a' i)
  RULES ITERATE (4)
      UNTIL ( (PREVIOUS(s[2001,3]) - s[2001,3]) < 100000 )
  (
    s[2001,3] = s[2001,3] / 2,
    i[2001,3] = ITERATION_NUMBER
  )
ORDER BY y, r, m;
```

R	Y	M	S	I
5	2001	3	70810.375	2
6	2001	3	79628.875	2
7	2001	3	81999.125	2

In this example, the previous value of the cell is compared to the current value after every iteration, and if that difference is less than 100,000, then the iteration stops. The PREVIOUS function provides a very useful means of constructing a termination condition. For problems requiring approximation solutions, you can use this approach to iterate till a point when the difference between the previous value and the current value is less than a threshold. You can then assume you have arrived at a reasonably approximate solution. For example, you could calculate pi to a resolution of 1/1000.

Iteration works only with the sequential ordering of rules. If you attempt to use ITERATE along with AUTOMATIC ORDER, you will get an error, as shown in the following example:

```
SELECT r, y, m, s
FROM sales_history
MODEL
  UNIQUE SINGLE REFERENCE
  RETURN UPDATED ROWS
  PARTITION BY (region_id r)
  DIMENSION BY (year y, month m)
  MEASURES (sales s)
  RULES AUTOMATIC ORDER ITERATE (4)
  (
    s[2001,3] = 20000,
    s[2002,3] = s[2001,3] / 2
  )
ORDER BY y, r, m;

  RULES AUTOMATIC ORDER ITERATE (4)
                   *
ERROR at line 8:
ORA-32607: invalid ITERATE value in SPREADSHEET clause
```

Reference Models

Commercial spreadsheet applications, such as Microsoft Excel, allow you to link cells from one spreadsheet to those in another spreadsheet. The same thing is possible with model queries in the Oracle database. A given model can reference one or more read-only spreadsheets, called *reference models*.

The REFERENCE clause can be used for referencing spreadsheets/models. The syntax of the REFERENCE clause is:

```
REFERENCE name ON (query)
DIMENSION BY (d)
MEASURES (m)
[ref_options]
```

The syntax elements are:

name
> A name for the reference model. You use this together with dot notation to reference values from the model.

query
> A SELECT statement that defines the reference model.

d   Dimension column(s) for the reference model.

m   Reference column(s) for the reference model.

ref_options
> Cell referencing options such as IGNORE NAV, KEEP NAV.

For example, the following query uses a REFERENCE clause to create a one-dimensional reference model containing monthly adjustment factors. Those adjustment factors are then referenced by the rule in the main part of the MODEL clause:

```
SELECT r, y, m, s
FROM sales_history
MODEL
  UNIQUE SINGLE REFERENCE
  RETURN UPDATED ROWS
  REFERENCE ref_adj ON
    (SELECT month, factor FROM monthly_sales_adjustment)
    DIMENSION BY (month)
    MEASURES (factor)
  PARTITION BY (region_id r)
  DIMENSION BY (year y, month m)
  MEASURES (sales s)
  RULES
  (
    s[2004, FOR m in (1,2,3)] = AVG(s)[y BETWEEN 1995 AND 2003,CV(m)]
                                  * ref_adj.factor[CV(m)]
  )
ORDER BY y, r, m;
```

R	Y	M	S
5	2004	1	687440.25
5	2004	2	858965.67
5	2004	3	747757.56
6	2004	1	824440.95
6	2004	2	598003.02
6	2004	3	840880.92
7	2004	1	511678.35
7	2004	2	862700.085
7	2004	3	865910.76

Look at the following component in the preceding query:

```
REFERENCE ref_adj ON
  (SELECT month, factor FROM monthly_sales_adjustment)
  DIMENSION BY (month)
  MEASURES (factor)
```

This code component defines the reference model, which has its own dimensions and measures. In this case, the reference model is a one-dimensional array filled in with adjustment factors from the monthly_sales_adjustment table. Those factors are dimensioned by month, making it easy to retrieve the adjustment factor for any given month.

The cells of the reference model are referenced from the main model in the following lines:

```
s[2004, FOR m in (1,2,3)] = AVG(s)[y BETWEEN 1995 AND 2003,CV(m)]
                              * ref_adj.factor[CV(m)]
```

The cells of the reference model are qualified using the name of the reference model. In this example, we used `ref_adj` for our reference model name. Thus, the single measure is `ref_adj.factor`. Use dot notation to qualify a measure name with the name of the reference model containing the measure. The cell reference `ref_adj.factor[CV(m)]` that you see here retrieves the adjustment factor for each month.

When a query contains more than one model, it makes sense to name each model such that it can be distinguished easily. In the preceding example, you saw how to name a reference model. You can actually name the main model, too, by specifying a name along with the MAIN option, as shown in the following example:

```
SELECT r, y, m, s
FROM sales_history
MODEL
  UNIQUE SINGLE REFERENCE
  RETURN UPDATED ROWS
  REFERENCE ref_adj ON
    (SELECT month, factor FROM monthly_sales_adjustment)
    DIMENSION BY (month)
    MEASURES (factor)
  MAIN sales_forecast
  PARTITION BY (region_id r)
  DIMENSION BY (year y, month m)
  MEASURES (sales s)
  RULES
  (
    s[2004, FOR m in (1,2,3)] = AVG(s)[y BETWEEN 1995 AND 2003,CV(m)]
                                 * ref_adj.factor[CV(m)]
  )
ORDER BY y, r, m;
```

In this example, the main spreadsheet is named `sales_forecast`. You can name the main spreadsheet irrespective of whether it references other spreadsheets.

The following rules and restrictions apply to reference models:

- The query defining the reference model cannot correlate to the outer (main) query.
- A reference model cannot have a PARTITION BY clause.
- Reference models are read-only. You can't update/upsert a cell in the reference model.

A model query can have only one main spreadsheet, but many reference spreadsheets.

Oracle's Old Join Syntax

The join syntax (involving the JOIN, INNER, OUTER, CROSS, LEFT, RIGHT, FULL, ON, and USING keywords) discussed in Chapter 3 was introduced in Oracle9i Database to make Oracle's join functionality compliant with the ANSI/ISO SQL92 standard known as SQL92. Prior to Oracle9i Database, Oracle supported the join syntax defined in the SQL86 standard. In addition, also prior to Oracle9i Database, Oracle supported outer joins through a proprietary outer join operator. Even though the new SQL92 join syntax is more elegant and powerful, the old join syntax and the proprietary outer join operator are still supported in Oracle Database 10g, for backward compatibility.

If you are writing a new application, we highly recommend that you use the SQL92 join syntax. However, if you have a pre-Oracle9i Database application, you need to understand both syntaxes—the old and the new. In this appendix, we illustrate the old join syntax, and show how it relates to the new syntax. This will help you to migrate an application from the old syntax to the new syntax, and it will help you when you are faced with maintaining an older application.

Old Inner Join Syntax

The following example illustrates the older inner join syntax:

```
SELECT d.name, l.regional_group
FROM department d, location l
WHERE d.location_id = l.location_id;
```

The corresponding query with the new syntax is:

```
SELECT d.name, l.regional_group
FROM department d JOIN location l
ON d.location_id = l.location_id;
```

Following are the two differences between the old and the new inner join syntax:

- The old syntax separates tables in the FROM clause using a comma.
- The old syntax specifies the join condition in the WHERE clause.

Since the old syntax uses the WHERE clause to specify the join condition as well as filter conditions, it may take awhile for you to figure out which component of the WHERE clause is a join condition, and which component is a filter condition.

Old Outer Join Syntax

The old syntax of the outer join is a bit different from that of the inner join, because it includes a special operator called the *outer join operator*. The outer join operator is a plus sign enclosed in parentheses: (+). This operator is used in a join condition in the WHERE clause following a field name from the table that you wish to be considered the optional table.

For example, to list all the departments even if they are not related to any particular location, you can perform an outer join between the department and the location tables as shown in the following example:

```
SELECT d.dept_id, d.name, l.regional_group
FROM department d, location l
WHERE d.location_id = l.location_id (+);

    DEPT_ID NAME                 REGIONAL_GROUP
---------- -------------------- ------------------
         10 ACCOUNTING           NEW YORK
         20 RESEARCH             DALLAS
         30 SALES
         40 OPERATIONS           BOSTON
```

Notice the (+) operator following l.location_id. That makes location the optional table in this join, in the sense that you want to display a row from the department table, even though there exists no corresponding row in the LOCATION table. A corresponding query using the new join syntax is:

```
SELECT d.dept_id, d.name, l.regional_group
FROM department d LEFT OUTER JOIN location l
ON d.location_id = l.location_id;
```

In the new outer join syntax, the LEFT (or RIGHT) keyword corresponds to the table from which you want all the rows. This example uses LEFT to point to department, because we want all the rows from the department table irrespective of whether there are coresponding rows in the location table.

Restrictions on Old Outer Join Syntax

There are some rules and restrictions on how you can use the outer join operator in a query. When you use the (+) operator in a query, Oracle doesn't allow you to perform certain other operations in the same query. We discuss these restrictions and some of the workarounds in the following list:

- The outer join operator can appear on only one side of an expression in the join condition. You get an ORA-01468 error if you attempt to use it on both sides. For example:

```
SELECT d.dept_id, d.name, l.regional_group
FROM department d, location l
WHERE d.location_id (+) = l.location_id(+);
WHERE d.location_id (+) = l.location_id(+)
                  *
ERROR at line 3:
ORA-01468: a predicate may reference only one outer-joined table
```

What this means is that the outer join operation using the (+) operator is unidirectional. You can't perform a bidirectional outer join (known as a full outer join) using the (+) operator.

 If you are attempting a full outer join by placing the (+) operator on both sides in the join condition, please refer to the section "Full Outer Join Using the Old Syntax," which follows this section.

- If a join involves more than two tables, then one table can't be outer joined with more than one other table in the query. Consider the following tables:

```
DESC employee
Name                                        Null?     Type
------------------------------------------- --------- --------------
EMP_ID                                      NOT NULL  NUMBER(5)
FNAME                                                 VARCHAR2(20)
LNAME                                                 VARCHAR2(20)
DEPT_ID                                     NOT NULL  NUMBER(5)
MANAGER_EMP_ID                                        NUMBER(5)
SALARY                                                NUMBER(5)
HIRE_DATE                                             DATE
JOB_ID                                                NUMBER(3)


DESC job
Name                                        Null?     Type
------------------------------------------- --------- ----
JOB_ID                                      NOT NULL  NUMBER(3)
FUNCTION                                              VARCHAR2(30)


DESC department
Name                                        Null?     Type
------------------------------------------- --------- ----
DEPT_ID                                     NOT NULL  NUMBER(5)
NAME                                                  VARCHAR2(20)
LOCATION_ID                                           NUMBER(3)
```

If you want to list the job function and department name of all the employees, and you want to include all the departments and jobs that don't have any corresponding employees, you would probably attempt to join the employee table with the job and department tables, and make both the joins outer joins. However, since one table can't be outer-joined with more than one table you get the following error:

```
SELECT e.lname, j.function, d.name
FROM employee e, job j, department d
WHERE e.job_id (+) = j.job_id
AND e.dept_id (+) = d.dept_id;

WHERE e.job_id (+) = j.job_id
                *
ERROR at line 3:
ORA-01417: a table may be outer joined to at most one other table
```

As a workaround, you can create a view with an outer join between two tables, and then outer join the view to the third table:

```
CREATE VIEW v_emp_job
AS SELECT e.dept_id, e.lname, j.function
FROM employee e, job j
WHERE e.job_id (+) = j.job_id;

SELECT v.lname, v.function, d.name
FROM v_emp_job v, department d
WHERE v.dept_id (+) = d.dept_id;
```

Instead of creating a view, you can use an inline view to achieve the same result:

```
SELECT v.lname, v.function, d.name
FROM (SELECT e.dept_id, e.lname, j.function
      FROM employee e, job j
      WHERE e.job_id (+) = j.job_id) v, department d
WHERE v.dept_id (+) = d.dept_id;
```

Inline views are discussed in Chapter 5.

- A condition containing the (+) operator may not use the IN operator. For example:

```
SELECT e.lname, j.function
FROM employee e, job j
WHERE e.job_id (+) IN (668, 670, 667);
WHERE e.job_id (+) IN (668, 670, 667)
                *
ERROR at line 3:
ORA-01719: outer join operator (+) not allowed in operand of OR or IN
```

- An outer join condition containing the (+) operator may not be combined with another condition using the OR operator. For example:

```
SELECT e.lname, d.name
FROM employee e, department d
WHERE e.dept_id = d.dept_id (+)
OR d.dept_id = 10;
WHERE e.dept_id = d.dept_id (+)
                    *
ERROR at line 3:
ORA-01719: outer join operator (+) not allowed in operand of OR or IN
```

- A condition containing the (+) operator may not involve a subquery. For example:

```
SELECT e.lname
FROM employee e
WHERE e.dept_id (+) =
(SELECT dept_id FROM department WHERE name = 'ACCOUNTING');
(SELECT DEPT_ID FROM DEPARTMENT WHERE NAME = 'ACCOUNTING')
                                                          *
ERROR at line 4:
ORA-01799: a column may not be outer-joined to a subquery
```

As a workaround, you can use an inline view to achieve the desired effect:

```
SELECT e.lname
FROM employee e,
(SELECT dept_id FROM department WHERE name = 'ACCOUNTING') V
WHERE e.dept_id (+) = v.dept_id;
```

Full Outer Join Using the Old Syntax

In the previous section, you saw that a full outer join using the (+) operator is not allowed. A UNION of two SELECT statements is a workaround for this problem. In the following example, the first SELECT represents an outer join in which department is the optional table. The second SELECT has the location table as the optional table. Between the two SELECTS, you get all locations and all departments. The UNION operation eliminates duplicate rows, and the result is a full outer join:

```
SELECT d.dept_id, d.name, l.regional_group
FROM department d, location l
WHERE d.location_id (+) = l.location_id
UNION
SELECT d.dept_id, d.name, l.regional_group
FROM department d, location l
WHERE d.location_id = l.location_id (+) ;

    DEPT_ID NAME                    REGIONAL_GROUP
---------- --------------------- ----------------
        10 ACCOUNTING              NEW YORK
        20 RESEARCH                DALLAS
        30 SALES
        40 OPERATIONS              BOSTON
                                   CHICAGO
                                   SAN FRANCISCO

6 rows selected.
```

As you can see, this UNION query includes all the rows you would expect to see in a full outer join. UNION queries are discussed in Chapter 7.

Using the ANSI/ISO-compatible join syntax introduced in Oracle9*i* Database you can perform a full outer join in a much more straightforward way than shown in the previous example. See the section "Outer Joins" in Chapter 3.

Advantages of the New Join Syntax

The ANSI join syntax represents a bit of an adjustment to developers who are used to using Oracle's traditional join syntax, including the outer join operator (+). However, there are several advantages to using the syntax introduced in Oracle9*i* Database:

- The new join syntax follows the ANSI standard, making your code more portable.
- The ON and USING clauses keep join conditions away from the filter conditions in the WHERE clause. This enhances development productivity and the maintainability of your code.
- The ANSI/ISO syntax makes it possible to perform a full outer join without having to perform a UNION of two SELECT queries.

We recommend that while working with Oracle9*i* Database and later Oracle releases, you use the new join syntax instead of the traditional join syntax.

Index

We'd like to hear your suggestions for improving our indexes. Send email to *index@oreilly.com*.

hash semi-joins, 89
HAVING clause, 74–77
    compared to WHERE clause, 353
    errors, 75
    scalar subqueries, 82
hierarchical data representations, 181–184
hierarchical queries, 191
    aggregating hierarchies, 198
    ascendancy, 196
    finding, 184
    leaf, finding, 186
    limitations of, overcoming, 98
    listing, 198
    parents, finding, 185
    PRIOR, hierarchical queries, 189
    restrictions, 204
    root nodes, listing, 197
    START WITH clause, 191
    START WITH...CONNECT BY
        clause, 188
    subtrees (hierarchical queries), 197
hierarchical trees, traversing, 187
hierarchies
    Database 10g, optimization of, 204, 209
    extensions, 187–193
    operations, 184–187
    ordering, 200
    paths, finding to nodes, 201
history of SQL, 3
horizontal partitioning, 231, 232–238
hypothetical analytic functions, 338

I

if-then-else functionality, 214
implicit type conversions, DATE data
        type, 128
IN operator, 24
    multiple-row subqueries, 85
indexes
    function-based, 162
    partitions, 231
    regular expressions, 399
inequality conditions, 23
inequality operator (!=), 23
inheritance of object types, 260
inline views, 91
    aggregate queries, overcoming limitations
        of, 100
    columns, hiding with WITH CHECK
        OPTION, 103
    creating data sets, 94–98
    DML statements, 102–103

errors, 102, 104
execution, 92
global, 104–106
hierarchical queries, overcoming
        limitations of, 98
mimicking analytic queries with, 322
overview, 92
selective aggregation, 225
inner joins, 36, 37, 39
    syntax, 449
INSERT statement, 11
    DML, 1
    join views, 56
    partitions, specifying, 238
    strings, converting to default date
        format, 128
inserting data (XML), 377
instances
    storing, 261
    XMLType, 369
International Standard ISO 8601, 121
INTERSECT set operator, 167, 170
interval data (date and time), 117
    INTERVAL DAY TO SECOND data
        type, 119
    INTERVAL YEAR TO MONTH data
        type, 118
    INTERVAL DAY TO SECOND data
        type, 119
    INTERVAL literals, 123
    INTERVAL YEAR TO MONTH data
        type, 118
IS ANY wildcard, 432
IS PRESENT condition, 433
ISO standards, dates
    overview, 143
    weeks, 143
    years, 144
ITERATION_NUMBER function, 443

J

joins
    anti-joins, 85
    conditions, 32–37
    conditions (WHERE clause), 7, 30
    cross, 37
    equi-joins, 37, 44
    hierachical query usage, 204
    inner, 37, 39
        syntax, 449
    key-preserved tables, 54–56
    mimicking analytic queries with, 322

natural, 35–37
new syntax, 454
non-equi-joins, 37, 44
    self, 46–49
outer, 37, 41
    full, 43
    left, 42
    LEFT/RIGHT, 356
    right, 42
    self, 45
    syntax, 450–453
placement of, 29
queries, 31
self, 37, 44
semi-joins, 89
stored functions, avoiding, 249
subqueries, 53
types of, 37–49
vertical, 166
views, DML statements on, 53–61

K

key-preserved tables, 54–56
keys
    foreign, relationships and, 4
    partitions, 231
    primary, comparing tables, 176
keywords, 283–295, 300
    ALL
        aggregate functions, 63
        multiple-row subqueries, 83
    ANY, multiple-row subqueries, 83
    CUBE, partial, 294
    CURRENT ROW, windowing
        functions, 341
    DBTTIMEZONE, 114
    DISTINCT
        aggregate functions, 62
        compared to EXISTS operator, 352
    GROUPI, 309
    NOCYCLE, 205
    RULES, 419
    SELF, object types, 259
    set operators, 166
    TRUST, stored functions, 253

L

LAST_DAY function, 146, 157
leaf nodes
    identifying, 207

leaf nodes hierarchical queries, 184
LEFT outer joins, 42, 356
less than (<) operator, 25
less than or equal to (<=) operator, 25
LEVEL pseudocolumn, 192
levels
    hierarchical queries, 184
    number of, finding, 193
lifecycles, 265
LIKE operator, 25
lines, definition of, 404
list partitioning, 235
literals
    dates, 120
    DAY TO SECOND interval, 124
    INTERVAL, 123
    TIMESTAMP, 120
    YEAR TO MONTH interval, 123
local indexes, 232
LOCALTIMESTAMP function, 147
logical models compared to physical models,
        entities and, 4
logical operators, WHERE clause, 20
loops, FOR, 429

M

maintenance, WHERE clause, 18
matching conditions, 25
match_parameter, 403
math, dates, 149
    addition, 149
    overview, 146
    subtraction, 152
MAX function, 63
MEASURES clause, 419, 420
MEMBER OF operator, 275
membership conditions, 24
merge anti-joins, 85
merge semi-joins, 89
Merge statement, 16
methods, partitioning, 232–238
MINUS set operator, 167, 170
    comparing tables, 173
minutes
    date math, 149
    representations of, 141
MODEL clause, 418
model queries
    elements of, 417–419
    iterative, 442–445
    reference models, 445–447

partitions *(continued)*
  key, 231
    hash partitioning, 233
    optimizer and, 240
  list, 235
  methods, 232–238
  naming considerations, 239
  performance, 230
  pruning, 239–242
  range, 232
  specifying, 238
  storage considerations, 231
  tables, overview, 230
  vertical, 231
  views, 239
paths
  nodes, finding, 201
  notation elements, 369
pattern-matching
  built-in functions, 26
  conditions, 25
patterns
  anti-patterns, finding, 409
  occurrence of, 403
percent sign (%), pattern-matching
    character, 25
PERCENT_RANK analytic function, 336
performance
  partitioning and, 230
  selective function exec, 219, 220
Perl, regular expression usage, 411
phantom columns, 8
pivot tables, creating dates, 162
placement of join conditions, 29
PL/SQL
  CASE expressions and, 215
  date pivot tables, 162
  deterministic functions, 250
  DML statements, stored functions in, 254
  including SQL, 256–257
  overview, 243
  restrictions on calling, 251–254
  stored functions
    avoiding table joins, 249
    calling from queries, 246–248
    views, 248
  stored functions compared to stored
    procedures, 244
  variables, converting to DATE data
    type, 127
PM indicator (time format), 138

populating data, XML, 372
POS (positive) transition types, 228
positional cell references, 420
positioning characters, 403
positive (POS) transition types, 228
pragmas, adding, 252
precedence
  operator/condition, 30
  set operators, 172–173
PRESENTNNV function, 435
PRESENTV function, 434
PREVIOUS function, 444
primary keys, comparing tables, 176
printing numeric amounts, 134
PRIOR operator, hierarchical queries, 189
programming languages, nonprocedural, 1
programming, style issues, 30
properties, key-preserved tables, 56
pruning partitions, 239–242
pseudocolumns, 8
  CONNECT_BY_ISCYCLE, 207
  CONNECT_BY_ISLEAF, 207
  LEVEL, 192
  ROWID, 8
purch_ord.xsd file, 376
purity levels, 252

Q

quantifiers, 394
queries
  CUBE, 289
    partial, 294
  filtering, 354
  joins, 31
  model
    elements of, 417–419
    iterative, 442–445
    reference models, 445–447
    rules, 427–441
  multilevel collections, 277
  reporting functions, 347
  ROLLUP, 283
    partial, 287
  UNION, 280
  (see also regular expressions)

R

range-hash partitioning, 234
range-list composite partitioning, 235
range-list partitioning, 234

U

underscore (_), pattern-matching
character, 25
UNION ALL set operator, 167, 168
comparing tables, 173
UNION clause, data sets, creating
custom, 94
union compatibility conditions, 166
UNION operation compared to UNION
ALL, 354
UNION query, 280
UNION set operator, 167, 169
UNIQUE SINGLE REFERENCE cell
reference, 423
Universal Coordinated Time (UTC), 113
UNTIL option, 442
UPDATE semantics, 440
UPDATE statement, 15
CASE expression, 221
collections and, 275
DECODE function, 220
DML, 1
inline views, 102
join views, 58
multiple-column subqueries, 86
selective aggregation, 223–225
WHERE clause and, 20
updating
cells, 440
XML documents, 380–382
UPSERT semantics, 441
user-defined constructors, object types, 260
USER_UPDATABLE_COLUMNS, 58
USING clause, 34
UTC (Universal Coordinated Time), 113

V

validity functions, XMLType object
types, 379
VALUE function, returning objects, 263
values
adding, 149
backreferences, 405–411
built-in temporal functions, 146
CONNECT_BY_ROOT operator, 204
NULLIF function, 212
NULLs, 64
references (PREVIOUS function), 444
VARCHAR2 data type, TO_DATE data
type, 127
variable arrays, 267

variables, bind, 359
varrays, 267
vertical joins, 166
vertical partitioning, 231
views, 103
data dictionary, USER_UPDATABLE_
COLUMNS, 58
DML statements on joins, 53–61
hierarchical queries, 204
inline, 91
aggregate queries, overcoming
limitations of, 100
creating data sets, 94–98
DML statements, 102–103
execution, 92
hierarchical queries, overcoming
limitations of, 98
overview, 92
selective aggregation, 225
join queries, 31
partitions, 239
stored functions, 248
WITH CHECK OPTION, 59–61

W

weekends, date math and, 163
weeks
date math, 149
ISO standard, 143
WHERE clause, 74
capabilities of, 19
columns, restricting access, 104
compared to HAVING clause, 353
conditions, 19
components of, 23
equality/inequality, 23
matching, 25
membership, 24
range, 25
evaluation, 20–22
conditions, 19
GROUP BY clause, 74
HAVING clause and, 76
join conditions, 30
logical operators, 20
noncorrelated subqueries, 82
NULL expression, 27–29
partition pruning, 239
SELECT statements, 7
subqueries, 81
tips for using, 30

About the Authors

Sanjay Mishra has more than 12 years of experience working with Oracle systems. His key areas of interest include database architecture, database administration, performance management, scalability, software development, and data modeling for mission-critical and decision support applications. He holds a Bachelor of Science degree in Electrical Engineering and a Master of Engineering degree in Systems Science and Automation. He is the coauthor of the books *Oracle Parallel Processing* and *Oracle SQL Loader: The Definitive Guide* (both published by O'Reilly). Sanjay has published several technical papers in *Oracle Magazine* and *SELECT Journal*, and has presented many technical papers at various regional, national, and international conferences. Sanjay can be reached at *Sanjay_Mishra0@yahoo.com*.

Alan Beaulieu has been designing, building, and implementing custom database applications for over 15 years. He currently runs his own consulting company, which specializes in designing Oracle databases and supporting services in the fields of financial services and telecommunications. In building large databases for both OLTP and OLAP environments, Alan utilizes such Oracle features as Parallel Query, Partitioning, and Parallel Server. Alan has a Bachelor of Science degree in Operations Research from the Cornell University School of Engineering. He lives in Massachusetts with his wife and two daughters and can be reached at *albeau_mosql@yahoo.com*.

Colophon

Our look is the result of reader comments, our own experimentation, and feedback from distribution channels. Distinctive covers complement our distinctive approach to technical topics, breathing personality and life into potentially dry subjects.

The animals on the cover of *Mastering Oracle SQL*, Second Edition are lantern flies. The lantern fly is mostly tropical, with a wingspan of up to six inches. The lantern fly's elongated head is an evolutionary adaptation called automimicry, in which parts of the body are disguised or artifically shifted to other areas to confuse predators: the lantern fly's head looks like a tail, and its tail looks like a head. On the rear it has artificial eyes and antennae.

Matt Hutchinson was the production editor for *Mastering Oracle SQL*, Second Edition. Octal Publishing, Inc. provided production services. Sarah Sherman, Marlowe Shaeffer, and Colleen Gorman provided quality control.

Ellie Volckhausen and Emma Colby designed the cover of this book, based on a series design by Edie Freedman. The cover image is from *Johnson's Natural History*. Emma Colby produced the cover layout with QuarkXPress 4.1 using Adobe's ITC Garamond font.

Melanie Wang designed the interior layout, based on a series design by David Futato. This book was converted by Julie Hawks to FrameMaker 5.5.6 with a format conversion tool created by Erik Ray, Jason McIntosh, Neil Walls, and Mike Sierra that uses Perl and XML technologies. The text font is Linotype Birka; the heading font is Adobe Myriad Condensed; and the code font is LucasFont's TheSans Mono Condensed. The illustrations that appear in the book were produced by Robert Romano and Jessamyn Read using Macromedia FreeHand 9 and Adobe Photoshop 6. The tip and warning icons were drawn by Christopher Bing. This colophon was written by Colleen Gorman.

Related Titles Available from O'Reilly

Oracle PL/SQL

Learning Oracle PL/SQL

Oracle PL/SQL Best Practices

Oracle PL/SQL Developer's Workbook

Oracle PL/SQL Language Pocket Reference, *3rd Edition*

Oracle PL/SQL Programming, *3nd Edition*

Oracle Books for DBAs

Oracle DBA Checklists Pocket Reference

Oracle RMAN Pocket Reference

Unix for Oracle DBAs Pocket Reference

Oracle SQL and SQL Plus

Oracle SQL Plus: The Definitive Guide

Oracle SQL Tuning Pocket Reference

Oracle SQL*Plus Pocket Reference, *2nd Edition*

Oracle SQL: The Essential Reference

Oracle

Building Oracle XML Applications

Java Programming with Oracle JDBC

Oracle Essentials: Oracle Database 10g, *3rd Edition*

Oracle in a Nutshell

Perl for Oracle DBAs

TOAD Pocket Reference

O'REILLY®

Our books are available at most retail and online bookstores.
To order direct: 1-800-998-9938 • *order@oreilly.com* • *www.oreilly.com*
Online editions of most O'Reilly titles are available by subscription at *safari.oreilly.com*

Keep in touch with O'Reilly

1. Download examples from our books

To find example files for a book, go to:
www.oreilly.com/catalog
select the book, and follow the "Examples" link.

2. Register your O'Reilly books

Register your book at *register.oreilly.com*

Why register your books?
Once you've registered your O'Reilly books you can:

- Win O'Reilly books, T-shirts or discount coupons in our monthly drawing.
- Get special offers available only to registered O'Reilly customers.
- Get catalogs announcing new books (US and UK only).
- Get email notification of new editions of the O'Reilly books you own.

3. Join our email lists

Sign up to get topic-specific email announcements of new books and conferences, special offers, and O'Reilly Network technology newsletters at:

elists.oreilly.com

It's easy to customize your free elists subscription so you'll get exactly the O'Reilly news you want.

4. Get the latest news, tips, and tools

www.oreilly.com

- "Top 100 Sites on the Web"—PC Magazine
- CIO Magazine's Web Business 50 Awards

Our web site contains a library of comprehensive product information (including book excerpts and tables of contents), downloadable software, background articles, interviews with technology leaders, links to relevant sites, book cover art, and more.

5. Work for O'Reilly

Check out our web site for current employment opportunities:

jobs.oreilly.com

6. Contact us

O'Reilly & Associates
1005 Gravenstein Hwy North
Sebastopol, CA 95472 USA

TEL: 707-827-7000 or 800-998-9938
(6am to 5pm PST)

FAX: 707-829-0104

order@oreilly.com
For answers to problems regarding your order or our products. To place a book order online, visit:

www.oreilly.com/order_new

catalog@oreilly.com
To request a copy of our latest catalog.

booktech@oreilly.com
For book content technical questions or corrections.

corporate@oreilly.com
For educational, library, government, and corporate sales.

proposals@oreilly.com
To submit new book proposals to our editors and product managers.

international@oreilly.com
For information about our international distributors or translation queries. For a list of our distributors outside of North America check out:

international.oreilly.com/distributors.html

adoption@oreilly.com
For information about academic use of O'Reilly books, visit:

academic.oreilly.com

O'REILLY®

Our books are available at most retail and online bookstores.
To order direct: 1-800-998-9938 • order@oreilly.com • www.oreilly.com
Online editions of most O'Reilly titles are available by subscription at *safari.oreilly.com*